T0330519

Intellectual Property in Global Governance

Intellectual Property in Global Governance critically examines the evolution of international intellectual property lawmaking from the build up to the TRIPS Agreement, through the TRIPS and post-TRIPS era. The book focuses on a number of thematic intellectual property issue linkages, exploring the formal and informal institutional interactions and diverse holder intrigues implicated in the global governance of intellectual property. Using examples from biotechnology, biodiversity, bioprospecting and biopiracy it investigates the shift or concentration in the focus of innovation from physical to life sciences and the ensuing changes in international intellectual property lawmaking and their implications for intellectual property jurisprudence. It examines the character of the reception, resistance and various nuanced reactions to the changes brought about by the TRIPS Agreement, exploring the various institutional sites and patterns of such responses, as well as the escalation in the issue linkages associated with the concept and impact of intellectual property law.

Drawing on multiple methodological approaches including law and legal theory; regime theory, globalization and global governance Chidi Oguamanam explores the intellectual property dynamics in the "global knowledge economy" focusing on digitization and information revolution phenomena and the concept of a post-industrial society. The book articulates an agenda for global governance of intellectual property law in the 21st century and speculates on the future of intellectual property in north–south relations.

Chidi Oguamanam is a Professor in the Faculty of Law, University of Ottawa, Canada and formerly the Director of the Law and Technology Institute at the Schulich School of Law, Dalhousie University, Halifax, N.S., Canada.

Intellectual Property in Global Governance

A Development Question

Chidi Oguamanam

Routledge
Taylor & Francis Group

LONDON AND NEW YORK

First published 2012
by Routledge
2 Park Square, Milton Park, Abingdon, Oxon OX14 4RN

Simultaneously published in the USA and Canada
by Routledge
711 Third Avenue, New York, NY 10017

Routledge is an imprint of the Taylor & Francis Group, an informa business

British Library Cataloguing in Publication Data
A catalogue record for this book is available from the British Library

Library of Congress Cataloging in Publication Data
Oguamanam, Chidi, 1965–
 Intellectual property in global governance : a development question /
 Chidi Oguamanam.
    p. cm.
 Includes index.
 1. Intellectual property (International law) 2. Intellectual property.
 3. International organization. 4. Globalization. I. Title.
 K1401.O387 2011
 346.04′8—dc22   2011004385

ISBN: 978–0–415–56417–5 (hbk)
ISBN: 978–0–203–80704–0 (ebk)

Typeset in Baskerville
by Keystroke, Station Road, Codsall, Wolverhampton

To my mother: Appolonia Nnuma Oguamanam:
1937–2010

Contents

Acknowledgements

In writing this book, I have explored and exploited diverse disciplinary convergences and resources to illuminate the interminable intellectual property issue linkages in global governance. They include research and scholarship in a wide range of disciplines in law, economics, science, globalization, world system theory, international relations, history, development studies, anthropology, and a host of other disciplines in the social sciences. I am indebted to those whose work in these areas provided the platform on which I stood and those on whose shoulders I have leaned to contribute in this complex conversation.

Intellectual Property in Global Governance is, in part, a product of the benefaction of the Canadian law firm of Borden Lardner Gervais (BLG) and the institutional support of the Schulich School of Law and the Law and Technology Institute at the Dalhousie University. In 2009 a committee of my colleagues recommended the book proposal for the BLG's generous annual summer fellowship designed to provide student research assistance for a law professor engaged in a "leading-edge legal research project". The fellowship served as a "seed" grant for which I retained the research assistance of the 2009 BLG fellow, Allan Doolittle. In addition to Al, I had the good fortune of working with two other dedicated assistants: Leon Tovey and David Dzidzornu. These three astounding gentlemen went beyond the call of duty in providing efficient research assistance and attending to many teaching and learning interactions that marked my experience working with them through this book project. I am grateful to them. My gratitude extends, as well, to my colleagues for selecting this project for the BLG grant and to Deans Philip Saunders and Kim Brooks for their kind support in the course of my tenure at the Dalhousie Law School where this project was conceived. The ideas canvassed here have been shaped through many formal and informal conversations and scholarly exchanges, in the course of conferences and speaking engagements in many countries and forums, especially in Canada, the United States, Israel, India, South Africa and Nigeria.

Thanks also to my other colleagues within and outside the Law School and several members of audience with whom I shared and received feedbacks on aspects of the ideas in this book. Specifically, Professors Teresa Scassa, Peter K. Yu, Ikechi Mgbeoji, Obiora Okafor, Wes Pue, Jeremy de Beer, Mike Hadshkis, David Michels, Amos Megged, Rochelle Dreyfuss, Barton Beebe, Dorris E. Long,

Jacqueline Lipton and Toshiyuki Kono, who, in one way or another, albeit unbeknown to them, have been instrumental in making this book possible deserve my special thanks. In addition, the students in my seminars in advanced intellectual property and in law and technology are well deserving of thanks for the insightful and mutually rewarding in-class exchanges, which not only challenged my thoughts and propositions but also helped in illuminating the complex issues explored in this book.

Last but not the least, I am grateful to my family: Ann and our children: Emma, John and Sinachi for their enduring graciousness in accommodating my awkward schedules through this project. Perhaps most important, I thank them for their tremendous show of affection and support following my mother's sudden passing on in the fall of 2010 as I was completing work on this book. Overall, it is impossible to name everyone whose kindness and support was invested in a project of this nature. For those silent and unnamed partners, especially the numerous reviewers of this book at the proposal and other stages, I am thankful.

Foreword

Commentators have widely noted the transformation of intellectual property law and policy from an arcane, obscure and technical area to one that now has a direct and pervasive impact on our daily life. Most of these commentators, however, did not discuss the growing complexity, fragmentation and incoherence in intellectual property law and policy at the international level. Professor Oguamanam's book, therefore, is a highly welcome addition to the intellectual property literature. It provides a rich narrative on how the protection of intellectual property rights has spilled over into other policy areas that have their own histories, cultures, philosophies, languages, institutions, players, norms, values, approaches and dynamics.

Drawing on the author's broad knowledge of intellectual property, international trade, public international law, political science, international relations, anthropology, and development studies, the book covers what commentators have described as the "international intellectual property regime complex." This ever evolving conglomerate regime was established by linking in a decentralized, nonhierarchical manner the various partially overlapping international regimes that have been implicated by the protection of intellectual property rights. These regimes cover areas ranging from public health to human rights and from biological diversity to information and communications.

The present regime complex builds on a decade-and-a-half-old, but highly turbulent marriage of intellectual property and trade through the Agreement on Trade-Related Aspects of Intellectual Property Rights (TRIPS) Agreement of the World Trade Organization. Entering into effect on January 1, 1995, the Agreement has adverse impacts on a wide range of areas in the developing world, including agriculture, health, the environment, education, culture and competition. To date, the international intellectual property regime complex remains one of the fastest growing but understudied conglomerate regimes in the international policy arena.

In this book, Professor Oguamanam introduces a wide and diverse array of actors, fora and issues that populate the emerging international intellectual property regime complex. The book also identifies many new battlegrounds, in particular those that provide developing countries with opportunities to restore the balance of the international intellectual property system. Although developments in this area are dynamic, entangled, multifaceted, rapidly changing and often messy, the author has successfully kept the discussion manageable for his readers without oversimplifying detail.

For lay readers, the book carefully breaks down the intriguing discussion into different policy areas. It situates the larger international intellectual property debate in the familiar contexts of globalization, global governance and post-industrial society. It explores the discourse on intellectual property law and policy in relation to the formation of a post-industrial global society driven primarily by creativity, innovation and a knowledge-based economy and also pays special attention to two issues that the TRIPS Agreement has failed to fully address: the information revolution and the advance of biotechnology. Such discussion is important because information technology and biotechnology have become key economic drivers in the 21st century.

For those well versed in international law, regime theory or international relations, or those who are already familiar with international intellectual property issues, Professor Oguamanam's highly informative account is equally insightful. It provides a deep understanding of the complex interrelationship between the many different nation states, state and non-state actors, global institutions and international regimes that have been implicated by the protection of intellectual property rights. The narrative not only shows vividly the dynamic nature of global standard setting in the intellectual property area, but also documents the alarming impacts the resulting standards have on scientific research, knowledge dissemination, technology transfer, industrial development, global competition, food security, environmental sustainability, cultural patrimony and wealth distribution.

Unlike other books that devote the last chapter, or last few chapters, to outlining solutions to address problems in the international intellectual property system, this book embeds the solution in itself. It reminds readers that, if we are to solve myriad problems in our existing system, we need to acquire a deeper and more sophisticated understanding of the international intellectual property regime complex. In short, *we need to read this book!*

The last chapter does, however, provide some concrete suggestions on how countries, in particular the oft mentioned BRIC countries, can team up with others to push for a proper recalibration of the international intellectual property system. The author rightly reminds us that the world is now at a crossroads. From climate change to global economic recovery, we are confronted with new issues and debates that have serious ramifications for the future development of the international intellectual property regime complex.

More importantly, how this regime complex develops will have serious implications for the developing world – for example, for access to medicines, textbooks, seeds, fertilizers, technology, knowledge and other development resources. As more developing countries migrate from the traditional agrarian and industrial economies to ones that are based on post-industrial, knowledge-based innovation, intellectual property can only become more important.

Thus, we should all be thankful that Professor Oguamanam has written this timely and important book. It shows how increased complexity, fragmentation and incoherence in the international intellectual property regime complex may place developing countries at a considerable disadvantage. Yet, the book offers hope by noting the possibility for these countries to better manage international regimes. In so doing, they can address global inequities, bridge the north–south divide and ultimately restore the much needed balance of the international intellectual property system.

Peter K. Yu
Drake University Law School
Zhongnan University of Economics and Law

List of abbreviations

A2K	access to knowledge
ABS	Access and Benefits Sharing (Convention on Biodiversity's Working Group on)
AFC	American Folklife Center
AKST	agricultural knowledge, science and technology
ARD	World Bank's Agricultural and Rural Development Department
ASEAN	Association of Southeast Asian Nations
AU	African Union
BIRPI	*Bureaux Internationaux Réunis pour la Protection de la Propriété Intellectuelle* (United International Bureau for the Protection of Intellectual Property)
BRIC	Brazil–Russia–India–China (alliance)
BWS	Bretton Woods System
CBD	Convention on Biological Diversity
CDC	Cultural Diversity Convention
CDIP	Committee on Development and Intellectual Property
CDP	Cooperation for Development Program
CDS	Center for Documentary Studies (Duke University)
CESCR	Committee on Economic, Social and Cultural Rights
CGG	Commission on Global Governance
CGIAR	Consultative Group on International Agricultural Research
CHM	Common Heritage of Mankind
CHP	Creative Heritage Project (for Strategic Management of Intellectual Property Rights and Interests) (WIPO)
CIGI	Centre for International Governance Innovation
CIPIH	Commission on Intellectual Property Rights, Innovation and Public Health (WHO)
CMH	Commission on Macroeconomics and Health (WHO)
COP	Conference of Parties (Convention on Biodiversity's executive body)
CPGR	Commission on Plant Genetic Resources
CPGRFA	Commission on Plant Genetic Resources for Food and Agriculture

CTE	Committee on Trade and Environment (WTO)
DNDI	Drugs for Neglected Diseases Initiative
DRIPS	Declaration on the Rights of Indigenous Peoples (UN)
ECOSOC	Economic and Social Council (UN)
EoF	Expressions of Folklore
FAO	Food and Agriculture Organization
FFM	Fact-Finding Mission, 2001 (WIPO)
FOD	Friends of Development
GATT	General Agreement on Tariffs and Trade
GIPID	Global Intellectual Property Issues Division (defunct) (WIPO)
GKE	Global Knowledge Economy
GNNTDC	Global Network for Neglected Tropical Disease Control
GPPPs	Global Private–Public Partnerships
GR	Green Revolution
HGDP	Human Genome Diversity Project
HGP	Human Genome Project
HYV	High-yield Varieties
IAASTD	International Assessment of Agricultural Science and Technology for Development
IARCs	International Agricultural Research Centers
IBSA	India–Brazil–South Africa (trilateral union)
ICANN	Internet Corporation for Assigned Domain Name and Numbers
ICCPR	International Covenant on Civil and Political Rights
ICESCR	International Covenant on Economic, Social and Cultural Rights
ICH	Intangible Cultural Heritage
ICJ	International Court of Justice
ICT	Information and Communication Technologies
ICTSD	International Centre for Trade and Development
IFAD	International Fund for Agricultural Development
IGC	Intergovernmental Committee on Intellectual Property, and Genetic Resources, Traditional Knowledge and Folklore (WIPO)
IGWG	Intergovernmental Working Group (on Public Health, Innovation and Intellectual Property) (WHO)
IK	Indigenous Knowledge
ILO	International Labour Organization
IMF	International Monetary Fund
IPC4D	Intellectual Property Coalition for Development
IPRs	Intellectual Property Rights
ITPGRFA	International Treaty on Plant Genetic Resources for Agriculture
IUPGR	International Undertaking on Plant Genetic Resources
IWG	Inter-sessional Working Group (WIPO)
MAT	Mutually Agreed Terms
MDG	Millennium Development Goals
MLS	Multilateral Systems
MSF	*Médicins Sans Frontières*

MTN	Multilateral Trade Negotiations on GATT (held in Uruguay from 1986 – 1993)
NAM	Non-aligned Movement
NCC	Nigerian Copyright Commission
OECD	Organization for Economic Cooperation and Development
PBRs	Plant Breeders' Rights
PCDA	Provisional Committee on proposals related to a WIPO Development Agenda
PCT	Patent Cooperation Treaty
PGD	Pre-implantation Genetic Diagnostics
PGRs	Plant Genetic Resources
PGRFA	Plant Genetic Resources for Food and Agriculture
PhRMA	Pharmaceutical Research and Manufacturers of America
PIC	Prior Informed Consent
PLT	Patent Law Treaty
PPP	Public–Private Partnership
PVPA	Plant Variety Protection Act (USA)
R&D	Research and Development
SAARC	South Asian Association for Regional Cooperation
SADC	Southern African Development Community
SAP	Structural Adjustment Program, an initiative of the BWS
SCP	Standing Committee on the Law of Patent (WIPO)
SPLT	Substantive Patent Law Treaty
SPS	WTO Agreement on the Application of Sanitary and Agreement Phytosanitary Measures
TCE	Traditional Cultural Expression
TK	Traditional Knowledge
TKDL	Traditional Knowledge Digital Library (India)
TKUP	Traditional Knowledge of Uses of Plants
TRIPS	Trade-Related Aspects of Intellectual Property Rights
UAEM	Universities Allied for Essential Medicine
UDCD	Universal Declaration on Cultural Diversity (UNESCO)
UDHR	Universal Declaration on Human Rights
UDRP	Uniform Domain-Name Dispute Resolution Policy
UNCED	United Nations Conference on Environment and Development
UNCHE	United Nations Conference on the Human Environment
UNCHR	United Nations Commission for Human Rights
UNCTAD	United Nations Commission on Trade and Development
UNDP	United Nations Development Program
UNEP	United Nations Environmental Program
UNESCO	United Nations Educational, Scientific and Cultural Organization
UNIDO	United Nations Industrial Development Organization
UPOV	Union for the Protection of New Varieties of Plants (International)

USAID	United States Agency for International Development
USTR	United States trade representative
WB	World Bank
WCT	WIPO Copyright Treaty
WFP	World Food Program (UN)
WHA	World Health Assembly
WHO	World Health Organization
WIPO	World Intellectual Property Organization
WPPT	WIPO Performances and Phonogram Treaty
WSSD	World Summit on Sustainable Development
WTO	World Trade Organization

Part I

1 Introduction and general outlook

Bio- and digital technologies are two defining technologies of our post-industrial society. The impacts of these often mutually dependent technologies are evident in virtually all aspects of society. Their advancements have radically transformed the conduct of research and the process of innovation in all fields, perhaps most evidently in health and pharmaceutical research, agriculture and food production, and communication, data processing and information management. These epochal technological transformations have also redefined business practices and services delivery, and are opening up unpredictable frontiers of commercial opportunities, as evident in the concept and conduct of electronic commerce. It is hardly in doubt that it is the influence of bio- and digital technologies that propelled analysts to characterize the present era in its historical context as a post-industrial global society (Bell 1973: 3).

The post-industrial global society is serviced by an information- and knowledge-propelled economic order. Knowledge and information are, perhaps, this order's most crucial factors of production and the most important assets in overall economic development. Intellectual property, the law's primary mechanism for allocating rights over knowledge, is the currency of the global knowledge economy. In their mutual dependence, bio- and digital technologies involve the generation, manipulation and application of critical information in diverse contexts (Takach 2003). Given the inherently non-rivalrous character of information and the ease with which it is generated in these two technological arenas, its ownership or proprietary control as supervised by intellectual property is critical to stakeholders in the knowledge economy. Intellectual property's pivotal role in that economy also accounts for the attention it generates from increasingly informed national and global publics.

In addition to its pivotal role in the consolidation of proprietary control over the gains of bio- and digital technologies, increasing global interest in intellectual property is also a factor of the phenomenon and logic of globalization. Intellectual property is an integral and instrumental part of the economic and regulatory harmonization birthed by globalization both as an ongoing historical process and as a unique descriptive feature of the new knowledge economic order. Today, intellectual property is an important item in the ever dynamic curriculum of global governance. The harmonization of the intellectual property order has hitherto followed a gradual and phased pattern from the national, to the international, and to the global stage (Drahos n.d.). Before the last stage, in both principle and practice, intellectual property remained a subject matter for national law and an instrument for leveraging the socioeconomic priorities of nations. Indeed, it was a conventionally acceptable system often strategically employed in the restraint of trade.

The principal governing institution for intellectual property, notably the World Intellectual Property Organization (WIPO) – a specialized agency of the United Nations (UN) since 1974 – was and has remained, at least on the face of its governance structure, a fairly democratic institution in which less developed countries exercised "numerical influence" in decision making.[1] Under that set up, arguably, the public-regarding aspects of intellectual property rights were inherently an aspect of WIPO's mission and, in a way, supposedly integral to WIPO's evolutionary history. Indeed, as a UN agency, WIPO ought to be evaluated more in regard to the extent it has kept faith with development objectives. It has remained under constant pressure to not lose sight of the imperative to balance those objectives with the core capitalist and free market end of the intellectual property spectrum. There is an absence of a clear textual commitment to development objectives in WIPO's enabling treaty and as well a paucity of its report card on that front. This is evident in the resurgence of interest in intellectual property and the development agenda (de Beer 2009a; May 2007). Even so, as a UN agency, the advancement of developmental objectives is inherently a complementary aspect of WIPO's mandate (Musungu and Dutfield 2003). Under the WIPO framework or, generally, the pre-TRIPS (trade-related aspects of intellectual property rights) international intellectual property regime, compliance with intellectual property treaties was secured by creative diplomacy rather than by crude coercion and crippling sanctions. There was enough leverage for less developed countries to pick and choose policies that enabled them to use intellectual property to advance national economic and development aspirations.

However, beginning in the mid-1990s, as a calculated act of protest and an overt vote of no confidence in WIPO (both as an institution and in its operational process), the US, its industrial interest groups and developed country allies elaborated the vision of a globalized intellectual property order by way of forum shifting. That regime *coup d'état* was typical of US hegemonic ambition in the advancement of its neoliberal economic agenda via the doctrine of market fundamentalism. A tightened global intellectual property order was prescribed for both developed and less developed countries alike, as a magic wand for economic emancipation. The pivotal role of intellectual property in the new global knowledge economic order makes it a strategic arsenal for the US in the continued consolidation of its ideological triumph over communism, its status as the world's sole superpower, and its head start in the development of the bio- and digital technologies that drive the new knowledge economy. Also, intellectual property is a crucial instrument in mitigating the increasing threat to the US' status as a prime economic power, especially from a consolidating Europe and the emergence of mid-level developing countries and new economic powers, especially China, India, Brazil, even a *new* South Africa. The new intellectual property order now envisioned marks a radical departure from the existing conventional wisdom around intellectual property.

First, in this new vision, intellectual property is no longer an acceptable trade-restraining instrument, but one crucial to the promotion of trade. Hence, the World Trade Organization (WTO) became a platform preferred to WIPO. Second, intellectual property practically ceased to be a subject matter within the exclusive jurisdiction of sovereign states. Third, the public-regarding and developmental objectives of intellectual property were constrained and compromised by an intensive promotional and norm-setting thrust. The US vision of a superlative intellectual property protectionist system crystallized in the upstaging of WIPO from being the most authoritative international governance framework for intellectual property to playing second fiddle. It elevated the WTO via one of its constitutive agreements, deceptively titled TRIPS. As a "floor without a ceiling," TRIPS sets a minimum standard of intellectual property protection that is applicable to all the member states of the WTO. Symbolically, TRIPS marked the globalization phase of intellectual property in a one-size-fits-all fashion.

The transformation in the international governance landscape for intellectual property occurred at a time of increased and continuing convergences in knowledge production, especially in the life sciences and biotechnology. For example, in the specific contexts of pharmaceutical, health, agricultural, agrochemical and allied research, scientists have developed a keen interest in insights from traditional knowledge of indigenous or local communities (Ten Kate and Laird 2002). Also, given that the mainstay of biotechnology and life sciences research are biological resources, there is also a heightened collective interest in the protection of the world's biological diversity. By most accounts, the centers of origin of more than 75% of global biological resources are in the less developed countries of the global south and in indigenous communities elsewhere. Most of these communities and the nation states in which they are embedded were reluctant parties or, at best, coerced converts to the TRIPS Agreement. They have not hidden their disaffection for that accord, especially as its complicity in the appropriation of their knowledge and expressive culture and in the escalation of their public health crises became obvious. This is notwithstanding the role of TRIPS, in aggravating the equity and access gap between developed countries, on the one hand, and disadvantaged peoples, communities and less developed states, on the other, to the overall benefits of innovation in various other sectors.

A prominent flashpoint of tension in the TRIPS Agreement is its apparent disdain for non-western scientific knowledge and innovative processes. TRIPS makes no provision for the protection or recognition of indigenous or traditional knowledge (TK) practices. Adding to the litany of disaffections over TRIPS, more than 10 years after it came into effect, it has yet to deliver on the issue of market access for less developed countries' produce, especially to the US and European markets. As part of bargain-linkage diplomacy, market access was one of the carrots that lured less developed countries into the cage of the TRIPS Agreement and the WTO-supervised global trade order (Long 2002: 223; Reichman 2000; Ryan 1998).

The TRIPS Agreement's omission of TK is made more glaring in relation to the approach adopted by the Convention on Biological Diversity (CBD), which came into effect at almost the same time as TRIPS. Clearly, the CBD is not an intellectual property regime, but it is one designed to facilitate "the fair and equitable sharing of the benefits arising out of the utilization of genetic resources" (CBD: Article 1). Given the centrality of biological resources to both life sciences research and indigenous biocultural knowledge and innovations, the importance of the CBD in the intellectual property discourse becomes quite significant. In this regard, the CBD member states' central commitment to:

> [R]espect, preserve and maintain knowledge, innovations and practices of indigenous and local communities embodying traditional lifestyles relevant for the conservation and sustainable use of biological diversity and promote their wider application with the approval and involvement of the holders of such knowledge, innovations and practices and encourage the equitable sharing of the benefits arising from the utilization of such knowledge, innovations and practices
>
> (CBD: Article 8(j))

strikes at the heart of TRIPS' disdain for local knowledge.

The contrasts in the approach of the CBD to the protection of local knowledge, *vis à vis* the TRIPS Agreement's approach to the same issue, becomes more pronounced in light of the role of TRIPS in the promotion of the unidirectional transfer of wealth from indigenous and local communities to the western industrial scientific complexes, especially through the patents system, a phenomenon now known as biopiracy (Mgbeoji 2006: 13; Shiva 1997, 1999). Also, since the TRIPS Agreement came into effect, global pandemics such as HIV/AIDS, hepatitis and resurgences in orphan and controlled diseases, such as polio, have escalated the public health crises in less developed countries (Oguamanam 2010; Oxfam 2008). Nowhere did the practical translation of the harsh consequences of the TRIPS Agreement become more apparent than in these contexts.

TRIPS' narrow and stringent prescriptions for compulsory licensing (TRIPS Articles 30 and 31) circumscribed the ability of less developed countries to respond to the prevailing public health crises. Only recently, those crises have reached historic proportions. Limited access to essential drugs and the high cost of patented pharmaceuticals became a sordid scar on the conscience of the international community, for which the globalized intellectual property order took a large portion of the blame. Recently, intellectual property has been identified as a clear obstacle to meeting the health needs of 90% of the global population. Such needs are now acknowledged as global public goods (Maskus and Reichman 2005; WHO 2002). These are goods that cannot be adequately provided within the matrix of the market-driven intellectual property framework; hence, the calls for a non-market approach as a panacea for the crises (WHO 2002; Oguamanam 2010; Oriola 2009).

Aside from the context of genetic resources of pharmacological value, changes in global intellectual property governance also had a practical impact in the context of genetic resources for food and agriculture. TRIPS radically extended the patent system to all spheres of innovation without discrimination, reflecting the 1980 elaboration of the ambit of patentable subject matter in the US "to all inventions under the sun made by man" (*Diamond v. Chakrabarty*). In the agricultural sector, an erstwhile elite club of countries with a head start in agricultural biotechnology development has reinvigorated their four-decade-old alliance under the aegis of the International Union for the Protection of New Varieties of Plants (UPOV). UPOV's stated objective is "the protection of new varieties of plants by an intellectual property right" (UPOV). That instrument's primary focus is the protection of scientific and hi-tech plant breeding practices by way of a *sui generis* regime known as plant breeders' rights (PBRs). Interestingly, TRIPS sanctions the protection of plant varieties by both PBRs and patents, and by combinations thereof or other special regimes of protection (TRIPS Article 27(3)(b)).

Similar to the approach adopted by TRIPS, UPOV does not give regard to informal or traditional innovation in plant genetic resources. Akin to the CBD's approach, in 2001, the Food and Agriculture Organization International Treaty on Plant Genetic Resources for Agriculture (FAO ITPGRA) was signed. The principal objective of the treaty is "the conservation and sustainable use of Plant Genetic Resources for food and agriculture and the fair and equitable sharing of the benefits arising from their use, in harmony with the Convention on Biological Diversity, for sustainable agriculture and food security" (ITPGRA: Article 1.1). Again, like the CBD, the treaty gave a strong recognition to the knowledge of indigenous and local communities by amplifying its objective through its elaborate provision on farmers' rights in recognition of:

> [T]he enormous contribution that the local and indigenous communities and farmers of all regions of the world, particularly those in the centers of origin and crop diversity, have made and will continue to make for the conservation and development of plant genetic resources which constitute the basis of food and agriculture production throughout the world.
>
> (ITPGRA: Article 9.1)

Juxtaposed with the UPOV, the FAO ITPGRA takes an opposing approach in its treatment of the sites and conception of knowledge and innovation in the context of plant genetic resources for food and agriculture.

In the meantime, the UN Educational, Social and Cultural Organization (UNESCO) has intensified its commitment to the revision of the 1982 WIPO–UNESCO Model Provisions on National Laws on the Protection of Expressions of Folklore Against Illicit Exploitation and Other Prejudicial Actions. Often perceived as a pejorative term, "folklore" refers to oral and "undocumented" forms of expressive culture and sites of local knowledge for many non-western peoples. Because folklore is a medium for expressive culture that traverses diverse forms of local knowledge, it poses a challenge for the intellectual property system, especially the copyright regime. For several decades, the fused relationship between knowledge and culture has made UNESCO a critical stakeholder and policy hub in matters of intellectual property rights. As part of its mandate, UNESCO fosters "collaboration among the nations through education, science and culture" (UNESCO Constitution: Article 1).

During the evolution of the global knowledge economic order in the last three decades, UNESCO adopted an intensified global and integrative approach to culture. More than ever before, it has become a global forum for the protection and promotion of creative industries. This approach embraces an inclusive construction of creativity and culture and has served as a source of positive energy for indigenous and local communities muzzled by the WTO/TRIPS exclusive approach to knowledge generation and protection. UNESCO has tapped into the link between culture and development, providing some comfort for many in less developed countries with fast waning expectations from WIPO on the issue of development. Significant impetus in these regards include the 2003 UNESCO Convention for the Safeguarding of Intangible Cultural Heritage (ICH), the 2005 Convention on the Protection and Promotion of the Diversity of Cultural Expression and a host of other legal instruments.[2] In a way, these initiatives serve as both the culmination and consolidation of historical international initiatives to accommodate creative enterprises in colonized societies – an important aspect of the historical evolution of the international intellectual property process.

For its part, WIPO has not capitulated completely to the WTO/TRIPS vision of intellectual property. As an organization, it has sought to recreate itself in ways that have enabled it to remain relevant in the new global reality in international intellectual property. Through its policies, it has also tried to push back at critics detailing the loss of confidence in its ability to sustain the development imperative of intellectual property for many in less developed countries.

WIPO has been actively involved through the activities of its Intergovernmental Committee on Intellectual Property, and Genetic Resources, Traditional Knowledge and Folklore (WIPO-IGC) since 2000. The committee was set up essentially as a forum for debate and dialogue concerning the interplay between intellectual property and TK, genetic resources, and traditional cultural expressions (TCEs)/(folklore) (WIPO-IGC 2009). The emergence of the WIPO-IGC is perceived as a strategy by developed countries to consign away or farm out policy discussions on TK to a powerless and obscure forum (Dutfield 2006b). However, the forum provides a critical platform for WIPO to continue to explore intellectual property matters that have ramifications for indigenous and local knowledge custodians in a way that underscores the urgency for those issues, particularly as they relate to knowledge convergences in biotechnology in particular and genetic resources in general. Perhaps more importantly, through the IGC-GRTKF, WIPO rekindles its collaborative engagement with UNESCO and also forges and advances a much needed rapprochement with the CBD. Thus, TK is amply embedded within the current intellectual property regime complex.

Aside from the activities of WIPO-IGC, internally since 2004, WIPO has been embroiled in responding to pressures from less developed countries to remedy the development deficit in its overall orientation and modus operandi. The development deficit is essentially in regard to lack of attention to the public-regarding aspects of intellectual property that are central to the interests of many in less developed countries. Glaring inequities in the north–south power and economic relations in the wake and continued implosions of the new technologies of the knowledge economy have compelled a rekindling of the developmental imperative in the elaboration of a new intellectual property order.

As a specialized UN agency, development objectives are integral aspects of WIPO's mandate (Musungu and Dutfield 2003). Due in large part to the tenacity of Brazil and Argentina, in 2007, less developed countries pushed WIPO into adopting 45 recommendations made by the Provisional Committee on Proposals Related to a WIPO Development Agenda (PCDA) (de Beer 2009a; May 2006, 2007). As a pushback against a strict market vision for the intellectual property order, this most recent campaign for a developmental thrust to intellectual property law and policy championed by developing countries gives vent to a counter-hegemonic aspect of the globalization of intellectual property.

Partly in response to a chronic intellectual property manpower shortage in less developed countries and the glaring need for technical assistance in intellectual property that became more pronounced with the coming into force of the TRIPS Agreement, WIPO set up the WIPO Worldwide Academy and distance educa-tion programs in intellectual property (de Beer and Oguamanam 2010). WIPO's commitment to intellectual property education and provision of technical assistance in intellectual property to less developed countries is part of that organization's foundational mandate in regard to promoting intellectual property across the globe (WIPO Convention: Article 3). The WIPO Worldwide Intellectual Property Academy promotes the training of intellectual property manpower, especially in less developed countries (de Beer and Oguamanam 2010; Takagi and Sinjela 2007). There are some reservations about the impact of the WIPO manpower training initiative (de Beer and Oguamanam 2010; May 2007). In the opinion of some, it underscores WIPO's complicity in the promotion of a US trade-centered vision of intellectual property, as elaborated in TRIPS, among African and developing country elites in order to shore up US global hegemony in intellectual property (May 2007). However, by means of this and other initiatives, WIPO has continued to maintain its link with less developed countries rather than adopt a policy of direct institutional indifference to the post-TRIPS disenchantments with international intellectual property lawmaking in those countries.

Also, in the post-TRIPS epoch, WIPO has brokered crucial intellectual property treaties that address the different interests of developed and less developed countries in digital technologies and in cultural heritage. WIPO upholds the 1996 Copyright Convention (WCT) and the WIPO Performances and Phonogram Treaty (WPPT)[3] as a win–win intellectual property package for the promotion of electronic com-merce and investment and for the promotion of local creativity and folklore in the advancement of overall economic development in rich and poorer countries.[4] The significance of these two treaties to WIPO's institutional integrity and WIPO's post-TRIPS relevance cannot be understated. For one reason, they demonstrate that WIPO is still a strategic institution in global intellectual property lawmaking, at least, one with a more moderate and less hawkish approach in comparison to the WTO.

Besides the WIPO, constitutive instruments of several organs or agencies of the UN provide ample anchor for the elaboration of intellectual property in both its development aspirations and in its cultural and political ramifications. For example, the UN's Universal Declaration on Human Rights (UDHR), and the International Covenant on Economic, Social and Cultural Rights (ICESCR) provide bases for intellectual property rights and its development imperatives, especially as they apply to indigenous and local communities. Beyond the UN, there are multiple regimes, including but not limited to hard and soft law instruments in international law-making, that re-enforce the nexus between intellectual property and development. More recently, intellectual property has been linked with human rights imperatives for developing countries and the world's indigenous and local communities. Indeed, after a time of inexplicable gulf between intellectual property and human rights, a period of engagement has dawned (Helfer 2004b: 167).

Helfer rightly observes that two significant events provoked the placement of intellectual property on the agenda of human rights lawmaking. The first is the neglect of the rights of indigenous peoples. Human rights interests in the UN initiated responses and reactions to this neglect. As far back as the 1980s, UN human rights bureaucrats began to design a framework for responding to the prevalent complaint of indigenous peoples in regard to their need to control their cultural rights and traditional knowledge and practices, especially those relevant to genetic resources, agriculture, food and medicines, which have been free-for-all assets for external industrial and western scientific interests. Through a checkered trajectory spanning several decades, and via multiple regimes, the international initiative climaxed in the adoption by the UN General Assembly in September 2007 of the UN Declaration on the Rights of Indigenous Peoples (DRIPS). That document articulates in a comprehensive and unprecedented way the significance of intellectual property and indigenous knowledge as integral aspects of indigenous peoples' rights to self-determination, placing this at the core of their human rights aspirations.

The second event that emboldened the location of intellectual property in the human rights framework is the consequence of linking it to trade via the WTO and the TRIPS Agreement. Essentially, TRIPS made intellectual property a tool for the promotion and consolidation of free trade. However, its key proponents, such as the US, Japan and the European Union, failed to deliver on their promise to open their markets to less developed country produce and textile exports. Not surprisingly, less than five years after TRIPS came into force, it became a source of apparent angst in these countries. TRIPS radically enclosed the intellectual property policy space for them and tightened their leverage or flexibility in regard to accessing patented medicines guaranteed under the pre-TRIPS era. Consequently, in many quarters, TRIPS is blamed for freezing access to essential medicines to needy peoples across the globe.

In August 2000 the UN Subcommission on the Promotion and Protection of Human Rights adopted Resolution 2000/7 on Intellectual Property and Human Rights (2000 Resolution). This was in response to the perceived impacts of TRIPS, potential and real, on access to essential drugs for combating public health crises in less developed countries. Essentially, that resolution restates the primacy of human rights obligations over economic policies, particularly in the context of intellectual property law under the TRIPS Agreement. It also restates the need to balance and preserve the social functions of intellectual property. The resolution and other responses of the UN human rights bodies[5] set the tone for articulating the reactions of many other agencies of the UN, including the World Health Organization (WHO) and the UN Commission on Trade and Development (UNCTAD). Indeed, there is hardly a single important agency or organ of the UN whose mandate is completely immune from the ubiquitous issue linkages that are now associated with intellectual property. The 2000 Resolution clearly anticipated the 2001 WTO Ministerial Council Declaration on the TRIPS Agreement and Public Health (the Doha Declaration).

As the pressure point that generated the global tension around intellectual property, the WTO has not remained aloof from the disaffections generated by the TRIPS Agreement, or so it appears. The Doha Declaration buttresses this point (Abbott 2002). In a way, however, the Doha Declaration was a hurried response by the WTO and its chief sponsors to the pressures of less developed countries and the damning publicity arising from the TRIPS-instigated public health crises, especially in those countries that symbolically exemplified the crises in the early 2000s through the prevalence of HIV/AIDS. The essence of the Declaration is captured in paragraph 6:

> We recognize that WTO members with insufficient or no manufacturing capacities in the pharmaceutical sector could face difficulties in making effective use of compulsory licensing under the TRIPS Agreement. We instruct the Council for TRIPS to find an expeditious solution to this problem. [. . .]
> (Doha Declaration)

The Declaration is perhaps the first major strategic concession by the WTO and the TRIPS Council to the fundamentally flawed and overreaching nature of the TRIPS Agreement regarding the social functions of intellectual property. This concession is one that has driven continuing but failed attempts to rethink TRIPS. The Doha Declaration and other provisions of TRIPS, such as Articles 30 and 31 that provide for compulsory licensing,[6] are often cited by WTO hardliners as evidence of its flexibility. But these provisions are easily criticized by opponents as reiterative of the inflexibility of the so-called flexibilities (Stiglitz 2008a: 1717). Despite the reservations that have attached to the Declaration, it must be given credit for engineering the first ever amendment to TRIPS. It will also remain pivotal to the ongoing and future review of the TRIPS Agreement.

Some important strands run through the foregoing outline of the state of the global governance of intellectual property, which is the main thrust of this book. First, the emergence of the WTO/TRIPS Agreement signals an historic and historical progression in the global economic framework. It is one that pushes the frontiers of hegemonic neoliberal market economic triumphalism to new heights. Second, a key feature or consequence of the WTO-driven global economic order is the centrality of intellectual property. Third, this new order was birthed at the cusp of significant technological revolutions that mark the advent of a post-industrial society (Bell 1973), the so-called global knowledge economy in which "knowledge or information now constitutes, perhaps, the most crucial factor or tool of production, and has become the most important matrix in overall economic development since the late 20th century" (Oguamanam 2009a: 131). Fourth, still on intellectual property, a recent shift and concentration of innovation from the physical to the life sciences is paradigmatic and, to some extent, catalytic of the important changes in our intellectual property jurisprudence. Such transitions are evolving in ways that position intellectual property or the control of knowledge assets as a complementary feature or integral aspect of the globalization phenomenon and a key driver of the global knowledge economy.

Fifth, in the global knowledge economy, intellectual property is a ubiquitous subject matter that traverses virtually every critical aspect of the global socio-economic experience. Sixth, one of the unintended consequences of the WTO's linking of intellectual property with trade is the escalation of issue linkages in intellectual property. Seventh, international intellectual property lawmaking presents an interesting place to not only attempt a further unraveling of the phenomenon of globalization, but also for the exploration of aspects of its dialectical consequences, i.e. the escalating of alterity, solidarity, and resistance. Eighth, the resistance or counterhegemonic side-effect of a globalized intellectual property order can be examined through multiple sites or regimes which provide the platforms of opposition to the TRIPS-driven WTO vision of intellectual property. Ninth, the serendipitous "regime shifting" or "forum shopping" that characterizes international intellectual property lawmaking is affirmative of the present state of "regime complexity" (Yu 2007b: 2) that has become the hallmark of the legal and policy landscape for intellectual property.

Consequently, intellectual property is a logical subject matter for global governance discourse. In that context, taking into consideration the increasing role of multivalent non-state and sub-state actors, including activist NGOs, civil society organizations and private charities in shaping the global intellectual property outlook, international intellectual property lawmaking implicates the democratic component of global governance. Tenth, the tensions imbedded or implicated in the discourse of intellectual property in global governance take the appearance and natural extension of the inherent conflict between the private and public-regarding aspects or social functions of intellectual property. In the globalized intellectual property order, such tensions escalate at a global scale, providing new micro-analytical sites for exploring the developmental inequity and ideological, cultural and epistemic schisms that characterize north–south relations over intellectual property.

Primarily, the purpose of the book is to critically examine the complex landscape for the evolution of international intellectual property lawmaking and the expansion of issue linkages to intellectual property from the buildup to the TRIPS Agreement, through the TRIPS and post-TRIPS era. The book explores the coalescence of diverse paradigmatic events, such as the globalization phenomenon, the emergence of the so-called global knowledge economy, advances in digital and biological technologies, the shift or concentration in the focus of innovation from physical to life sciences and the ensuing changes in international intellectual property law-making. In underlining the implications of these events for intellectual property jurisprudence, the book also evaluates their ramifications for development and equitable distribution and access to the benefits of knowledge and innovation, especially in regard to critical needs in less developed countries. Identifying the TRIPS Agreement and the WTO regime as perhaps the single most important composite touchstone for global consciousness over intellectual property, the book examines the character of the reception, resistance and various nuanced reactions to the changes brought about by the TRIPS Agreement. It explores the various institutional sites and patterns of such responses, as well as the escalation in the issue linkages associated with the concept and impact of intellectual property law. Within the framework of that analysis, the book seeks in part to locate the acute perceptions of the important role of intellectual property as an integral aspect of the globalization narrative (Drahos and Braithwaite 2002; Maskus and Reichman 2005; Sell 2003; Stiglitz 2008a).

Further, in recognition of the historical evolutions and multiple interpretative and variegated disciplinary paradigms of globalization (Santos 2006), the book attempts to interrogate, as well as speculate on the real implication of that phenomenon in the context of the exponential increases in diverse legal and non-legal regimes that provide alternative platforms for discussions and elaboration of intellectual property policies. The book capitalizes on the ubiquity of intellectual property in the global socioeconomic and political spheres as a subject matter of global governance. Primarily, the uncontested nesting of intellectual property within the discourses of globalization provides the basis for its induction into the global governance project. As an aspect of globalization's many byproducts, as well as its sociopolitical, legal and political infrastructure (Söderberg 2006: 1, 21), global governance provides the lens for viewing the practical translation and appreciation of the significance of intellectual property in the globalization dynamic. Overall, the book explores how various multiple and intersecting disciplinary interests in select institutional and regime contexts coalesce in a constitutive fashion to provide the global governance dynamic of intellectual property law in the 21st century. It highlights the critical need for balancing the tensions that shape the formation of intellectual property laws and policies in the knowledge economy in ways that plug the extant equity gaps while addressing development imperatives.

Methodological framework

Arising from its association with diverse issue linkages, perhaps one of the most obvious features of intellectual property since the 20th century is its interdisciplinary thrust. Time and again, we are reminded that intellectual property has ceased to be a matter within the purview of esoteric lawyers and exclusive clubs of experts or elite policy bureaucrats (Sell 2003: 99; Yu 2007b: 33). The ubiquity of intellectual property is self-evident, especially in the current global phase of its development

(Drahos n.d.). This is not only in regard to the subject matters of innovation and creativity but also in regard to variegated stakeholders that include creators and consumers of intellectual property and in regard to its impact. In the latter regard, Professor Madhavi Sunder makes a poignant observation: "Intellectual property has grown, perhaps, exponentially [. . .] march[ing] into all corners of our lives and to the most destitute corners of the world [. . .] bringing with it patents in everything from seeds to drugs, intellectual property has literally become an issue of life or death" (Sunder 2006: 257).

Similarly, theorists of globalization and global governance operate from multiple, interlinked and open-ended disciplinary platforms. Like intellectual property, globalization analyses are located at economic, cultural, political, regulatory and diverse disciplinary sites. Disparate analyses of intellectual property rights and globalization have tended to implicate hegemonic or regime dynamics that shape the nature of contestations or resistances that characterize the two subjects (Drahos and Braithwaite 2002, 2004; Helfer 2004a; Maskus and Reichman 2004, 2005; Sell 2003; Stiglitz 2008a).

Therefore, a book that focuses on intellectual property in the context of global governance is inherently an interdisciplinary project. To the extent possible, this book has benefited from diverse disciplinary insights necessary for the exploration of the issues under its conceptual framework. Most especially, the book has drawn from research and scholarship in law, political science, international relations, anthropology and various social sciences. Also, it has blended knowledge from multiple methodological approaches: law and legal theory, regime theory, globalization, and global governance in an arguably organic fashion to advance its analysis of intellectual property in the global governance context. The legal doctrinal analytical method, nonetheless, provides the fundamental or overarching methodological platform for the research and writing that have yielded this book. I have relied on diverse primary, secondary and tertiary legal sources dealing with national, international, regional and customary or local intellectual property lawmaking.

In regard to globalization, I recognize the interpretative dilemma posed by the concept and have exploited it in a critical manner, especially capitalizing on its dialectical character. Globalization, whether as process or phenomenon, or as descriptive thesis, is both a hegemonic and counterhegemonic experience. The local and global are, indeed, flipsides of the same coin. These inherent features of globalization are implicated in a parallel fashion to the resistances that now characterize the role of intellectual property in the entrenchment and consolidation of the WTO neoliberal global knowledge economic order. Those resistances manifest in the form of multiple regimes that represent what prominent analysts agree to be the current international intellectual property regime complex (Helfer 2004b; Okediji 2007; Yu 2007b).

Raustiala and Victor characterize an international regime complex as "a collective of partially overlapping and even inconsistent regimes that are not hierarchically ordered, and which lack a centralized decision maker"[7] (Raustiala and Victor 2004: 279). Stephen Krasner defines international regimes more broadly "as sets of implicit or explicit principles, norms, rules or decision-making procedures around which actors' expectations converge in a given area of international relations" (Krasner 1983: 186, 2009: 12). Rosenau reiterates the same or similar notion of a regime as "rules, norms, principles, and procedures that constitute control mechanisms through which order and governance in particular issue areas are sustained" (Rosenau 1995a: 28). Thus, these identical constructs of regimes echo some, albeit, subtle distinctions between macro- and micro-paradigms useful in my deployment of regime analysis.[8] According to Rosenau:

> [I]ssue areas are essentially a conglomeration of related smaller issues and each of the latter evolves identifiable mechanisms for governance that are at variance with other issues in the same area. The global agenda is conceived in terms of large-issue areas only because those are easily grasped and debated, but it is on the smaller issues that particularistic activities requiring special governance arrangement focus.
>
> (1995a: 30)

Intellectual property in global governance implicates both micro- and macro-interplays of regime theory. The prevailing regime complex that contextualizes international intellectual property assists in the deployment of regime theory to explore the tensions and the overall counterhegemonic landscape that characterizes oppositions to the TRIPS Agreement. Consequently, one of the operational features of the intellectual property regime complex is the politics and process of "regime shifting" or forum shifting (Braithwaite and Drahos, 2000; Helfer 2004a, 2009) by both developed and less developed countries through specific and multiple treaty and non-treaty forums that are now part of the global governance framework for intellectual property. According to Peter Yu (2007b: 15):

> As the international intellectual property regime complex evolves, countries from both the developed and less developed worlds have been actively engaging in what commentators describe as regime shifting or forum sifting. As Laurence Helfer defined it, regime shifting is "an attempt to alter the status quo ante by moving treaty negotiations, lawmaking initiatives, or standard setting activities from one international venue or another".

The evolution, interaction and unraveling of globalization and international regime dynamics in the intellectual property arena makes intellectual property a subject matter for global governance.

According to the Commission on Global Governance (CGG 1995a, 1995b), the concept of governance depicts enduring multifarious ways, processes and dynamics through which individuals, many institutions (private and public) and regimes manage common, diverse and conflicting interests "in a way that accommodates a broad range of stakeholders and publics" (Sell 2004: 363–4). Without a doubt, intellectual property is a subject of common, diverse and conflicted interests in north–south global geopolitics.

From yet another perspective, global governance is characterized as globalization's byproduct or an aspect of its social political infrastructure (Söderberg 2006). Like globalization, global governance has yielded a decrease in the power of nation states and a deflection of hierarchical power relations in ways that may be beneficial to the interests of less developed countries. The accommodation of a diversity of actors, including conventional and non-conventional actors in global governance, fosters the democratic component in the international policy and legal development process. International intellectual property lawmaking, as a site and process for aggregation of diverse actors with diverse and often conflicted interests, provides a suitable framework for the elaboration, testing and application of global governance theory in an organic way that consolidates the application of regime and globalization theories within the book's analytical framework.

Finally, I recognize the amorphous nature of the relationship between globalization and the intellectual property regime complex. But I eschew speculating on the nature of that relationship in a definitive way. Instead, I am more interested in the timing of bio- and digital technological advances at the core of the new global knowledge economy and the emergence of post-industrial society and suggest that globalization could not have been a coincidence in that matrix. In a way, it drives and is driven by these technological advances. Intellectual property is pivotal in pushing the frontiers of these technologies. Whether it does that in a one-sided hegemonic triumph, or in a way that accommodates or balances counterhegemonic interests would have ramifications for equity in the new global knowledge economy.

Some caveats

This book is not about global governance of intellectual property rights. Neither is it about globalization or global governance in any rigorous way. Rather, it deploys the two concepts and explores the intricate relationship between them in limited ways as both theoretical and analytical tools to investigate how the dynamics of intellectual property in the new global knowledge economy implicate aspects of the globalization and global governance narrative. To that extent, this book is more about intellectual property in the context of global governance than it is about globalization or global governance. Even then, in terms of scope, the book does not cover the density of issues implicated within the ambit of intellectual property in global governance. Rather, the scope of issues covered is moderated by those predominately implicated in the different forums that drive the intellectual property regime complex and which also help to highlight the development question in the contemporary intellectual property discourse. Even so, the book's analysis is hardly exhaustive on that count. For instance, although the book demonstrates the pivotal nature of digital technologies as an important aspect of the discourse of intellectual property in global governance, the vexed issue of how intellectual property is implicated in the digital divide and aspects of access to information/knowledge, and electronic commerce, are outside its scope. Similarly, in spite of discussions on TK, traditional cultural expressions/expressions of folklore (TCE/EoF), and other aspects of tangible and intangible cultural heritage, the book does not fully engage with the subject of intellectual property and traditional cultural expressions in the context of the challenges of the digital environment.

Chapter synopsis

Excluding the concluding chapter, this book is divided into three parts. In addition to the present introductory chapter, Part I comprises two other chapters. As a whole, this part elaborates on the conceptual framework and provides the general analytical backdrop and context for the book. Chapter 2 throws some light on the deployment of the triple concepts of global governance, globalization and regime theory as the overarching methodological thrust of the book. It examines the complex but logical relationships and roles that these concepts play in the effort to understand the major and mutually re-enforcing technological transformations of the 20th and 21st centuries, specifically, the advances in bio- and digital technologies and the birth of the post-industrial society. The roles of intellectual property in the shift in innovation from physical to life sciences are covered in this chapter. As aspects of the post-industrial society, the chapter explores the ramifications of the new innovation dynamic within the matrix of the quadruple phenomena of biodiversity, bioprospecting, biotechnology and biopiracy. More importantly, the chapter looks at how the changing innovation matrix conditions for inequity, appropriation and the unidirectional transfer of knowledge from developed to less developed countries as an important consequence of globalization in the intellectual property arena. It argues that the new innovation matrix has provoked "regime tension" and "regime shift" in intellectual property, opening it up as a subject matter for global governance. Chapter 3 focuses on WTO/TRIPS and WIPO as pivotal sites for exploring global governance and regime dynamics in the transformations of intellectual property in the global knowledge economy. The chapter underscores the symbolic and critical role of these players in advancing the emergence of a global governance regime on intellectual property.

Part II comprises Chapters 4 and 5 and it focuses on a number of thematic issue linkages implicated in the global governance of intellectual property. It explores the formal and informal institutional interactions and multi-stakeholder intrigues that drive the global governance of intellectual property. Each of the two chapters addresses a specific issue linkage to intellectual property within the global governance paradigm. Chapter 4 explores the relationship between the international intellectual property regime and human rights questions at the heart of the prevailing global public health crises, especially in less developed countries. Chapter 5 focuses on the role of intellectual property in the recent exponential advances in agricultural biotechnology in relation to traditional or informal agricultural practices in indigenous and local communities and its implication for food security.

Part III is made up of Chapters 6 and 7. The focus of both chapters is on TK in its conceptual complexity as an important constitutive element of the intellectual property dynamic in global governance. Both chapters recognize that TK is an area of diverse issue aggregations that are constitutive and integral aspects of the global governance discourse in the intellectual property arena. However, they underscore the point that the subject of TK presents a more complex analytical challenge. TK does not necessarily represent a single issue linkage to intellectual property in global governance in the manner presented by the specific heads of issues canvassed in Part II.

Specifically, Chapter 6 explores the conceptual challenges posed by TK in the discourse about intellectual property and attempts to provide the basis, and to speculate on the justification for the increased interest this subject has garnered recently in intellectual property policy and lawmaking. On a conceptual level, Chapter 6 highlights the bifurcation of TK between "traditional knowledge" *stricto sensu*, which focuses on those dealing with genetic or biological resources, on the one hand, and those dealing with expressive culture, a.k.a. TCEs/EoF, on the other. The rest of that chapter is devoted to the exploration of key institutional sites, major instruments and diverse issues involved in the governance of TK, such as those undergirding the subject of access and benefit sharing (ABS) in regard to genetic resources and associated TK.

Chapter 7 discusses both regime shift and regime overlap, especially in regard to WIPO-IGC and UNESCO over the subject of TCE/EoF within a broader analysis that incorporates developments in the realm of tangible and intangible cultural heritage. Building on earlier discussions in Chapter 6 (which broached the role of biotechnology), Chapter 7 draws attention to the role of digital technology in escalating the tension between intellectual property and TCE/EoF as a complementary feature of intellectual property in global governance. Bio- and digital technological frameworks are identified respectively in the two chapters of Part III as technologies of globalization that are critical in the appropriation of various forms of expressive or intangible culture, even as their practical relevance in the protection and safeguarding of expressive culture is an aspect of the dialectics which technological poses for TK stakeholders in the narrative of intellectual property in global governance. Overall, Chapter 7 provides the historical backdrop of the interminable negotiations and transformations around TCE/EoF across diverse regimes by stakeholders, which has now predominantly crystallized in the activities of the WIPO-IGC as a crucial feature of the global governance narrative in the intellectual property context.

Chapter 8 articulates some conclusions that follow from the entire analysis in the three parts. It x-rays the crisis-ridden nature of the global intellectual property order and its potential to upset the technological leadership of present technology-exporting countries. Aswell, the chapter reflects on the overall implication of this state of affairs for the future of innovation and creativity. Noting the limitations of the market-driven ideology and present maximalist outlook of intellectual property jurisprudence, the chapter restates the imperative for balancing or moderating that approach with public-regarding considerations. It argues for a reconfigured global intellectual property order, one in which the development imperative is pivotal. Chapter 8 re-enforces the argument that as part of its ideal outcome, global governance in intellectual property could take advantage of its inherent democratic components to create a robust policy space in which the new emergent economic powers from the less developed world and critical intellectual property constituencies in the developed world could forge the urgently needed partnership for change. It argues that through the strategy of coalition building, these crucial economic blocs are in a position to lead the charge in shaping the global governance in intellectual property order with development-oriented interventions as a way to tackle the crisis of inequity in the global knowledge economy. Thus, the reproduction of development issues is an integral and essential part of intellectual property in global governance. This can be done by moderating normative production by development reproduction in global intellectual property policy and lawmaking.

Notes

1　WIPO is essentially an administrative organization, overseeing more than 20 treaties. Both on the basis of its enabling instrument and specific treaties administered by WIPO, the extent to which less developed countries have influence on the WIPO is a subject of debate. Despite the numerical advantage of less developed countries at the WIPO, especially in the wake of WIPO's transformation into a special agency of the UN in 1974, many analyses insist that the true measure of the influence of less developed countries (or lack thereof) at the WIPO is the extent to which development is mainstreamed in the WIPO. The continued marginalization of development issues at the WIPO is an affirmation of the historic gulf between that organization and the aspirations of less developed countries.

2　For example, the 2001 Convention for the Protection of Underwater Cultural Heritage, the 2001 Universal Declaration of Cultural Diversity, etc.

3　Recently, WIPO entered into partnership with the African Regional Intellectual Property Organization (ARIPO) and the Africa University in Harare, Zimbabwe, for a scholarship and training program in intellectual property. The program targets young African professionals from academic and research and development institutions who are expected to contribute to manpower development in intellectual property on the continent.

4　See WIPO, "The Significance of Adherence to the WIPO Copyright Treaty and the WIPO Performances and Phonogram Treaties." Available online: http://www.wipo.int/copyright/en/activities/wct_wppt/pdf/ advantages_wct_wppt.pdf (accessed 17 November 2010).

5　See Resolution 2001/33, April 2001 of the Commission on Human Rights on Access to Medicine in the Context of Pandemics Such as AIDS.

6　Appearing respectively in the text of the TRIPS Agreement under the titles of "exceptions to rights conferred" and "other uses without authorization of right holder."

7　As quoted by Yu (2007b: 13–14).

8　Quoting Arthur Stein, Rosenau (1995a: 29, n. 29) observes that "scholars have fallen into using the term regime so disparately and with such little precision that it ranges from an umbrella for all international relations to little more than a synonym of international organizations."

2 Global governance, intellectual property and the knowledge economy

> Intellectual property has become one of the major issues of our global society. Globalization is one of the most important issues of the day, and intellectual property is one of the most important aspects of globalization, especially as the world moves toward a knowledge economy. How we regulate and manage the production of knowledge and the right of access to knowledge is at the centre of how well this new economy, the knowledge economy, works and of who benefits. At stake are matters of both distribution and efficiency.
>
> (Stiglitz 2008b: 1695)

Globalization

To understand this book's conceptual focus on global governance and intellectual property, we start by looking at the notion of globalization. Globalization is a legally elusive and politically seductive subject, one that appears to have been demystified, yet about which curiosity has yet to abate. In the preface to his book, *In Defense of Globalization*, Jagdish Bhagwati wonders: "Does the world need yet another book on globalization?" He then observes that "[n]ot a day passes by without impassioned authors and activists, whether anti- or pro-globalization, putting their oars into these agitated waters ... But when all is said the fact is that we lack a clear, coherent, and comprehensive sense of how [economic] globalization ... works and how it can do better" (Bhagwati 2004: xi).

The lack of clear understanding of globalization's modus operandi is also indicative of a general lack of consensus on what globalization is. These gaps partly account for why globalization is indeed a thriving subject of scholarly inquiry and will remain so for a long time to come. Furthermore, the inconclusive attempts to grapple with the concept indicate its multivalent and elusive nature, and its impact on virtually all aspects of contemporary life. Most discourses of globalization appear to focus on its economic aspects or ramifications. However, the treatment of the concept as a "new academic industry" (Kumar 2003: 88) has mushroomed into virtually all conventional disciplinary classifications, providing a suffix and adjunct of choice for folks who want to take the globalization ride from their disciplinary vantage points. For example, there is no dearth of literature on such topics as cultural, political, regulatory/administrative, financial, institutional globalization.

Similarly, the litany of "globalization-and" studies remains robust and interminable. Thus, for a subject that is tackled at every conceivable front, it is perhaps natural that there will be some inadequacy of clarity and comprehensiveness as to what it is, let alone how it works.

Almost every author on globalization proffers his own, albeit restricted definition of the concept, giving regard to his disciplinary and conceptual outlook. A few perspectives on globalization that run through the definitions include those emphasizing the process of the breaking down of national systems or denationalization (Sassen 1996,[1] 2003); and the removal of restrictions and facilitation of diverse exchanges across national boundaries via regulatory harmonization and technological interventions (Braithwaite and Drahos 2000). Because of the prominence of economic analyses of globalization, the bulk of the definitions emphasize its role as a process in the consolidation of a world economy and its ensuing dynamics. For instance, Bhagwati (2004: 3) defines economic globalization as constituting the "integration of national economies into the international economy through trade, direct foreign investment (by corporations and multinationals), short-term capital flow, international flows of workers and humanity in general, and flows of technology."

From an international governance perspective, Dutfield and Suthersanen (2008: 3) offer a more embracing but hardly comprehensive description of globalization as "a process, or series of processes, which create and consolidate a unified world economy, single ecological system and a complex dynamic network of communication that covers the world". Similarly, for Stiglitz (2006: 4), "[g]lobalization encompasses many things [including]: the international flow of ideas, the sharing of cultures, global civil society and global environmental movements". He defines economic globalization as "the closer economic integration of countries of the world through increased flow of goods and services, capital and even labour."[2]

From doctrinal and often more critical points of view, globalization is associated with the global dispersal of neoliberal forms of economic imperialism in an extremely hegemonic fashion, as demonstrated or symbolised in various neoliberal economic strategies deployed by America in what Noam Chomsky characterizes as that country's quest for global dominance (Chomsky 2003). According to Santos (2006: 396) globalization "is a set of unequal exchanges in which a certain artefact, condition, entity or local identity extends its influence beyond its local or national borders and, in so doing, develops an ability to designate as local another rival artefact, condition, entity or identity". Santos argues that, under his process-based definition, there is no original global condition. Rather, he identifies two modes of the production of globalization: *globalized localism* in which one local system wins over other local regimes and becomes the global; and *localized globalism*, which depicts the damning impacts of globalized localism on specific local conditions. Such impacts include the oppression, exclusion, restructuring and general subordination of local conditions and their cooptation and uptake by the now triumphant localism that has now assumed a global status. As Santos points out, the two processes of globalisation "operate in conjunction and constitute the hegemonic type of globalization, also called neoliberal, top-down globalization or globalization from above" (2006: 397). He surmises that "what is generally called globalization is a vast social field in which hegemonic or dominant social groups, states, interests and ideologies collide with counter-hegemonic or subordinate or social groups, states, interests and ideologies on a world scale" (2006: 393).

This thumbnail sketch of the definitional perspectives on globalization is representative of the diverse approaches taken in the attempt by analysts from different disciplinary backgrounds to grapple with the concept. As well, it indicates the variegated tones through which scholars have tackled the subject of globalization. Implicit in these definitions are sentiments indicative of pro- and anti-globalization, and of subjective and objective approaches to globalization. However, the demarcation between an objective and subjective approach to globalization is hardly exact. Objectively, globalization as a process can be approached from a descriptive perspective. Despite doubts about the objectivity of a description, in a way, such a perspective may become a resourceful tool of analysis, even if it is not fully immune from the ideological tussle that has shaped globalization discourses, especially in the social sciences, as evident in de Sousa Santo's profound contributions to the subject.

Whether one's approach to globalization is supportive or oppositional, subjective or objective, there seems to be a consensus that the globalization experience or processes could be made to work better than it presently does (Bhagwati 2004; Long 2002; Stiglitz 2006). The challenge for the continuing unravelling of the concept of globalization is how to address its deficits in fairness and equity. Plugging the fairness and equity gap constitutes the "fierce urgency" of globalization, and both proponents and opponents seem to agree on the need to respond to it. In the pursuit of that imperative, the distinctions over various forms of globalization falter. The effects of economic globalization, negative or positive, are readily felt in the sociocultural and lived experiences of otherwise remote communities in hidden corners of the globe.

For example, the harmonization of trade regulation under the World Trade Organization's Agreement on Trade-Related Aspects of Intellectual Property (WTO/TRIPS) resulted in scuttling the ability of less developed countries to intervene in the patent system to cut back on the price of brand-name pharmaceuticals. Consequently, a strong globalized patent regime under TRIPS has continued to nail the coffins of many sick people in those less developed countries not able to afford essential medicines. Conversely, the explosion in information and communications technologies (ICTs) has had, by many accounts, positive sociocultural impacts on many peoples and communities, especially in less developed countries. The use of computers, access to the internet and affordable cellular phones not only boosts business transactions in many communities; it also advances their sociocultural and networking experiences. The point here is that the pervasive nature of the globalization process and its unlimited impacts on sociocultural and economic ordering do not make the distinctions between various kinds of globalization compelling.

Economic globalization would hardly make any sense if appraised in isolation from its sociocultural and other innumerable ramifications. Similarly, the economic impacts of other sites or processes of globalization including, for example, on culture, immigration, labor, communication, social networking, and knowledge production are conceivably the basis for their being taken seriously. In all, although economic globalization provides a pivotal traction for the elaboration of the phenomenon, increasingly it is becoming difficult to draw definitive lines of distinction between forms of globalization. To insist on drawing distinctions chips away the "global" in globalization. The inherently interlinked nature of the pervasive impacts of globalization, both from the vantage point of its disciplinary reach and convergences and in relation to its effects on virtually all aspects of people's lived realities in distance, space and time depicts globalization, rightly or wrongly, as a touchstone for a contemporary discourse on the "global process" and, by logical implication, on the notion of "global governance."

Global governance

That last sentence suggests a symbiotic relationship between globalization and global governance. This is certainly tenable but not in absolute terms, and so, requires clarification. The challenges of navigating, managing or trying to appraise the nature of a world order, if ever there were one, predates our current consciousness over globalization, which is only but a descriptive or discursive paradigm that attempts to capture a particular phase in the evolution of the so-called world system. World system theorists, or scholars of the world system or world politics committed to inquiries into the nature of that system, contend that as a concept and a discursive endeavour, global governance is as old as the inquiry into the nature of human interaction across diverse natural and artificial barriers (el-Ojeili and Hayden 2006; Held et al. 1999; Wallestein 2005).

Some chroniclers of the globalization experience (e.g. el-Ojeili and Hayden 2006: 17; Held et al. 1999) divide its evolution into phases. They distinguish between premodern globalization (from the Nordic Revolution to the 1500s – about 11,000 years of history); early modern globalization (from 1500–1850); modern globalization (1850–1945); and contemporary globalization (end of World War II–present). The early accounts of the dynamics of human experience on earth through its epochal phases pervaded by wars, conquests and anarchic experiences, peace, prosperity, trade, resource control, environmental and natural disasters, racial conflicts to more contemporary ideological and imperialist battles, colonialism, post-colonialism, technologically enhanced contacts are, arguably, constitutive of global governance. This form of constructing global governance accommodates the cooptation of the term by those who trace the origins of globalization far back in time predating the emerging consensus that points to the last three to four decades (Long 2002: 228).[3]

Despite doubts over the obligatory association of globalization with global governance, such an association takes the form of received wisdom in the narratives of globalization and global governance (Söderberg 2006: 21). Indeed, "globalization and the rise of global governance" is often an all-too-familiar expression in these field(s) (Krisch and Kingsbury 2006: 1). For instance, Santos (2006: 393) argues that "[t]he term 'global' today is used to refer both to the processes and to the results of globalization," while Söderberg (2006: 1, 21) notes that global governance is perceived as a byproduct of globalization and "is often used by policy-makers and scholars to describe and explain the social-political infrastructure of globalization." Similarly, she posits that, in its seminal elaboration of the concept of global governance, the Commission on Global Governance (CGG) takes the position that the imperative for global governance arises in part because of "the transformations brought about by globalization" (Söderberg 2006: 17). In the same vein, Stiglitz (2008b) ties the reformation of global governance to the imperative to keep pace with the challenges of economic globalization. Writing in the context of global health, Novotny (2007: 21) characterizes "[g]lobalization as the driving force for global governance."

As noted by Kennedy (2008: 848), in the legal context, the "sheer densities of rules and institutions in the global space" which are a result of globalization, easily links globalization with global governance. Globalization has not only "*fragmented* both economic and political power, but it has not de-legalized it" either.[4] He further notes:

> [t]he globalization of law, the legalization of politics and economics, has brought with it a tremendous dispersion of law. All manner of rules, enforced and un-enforced, may, as a matter of fact, affect any global transaction. [. . .] Some of this disorder is structured in one or another way [. . .] But some is also a matter of struggle and conflict, between legal orders, ideas, powers and traditions.
>
> (Kennedy 2008: 848)

Consequently, global governance is an experience in which some will gain and others will lose, warranting the need "to assess the dynamic and distributive effects of the disorderliness of global governance" (Kennedy 2008: 848–9).

Two points must be made in the light of the clear association of globalization with global governance. First, that association appears to find favor as a conceptual template that focuses on the abridgment of the chronicle of the evolution of the world system from its earlier to its latter day epoch: global governance is readily associated with postmodern or contemporary globalization. Second, the association of global governance with globalization emboldens a departure from traditional approaches to governance in conventional settings, including at corporate, national, and global levels of governance (Fratianni et al. 2007: 4). In the observations of Krisch and Kingsbury (2006: 10), "[g]lobal governance does not fit easily into the structures of classical, inter-state, consent-based models of international law; much too often it operates outside the traditional binding forms of law."

Clearly the "governance" in global governance is hardly a synonym of government; "rather it is broader concept necessary to address complex issues of a globalized world, a world where sovereign nations cannot individually respond to problems that span national boundaries" (Novotny 2007: 19). It is also a world in which, despite its enduring sanctity, the doctrine of the sovereignty of nation states as known in international law is now negotiable and readily compromised by overriding global contingencies (Long 2002; Sassen 1996), one in which non-state or sub-state actors are increasingly influential in the global process, often through the agency of unprecedented private–public partnerships. In short, "[i]n the era of globalization, governance no longer exclusively entails the activities of governments" (Söderberg 2006: 19).

Defining global governance

Following this outline of the nature of global governance, we now explore a few definitional perspectives on the concept. Before defining global governance, Söderberg counsels that its growing popularity notwithstanding, and but for a few exceptions, the concept of global governance "is notoriously ill-defined and devoid of any critical theorization" (2006: 1; Kennedy 2008). Rosenau and the CGG provide two leading definitions of global governance that have shaped recent dialogues on the subject. According to the CGG:

> [g]overnance is the sum of the many ways individuals and institutions, public and private, manage their common affairs. It is a continuing process through which conflicting or diverse interests may be accommodated and co-operative action may be taken. It includes formal institutions and regimes empowered to enforce compliance, as well as informal arrangements that people and institutions either have agreed to or perceive to be in their interest.
>
> (Söderberg 2006: 19)

Rosenau's work on global economic governance is credited with having analytically amplified the CGG work on the subject[5] (Söderberg 2006: 16). Both Rosenau and the CGG agree that the changes brought about by globalization necessitated a global governance system. Rosenau (1995a: 13–14) commenced his famous essay, "Global Governance in the Twenty-first Century," on a sober note:

> To anticipate the prospects for global governance in the decades ahead is to discern powerful tensions, profound contradictions, and perplexing paradoxes. It is a search for order in disorder, for coherence in contradiction, and for continuity in change, it is to confront processes that mask both growth and decay. It is to look for authorities that are obscure, boundaries that are in flux, systems of rules that are emergent. It is to experience hope embedded in despair.

Rosenau (1995a: 14, 16) endorses a notion of global governance that embraces both the activities of conventional governments and perhaps, more importantly, one that includes diverse channels for enhancing or facilitating the flow of "commands" or, preferably, "control mechanisms" that are represented in the nature of "goals framed, directives issued, and policies pursued." For him, however, it is critical that the reference to 'command' does not entail a hierarchical relationship. He argues that although such a relationship is typical of governments, in the global governance context, "it is certainly not a necessary prerequisite to the framing of goals, the issuing of directives, and the pursuit of policies." He further observes that "the central theme of this analysis is that often the practices and institutions of governance can and do evolve in such a way as to be minimally dependent on hierarchical, command-based arrangements" (1995a: 13). This can happen by substitution of command mechanisms with control or steering mechanisms.[6] Hence, he defines global governance as resting "on no single organizing principle but [being] the sum of myriad – literally millions of – control mechanisms driven by different histories, goals, structures, and processes . . . [in which] there is no characteristics or attributes common to all mechanisms" (1995a: 16). Rosenau's novel approach to grasping the nature of the concept reflects the prevailing modus operandi employed by non-governmental, intergovernmental and other entities in the pursuit of their activities within the interstices of complex mechanisms that influence and are influenced by macro- and micro-processes but devoid of hierarchical relationships.

Both Rosenau and the CGG's approach to global governance have been critiqued by Söderberg. Among other things, she charges that the "CGG's approach lacks historical insights into unequal human relations that compromise its multi-level governance structure" (2006: 2). She also disagrees with both Rosenau and the CGG's use of globalization as the premise for explaining the emergence of global governance. In her view, the playing field for Rosenau and the CGG's vision of globalization is hardly a level one. Consequently, Söderberg (2006: 21) prefers to locate globalization away from the emergence of global governance and rather, to identify it as "a moment of wider neoliberal-led forms of capitalist restructuring."

Söderberg's observation in regard to unequal human relations in the exploration of the dynamics of multilevel governance structures is a tenable argument. However, it is not clear why she seems averse to a direct association of global governance with globalization, but prefers to locate global governance within a neoliberal capitalist hegemony. Both frameworks are mutually re-enforcing and are not mutually exclusive, even in regard to the theme of unequal human relations and in terms of aspects of the evident negative impacts of globalization and global governance in contemporary society. Söderberg appears unimpressed with Rosenau's perceived apolitical and perhaps non-normative treatise on global governance. Specifically, reading from his seminal 1995 essay on which a significant part of Söderberg's intervention focused, one gets a sense of Rosenau's nuanced insensitivity to the neoliberal and capitalist ideological undercurrents of globalization and global governance.

Setting aside these sophisticated quibbles over the proper setting for engaging global governance, there is no scarcity of more accessible definitions of the term. Interestingly, Rosenau (1995a: 13) comes in handy when he avers that "global governance is conceived to include systems of rule at all levels of human activity from the family to the international organization – in which the pursuit of goals through the exercise of control has transnational repercussions." Weiss and Thakur

(2010: 6) define global governance as "the sum of laws, norms, policies and institutions that define, constitute and mediate relations among citizens, society, markets, and the state in the international arena – the wielders and objects of international public power." Elsewhere, the United Nations Economic and Social Council (ECOSOC) endorses several definitions of global governance, including the following which it associates with Weiss and Thakur:

> [T]he complex of formal and informal institutions, mechanisms, relationships, and processes between and among states, markets, citizens and organizations, both inter- and non-governmental, through which collective interest on the global plane are articulated, rights and obligations are established and differences are mediated.
>
> (ECOSOC 2006: para. 15 and n. 12)[7]

Global Governance,[8] the pioneer and flagship journal on the subject does not endorse a normative approach to the concept, but perceives global governance as an ongoing inquiry into managing the dynamics of "a more global world order" (Carin et al. 2006: 1). Along similar lines, Kennedy (2008: 832) notes that:

> We will need to think of our work on global governance not only as description, but also as program for a world in transition [. . .] We will need to think about global governance as a dynamic process in which political and economic arrangements unleash interests, change the balance of forces, and lead to further reinvention of the governance scheme itself.

Indeed, as a descriptive, conceptual, empirical and yet theoretical enterprise, global governance does not presuppose a global government (Söderberg 2006; Weiss and Thakur 2010). But it is an inherently multi- and interdisciplinary attempt at appraising the ongoing and ever unravelling regulatory dynamics, or lack thereof, in regard to grappling with the challenges of an ever increasing interdependent human society on a global scale wherein there is an absence of a hierarchical or overarching political authority.

On reflection and to sum up, a few points about global governance can be confidently asserted. First, global governance is deliberately associated with globalization, and we explore that association shortly. But, depending on one's conceptual outlook, global governance transcends globalization. Second, global governance is an ongoing conceptual and descriptive enterprise. It is neither prescriptive of what ought to be or is desirable nor is it about world government. Third, the relevance of global governance is enunciated against the backdrop of a perceived thinning of state sovereignty and the emergence of multivalent non-state or sub-state entities and new networks of actors on the global stage that, together, have assumed the nature of disaggregated sovereignty. At the same time, governments or nation states are key constitutive players in global governance. Fourth, global governance unfolds more in the sense of a concerted horizontal interaction of actors at the global level without the necessity of an overarching hierarchical authority. Fifth, of necessity and logic, the tensions and hegemonic and counter-hegemonic dialectics implicated in globalization also unravel in global governance. Finally, like globalization, global governance cannot be wished away. Rather, we face the challenge of how it could be made to work, or how it could continue to unravel in ways that are fair and equitable to those most at risk from the negative impacts of globalization.

Globalization and global governance in mutual tangle

Although segments of world systems theorists and analysts (el-Ojeili and Hayden 2006: 18; Held et al. 1999; Wallestein 2005) trace the evolution of world inter-connectedness or globalization back in time, global governance appears to enjoy more traction in reference to the contemporary globalization era which, many suggest, started three to four decades ago. What is it about globalization the buoys the notion of global governance? Framed differently, why did the notion of global governance as herein explored not gain traction earlier? Why did it not apply convincingly to earlier phases of globalization and earlier progressions in global interconnectedness?

I provide no exhaustive response to this question. I am content to highlight a few issues in response. First, the last three or four decades of the contemporary globalization phase also make up a period of intensified proliferation of control mechanisms implicated in global governance. For example, from the original 51 members at the end of World War II in 1945, to the addition of the Republic of Montenegro in 2006, the membership of the United Nations (UN) has increased almost fourfold to 193 countries. Rosenau (1995a: 15) notes that "the density of Non Governmental Organizations (NGOs) has increased at a comparable pace. More accurately, it has increased at a rate comparable to continuing growth of the world's population beyond five billion and a projected eight billion in 2025."

A combination of factors accounts for this rise in the steering mechanisms of global governance. They include new technological advances in bio- and digital technologies, and the latter's role in fueling recent democratic appetite in the Arab Middle East and North Africa; a renewed global consciousness regarding the environment (e.g. biodiversity, global warming/climate change); global public health crises (a rise in incidents of new diseases and a resurgence of old ones); heightened regional political rhetoric that fuels hardened religious and ideological divisions between the "axis of evil" and the forces of good; the unofficial reopening of the nuclear arms race; the September 11, 2001 terrorist attack on the United States (9/11); America's subsequent Invasion of Iraq; recent natural disasters such as the 2004 historic Indian Ocean Tsunami; the 2009 Haitian earthquake; the 2011 historic devastations from flooding, earthquakes and tsunamis in Australia, New Zealand, Japan and elsewhere; rampant forest fires and flooding; and not least, the resurgence of the issue of the rights and the place of indigenous peoples in national and international political and legal governance, heightened global poverty, food insecurity and the north–south development asymmetry. In response, new non- and intergovernmental organizations and forms of public–private partnerships have arisen in concert with state-sponsored and various new role players and stake-holders as part of the new control or steering mechanisms that dot the global governance landscape in the service of a global order. As well, existing NGOs have continued to reinvent themselves to respond to the perceived challenges of a global order. In this regard, the following observation could not be more apt:

> [I]f it is the case – as I believe it is – that global life in the twentieth century is more complex than ever before in history, it is because the world is host to ever greater numbers of organizations in all walks of life and in every corner of every continent. And it is this complexity, along with the competitive impulses that lead some organizations to defy steerage and resort to violence, that makes the task of governance at once difficult and so daunting.
>
> (Rosenau 1995b: 372)

Second, technological advances, especially in transportation, information and communications, remain a constant driver of earlier and contemporary globaliza-tion. In regard to the former, such advances are reflected in roads, navigation, rail-ways, and communications technologies such as the telephone, telegraph, telegram, etc. For the latter, technological advances concentrate around the computer-driven digital information and communication technological revolution and their ubiqui-tous multiplier effects manifested in the internet, email, e-commerce and the general internet platform with its new social networking culture, mobile and smart phones and various sophisticated and portable or non-portable digital electronic devices.

However, according to Bhagwati, the impacts of direct policy or regulatory changes were not the same on both phases of globalization. He argues that "today's most dramatic change is in the degree to which governments have intervened to reduce obstacles to the flow of trade and investments worldwide".[9] Hence, "[t]he story of globalization must be written in two inks: one colored by technical change and the other by state action" (Bhagwati 2004: 17). Comprising a total of approxi-mately 60 different agreements and associated legal instruments in various areas, the introduction of the WTO, which replaced the General Agreement on Tariffs and Trade (GATT), was an unprecedented act of multilateral state intervention to break down barriers to trade and to open up markets. Since the mid-1990s, the WTO, in terms of its institutional profile, processes, general outlook and its immense impact on peoples globally, remains an important flagship and catalyst for globalization. It is a state-sponsored institutional control mechanism and a critical site for dialectical convergences of states and non-state actors and other stakeholders in ways that demonstrate global governance at work in contemporary globalization.

Third, the commonality of technology as a driver of earlier and extant global-ization is already acknowledged. There is no doubt that the technological revolu-tions of the last three to four decades have had more impact on the rapid integration of the world economy and on the density of sociocultural experiences of peoples and cultures on a global scale than what happened before. The revolutions in computer-driven digital technology have left their imprint on all spheres of human interactions across the globe, both in the elimination of distance or space and in the abridgment of time. The economic and social impacts of these technologies are evident on both negative and positive templates. The emergence of electronic commerce, email, e-government, use of domain names (website addresses) in cyberspace, text messaging, social networking sites (YouTube, Facebook, MySpace, Twitter, etc.), the blogosphere and various internet-driven platforms has not only advanced communication; it has also radically expanded the scope of social-cultural, political and commercial activities to a global range with minimal jurisdictional inhibitions. Conversely, these same resources and opportunities are readily deployed for criminal and other negative ends, including but not limited to terrorism, paedophilia, violence, large-scale scams, national security breaches (e.g. Wikileaks) personal privacy infractions, etc. The information revolution re-enforces the collective vulnerabilities and collective strengths of peoples and nations globally.

Coming within the era of contemporary globalization, the computer-driven digital technology revolution has an enigmatic relationship with globalization. Such a relationship defies a precise analytical contour, but it is of a mutually reinforcing nature. Access to and use of these technologies is contentious and raise equitable and developmental concerns usually characterized as the digital divide. Similarly, there are frequent oppositions or resistances to these technologies expressed in the form of counterhegemonic sentiments. Finally, given their role in making our collective global security susceptible to breaches, the use of control or regulatory mechanisms to mediate converging interests in the new technologies of the contemporary globalization era draws in the global governance imperative. Atypical of global governance, the regulatory climate for digital technologies traverse virtually the gamut of control mechanisms, ranging, for example, from parent-installed child safety computer access devices, through specific industry self-regulation, to international treaties on electronic commerce.

Fourth, the application of information and communication technologies, especially digitization, has transformed the conduct of business, the practice of innovation via research and development, and the provision of special as well as general services delivery. Also, these technological revolutions have created diverse new professional categories, penetrated traditional professional groups (yielding unprecedented professional convergences), and thereby changed the nature and quality of service delivery within and across professions. And they will continue to do so. Specific examples are easily taken from developments in agricultural biotechnology, pharmacology and pharmaceutical productions, medicines, medical research, and the health professions in general, and of course, educational training at institutional and other disaggregated levels. In virtually all of these contexts, data generation assumes a concerted engagement. It often takes place on a networked scale and involves multiple but divergent stakeholders with competing interests. Consequently, the use and control of such data as electronic health records, genetic information and vital statistics are highly contentious issues that have global repercussions.

Responsible use and control of and access to critical data generated in diverse contexts (including basic and applied research), whether of general, genetic or of other special nature, are paradigmatic of the character of the technological currents surging in the sea of contemporary globalization. Given their pivotal role in this new knowledge and innovation paradigm, data or information management provides the touchstone for mapping new research ethics, for negotiating access to the benefits of innovation, and for addressing variegated equity concerns. All of these happen via the agency of multiple control or steering mechanisms embedded at professional, national, regional and international levels of global governance. Indeed, the technologies of globalization and the globalization of technologies are phenomenally situated at the core of what analysts have defined as the knowledge economy that has birthed post-industrial society.

In sum, the association of global governance with globalization is justified on many tenable grounds, including but not limited to: the heightened proliferation of control mechanisms, unprecedented technological advances with pervading and transformative impacts on all aspects of socioeconomic experience, and direct policy and regulatory changes that have resulted in a significant advancement of free trade. All of these lend credence to the notion of "fundamental differences that give globalization today a special, and at times sharp, edge" (Bhagwati 2004: 11) that, nevertheless, draws in the narrative of global governance.

The post-industrial society

More than three and a half decades ago, at the early onset of contemporary globalization and before global governance gained its current popularity, Daniel Bell in 1973[10] wrote his prophetic treatise, *The Coming of Post-Industrial Society: A Venture in Social Forecasting.*[11] Bell's notion of post-industrial society has an organic link with the post-industrial economy.[12] His elaboration of post-industrial society is not without criticisms (e.g. Ferkiss 1979; Veneris 1984,[13] 1990). To mention a few, Bell's elevation of the service sector (which is a tertiary sector in capitalist economic production) in his analysis of factors undergirding a post-industrial society (Bell 1973: 127),[14] tends to unduly undermine the enduring role and the constant nature of the industrial sector in the overall capitalist economic production scheme. Also, the post-industrial label is perceived to be problematic as an analytical tool with which to capture this historic transformation in the global economic matrix. Thus, without dismissing Bell's original idea, some (e.g. Crawford 1983; Machlup 1973)[15] have suggested the term "information society" as more appropriate, a term Bell considered but insistently did not favor.[16] The reservations about Bell's use of the term "post-industrial society" notwithstanding, the phrase invokes an apt or compelling imagery that captures, in a way, paradigmatic technological transitions in the "knowledge economy," a phrase which by itself both captures and nicely mediates Bell's post-industrial society and his critic's favored substitute, the "information society." Without allowing terminological hair splitting to detain us here, Bell's argument for the choice of the "post-industrial society" label is coupled with a tinge of counsel. He writes:

> I employed the term "post-industrial society" [*inter alia*] . . . to underline a major axial principle, that of intellectual technology. But such emphasis does not mean that technology is the primary determinant of all social changes. No

conceptual scheme ever exhausts a social reality. Each conceptual scheme is a prism which selects some features, rather than others in order to highlight historical change, or more specifically, to answer certain questions.

(Bell 1973: ix–x)

Post-industrial society, knowledge economy, information society, digital revolution, digital age, computer age, biorevolution, etc., are collectively indicative of the competing, sometimes complementary and non-exclusive attempts to characterize the results of recent technology-driven historic and historical transitions in our global socioeconomic experience.

Since no conceptual scheme ever exhausts a social or, indeed, an economic reality, it serves our purpose here to map, in a non-exhaustive fashion, a few critical and evident features of this new society that are at the core of these multiple characterizations. To conduct this task, we will build on the earlier discussions by exploring the complicity of bio- and digital technologies in globalization and global governance. Collectively, the terms bio- and digital technologies carry no precise analytical levers. But they are used frequently without discrimination to nuance:

[T]he ascendancy and rapid transformation of information (often depicted as a synonym of knowledge) and its generation and management, mainly with the help of computer-driven digital technologies in the spheres of economic, research, administration, service delivery and diverse industrial activities often with special interest in data mining and biotechnology or biological/genetic engineering.

(Oguamanam 2009a: 131)

Whether we place the emphasis on biotechnology, digitization or computers in general, or on their impact in revolutionizing the role of information in innovation and wealth generation, information or knowledge is at the core of the functioning and regulation of post-industrial society. Perhaps nothing emboldens analysts to contemplate the dawn of a post-industrial society or the knowledge economy more than the commodification of information and/or knowledge. In locating the new society in its historic context, Bell (1973: 126–7) distinguishes between pre-industrial, industrial and post-industrial societies. He avers that in pre-industrial society, labor was deployed overwhelmingly in natural resource exploitation, for example, in mining, fishing, forestry, agriculture, etc. He notes that industrial societies are goods-producing societies, where energy and machines are key sources of labor that transform the nature of work. In post-industrial society, labor is concentrated in the professions and "[w]hat counts is not raw muscle power or energy, but information" (1973: 127). Thus, whereas in pre-industrial society "life is primarily a game against nature," in the industrial and post-industrial epoch, it assumes the nature of "a game against fabricated nature" and "a game between persons" in regard to the contestation over the control of information (1973: 126–7).

From a similar but slightly different conceptual outlook, George Takach (2003: 48–9) argues that land was the primary economic asset and critical determinant of social relations in the era of the Agricultural Revolution. In regard to the Industrial Revolution, he points out that mass-produced factory goods of a physical nature constituted the defining asset of that period. Processing information/symbols, data generation/mining and data management constitute the defining economic activity of the information age. The uniqueness of the information age, Takach rightly argues, lies not in the displacement of two previous eras, but in its strategic relevance as an additional layer for injecting efficiency and minimizing the operational and overall cost of activities such as agriculture and other forms of industrial production. Perhaps what sets that age apart is how it is able to revolutionize preexisting economic activities while opening up novel opportunities and facilitating unprecedented convergences in production, research and service delivery. For example, it is hard to contemplate an industrial activity that is not serviced by computer technology in one form or another. The same is true in the use of land, whether for agricultural or other purposes. The significance of computer-driven digital technology is, in a way, symbolically represented by the rise of ICT corporations,[17] large and small, and their multiplier effects in virtually every sphere as the most lucrative economic sector over, for example, real estate and other hitherto traditionally viable sectors. In Canada, dated statistics indicate that the ICT sector accounts for over 60% of the economy while the rest is shared between agriculture, industry and general services (Takach 2003: 50). This trend is no less different in the rest of the developed countries of the North Atlantic littoral and a few others elsewhere.

Critics may rightly question the basis for the exclusion of a particular society or economy from being knowledge based (el-Ojeili and Hayden 2006: 32). Surely, knowledge is and has been at the core of social and economic ordering at all times now and in the past. However, in the contemporary globalization era, like no other time in history, information or knowledge constitutes, perhaps, the most crucial factor or tool of production and has remained the most important matrix in the overall economic development of this period (Oguamanam 2009a: 131). In this account, the generation, ownership, and management, including the manipulation of information are considered pivotal in the new global knowledge economy. In a way, the last is a feature of a post-industrial society, and it services, and is in turn serviced by, information.[18] The practical visibility of digital technology – i.e. simply the reduction of all forms of information representation into numeric-based signals recordable electronically or on an optical medium[19] for ease of manipulation, storage and overall application and management in the deployment of vital information and knowledge toward the neutralization of jurisdictional boundaries, is a hallmark of post-industrial society. It is one that demonstrates post-industrial society's fusion with globalization and the nascent knowledge economy.

Next to the facilitation of a global knowledge economy as a fundamental application of computer technology, the malleability, relevance and overall application of digitization in diverse sectors of critical economic and social activities is its greatest contribution to globalization. Digital technologies supervise the intensification of information linkages and application of knowledge across sectoral boundaries with unprecedented socioeconomic ramifications and global repercussions.

The impact of this trend is easily demonstrated by an exploration of the changing innovation matrix under what we call here the 4Bs.

The 4Bs: biodiversity, bioprospecting, biotechnology and biopiracy

Biodiversity

The year 1992 marked the start of a sea change in international environmental governance pursuant to the United Nations Conference on Environment and Development (UNCED) held in Rio de Janeiro, Brazil, that year. Indeed, narratives of globalization from the environmental perspective are incomplete without the mention of the "Rio Earth Summit." This summit produced several environmental control mechanisms by way of soft and hard law instruments[20] that remain of strategic significance to subsequent developments in global environmental governance. Specifically, for our present purpose, the Convention on Biological Diversity (CBD) is perhaps one of the most prominent legal instruments to emerge from Rio. In a nutshell, the Convention's objectives are:

> [T]he conservation of biological diversity [also biodiversity], the sustainable use of its components and the fair and equitable sharing of the benefits arising out of the utilization of genetic resources, including by appropriate access to genetic resources and by appropriate transfer of relevant technologies, taking into account all rights over those resources and to technologies, and by appropriate funding.
>
> (CBD: Article 1)

The urgency for a legal and policy intervention in the conservation of biodiversity is in response to incontrovertible accounts of unparalleled decline or loss of biodiversity and, by extension, biological resources (McManis 2007; Oguamanam 2006a; Raven 2007; Raven and Yeates 2007). At an estimated rate of a hundred species a day and four species per hour, the current state of species extinction is said to be in a magnitude beyond any previous experience in history (Oguamanam 2006a: 41; Wood 2000: ix):

> Biodiversity encompasses all species of plants, animals and microorganisms and the ecosystems, and the ecological processes of which they are parts. It is an umbrella term for the degree of nature's variety [. . .] usually considered at three levels: genetic diversity, species diversity and ecosystems diversity.
>
> (Oguamanam 2006a: 37)[21]

Biodiversity is the principal source of biological resources, which then is the basis of its obligate value to humanity. From a holistic environmental point of view, the alarming loss or threat to global biodiversity has severe implications for human subsistence and for the general dynamics of earth life. At no point in time has this awareness become more obvious than in the late 20th century. Whether by coincidence or inexplicable design, that period marks a paradigm shift in innovation from mechanical inventions of the previous industrial era to a monumental focus on life sciences often depicted as a biorevolution. Thus, the time of the increased awareness of the prevailing exponential threat to global biodiversity is also one of heightened appreciation of its value as the reservoir of core raw material for the sustenance of new technological breakthroughs based on the use of life forms, loosely referred to as biotechnology, a subject to which we shall turn shortly.

The significance of biological diversity is evident in yet another contentious context. By some accounts, an estimated 75% of the world's biological resources and, by extension, its biological diversity, are located in the global south and in the homes of the world's local or indigenous communities (Oguamanam 2006a: 23, 39, 50). For many of these communities, located mainly in the less developed countries of the south, direct relationships with biological diversity and resources, including a methodical engagement with ecological forces, is key to their survival (Brush and Stabinsky 1996). Such relationships are sites for the expression of their epistemic identity, overall worldview and self-determination. However, control of critical technologies used in exploiting the world's biological resources lie within western industrial and techno-scientific establishments. Hence, policy around access to biological resources and biodiversity conservation are critical to the post-industrial era and the global knowledge economy.

Bioprospecting

From this analysis we surmise as follows: first, in the new economic order, there is a boost in the innovation matrix in the direction of engineering of life forms or biological diversity/resources in comparison to the traditional technical inventions. Second, biological diversity and, by extension, biological resources are under alarming threat of extinction due to overexploitation; and, third, the natural dispersals or distributions of the world's biological diversity are clearly uneven in regard to the two global geopolitical and economic blocks of north and south. Consequently, access to biological or genetic resources in their centers of origin, especially in the global south, has become a key subject for global governance. Clearly, the reference in the CBD objective cited earlier to "fair and equitable sharing of the benefits arising out of the utilization of genetic resources . . . [and] appropriate access to genetic resources" (CBD: Article 1) is indicative of the role of CBD as a control or governance mechanism for global biological resources.

In marked departure from the period when biological, including, of course, genetic resources were referred to as the common heritage of mankind, the CBD confers on states "the sovereign right to exploit their own [biological] resources" (CBD: Article 3) within their respective national boundaries, and to determine terms of engagement with external interests. Even so, biological diversity and resources have the status of a common concern of mankind (Brunnée 2009: 44; Oguamanam 2006a). At least, theoretically, this provides the reasons for the concerted global effort to conserve it, notwithstanding the unevenness of their location across the two geopolitical blocs. Also, that status provides the justification for accommodating the imperative for access to genetic resources to those who are not as endowed with them.

Since 2000, through its Working Group on Access and Benefits Sharing (ABS), the CBD has continued to elaborate on the appropriate modality for ABS pursuant to its principal objectives. In this regard, the CBD's governing body, the Conference of Parties (COP), issued the 2002 Bonn Guidelines on access to genetic resources and the fair and equitable sharing of the benefits arising from their utilization developed by the Working Group. Among other things, that document endorses the notion of prior informed consent (PIC) of owners of sought-after genetic resources and a framework of engagement with second comers under mutually agreed terms (MAT). The CBD's Bonn Guidelines provided the framework for the 2010 Nagoya Protocol on ABS regarding which negotiations were concluded on October 29, 2010.

Biological diversity provides a critical contact point for geopolitical tension between the north and the south. The framework for the conduct of bioprospecting and, by extension, biotrade is now at the center of equity, efficiency and distributional concerns in the knowledge economy. This is critical because more often than not, biological resources have inherent association or relationship to local knowledge. For example, reliance on local knowledge to screen for variable compounds in medicinal plants prods the success rate for drug discovery by 78% (Horton 1995: 5; Oguamanam 2004b: 140).

The relationship between biological resources and local knowledge is sometimes direct and clear. At other times, it can be nuanced; hence, the process of bioprospecting is often one of surreptitious unidirectional knowledge transfer. Bioprospecting refers to the search by external interests for biological and genetic resources of economic value, especially those at the center of biodiversity origins, while biotrade simply refers to transnational trade in those resources (Oguamanam 2006a: 10–11). The practice of foraging the tropical rainforests is an ongoing historical, exploitative adventure dating back to colonialism. In fact, even the issue of equitable access and extension of the benefits of genetic resources via public gene banks, under discussion in the Consultative Group on International Agricultural Research (CGIAR),[22] has remained unresolved (Mgbeoji 2006; Oguamanam 2006b). However, the period immediately preceding and following the emergence of the CBD marks the bourgeoning of a range of institutional scrutiny and other interventions over the conduct of bioprospecting. This is sustained by a combination of multiple control mechanisms, including NGO public interest advocacy, self-initiated and ethically based corporate best practices, national, regional and country-specific direct regulatory and legislative interventions mainly based on the CBD framework.[23] I have noted elsewhere that "[i]n recent times, access and benefits sharing (ABS) and other contractual frameworks for the exploration of local knowledge between indigenous communities and second comers are as diverse as there are such communities" (Oguamanam 2008a: 46). An equitable framework for the conduct of bioprospecting from the onset is imperative to ensure the extension of the benefits and results of biotechnology activities that depend on the acquired genetic resources. It is also a necessary way of nipping biopiracy in the bud. The next sections explore the significance of biotechnology and the concept of biopiracy as components of the new innovation matrix of the knowledge economy.

Biotechnology

Advances in biotechnology constitute one of the most paradigmatic trends in the technological transformations of the post-industrial society. Such advances lie at the heart of the new knowledge economy. In many ways, biotechnology is symbolic of the transition in innovation from the technical inventions of the industrial era to the recent focus on life forms and life sciences. In a nutshell, biotechnology depicts diverse techno-scientific interventions over life forms, especially including techniques for manipulating the genetic materials of living organisms and for exploring the complex chemistry of biological systems for, *inter alia*, therapeutic intervention, agricultural production, environmental management and various industrial and life style applications (Oguamanam 2007b: 222). Tinkering with biological systems is not new to science. But since the discovery of the DNA structure in the mid-20th century as a medium of transmission and encoding of genetic information and pattern in replication of life (Oguamanam 2009b; Watson 2001), and subsequent developments in rDNA research, genetic engineering and its applications have gained prominence as drivers of cutting-edge innovations especially in agriculture, health and pharmaceutical production. Genetic engineering, also referred to as genetic modification or gene splicing, differs from other forms of techno-scientific intervention with life forms. This is because its direct focus on genes and gene functions enables a deliberate and targeted alteration of gene characteristics within and even across different organisms for a given objective. For instance, in agriculture, while conventional breeding is a science-based extension of artificial seed selection practiced by farmers from time immemorial, genetic engineering involves the mapping of genes and their functions with a view to discovering and exploiting desirable traits for faster and bigger products output and longer timespan preservation in their "natural" forms.

In addition to plants, animals and microorganisms, humankind and its diversity are also a critical focal point for the genetic engineering enterprise. In a way, this is epitomized in the 1990 joint initiative of the US Department of Energy and National Institutes of Health called the Human Genome Project (HGP). This was designed, *inter alia*, to map or identify all genes in the human DNA genome and then to sequence the three billion letters, also known as the chemical base pairs of the human genome, i.e. the human DNA code and the project has since assumed global significance. At the completion of the project in 2003, scientists discovered that of the three billion letters of the human genome, 99.9% are identical between individuals. Consequently, only 0.1% of the human genome differentiates for variation between humans and is responsible for individual susceptibility to disease. Just before the formal completion of the HGP, a consortium of six countries (Canada, China, Japan, Nigeria, the UK and the US) became the focus of the

Haplotype Mapping (HapMap) initiative, which focuses on that 0.1% of the human genome to investigate the chromosomal regions that constitute the core sites of genetic variation (Oguamanam 2009b). This is with a view to identify and catalogue genetic similarities and differences in human beings so as "to locate genes associated with [specific] diseases and their likely responses to therapeutic drugs and overall individual responses to modifications and environmental factors" (Oguamanam 2009b: 945).

The ramifications of the HGP for the future of research and innovation in medicine, pharmaceutical production, diagnostics and therapy is already evident in the phenomena of genomics, proteomics and personalized medicine and, generally, in the recent focus on medical care delivery for individual genetic profiles. Francis Collins, director of the US National Genome Human Research Institute, calls the completion of the HGP the real beginning of genomics (Collins 2005). Others describe it as "the single most important project in biomedical sciences, predicated to have unprecedented impact and long-lasting value for basic biology, biomedical research, biotechnology and health care" (Shan and Busia 2002: 194). Like most other biotechnology endeavors, the HGP project poses ethical, legal and social challenges in its wake (Gold and Knoppers 2009; Knoppers 2000). For example, increasing interest in the collection of DNA samples of indigenous peoples for research arising from their incredible diversity and spurred by their rapid extinction rate, or threats thereof, has come under fierce opposition and criticism by a coalition of indigenous peoples' groups on ethical, legal (including human rights) and social grounds.[24] The criticism dogged and scuttled the Human Genome Diversity Project (HGDP) – a population-centered research initiative designed to map human DNA variations.[25]

An interesting aspect of biotechnology is the shrinking or leveling of disciplinary gulfs between the basic and applied sciences. For example, the outcome of scientific research activities around life forms blurs the boundary between food and medicine, expanding the scope of techno-scientific possibilities around life forms to unprecedented levels. Biotechnology is conditioned for the uptake of advances in basic biomedical sciences, facilitating the emergence of scientific networks and the expansion of scientific opportunities (DiMasi and Paquette 2004: 11). In the pharmaceutical sector, this has resulted in a gradual transition from random screening to targeted drug design and diagnostics, and in a slow change in marketing dynamics from blockbuster to designer drugs (Oguamanam 2009b).

Also, biotechnology is naturally linked to nutritional enhancement or functional food production and public health in general (Ryan-Harshman 1997). For example, food biotechnology facilitates the advancement of micronutrients such as vitamins and irons in most staple food crops, a process called biofortification, a process used to address nutritional deficiencies in endemic populations. Practices ranging from pre-implantation genetic diagnostics (PGD), xeno transplantation, human and animal cloning, stem cell research, biofortification, biopharming and terminator technologies, to exploits in cosmeceuticals, nutraceuticals, genetic modification or biotechnology, raise complex ethical challenges outside the scope of this book. But access to the benefits of biotechnology, especially by segments of the global population that are the sources of global biodiversity, biological resources and local knowledge including the human and genetic diversity critical to biotechnology, is a major issue for the distributional equity and efficiency of the new knowledge economy.

Biotechnology in general, and in genetic engineering in particular, are essentially interdisciplinary ventures involving the convergence of disciplines in basic sciences, including molecular biology, genetics, genomics, pharmacogenomics, proteomics, cloning technology and new and emerging peripheral fields such as health information/communication technology, bioinformatics – the application of information technology to the field of molecular biology. Perhaps more importantly, advances in biotechnology and genetic engineering are amply supported and serviced by computer-driven digital technology. Because biotechnology is, for the most part, an information-based enterprise, the management and translation of critical information generated in the biotechnology context is facilitated by digital technology resources and information technology professionals. The biotechnology enterprise is unfeasible without digital technology. Few examples illustrate this more than how advances in digital technologies facilitated the early completion of the sequencing of the human genome far ahead of its projected target date.

Elsewhere I have noted that:

> [b]iological resources are the critical raw materials for biotechnology. In the GKE [global knowledge economy] increased concentration of research and development by Western industrial and scientific complexes on plant and animal [including human] genetic resources targets the biological resources in developing countries and other centres of origin of biodiversity. A combination of bio- and digital technologies facilitate the harnessing of biological resources and associated indigenous or local knowledge in developing countries of the South; a trend which analysts have associated with unidirectional transfer of wealth and knowledge.
>
> (Oguamanam 2009a: 136)[26]

Biopiracy

The inequitable south–north knowledge transfer via the intense increase in the applications of biotechnology is more appropriately captured by the buzzword "biopiracy." The word is credited to foremost Canadian activist and Executive Director of the Action Group on Erosion Technology and Concentration (the ETC Group) Pat Mooney (Mgbeoji 2006: 12). It is used as a counterhegemonic defense and attack strategy of retort by less developed countries long accused by the industrialized world of acts of piracy or illegal appropriation of the latter's technologies through lax intellectual property laws, especially in published materials, agriculture, chemicals, pharmaceuticals and physical innovations in general.

As both counter-argument and play on words, biopiracy describes the activities of western-based transnational corporations backed by their home governments in regard to the acquisition of biological resources and or associated knowledge of indigenous and local communities of the global south and elsewhere. These corporations and research concerns take advantage of the global and domestic intellectual property systems to obtain questionable patents (piracy) over those resources and associated knowledge, neither acknowledging nor recognizing the contributions of the local peoples to the generation of the knowledge. Mgbeoji (2006: 12) defines biopiracy in secondary terms as "the asymmetrical and unrequited movement of plants and TKUP [traditional knowledge of uses of plants] from the South to the North through the processes of international institutions and the patent system." He argues further:

> [i]f the infringement of patents, copyrights and trademarks constitute intellectual piracy, then so does the failure to recognize and compensate indigenous and traditional peoples for the creations arising from their knowledge. Inherent to the biopiracy rhetoric are the notions of unauthorized appropriation/theft of biological diversity and its associated traditional knowledge. The concept of biopiracy concerns law, ethics, morality and fairness.
>
> (Mgbeoji 2006: 12)

This process of knowledge transfer, or funneling of precious natural resources from the global south to the north, dates back to early colonial encounters under the international division of labor when one region (the colonized south) provided the raw materials for the other, the colonial industrialized powers which laid exclusive claim to the scientific prowess required to transform the so-called raw materials into industrial applications (Oguamanam 2008a: 33). The colonial appropriation of science and technology legitimized the exclusion of indigenous knowledge from the scientific narrative. Consequently, indigenous and local peoples' dealings with their biological resources and their experience with biodiversity is seen as bereft of intellectual content in accordance with colonial hierarchies of culture and power (Arewa 2006a; Oguamanam 2008a: 32–3).

It must be noted that in the post-industrial or knowledge economy, the focus of innovation via the life sciences has yielded increased interest in the biological resources in indigenous and local communities, which also double as centers of global biodiversity. Recently, the association of biological resources with indigenous knowledge has become part of the received wisdom in agriculture, pharmaceuticals, phytomedicine, and forms of therapeutic intervention. Increasingly, in general terms, it has become difficult to deny the intellectual content of indigenous knowledge in the context of innovation in life sciences. However, because of the prevailing gap in the conventional legal regime for the protection of knowledge systems, indigenous knowledge and associated resources remains the subject of legal and illegal appropriation by agents of western science. Such appropriations elicit accusations of biopiracy that evoke concerns over access to knowledge (A2K). Such concerns range from general issues in regard to equity and distributive justice over the products of biotechnology, to the need for adequate reward for the contributions of indigenous and local communities in the convergent process of knowledge production in the new global knowledge economy.

The biopiracy debate often focuses on the appropriation of indigenous knowledge of plant and animal genetic resources especially in agriculture, medicine and associated contexts. However, as discussed in Chapters 6 and 7, it has acquired special meaning and now encompasses references to the appropriation of the tangible and intangible cultural heritage of non-western peoples, including their expressive culture and the misappropriation of sacred images or symbols of indigenous peoples for commercial purposes via the use of high-technologies and diverse new digital media. Biopiracy appears no longer to be limited to abuses in the patent regime of intellectual property. For example, as also illustrated in Chapter 7, the Ami Song of Joy, also called "Jubilant Drinking Song," was a commercial sample of a live recording of the voices of Taiwan's largest indigenous peoples, the Ami (Taylor 2003). The song was sampled in another song, "Return to Innocence," by the German electronic pop group Enigma, and was licensed for use in the 1996 Atlanta Olympics without the consent of the Ami. The song sold five million copies. The Ami's objection resulted in a lawsuit that was settled out of court. A similar experience trailed "'Deep Forest,' a techno-house rhythm album created in 1992 that fused digital samples from Ghana, the Solomon Islands and African Pygmies" (Arewa 2006b: 177). These and a few other examples are elaborated in Chapter 7 in the discourse on the role of digital technology in cultural appropriation. There are also analogous experiences of exploitation of indigenous knowledge via the commercial appropriation of native symbols. Notable examples include cases involving challenges to the use of sacred symbols of New Zealand Maori and Native American peoples (Anderson 2009).[27]

Beyond expressive culture and intangible cultural heritage, at the global level, the litany of cases of biopiracy involving medicinal plants and agricultural crops has continued to increase since the 1990s when the biopiracy debate gained prominence.[28] Without exploring their specific accounts, which have been dealt with elsewhere,[29] it should be noted, for example, that the following medicinal plants or agricultural crops with origins in several less developed countries have contributed in one way or another to the documented narratives of biopiracy: the neem tree, basmati rice, turmeric, Karela juice, Enola bean, arogyapaacha, hoodia cactus, rooibois tea, rosy periwinkle, Nigerian cow pea, cinchona bark, pozol, etc. Despite skepticism over the juridical status and emotive nature of biopiracy (Dutfield 2006b; Heald 2003: 521), the concept appears to have caught on. It now constitutes an entrenched subtext in the narrative of appropriation and an important aspect of the intellectual property debate in the new innovation matrix of the knowledge economy. In the colonial experience, biological resources were removed physically via briefcases and cages by sheer colonial authority from centers of biodiversity origins, most of which doubled as colonial outposts. Today, digital technology enhances the transfer of such resources. Indeed, the genetic profile of vital biological resources or even of indigenous peoples can easily be disguised and compressed in a flash drive or other digital capturing devices in mind-boggling quantities for illegitimate objectives.

Conclusion

This chapter elaborated in a conceptual and critical manner, and deployed the ideas of global governance and globalization to provide some explanation for the association of the two concepts, especially in the analysis of contemporary globalization. I have also examined the complex but logical relationships that these concepts bear to one another, and the roles that they play in our effort to understand the major and mutually re-enforcing technological transformations of the 20th and 21st centuries, specifically the bio- and digital technologies and the birth of the post-industrial society. In situating biodiversity, bioprospecting, biotechnology and biopiracy – the 4Bs – as the composite focal point of the new innovation matrix, I highlighted the complementary roles of the two dominant technologies of the post-industrial, epoch – bio- and digital technologies – and how they are implicated in the unidirectional knowledge transfer from the south to the north. The next chapter draws in the significance and contentious role of intellectual property in the post-industrial era, and in supervising the process of south–north knowledge transfer. Building on this contentious role, I demonstrate how intellectual property has become a veritable site for regime dynamics and for the aggregation of diverse control mechanisms that map the global governance landscape for intellectual property.

Notes

1 Sassen (1996) alludes to the importance of state sovereignty as an enduring feature of the national system despite the influence of supranational institutions in pushing a partial denationalization of sovereign states.

2 See also Stiglitz 2002.

3 Long argues that globalization, as an integrative market phenomenon, has existed at least from the days of the development of commerce later in the Middle Ages and has existed in its present form, at least, since the Industrial Revolution. Additionally, Ladner and Dick (2008: 63) contend that "[i]n many ways, 1492 represents the onset of globalization in the Americas." Prior to that period, indigenous nations had integrated trade networks that became global when indigenous peoples and Europeans mutually attempted to integrate each other into their respective political, social and economic systems via the colonial encounter.

4 Emphasis in the original.

5 See, for example, in addition to his other profound contributions, Rosenau 1995: chs 1,13 and 16.

6 In rejecting the use of "command" by the Council of Rome formulation of global governance, Rosenau, citing King and Schneider (1991: 181–2) substitutes that word "with the concept of control or steering mechanism, terms that highlight the purposeful nature of governance without presuming the presence of hierarchy." He endorses the notion of governance as a process through which organization or society steers itself whereof communication and control dynamics are critical to that objective.

7 The ECOSOC study credits Weiss and Thakur's (2010) book as the source of the definition when the book was in a pre-publication stage under a slightly different title.

8 Fully titled *Global Governance: A Review of Multilateralism and International Organizations*, this is an authoritative pioneer journal in the field of global governance. Since 1995 it has continued to shape conceptual, empirical and public policy centered interdisciplinary research on the subject of global governance and has had on its editorial teams, now

and at various times, leading scholars and policy experts in the field of global governance.

9 Long (2002: 228) shares similar sentiments. She notes that, "[t]he primary impact of present-day economic globalization has been the inexorable integration of markets, nation-states and technologies to a degree never witnessed before."

10 Bell's other work of the same era is titled *The Cultural Contradictions of Capitalism* (1976). In addition to Bell's several works written together with other scholars, these two works are, in the social sciences, central to the debate over the nature of a post-industrial society.

11 Even before and after Bell's treatises, there was much literature and scholarly discourse on the characterization of the nature and potential impact and scenarios regarding the emerging technological transformations of the late 19th century. For example, Ferkiss (1979) cites several scholars who began to push the concept of post industrial society perhaps earlier than Bell: Kahn, H. and Weiner, A.J. (1967) "The Next Thirty-Three Years: A Framework for Speculation," in Bell (ed.), "Toward the Year 2000: Work In Progress," *Daedalus* 96: 726; Kahn, H. and Bruce-Briggs, B. (1972) *Things to Come: Thinking About the '70s and '80s*, New York: Macmillan; Kahn, H. and Martel, L. (1976) *The Next 200 Years*, New York: William Morrow.

12 In fairness to Bell, he disclaimed that his essay was not a point-in-time prediction of the future but a speculative initiative concerned mainly with determining the operative factor in effecting social change. He argued that the idea of a post-industrial society is neither a "definition" nor a "forecast" but a scenario. See also Tilton, T.A. and Bell, D. (1973) "Dialogue: The Next Stage of History," *Social Research* 40: 747.

13 Veneris's 1984 PhD thesis explored trends and theories (general economic and regional), and developed a large-scale dynamic simulation model of the transition from an industrial to an informational economy.

14 Bell argues that "[a] post-industrial society is based on services. Hence, it is a game between persons. What counts is not raw muscle power, or energy but information."

15 Crawford (1983) credits the origin of the phrase to the eminent economist, Fritz Machlup.

16 In the 1976 preface to *The Coming of Post-Industrial Society*, Bell responds to his critics who questioned the appropriateness of the term "post-industrial society" by charging that "perhaps a major misconception is to identify the idea of the post-industrial society with the expansion of the service (or tertiary) sector of the economy and dispute its importance ... To the extent that some critics identify me with the centrality of a service sector, it is either ignorance or wilful misreading of my book." Note: Bell identifies Herman Kahn (a friend of his) as one of his misguided critics, see Kahn and Bruce-Briggs 1972.

17 This is exemplified by Microsoft, Apple and other internet-dependent platforms such as Google, YouTube, Facebook and Twitter.

18 See Machlup 1973 and Crawford 1983.

19 Takach 2003: 35.

20 The soft law instruments include the Rio Declaration, Agenda 21, and the Non-Legally Binding Authoritative Statement of Principles for Global Consensus on the Management, Conservation and Sustainable Development of All Types of Forests (the Forest Principles). Hard law instruments from Rio include: the Convention on Biological Diversity and the Convention to Combat Desertification in those Countries Experiencing Serious Drought and/or Desertification, Particularly in Africa.

21 See also CBD Article 2 for the definition of biological diversity.

22 CGIAR was established in 1971 as a private–public initiative that manages the use and access to plant genetic resources in *ex situ* seed banks for agricultural research, including plant breeding. It is a consortium of 15 federated international agricultural research centers that operate with national agricultural research centers and a host of private sector and civil society organizations in the agricultural, food and seed sectors.

23 See, for example, Ten Kate and Laird (2002), McManis (2007), and Kamau and Winter (2009).

24 For accounts of indigenous peoples' opposition to specific projects, see the US- and Canada-based Indigenous Peoples Council on Biocolonaliasm (IPCB), and Erosion, Technology and Concentration (ETC) Group, both of whom are vociferous in their criticism of genetic research that targets indigenous peoples, and which they perceive as exploitative acts of biopiracy and colonialism that are insensitive to indigenous peoples' interests and aspirations. See especially "Indigenous Peoples Oppose National Geographic and IBM Genetic Research Project that Seeks Indigenous Peoples DNA." Available online: http://www.arena.org.nz/indbiop.htm (accessed 17 November 2010). See also Debra Harry, "Biopiracy and Globalization: Indigenous Peoples Face a New Wave of Colonialism." Available online: http://www.ipcb.org/publications/other_art/globalization.html (accessed 17 November 2010).

25 The HGDP is distinct from HGP. The latter is a broader initiative that mapped all genes in the human genome, while the former is a narrower population health platform research targeting less than 1% of the human genome with a view to mapping specific DNA variations between humans. The national Research Council declined to support the HGDP because of objections on its overall concept and procedure.

26 Footnotes omitted.

27 Logos of contention in the US include those of the Washington Red Skins, Cleveland Indians, Atlanta Braves, Chicago Black Hawks and Kansas City Chiefs. In New Zealand, following protestation over Air New Zealand's placement of Maori-derived koru logo on its floor mats, which the Maori perceived as debasement of the sacred symbol, the airline removed it, but retained the "koru symbology" in its official logo. See Arewa (2006b: 179).

28 See Heald (2003).

29 See Arewa (2006b), Mgbeoji (2006) and Rattray, G.N. (2002) "The Enola Bean Patent Controversy: Biopiracy, Novelty, Fish-and-Chips," *Duke Law and Technology Review* 0008.

3 Global governance structures and regime dynamics in intellectual property

Intellectual property in the global economy

The last chapter made reference to Daniel Bell as one of the leading theorists on the emergence and characteristics of the information age, and the proponent of the concept of a post-industrial society. Bell distinguishes between the pre-industrial, industrial and the post-industrial eras as different epochal phases in human history. From a more conventional, historical, and sometimes atheoretical position, analysts are inclined to distinguish between the agricultural, industrial and the information revolutions. I note, in agreement with Bell, that no conceptual scheme ever exhausts a social or economic reality. As such, I am not concerned with interrogating the accuracy of these categories in the present exercise. Indeed, law does not have a separate or neutral existence. Rather, it "is a reflection of the economy and the society from which it emanates" (May and Sell 2006: 38; Takach 2003: 57), and thus, each of the identified phases is essentially supervised by one dominant legal regime or the other, even if not in an entirely exclusive fashion.

For example, according to Takach (2003: 57), "it is not surprising that land-related laws [especially mortgage legal principles] first developed with the ascendancy of the role of land as the principal asset in the agrarian era." Similarly, he avers that given the focus of the Industrial Revolution on the production and distribution of physical goods, the enactment in 1894 of the first Sale of Goods Act in England was a "quintessential legal development in the industrial era" (2003: 57). Takach suggests that in the information age, information is the pre-eminent asset, or according to Drahos (n.d.), the "prime resource" analogous to the status of land and physical goods in the agrarian and industrial revolutions. Consequently, he wonders if our laws have stayed current with the rise of information and knowledge as the single most important economic asset of our time. In the post-industrial or information and knowledge economic order, the challenge for law is whether "we need to develop new laws and legal principles for the new era, or can we make do relying on, for the most part, laws intended for a previous era?" (Takach 2003: 58).

If land-related law received a boost in the agrarian era, then intellectual property has been, and rightly so, on target for the information or knowledge age. Not many dispute the unprecedented attention which intellectual property has attracted since the dawn of the knowledge economy. This is simply because intellectual property is law's primary mechanism for the allocation of rights and general control over information or knowledge, including knowledge-based assets. Drahos (n.d.) describes it as a "right of exploitation in information." It is a generic label that encapsulates diverse legal regimes "each of which, to a different degree, confers rights of ownership in a particular subject matter," mostly knowledge and information. For the most part, as distinct from tangible property, intellectual property applies to information, knowledge or intangibles or so-called products of the intellect or of the mind (Drahos n.d.). Neither the subject matters of intellectual property protection nor the categories of intellectual property regimes are closed. Not surprisingly, the last several decades have witnessed radical adjustments to hitherto settled legal boundaries in order to accommodate intellectual property claims on the new technological advances of the new knowledge economy (Oguamanam 2009a). Thus, intellectual property expansionism is one of the hallmarks of the post-industrial society. Clearly, the malleable character of intellectual property has been drawn out onto a near superlative pedestal in the post-industrial era.

In suggesting that intellectual property is the most suitable legal regime for the information age, one should be careful to not stretch the proposition too far. It is not as simple as the analogy made in relation to land and the agrarian revolution. First, in our computer-driven information society, I recognize the ubiquitous or embedded nature of the computer for the generation of information and in facilitating capitalist production processes in virtually all the economic and diverse social activities of this new era (Takach 2003: 54). Consequently, instead of isolating intellectual property as a standalone regulatory scheme for the knowledge economy, intellectual property is best appraised as a pliable, albeit pivotal legal design that interacts with, influences, and is influenced by other legal and socio-economic regimes and activities in the knowledge economy. In this legal order, therefore, intellectual property is an inherently transdisciplinary subject matter that "affect[s] virtually everyone on the planet in one way or the other" (May and Sell 2006: vii), insofar as no one is immune from the effects of knowledge and information.

Intellectual property is implicated in a range of ways in the following examples, and many others besides: the appropriation of information and knowledge relating to a farmer's prized genetic resources; a record publisher's bid to control P2P file-sharing practices on a website; a celebrity's opposition to the appropriation of her persona on the internet; a pharmaceutical company's bid to shut down a website that distorts its logo and associates it with the deaths of people with AIDS in less developed countries; an indigent third-world student's earnest desire to obtain a copy of a bestselling text by a Canadian publisher and author; and a patient's discovery, after the fact, that his body part or medical information was the subject or component of a patent application by surgeons who treated him. In these examples, there is a palpable intersection of intellectual property and its different regimes (including patents, copyright, and trademark) with agricultural law, the law of libel, constitutional law (freedom of expression), entertainment law, public health law, and ethics and morality. Thus, as the most implicated legal regime for the information age, intellectual property law is faced with challenges that extend beyond its conventional formulation and jurisprudence. As an aspect of its new found prominence, it is forced to interact and contend with the claims of other branches of the law. It must adapt, and has, therefore, been in transformation both on its own and in regard to its complex interactions with several public-regarding challenges in the new knowledge economy.

Second, because the knowledge economy and its undergirding technological changes are still developing, the role or extent of the application of intellectual property on knowledge and information-based assets has yet to crystallize and will remain in a state of flux for a long while. For example, advances in technologies continue to finetune new technological control mechanisms of knowledge and information, such as encryption devices and genetic use restriction (so-called terminator) technologies as alternatives to the legal control mechanisms represented by intellectual property (Oguamanam 2005). Even if the contours of the technological advances in the knowledge economy were determinate, intellectual property has been a historically malleable and instrumental mechanism deployed on contingent bases for political and other economic ends, despite being masked by ostensible philosophical considerations.

These inherent features of intellectual property notwithstanding, its application to information-based assets is in a state of constant flux. In the opinion of one analyst, the reason for this is, in part, a function of four factors identified under a narrow conceptual framework as the dynamics of computer law, factors that are relevant and adaptable as part of the dynamics of the knowledge economy: The rapid pace of technological change, the elusive nature of information, the blurring of private and public, and blurring of national and international range of activities in the use of new information technologies (Takach 2003: 73–4). The short point here is that because the technological drivers of the new knowledge and information society are still developing, they present enormous challenges to intellectual property as the most appropriate legal regime amenable to the regulatory demands of that order. Thus, the extent to which intellectual property serves this purpose for the knowledge economy is a subject of negotiation in regard to its overall jurisprudence and in relation to its interaction with other legal norms arising in the context of new technological developments.

According to May and Sell (2006: 5, 38) "[i]ntellectual property constructs a scarce resource from knowledge or information that is not formally scarce." In my adaptation of George Takach's four dynamics, the elusive nature of information serves as the second dynamic of the knowledge economy. The elusive nature of information is readily linked to the other three dynamics. Among other things, it is made possible by the rapid pace of technological change which in turn fuels the ease at which information is generated and manipulated, aggregated and segregated, transformed and transposed via multimedia platforms, especially by means of computer-driven digital technologies. Indeed, the rapidity of information transformation in the digital age is part of the first dynamic, which points to the heightened pace of technological change.

Many older researchers speak of the pre-digital era when, for example, library research basically involved manual navigation of card-filing systems. Today, digitization, "Googlization," "Wiki-," and the overall application of the enormous resources of cyberspace in the conduct of research has yielded an information explosion that not only compresses space, time and distance, but has made the world a virtual library only as far away from the researcher as a click of the mouse. Beyond library research, the same trend occurs in all fields in which knowledge, information and communication are the drivers of innovation and creativity. Increasingly, the elements of good research skills turn on a researcher's creative discipline to discern wisely, select judiciously, and exclude radically, as opposed to the obsolete quest of the old era to "cover the field." Indeed, today, it is no longer possible to cover the field, whatever that means. Information and knowledge continue to overflow and sometimes overwhelm, requiring deft management skills in their use and application. Yet they are elusive, easily defying and blurring the private–public divide and the national–international precincts.

Because knowledge and information are the critical assets of the information age, those who control information and knowledge are the captains of the knowledge economy. The tool for the exercise of this control is intellectual property. As evident from May and Sell's definition, an important objective of intellectual property in the post-industrial society is to impose artificial scarcity over information. Ironically, the exponential nature of information in the new digital environment does not necessarily mean that the process of information generation is cheap. For instance, to audit or sequence the genome of a plant or animal involves a complex and expensive process, including hi-tech computer software, expert knowledge and an extensive length of time deployed in a painstaking fashion. The same is true with regard to gathering the complex information or vital data sets critical for specialized or automated service delivery. However, once these critical stages are passed, the replication of information by second comers is as simple as a click of the mouse.

Basically, however, not many are aware that whenever they open a webpage, or e-document, they automatically make a virtual copy of the document. In this context, information and knowledge are essentially non-rivalrous and can be deployed simultaneously by as many people as possible without necessarily interfering with the ability of others to access that same information. The non-rivalrous nature of knowledge and information finds practical demonstration in the applications and modus operandi of digitization. In the new knowledge economic order, information and knowledge are expensive to generate, easy to replicate, yet inherently non-rivalrous. Consequently, their control is a matter of intense contestation involving multiple dialectics. These dialectics take the form of competition between economic and social interests; conflict between rights holders and users; private and public rights; exclusion and diffusion; monopoly and competition; trade and development; public enclosure and private domain expansionism; rights elongation and reduction of obligations, etc. These binaries of parallel dynamics are not necessarily exclusive and are hardly exhaustive.

Among them, intellectual property is required to play a critical role in supporting the "efficiency and distributive effects of the global knowledge economy" (Drahos and Braithwaite 2002: 204). Echoing similar sentiments, May and Sell (2006: 159) contend that "[d]espite the rhetoric of efficiency, property rights are fundamentally about distributive policies." However, the unprecedented technological break-through in digitization and its ramifications in all sectors of socioeconomic activity, as well as advances in biotechnologies, have compelled a strong intellectual property regime in which the propertization of knowledge is as central as the aggressive attempt to create artificial scarcity over information (Oguamanam 2009a). This approach to intellectual property has been described by Drahos and Braithwaite (2002, 2004; Oguamanam 2009a) as a perpetuation of hegemony based on knowledge. In their words, "[t]he logic of hegemonic power based on knowledge is to lock up knowledge . . . to create a morality that judges knowledge to be a private good and punish through the criminal apparatus of the state those who steal knowledge."

The contestation over the control of knowledge is hardly a new development (Drahos n.d.; May and Sell 2006). Throughout its history, intellectual property, as the legal mechanism for allocating rights over knowledge and information, has been no stranger to controversy and contest (Mgbeoji 2003; Oguamanam 2009a: 106). For the most part, intellectual property is about the history of making knowledge and information ownable, a history characterized as not only contingent and contested and one in constant evolution (Raustiala 2006). Nonetheless, in the overall technological paradigms of the new global knowledge economy, the stakes could not have been higher. In the wake of the monumental possibilities of technological transformation in the digital and biotechnology arena, explored under the 4Bs in the preceding chapter, access to those technologies are critical for all, especially the most vulnerable. In short, it boils down to determining who dies and who lives (Drahos and Braithwaite 2004: 205; Sunder 2006: 257). Hence, lately, nothing has provoked so much tension in the global sphere, or sharpened the north–south tension, than the issue of access to knowledge (A2K), especially as it relates to bio- and digital technologies.

Because of the huge socioeconomic import of these technologies, which traverse health, food security, the environment, wealth creation, poverty alleviation and development, human rights and self-determination, etc., they raise enormous political stakes. According to May and Sell (2006), intellectual property is not neutral; it is politically driven and politically constructed. Clearly, the contest over the ownership and control of knowledge and information as the key drivers of the knowledge economy is both political and legal. It is played out on the intellectual property chessboard. To echo the sentiments of Drahos and Braithwaite (2002) and Stiglitz (2008a: 1695), how we define and arrive at the distributional efficiency of the new global knowledge economy will depend on how we regulate and manage the production of knowledge, and invariably how we explore and play the politics of intellectual property. At the center of this will be how we resolve or balance the multiple dialectics of intellectual property highlighted above. A number of commentators, including Deere (2009), Drahos and Braithwaite (2002, 2004), Helfer (2004b, 2009), Okediji (2003, 2004), Reichman (2009a), and Yu (2004, 2007b), indicate that the pathway to this delicate balance is not being trodden in any dedicated and deliberate manner; rather, it is being driven by hegemonic and counterhegemonic currents and cross-currents. This hegemonic template provides a defining insight into the global structures and overall dynamics of intellectual property in global governance, which the next sections examine.

Intellectual property: a preview in global governance

> To think fruitfully about the future of the global governance of IPRs, we must examine their past. . . . Only by understanding the long history of intellectual property can the problems of its contemporary global governance be assessed.
>
> (May and Sell 2006: 5, 215)

The World Intellectual Property Organization (WIPO) represents the first major multilateral institutional framework under the auspices of the United Nations for the purpose of the global governance of intellectual property. In-depth historical examinations of the WIPO, and for that matter, intellectual property and its component regimes, have been carried out by several analysts (e.g. May 2007; May and Sell 2006; Mossinghoff and Oman 1997; Salmon 2003) and are outside the scope of this book. The WIPO's evolutionary development indicates, for the most part, the contested and constantly evolving nature of intellectual property. My interest is to explore how the WIPO story provides insight into aspects of the global governance of intellectual property, including WIPO's institutional transformations and the tensions between balancing a neoliberal economic imperative with a public-regarding consideration, not the least of which is the development imperative in intellectual property which largely drives the undergirding regime dynamics that supervise the contest for the ownership of knowledge.

Peter Drahos conveniently delineates three phases in the evolution of intellectual property: territorial/national, international and the extant global phase (Drahos n.d.). Before the formal "birth" of WIPO in 1970, all important control mechanisms for the global governance of intellectual property had deployed at one level or another, and have remained active features of the structure through to the extant global phase. Drahos locates this phase "in the linkage that the United States of America made between trade and intellectual property" (Drahos n.d.) that eventually resulted in the TRIPS Agreement. The territorial phase of intellectual property underscores the inherently national character of intellectual property whereof nation states were the key determinants not only of the subject matters for intellectual protection or exclusion within their territories, but also the legal details of such schemes. As a result, intellectual property rights were limited to the territorial boundary of the right-granting sovereign.

Whether dated to royal grant of privileges as far back as the 14th century in most of continental Europe, or to other contingent historical experiences of the "new world," the interests of individuals, special industrial sectors, and trade and occupational groups have been critical influences on nation states in the evolution of intellectual property law (Drahos and Braithwaite 2004; Feather 1988; Goodman 2006; Mossoff 2001; Yu 2006). For instance, King Edward III's grant of the first ever letters patent to John Kempe of Flanders in 1331 laid the foundation for the checkered history of patents in England, mired as it was in royal corruption and abuse through the reign of Queen Elizabeth and King James until parliamentary intervention via the Statute of Monopolies in 1623. All through its early evolution, the influence of courtiers or those with access to seats of power, similar to the influence of modern day industry and special interest lobbyists, was apparent. Similarly, Venice's 1474 patent statute, known as the first modern patent, is owed to the tenacity, or some would say, the blackmail of a single individual. In that account, Philipo Brunelleschi insisted that he would not deploy his new invention for use to transfer materials across Lake Arno for the construction of the historic suspended dome of the cathedral of Florence until he was guaranteed some protection for his, afterward embarrassingly, ill-fated invention (Mgbeoji 2003: 411).

In regard to copyright and trademark law, disparate accounts of their early history implicate the role of diverse stakeholders, ranging from individuals to industrial and special interest trade groups, in determining the details of common law and legislative schemes around these two regimes of intellectual property. For instance, in the copyright realm, the legal scheme is rooted in, and results from political resolutions of the dynamics of the often tense relationship among various stakeholders, including stationers' companies, book publishers, printers, writers or members of the scribal industry (Yu 2006). These tensions continue to characterize the evolving definition of literary property, creativity and authorship (Craig 2002; May and Sell 2006: 49). They also shape the contours of copyright jurisprudence by the (re)alignment of stakeholders' interests regarding technological transformations in copyright industries, from Gutenberg to digitization. Similar dynamics characterize trademark jurisprudence from the early history of passing off (Schechter 2000; Stolte 1998), through the emergence of statutory trademark, to the rise of cybersquatting and domain naming.

When all is said and done, the 19th century represented a period when more dedicated attempts were made to develop an international or multilateral approach to intellectual property law. In part, this shift was to check free riding, which the territorial approach encouraged. Given that intellectual property was limited to the territory of the granting sovereign, outside that territory, there was no disincentive to free riding. Also, earlier but limited bilateral or reciprocal arrangements on intellectual property among European countries did not seem to have equitable effects on collaborating parties (May 2007: 17). Moreover, states such as the US that stood to gain if they remained outside any collaborative arrangements on intellectual property (as recipients of a positive externality), strategically decided to remain outliers. Also depicting a debate yet to be settled, it is said that the imperative for wider collaboration on intellectual property on a transnational level was driven by the ideological triumph of intellectual property proponents over their free trade counterparts at a time when the two concepts were perceived to be in conflict (May and Sell 2006: 116). The initial bilateral approach was more of a precursor "towards serious international co-operation on intellectual property [which] arrived in the form of two multilateral pillars" (Drahos n.d.) that formed the backdrop for the emergence of the WIPO.

The two multilateral pillars in the international phase of intellectual property are the 1883 Paris Convention for the Protection of Industrial Property and the 1886 Berne Convention for the Protection of Literary and Artistic Works. The historical context of the emergence of the two treaties is instructive for appreciating the contemporary global governance dynamics in intellectual property. Paris and Berne were birthed at a time when the idea of property in knowledge was shared among governments, policymakers, and industrial and commercial stakeholders in the industrialized world. May and Sell observe that this affirmation of the propertization of knowledge and the favourable disposition toward intellectual property between 1870 and the early 1900s happened at a time when economic and technological leadership began to shift from Britain to Germany and the US. Britain presided over the first phase of the Industrial Revolution through the invention of the steam engine, diverse machine tools, and advancements in other industrial developments such as in textiles, iron and shipbuilding (Dutfield 2009; May and Sell 2006: 117).

The period from 1870 to 1914 marked the second phase of the Industrial Revolution. That phase was spurred by innovations around chemicals, steel, oil and electricity for which Germany (chemicals, steel) and the US (oil and electricity) took economic, technological and corporate leadership (Dutfield 2009). Advances in communication, transportation, and especially the development of functional railways propelled mass production, resulting in an increase in both America's domestic market and the rise of its corporations. The latter capitalized on that country's economies of scale, supported by the sheer size of its domestic market and abundant natural resources, and reached out to exert a global influence that marked the onset of American capitalism. As for Germany, its exploits in the second phase of the Industrial Revolution were partly accounted for in its steel resources, its innovation in chemicals and its strong track record in scientific and technological education (Dutfield 2009; Dutfield and Suthersanen 2005).

By many accounts, the tenacity of two individuals and corporations: America's Thomas Edison and Germany's Werner Siemens,[1] notably in electricity, on the one hand, and dyestuff, chemicals and pharmaceuticals, on the other, hugely influenced changes in the American and German patent regimes. In the US and Germany, the duo secured legislative accommodation for the transfer of ownership of innovation from employee to employer. They also established and entrenched an R&D-propelled model of business practice that is based on in-house research laboratories and workshops. The success of this model was premised on unprecedented aggressive patenting and overall intellectual property protection (May and Sell 2006; Dutfield 2009). Simply stated, it was "a business strategy of market dominance [exercised] by controlling the fruits of innovation through control of existing patents and of future patented inventions. The idea was to maintain control over innovation, manage patents so as to create barriers to entry, and prepare patent applications with broad claims" (May and Sell 2006: 122).[2]

More than a century later, this strategy seems to be an excerpt from the operational manual of biotechnology and allied industries in their gold rush for gene patents. Even though, as time went on, skepticism over intellectual property and the benefits or justifications claimed on its behalf moved the pendulum occasionally toward abolitionism (Dutfield 2009; Jaffe and Lerner 2005; May and Sell 2006: 119), there was no doubt that powerful industrial sectors in Europe and America promoted intellectual property or hegemonic control over knowledge above other rival considerations.

In the 21st century, that ideological triumph is aptly depicted in Drahos and Braithwaite's (2002, 2004) reference to the logic of hegemonic power based on knowledge which entrenches the psychology of knowledge hoarding and a morality that judges knowledge to be a private good in which all public-regarding claims are barely tolerated if not subdued. Intellectual property triumphalism – the privileging of owners of knowledge assets over competing public-regarding considerations – was the moral high ground for the onset of the international phase of intellectual property. That triumphalism remains an integral part of the neoliberal economic framework that demarcates the global phase of intellectual property in the post-industrial society, which we explore in the next section.

The build-up to WIPO

Our brief exploration of the background of the Paris and Berne Conventions helps to understand the place of those two treaties in the global governance of intellectual property. Because of intellectual property triumphalism, American inventors boycotted the Weltausstellung 1873 Wien World Exposition, which was held in the Austro-Hungarian capital of Vienna. They expressed reservation over lack of adequate protection of their inventions from free riders. The same sentiments were shared by German inventors. Given the technological and economic leadership of the two countries, these reservations were taken seriously. Not only did the empire adopt ad hoc legislation that protected the inventions of foreigners for the duration of the exposition (May–October), it followed up by holding a conference the same year in Vienna to tackle the issue (May and Sell 2006: 118). Subsequent conferences in Paris (1878 and 1880) led to the conclusion of the Paris Convention for the Protection of Industrial Property 1883. The latter was amplified by the 1891 Madrid Interpretative Protocol. The Convention is essentially a system that enables states to accord recognition and protection to the rights of foreigners in their jurisdictions in relation to patents, trademarks, and industrial designs. Paris Union member countries constituted the membership of the International Union for the Protection of Industrial Property.

Like the Paris Convention, the Berne Convention for the Protection of Literary and Artistic Works 1886 also came about in the dramatic circumstance of a general mood of intellectual property triumphalism and disillusion over existing bilateral arrangements on copyright. As if testing the waters, in 1852 Napoleon III of France unilaterally extended copyright protection to all foreign works in France by criminalizing counterfeit production of such works. In a period of 10 years, May reports, 23 countries entered into treaty relationships with France on the subject of copyright (May 2007: 17; May and Sell 2006: 120), indicating the feasibility for the emergence of a broader multilateral treaty.

French author, Victor Hugo, seizing the momentum, became a vocal champion of the notion of extending national treatment to foreign artists and authors, and was the convener of the 1858 Congress of Authors and Artists in Brussels which affirmed those principles. He subsequently founded the International Literary Association, which later became the International Literary and Artistic Association. He used the platform of this body to convene a number of meetings in Europe aimed at replicating the idea of the Paris Convention in the copyright realm by means of a multilateral copyright treaty. His effort paid off in the Berne Convention (May 2007: 17; May and Sell 2006: 118–19). The US did not become a member of the Berne Convention until 1989, not only because its domestic legislation created more onerous terms for the protection of foreign works (May 2007: 18; May and Sell 2006: 120), but also because it was taking advantage of positive externalities by remaining outside the Berne Convention. This was a source of conflict between it and the UK, as the work of the latter's nationals was being pirated in the US (Yu 2009: 12).[3]

Neither the Paris nor the Berne Conventions warranted an enactment of new laws by member states. They were an affirmation of the emerging consensus among state parties that were, for the most part, already entrenched in their domestic laws. Essentially, the letter and spirit of the conventions encompassed the principles of non-discrimination, national treatment and priority on the basis of the first-to-file or produce as opposed to first-to-invent/create system of priority (Mossinghoff 2005). America's patent law remains at cross purposes with the rest of the world's first-to-file system of priority, as it only sanctions the longstanding American patent tradition of first-to-invent. That policy has remained a target for patent law revision since its adoption. Some hold out the hope that its days are already numbered (Martin 2009).

Both the Paris and Berne initiatives share important similarities in terms of the role of individuals, trade groups, industry stakeholders and, of course, nation states as crucial constituencies in the emerging governance regime on intellectual property. From this compressed account, we note that intellectual property triumphalism sets the tone for the internationalization and globalization of intellectual property, subduing public-regarding considerations. In the tension between hardcore intellectual property protectionism and the forces advocating balance on the basis of diverse public-regarding considerations, protectionism appears to have assumed a normative status and to have gained the moral high ground. In this mix, the idea of politics and instrumentalism as important underlying factors that shape intellectual property law and policy is evident. Often, the appeal to theoretical justifications is only attractive when it advances a state's economic and political contingencies. For instance, states are willing to explore a bilateral approach only when it serves their interests. When it does not, they are inclined to explore other options, including multilateralism. In viewing these actions, we see situations where the interest of states may converge with those of their nationals. The last point may seem quite palpable, but it is not always the case. Also, as part of the political stake, where a state's interests attract positive externalities, it may be inclined to not participate in any collaborative arrangement, but to remain an outlier. America's initial interest in remaining outside the Berne Convention and, as we will see later, its willingness to support a different regime under the auspices of UNESCO, namely, the Universal Copyright Convention (Halbert 2007: 256), is also indicative of the regime dynamics that characterize intellectual property in global governance.

In a way, the Berne Convention was inspired by the Paris Convention. The Berne Convention replicated a Paris-like regime for copyright within a period of three years. Thus, the foundation for a multilateral approach to the key regimes of intellectual property was laid. Apparent commonalities in the objectives of Paris and Berne, as well as the proliferation of treaties and the rise in international organizations around intellectual property,[4] led to the consolidation in 1893 of the administrative offices of the two conventions under one secretariat, called the United International Bureau for the Protection of Intellectual Property (BIRPI). BIRPI offices were originally in Berne, and relocated to Geneva in 1960. According to May (2006: 436, 2007: 19), BIRPI became a pivotal part of a growing network of multilateral governance agencies and, therefore, was at the forefront of the nascent governance mechanisms of the early organizational developments instrumental to the late 20th-century efforts directed at the global governance of intellectual property. The Swiss maintained administrative and financial control of BIRPI. This was done, putatively, on behalf of the majority of BIRPI member states, most of which were developed countries responsible for the elevation of intellectual property triumphalism to a normative level.

Following the wave of decolonization that swept through many of today's less developed countries beginning in the late 1950s, not only did the membership of BIRPI increase, but also, the later entrants had begun to inject their unique national interest perspectives into the elaboration of intellectual property policy. For the most part, those interests centered on development and other public-regarding imperatives under the regime of intellectual property hitherto sidelined by developed countries. Also, new technological developments of that era, especially radio and television technologies, warranted new negotiations and amendments to existing treaties on intellectual property. All of these yielded a consciousness for a more expanded and consolidated governance framework for intellectual property. The BIRPI's 1967 Stockholm Conference formalized this new vision. It instituted an independent intergovernmental organization that became the WIPO, and provided for the latter's budgetary and operational control. That singular act effectively took BIRPI out of Swiss control. Three years later, in 1970, the World Intellectual Property Organization was formally established pursuant to the Stockholm Convention.

WIPO and the development imperative

According to its enabling instrument, the WIPO's principal objectives include the *promotion* and the *development* of measures for the *protection* of intellectual property throughout the world. Among other things, this is to be achieved through the harmonization of national legislation, the provision of technical and legal assistance, and the dissemination of information aimed at promoting awareness in the intellectual property field (WIPO 1967). Essentially, the WIPO's enabling treaty is an administrative instrument. The organization is fundamentally charged with the administration (including registration) of, provision of technical support for, and the development of control mechanisms or governance frameworks for intellectual property on a global scale. Seven years later, through the tenacity of Arpad Bogsch, a seasoned bureaucrat and strategist involved in the transition from BIRPI to the consolidation of the WIPO, the latter became a specialized agency of the United Nations in 1974.

Embedded in Bogsch's vision of WIPO membership in the UN system were two ideological conflicts over intellectual property that have continued to dog the WIPO. In fact, these conflicts reflected the characteristic tension and constant dialectics that played a role in defining the debate on the role and overall purpose of intellectual property. In a nutshell, WIPO's status as a specialized agency of the UN meant that as an incidence of that membership, WIPO's mandate inherently incorporated a developmental imperative. As well, membership would clear the cloud of suspicion hanging over the BIRPI/WIPO in the eyes of newly independent countries concerned with the organization's commitment to their national interests. The interests in question aligned with the developmental objectives of intellectual property, and their desire to pursue its realization launched a debate that started at a multilateral level in BIRPI's early history. Also, the expectation was that WIPO's status as a UN specialized agency would phenomenally increase its membership, and it did.[5] But decision making by these many members was based on the "one member, one vote" formula of the UN system. This meant that the majority of WIPO members would be those inclined to accept and support a developmental orientation to intellectual property regulation, and implied that this was the direction in which the organization would move. Consequently, the continuing sway of intellectual property triumphalism under which the BIRPI was born, faced an imminent threat in the new WIPO. As concisely stated by Halbert, the "WIPO was born into the controversy of how intellectual property would impact the developing world" (2007: 262). At the same time, advancements in bio- and digital technologies, especially in developed countries in the late 20th century, foreshadow the tightening of control over knowledge in consolidation of intellectual property triumphalism.

In her insightful study of the politics of the creation of the WIPO, Halbert (2007: 256) observes that the powers behind WIPO's precursor, BIRPI, considered the need for WIPO as a universal intellectual property regime in stark "'clash of civilization' terms." The battle to extend intellectual property to the entire world, as championed by Europe, was perceived as one that behooved enlightened Europe; it had to be pursued aggressively in order to arrest the threat intellectual property infringement presented. That threat was likened to a global anarchy undermining the foundations of western civilization itself. The director of BIRPI, Jacques Secrétan (as quoted in Halbert 2007: 256), observes regarding the imperative for WIPO as follows:

Most precious assets for the development of our civilization, namely, the opportunity for the author and the artist to work and the right of the inventor and manufacturer to benefit from the fruits of their labour [. . .] have enabled the civilized world to bring a ray of hope throughout the world[. . .]

Halbert (2007: 263–6) finds that the list of NGOs that witnessed the creation of the WIPO at the Stockholm Conference in 1967 reflected the tone of Secrétan's comment.[6] Virtually all the NGOs present at the Conference represented intellectual property-producing classes and not users. Despite the US' attempt to obscure what turned out to be an elaborate deliberation on development concerns over intellectual property, especially copyright, as championed mainly by Cuba and Switzerland, that initiative yielded a special Protocol Regarding Developing Countries.[7] The protocol allowed special dispensation from the Berne Convention on categories of countries. Pursuant to this, those countries could make reservations to restrict application of core Convention provisions, for example, in regard to copyright terms on literary and artistic works. They could also impose compulsory licenses, especially for translated works, and implement other miscellaneous accommodations on terms allowed under the Protocol (Ndiaye 1986).

It is not surprising then, that when the WIPO became a specialized agency of the UN, the move did not necessitate an amendment to its enabling instrument. Rather, it was accomplished by a special agreement between the two bodies, which outlined the details of that relationship.[8] If the truth be told, it will require stretching the text of the WIPO's enabling instrument to obligate WIPO to any significant commitment to a development or public-regarding approach to intellectual property. Rather, seekers of such a commitment are better served by looking at the agreement between WIPO and the UN under which the former became a UN specialized agency. Musungu and Dutfield (2003: 18) have observed that:

A restrictive reading of the objectives set out in the WIPO Convention may suggest that the organization should not be concerned with development-related issues connected with intellectual property [. . .] Such a reading would, however, be erroneous. The ultimate purposes which should be served by WIPO's activities should include broad development objectives and measures to ensure that developing countries benefit from modern scientific and technological advances in health, environment, communication, information technology, food and nutrition among others. This broad reading of WIPO's mandate and its ultimate purpose is based on a review of its agreement with the UN and by seeing the organization as a member of the latter's family, bound by the broader development objectives of the UN.

Before returning to the development debate, the next paragraphs outline the status of WIPO as a unique creature of the international system. That status includes and transcends WIPO's membership in the UN and leaves it in the crossfire between intellectual property triumphalism and the development debate. It does seem that despite nearly 40 years of official membership in the UN, WIPO has been on the side of the neoliberal forces promoting a stronger global intellectual property regime, rather than on the side of the peripheral forces that harp on development. Pressures on the development side arise first as an incidence of WIPO's historically unique status as an organization formed by mainly industrialized countries insensitive to the needs of less developed countries. Second, WIPO's delicate attempts at continuing transformation arise largely in response to the increased assertiveness of its less developed members whose numerical strength and shared interest have put more pressure on WIPO than is impelled by its 1974 agreement with the UN.

To date, WIPO administers a total of 24 treaties categorized under three heads: intellectual property protection, global protection systems, and classification. These treaties are quite fragmented not only in respect of their subject matters and in regard to their constitutive membership, but also in relation to the extent of their individual member obligations. Beyond the principles of national treatment, non-discrimination and, to some extent, priority, the details of a state's obligation in a WIPO-administered multilateral treaty often take the form of tangled legal knots and are quite difficult to untie. In fact, states can strategically opt out of treaties or make reservations to specific treaty provisions to safeguard their interests (Musungu and Dutfield 2003: 20). Before the TRIPS Agreement came into effect, WIPO presided over a world intellectual property system that was the subject of immense rule diversity, leaving much room for flexibility regarding the extent or detail of applicable treaty regimes in any given country. Nation states had leverage to determine the subject matters for intellectual property protection within their domains.

For example, although members of the Paris Union, least developed countries did not extend patent protection to pharmaceuticals, chemicals and aspects of innovation in agriculture. Also, as noted earlier, while a member of the Paris Union, the US retained the first-to-invent rule in regard to its domestic patent over the first-to-file that applied to the rest of the members of that body (Martin 2009).[9] In addition, membership in WIPO did not necessarily correlate with that of BIRPI or the UN. The establishment of WIPO did not extinguish BIRPI, which remained the governing organization for those members that did not immediately join WIPO. The WIPO General Assembly reserved the right to invite any state not party to the Berne or Paris Union or even the UN to join WIPO.

The pre-TRIPS WIPO world was by no means one in which there was a harmonization of technical rules on intellectual property (Drahos n.d.). This meant that states actively capitalized on their enormous sovereign rights and discretion to set intellectual property standards. Developed and less developed countries used WIPO as a chessboard to advance their often conflicted approaches to intellectual property. Given the power in numbers wielded by many less developed countries that have now joined WIPO, but who were visibly absent in Berne and Paris and in the founding of BIRPI, the development imperative threatened to assume the upper hand in WIPO deliberations. Already, developing countries led by India secured revisions to the Berne Convention to accommodate folkloric expressions and aspects of traditional knowledge (Arewa 2006a: 45; Bentley 2005). These were hardly in issue when the Berne Convention was first negotiated. In recent times, diverse regional blocs and frontline countries of the global south, notably the Andean and African regional blocs, China, India, Brazil, Argentina, etc., continue to articulate alternative visions for an equitable global intellectual property regime. Perhaps the tension in WIPO over the development agenda was contingent on the increase in the membership of less developed countries, rather than on WIPO's perceived consciousness or lack thereof, regarding the developmental ramifications of its membership in the UN.

Turning now to key development aspects of the agreement between WIPO and the UN,[10] it must be pointed out that, by recognizing WIPO as its specialized agency, the UN imposed an obligation on WIPO in many respects. Notably, WIPO was obligated to facilitate technology transfer in regard to industrial property to developing countries with the objective of expediting economic, social and cultural development.[11] Also, WIPO was expected to use its specialist competence in the areas of intellectual property to work in concert with the UN and several of its identified organs, specifically, the UN Conference on Trade and Development (UNCTAD), UN Development Program (UNDP), UN Industrial Development Organization (UNIDO), UNESCO, etc., to realize the development objectives of the UN and to pursue the "broader objective of achieving international corporation in solving problems of an economic, social, cultural, or humanitarian matter and in promoting and encouraging aspects of human rights and fundamental freedoms" (Musungu and Dutfield 2003: 19). Although the overall text of WIPO's agreement with the UN may be subject to diverse interpretations, the specific mention of the key development-oriented agencies of the UN in association with WIPO's status as a UN specialized body ties WIPO unequivocally to pursuing a developmental mandate. It is clear, as Musungu and Dutfield (2003: 19) affirm, that "an important prerequisite for an organization to attain the status of a specialized agency is that its purposes must be compatible with those of the UN and its agencies."

Finally, WIPO committed to accept recommendations from the UN in regard to promoting and giving effect to the latter's objectives and, generally, working in concert with other UN agencies to provide requisite support for effective implementation of the activities and policies of the UN, including those of its organs and agencies.[12] One conclusion is now unequivocal: WIPO's agreement with the UN provides the cornerstone for pushing the development imperative within WIPO. This contrasts with the sketchy objectives in WIPO's enabling document, which centered mainly on universal promotion and protection of intellectual property without any clear mention of a development objective.

Despite WIPO's pact with the UN, it would appear that Arpad Bogsch's vision of embedding the organization within the UN was not, at least after the fact, motivated by a quest to promote the cause of intellectual property in development – at least not in regard to less developed countries. Rather, the UN was to serve as a prime legitimate platform providing much needed diplomatic cover for WIPO to foist a narrow vision of intellectual property, one without development content, on less developed countries from the onset of their new found independence. WIPO's lip service to development was evident in the following symbolic event, as observed by May (2007: 24):[13]

[WIPO] agreed to be listed as the co-author on the 1974 United Nations Conference on Trade and Development (UNCTAD) report *The Role of the Patent System in the Transfer of Technology to Developing Countries*,[14] despite the report's thrust being widely divergent from WIPO's position on the role of patent in technological transfer.[15]

Given the specific mention of a few UN agencies in the agreement between the WIPO and the UN, the expectation is that if WIPO was genuinely committed to development, it would have played by the scripts of that agreement to draw in and collaborate with those agencies in the spirit of the accord with the UN. Regrettably, analysts (Halbert 2007: 261;[16] May and Sell 2006: 215; Musungu and Dutfield 2003) agree that UNCTAD, and other UN agencies with significant interests in intellectual property rights, such as UNESCO and UNDP, were notably marginalized, if not excluded from policy deliberations at the WIPO. Musungu and Dutfield (2003: 11)[17] charge that WIPO was a direct "beneficiary of the strategy [by the US] to weaken the UNCTAD in the early 1980s." But with their numeric advantage, less developed countries never let up on drawing attention to the development imperative mandated under WIPO. Their persistence resulted in a crisis of confidence in the organization, especially from its developed founding members. One significant issue provided the straw that broke the proverbial camel's back in WIPO and paved the way for the high stake intrigues and regime dynamics that have since shaped intellectual property in global governance.

In order to benefit from the technological advances of the late 20th century, especially from the 1960s, less developed countries pushed for new treaties and revisions of old ones that would extend to them the benefits of the new technologies (Braithwaite and Drahos 2000: 61; Musungu and Dutfield 2003: 20). We have already noted that, in 1967, they succeeded in securing the Stockholm Protocol to the Berne Convention that provided for increased access to copyright materials to needy countries, similar to the Indian-led initiative for the 1971 revisions of the Berne Convention to accommodate folkloric expressions. In the 1980s the Paris Convention became the site of intense contestation. While less developed countries pushed for a generous compulsory licensing of patents and new technologies, developed countries insisted on a more stringent regime beyond the status quo, one designed to lock up new technologies. A series of four-yearly Diplomatic Conferences of Revisions to the Paris Convention, from 1980 to 1984, were "deadlocked by the opposed views of the purposes of IPR [intellectual property rights] protection, frustrating attempts of developing countries' negotiators to widen the public realm of intellectual property" (May and Sell 2006: 156). Yu (2009) identifies these initiatives as the first development agenda.

The failure of the WIPO to revise the Paris Convention was to mark a turning point in its fortune and status, changing the global governance of intellectual property in a very strategic and structural manner. That failure cast serious doubts on the status of the WIPO as a credible forum for multilateral negotiations on intellectual property for both developed and less developed countries. Cheek (2001:

287) is of the impression that the "failure discredited the institution as a forum for meaningful reform."

Intellectual property in global economic re/structuring

In terms of timing, the failure of the Diplomatic Conferences was instructive for a number of reasons. Before then, in the US and Europe, ambivalence over support for a stronger and a public-regarding intellectual property regime had definitely settled after a period of vacillation. Patents and intellectual property rights were now perceived not as anti-competition tools or instruments of monopoly to be frowned on, but as promoters of innovation for competitiveness in the market place. In the US in particular, there had come about a marked relaxation of anti-trust regimes that leveraged the monopolistic impacts of strong patents and discouraged corporate amalgamations aimed at market control. The new Patent Act of 1952 had set the tone to affirm the mood for strong patent protection and to lay the foundation for America's competitiveness in the post-World War II era. The American experience during the war was such that it could no longer allow or rely on Germany as the source of critical pharmaceutical supplies. America deployed patent as an instrument for safeguarding national security by adopting a targeted compulsory license regime (Braithwaite and Drahos 2000: 465) and other measures that actually laid the basis for the modern American pharmaceutical industry as, perhaps, the most successful globally (Dutfield 2009; May and Sell 2006).[18] In intellectual property, as in most other things, interests are contingently rotated on values.

Second, general skepticism in the US and elsewhere about intellectual property in the post-World War II era was to be short lived, especially given Japan's aggressive appropriation of America's technologies and America's continuing descent into a balance of payment abyss. The 1952 Patent Act, which laid the legal foundation for the shift toward a strong patent regime, is said to reflect "the wishes of [American] corporations that had amassed huge patent portfolios for greater protection and clarifies the notion of patent power as the power to withhold" (May and Sell 2006:141). In addition to this legislative intervention, judicial intervention in the 1980s was perhaps more indicative of the pro-intellectual property mood. May and Sell's (2006: 141)[19] summary of this trend merits cooptation *in extenso*. According to them, beginning from 1980, the US Supreme Court rulings:

> [B]egan to signal a new attitude toward patents. In its ruling in *Dawson Chem. Co. v. Rohn & Hass Co.*, the Court stated that "the policy of free competition runs deep in our law . . . but the policy of stimulating invention that underlies the entire patent system runs no less deep" . . . for the first time [since 1912] the Supreme Court placed public policy of supporting patent rights on an *equal footing*[20] with public policy of supporting free competition, [and by so doing] "effectively ended the era of anti-trust dominance over patent law in the eyes of the judiciary".[21] This "equal footing' was short lived, however: the rights of owners of intellectual property soon became *more*[22] important as these owners

were increasingly likely to deliver economic and competitiveness objectives valued by the US government. This led the US government to establish the Court of Appeals for the Federal Circuit (CAFC) in 1982 that institutionalized a more pro-patent approach.

The period of the failed diplomatic conferences was also one of expansive technological changes, especially in the information, communication, biotechnology and general life sciences, changes which have paradigmatic ramifications for agriculture, nutrition, environmental control, pharmaceutical, health and therapeutic interventions and research. The US' head start in these technological arenas was to shape the face of global capitalism under an information and knowledge-based economic order. So, the technological and economic developments of the 1980s warranted a fundamental shift in the US' attitude to intellectual property rights. High-technology and entertainment goods constituted a significant portion of US exports (Cheek 2001: 284–5). At a time when the US faced myriad challenges, including a balance of payment crisis, a slowing economy, and threat from new economies such as Japan and the Asian tigers that rely on its high-technologies, America's competitiveness in the unfolding knowledge economy hinged on the protection of its critical hi-tech export and most valued asset. According to Cheek (2001: 285), "[s]ince the main value of high-technology products is intellectual property, rather than traditional inputs such as raw materials, intellectual property became a fundamental part of the United States trade strategy."

On the global political and broader socioeconomic side, the world was at the cusp of a significant political change: the collapse of the Soviet Union, the decimation of communism, and the ascendance of globalization. Admittedly, the nature of the interrelationships between these developments is hardly amenable to any settlement and remains open to sociopolitical interpretation. However, in a collective fashion, they represented a rare historic and opportune moment for the consolidation of American-led neoliberal ideological hegemony in a post-Cold War economic order, not to mention the consolidation of America's status as a lone super power. Under the emerging equation, less developed countries were no longer beautiful brides of the Cold War to be courted to advance ideological and political objectives of the then superpowers. Now, they were vulnerable to coercion by a lone superpower and its allies basking in capitalism's triumph and vindication.

Meanwhile, the foundation for the emergent neoliberal economic order was already laid by the US and its allies immediately after World War II, a period Cox identified as the hegemonic period (Cox 1993; Cox and Sinclair 1999). According to Söderberg (2006: 6) a hegemonic period is a reference to:

> [T]he manner in which a dominant state and other social forces (such as powerful capitalists in the form of transnational corporations and financial institutions) sustain their position through the creation of and adherence to universal principles that are accepted and or acquiesced to by sufficient proportion of subordinate states and social forces through both consensual or coercive means.

The US and its allies were quick to set up institutional frameworks aimed at the regulation of global trade, the control of financial relations and, by implication, the flow of global capital. This was accomplished through the agency of the Bretton Woods institutions, such as the International Monetary Fund (IMF), the World Bank (WB) and the General Agreement on Tariffs and Trade (GATT) framework. While the IMF ensured financial stability, the World Bank's mandate was to finance post-war economic recovery. GATT's principal objective was to ensure equitable trade practices. For strategic reasons, the US and its allies ensured that control of these three institutions was placed outside the more democratic UN structure. Equities in the IMF and the WB are based on the amount of capital member states contributed to it. Thus, while the G7/8 industrialized countries and members of the EU constitute 14% of the global population, they hold 56% of the voting rights on the board of the IMF (Södeberg 2006: 8).

The separation of the operational framework of the Bretton Woods system from that of the UN reflects the ambiguous place of social policy in the international economic and political institutional framework of the post-World War II era. The classical view of international economic institutions (i.e. the Bretton Woods system), in relation to the UN, its organs or specialized agencies, reflects the conceptual bifurcation of private and public international law (Gathii 2002). While these institutions narrowly construe their mandate to be mainly economic and financial, and as having limited, if any, social agenda, the UN's role was acknowledged as essentially sociopolitical and inherently development oriented (Oguamanam 2006c). Until recently, historically, the Bretton Woods institutions have eschewed social and political exigencies in the implementation of their mandates. This distancing from political, social or public-regarding agendas is a mindset further elaborated in what has been known as the Washington Consensus. In a nutshell, according to Williamson, Serra, Spiegel and Stiglitz, the Washington Consensus is a strategic ideology to pull back on the role of the state in initiating industrialization and import substitution, and to allow a free reign of "market economy, openness to the world [or globalization] and macroeconomic discipline" (Serra et al. 2008: 3;[23] Williamson: 2008: 14).

Thus, in the new economic order, the norms of the Bretton Woods system and the Washington Consensus correlate with those of the hegemonic states led by the US. These norms center on the fetish of the market economy, the sanctity of market forces, and a myopic separation of economic from sociopolitical exigencies. They constitute the ideological mantra of neoliberal economic thinking. The Bretton Woods institutions are instruments used to subordinate other states, especially those that are less eveloped, to the new universal norms of the hegemonic states.

When in 1986, the US, under pressure from its private sector, capitalized on the international trade negotiations to incorporate the regulation of intellectual property into the WTO, the successor organization of the GATT, the significance of that move was not lost on analysts (Drahos and Braithwaite 2004). Nothing demonstrates the marginalization of public-regarding considerations in global intellectual property governance more than the location of intellectual property within an international economic institution and framework. Given the dichotomization of the economic and sociopolitical roles of the international economic institutions and the UN and its specialized agencies, the location of intellectual property in the WTO (the prime global international economic institution), was in radical conflict with the status and putative development mandate of the WIPO as a special agency of the UN pursuant to the 1974 agreement. Perhaps, more importantly, when TRIPS became one of the component agreements of the Uruguay Round of Multilateral Trade Negotiations and was placed under the auspices of the new WTO, there was little doubt that intellectual property was now strongly entrenched within the international economic institutional and regulatory framework as an integral part of the Bretton Woods system.[24]

The TRIPS agreement and intellectual property regime dynamics

As Drahos rightly noted, TRIPS marks the global phase in the evolution of intellectual property lawmaking (Drahos n.d.). Consequently, it is critical in understating the place or role of intellectual property in global governance. Also, TRIPS represents a quintessential breaking point and a touchstone for locating the regime dynamic in the new international intellectual property order. International regimes have been characterized as not amenable to theoretical neutrality because they represent "sets of implicit or explicit principles, norms, rules, and decision-making procedures around which actors' expectations converge in a given area of international relations" (Krasner 1983: 2). Krasner argues that what matters most in the international system is the power and interest of states. In the pursuit of such interests, states "are makers and breakers of regimes and the international systems more generally" (Krasner 2009: 6). In the international arena, interests change; they are contested and are rotated, especially by powerful states ever willing to change institutions and structures to suit their interests so long as the transaction or organizational costs for such shift do not outweigh anticipated benefits (Helfer 2004: 7; Krasner 2009: 8). Krasner notes that since World War II, the US has been making and breaking regimes as it suits its national and international interests, and its ideational beliefs (2009: 8).

America's sacrosanct economic interest is premised on the market economy. Its prime export in the late 20th and early 21st centuries has been high-technology, which is leveraged by intellectual property rights. For America and its European allies, the emergence of an intellectual property regime that was not encumbered by the social interests or development debates which threatened to cripple the WIPO, was overdue. Essentially, such a switch in regime would check the perceived obstructing influence of less developed countries. The incorporation of intellectual property into a more encompassing WTO was an attempt to expand the scope of market-oriented neoliberal economic rules into new issue areas. Again, Krasner (2009) observes that though many less developed countries were uncomfortable with this change, they had little choice. Not only were they lured by the carrot of access to the largest markets in the world, they were also faced with the stick of coercive crippling sanctions under the US' new trade regime headed by the office of the US Trade Representative (USTR) (Drahos and Braithwaite 2004; Reichman 2000). Also, less developed countries were promised some respite from US-led bilateral pressures if a uniform comprehensive multilateral regime on intellectual property could be put in place (Reichman 2000).

There is no scarcity of literature on the changes brought about by the TRIPS Agreement. Here, a highlight of those changes will suffice. TRIPS sought to resolve the issue of rule diversity that had plagued the WIPO system. It sets out a global intellectual property system that covers all regimes of intellectual property with binding, albeit minimum, substantive content and incorporated by reference the agreements administered by the WIPO. Under TRIPS, states' obligations to protect intellectual property are no longer optional, neither is there any crippling ambivalence regarding the substantive content of the international intellectual property regime, or the extent of states' commitment to them. Accession to the TRIPS Agreement is automatic and compulsory for all members of the WTO, thus ensuring a more streamlined membership register, in contrast to the confusion with the WIPO-administered treaties. TRIPS draws in the resolution of intellectual property disputes among the WTO members states, into the hard-edged WTO binding dispute settlement system which incorporates retaliatory trade sanctions for erring states. This is a sharp contrast to the pre-existing WIPO mechanism in which the International Court of Justice (ICJ) had jurisdiction over intellectual property disputes emanating from the WIPO administered treaties – a jurisdiction that was never exercised.

TRIPS' one-size-fits-all global regime of intellectual property (Dutfield 2000) is exacerbated by the extension of patents and, indeed, intellectual property rights broadly, to virtually all areas of technology and creativity with little or no discrimination. This includes the expansion of the scope of patentable subject matter to key areas, including pharmaceuticals, life forms, especially genetic resources and even plant varieties, reflecting the influence of American patent jurisprudence. In a 1980 landmark decision, *Diamond v. Chakrabarty*, the US Supreme Court endorsed an expansive interpretation of section 101 of the US Patent Act and extended patentable subject matter to "anything under the sun that is made by man," (*Diamond v. Chakrabarty* at 309) opening a floodgate for patents on life forms.

TRIPS' expansion of the scope of patentable subject matters meant that the flexibility enjoyed by developing countries under the pre-existing WIPO framework to exclude specific items from patentability, such as pharmaceuticals and life forms in accordance with social, economic and cultural considerations could no longer be guaranteed. Similarly, TRIPS created stringent conditions for the exercise of the option of compulsory licensing. The latter was of critical attraction to many less developed countries in regard to addressing price distortions behind local supply and access gaps for basic necessities such as pharmaceuticals and agro/industrial chemicals. I have noted elsewhere (Oguamanam 2006c: 427) that:

> In their detailed enunciation, these changes [by the TRIPS Agreement] represent "a marked strengthening of substantive intellectual property standards"[25] in a direction [radically] opposed to the social interest sensitivities of developing

countries and their economic sovereignty guaranteed under the pre-TRIPS framework. Consequently, the entrance of TRIPS into the global intellectual property equation has yielded a culture of disaffection against the agreement by developing countries akin to one that prevailed against the [pre-TRIPS] WIPO framework by developed countries.

A combination of these changes and other omissions in the TRIPS Agreement, notably the non-accommodation of indigenous or traditional knowledge, underscore TRIPS' social interest deficit. In addition, post-TRIPS, less developed countries became quickly frustrated with the failure of the US and its European allies to deliver on the promised "carrot," i.e. the opening of their markets to less developed countries, especially in regard to access to agricultural produce, textile and other export opportunities in foreign markets, including reductions in agricultural subsidies and concessions on imports of tropical products (Abbott 1989; Correa and Musungu 2002: 2). Also, despite assurances to the contrary, the US did not relent on the use of unilateral trade sanctions and other acts of coercive bilateralism. Instead, it took advantage of the minimalist nature of TRIPS prescriptions[26] to enter into post-TRIPS contractual arrangements with weaker states, while stepping up pressures via the office of the USTR to coerce and rein in perceived recalcitrant states.

Generally known as "TRIPS-plus," these latter-day agreements bind its parties to more stringent intellectual property protection than does TRIPS (Helfer 2003: 59; Maskus and Reichman 2005: 5; Morin 2009; Musungu and Dutfield 2003; Reichman 2000: 454; Sell 2007). Thus, more than 15 years after TRIPS, the US and its allies, the European Union and Japan, have neither delivered nor shown commitment to deliver on the promise of bargain diplomacy, treating coldly the issue of new trade concessions for less developed countries. The prevailing impression is that in relation to those countries, TRIPS has left in its wake a sobering litany of negative impacts (Long 2002: 256; Reichman 2000: 456). Yet the pressure on less developed countries has continued to affirm an international intellectual property protection standard that transcends those set by the TRIPS Agreement (Musungu and Dutfield 2003: 10–17).[27]

Meanwhile, technological innovations in digital and biotechnologies, as well as the impact of globalization continue to be felt in far flung places in the less developed world. In the wake of new global public health, environmental, biodiversity and food security crises, the TRIPS Agreement and intellectual property are readily implicated in the inequity or asymmetry over access to the benefits of new technologies. Increased consciousness over the values and contributions of the knowledge and cultural resources of indigenous and local communities in various forms of innovation, especially in the life sciences, became a source of pressure for, at least, accommodation. That pressure came mainly from less developed countries and various indigenous and local community stakeholders in traditional knowledge, including various aspects of expressive culture. In a way, these countries sought to challenge the normative template of the international intellectual property regime and its continued disdain regarding the protection of traditional knowledge. Partly, the pressure has since translated or manifested in what analysts have variously characterized as an aspect of the escalation of "regime shifting," "regime shopping," "regime proliferation," "regime tension," and "counter-regime dynamics" that are collectively part of the new "intellectual property regime complex." The pressure attempts to resist TRIPS and its underlying ideology, and to force an expansion of its interpretative space to accommodate the crucial social policy, cultural sensitivities, and the developmental desires of the less developed countries. This dual culture of resistance to, and pressure for reinterpretation of TRIPS is essentially pursued through the strategy of issue linkages that ventilate in diverse agencies and institutional arenas, and coalesce as part of the global governance dynamic in intellectual property. To set the stage for exploring the specific heads of the key issue linkages that map the global governance landscape for intellectual property in the next three chapters, we turn to the interaction between the WIPO and the WTO/TRIPS.

WIPO and TRIPS: opportunity and strategic engagement

Despite TRIPS' far reaching interventions, it did not compromise WIPO's standard-setting role or WIPO's status as the mainstream technical agency on global intellectual property matters. Counter-intuitively, TRIPS was after all "a good business for WIPO," not only "because it incorporated as its basis the provisions of WIPO's fundamental treaties, the Paris and Berne Conventions" (Salmon 2003: 434), but also because it provided WIPO the opportunity to quickly restore itself into the confidences of the developed countries. It did not take long before WIPO figured out a strategy to take advantage of that opportunity. Despite not being invited and, in fact, being opposed to the process that made the WTO the overarching body for global governance on intellectual property, by its own volition in 1994, WIPO adopted a resolution requiring its secretariat (the International Bureau) to provide technical assistance to WTO members in regard to TRIPS-related matters.

The following year, WIPO entered into a formal cooperation agreement with the WTO, known as the Cooperation for Development Program (CDP), to provide technical assistance to member countries of the WTO without regard to their non-membership in WIPO (May 2006: 439; Musungu and Dutfield 2003: 11). For many developed countries, especially the US, WIPO's proactive role in partnering with the WTO over the implementation of the TRIPS Agreement is consistent with its mandate under the 1967 Stockholm Convention. More importantly, given the WTO's nascent and inexperienced involvement in intellectual property matters, capitalizing on the WIPO's technical support and pre-existing expertise is not only logical but also attractive. Killing two birds with one stone, the WTO is able to avoid duplication of bureaucracy or reinvention of the wheel for a cost-effective global governance regime on intellectual property.

WIPO's CDP is now the centerpiece for the implementation of its technical assistance mandate. Since early 1993, through its academy in Geneva, WIPO offers a diverse range of courses and programs, including residential and online long-distance modules that target the elite and technocrats from less developed countries. For the most part, these programs are aimed at capacity building, including the provision of legal and technical infrastructure for the calibration of domestic legal regimes, especially in less developed countries, to bring them into compliance with the TRIPS Agreement (de Beer and Oguamanam 2010). The WIPO's extensive engagement in this regard, especially pursuant to the post-TRIPS CDP initiatives, has been the target of suspicion and scathing criticism by commentators. Steven Gill and Christopher May point to the hegemonic undertones of WIPO activities under the CDP, locating them within "a wider political economic dynamic of 'new constitutionalism,' [as] an attempt to make 'transnational liberalism, and if possible liberal democratic capitalism, the sole model of future development'" (Gill 2003: 132).[28]

The WIPO's CDP is premised on a blanket imposition of a TRIPS and TRIPS-plus standard, and is not oriented toward a critical approach to TRIPS implementation in less developed countries. Under the CDP, TRIPS is the gold standard for legislative intervention in less developed countries, irrespective of compelling constraining factors, such as poor national economic and industrial profile, dearth of R&D and a paucity of intellectual property expertise, as well as differences in domestic legislative models. For May (2006: 440), the CDP translates into "an important political (or even ideological) program of social re-orientation" by WIPO, involving the socialization of less developed country elites and policymakers in a manner that transforms them into advocates for stronger intellectual property protection bereft of development considerations. In a way, this may help to silence domestic objections and assuage concerns over the WTO/TRIPS' legitimacy deficit (de Beer and Oguamanam 2010; May 2006).

Similar to the CDP, in 2001, WIPO enunciated the "Patent Agenda" which aims at harmonizing the international patent system under the vision of a universal patent regime, and mapping a course for its future development. This elaborate program, which falls directly within the registration, administration and treaty-negotiating mandates of the WIPO, is being explored on three fronts: Revision of the Patent Cooperation Treaty (PCT), the ratification of the Patent Law Treaty (PLT) adopted in 2000, and the negotiation of the Substantive Patent Law Treaty (SPLT). Under the Patent Agenda, the WIPO seeks to amend the PCT, which is the procedural part of the Paris Convention, in a way that streamlines and simplifies its operative procedures for an efficient international patent registration process. Such a process is envisaged to align with the new PLT, which is primarily concerned with the harmonization of formal procedures for patent application, for example, in regard to filing date, form, content, etc. Perhaps to underscore the contentious and horizontal nature of the issues implicated in the Patent Agenda across regimes, in 2000, less developed countries pressed for inclusion of disclosure of source or origin of genetic materials implicated in new patent applications (Arezzo 2007). This subject threatened to derail deliberations on the PLT until WIPO agreed to move the discussions onto the SPLT negotiations. The resolution of the issue of disclosure of source/origin of genetic resources remains critical to the future of the SPLT negotiations.[29]

Perhaps more contentious than the PLT negotiation is the WIPO Standing Committee on the Law of Patent (SCP)'s continuing negotiation of the 2001 draft of the SPLT.[30] The content and scope of the SPLT touches sensitive nerves in both less developed and developed countries. Essentially, the SPLT aims at establishing and elaborating a harmonized standard for patentability in key areas, including prior art, novelty, utility and inventiveness, as well as a common benchmark for claim drafting, the nature of "sufficient disclosure," and the fixing of a grace period, all of which will, among other things, facilitate and streamline the process of patent examination and searches for prior art. Most of the critical issues in the negotiation agenda for the SPLT just mentioned underlie the epistemic conflict between western science and indigenous knowledge practices; they are at the root of the hierarchies of culture and power that have for too long excluded local knowledge from the innovation matrix, denying it intellectual content (Oguamanam 2008a).

At the core of this contention is how the benchmarks could accommodate the protection of biological diversity, genetic resources, the environment and indigenous biocultural knowledge in particular, and traditional knowledge practices, in general. The SPLT debates have implicated aspects of diverse intellectual property regime dynamics, as some of the issues are also open to exploration by way of forum shopping and regime proliferation at other avenues, as discussed in the subsequent chapters of this book. Predictably, in 2005, less developed countries under the aegis of Friends of Development (FOD), sought to link the ongoing negotiations on the draft of SPLT to the broader Development Agenda in WIPO, a matter to we return shortly.[31]

Not surprisingly, analysts have expressed concern over the nature of the SPLT negotiations. Most importantly, they point to the marginalization of the voices of less developed countries and the suspicious role of the WIPO via the International Bureau in the negotiations. The WIPO has been criticized as a partial facilitator with a self-serving agenda that aligns more with the interests of developed countries than with the less developed ones. According to Musungu and Dutfield (2003: 12), overall, the implementation of the SPLT, as presently drafted, would yield a more stringent TRIPS-plus standard of patent regime, one that would "compromise the ability of developing countries to use the various TRIPS flexibilities, including even the Doha Declaration, for development objectives." The involvement of WIPO in instituting a TRIPS-plus initiative may, in some way, be attuned to the new vision of intellectual property under the WTO. However, it is clearly antithetical to WIPO's status as a special agency of the United Nations supposedly committed to working to realize its development objectives. As such an agency, WIPO is caught at the crossroads of the ideological conflict between strong private claims versus public interest or developmental claims over the control of knowledge, a conflict that has historically shaped intellectual property jurisprudence. In the post-TRIPS era, the WIPO appears to have clearly aligned with the strict private proprietary control end of the intellectual property spectrum at the expense of the development imperative. In the words of Musungu and Dutfield (2003: 11):

Ultimately, the circumstances leading to the adoption of the TRIPS Agreement in the WTO demonstrate that for WIPO to remain the main forum on intellectual property matters, it must show to the United States and its industry that it can deliver new standards faster and more efficiently. This reasoning underlies WIPO's TRIPS-plus agenda.

In addition to its Patent Agenda, the WIPO has been active in instituting and implementing, via its Arbitration and Mediation Center, regulatory and dispute resolution mechanisms for the control and use of domain names under the Uniform Domain-Name Dispute Resolution Policy (UDRP) of the Internet Corporation for Assigned Domain Name and Numbers (ICANN). Also, while coordinating discussion of internet-related intellectual property policy matters, WIPO has supervised two important TRIPS-plus treaties under its Digital Agenda. They are the 1996 WIPO Copyright Treaty (WCT) and the WIPO Performances and Phonograms Treaty (WPPT) of the same year. Collectively, the two treaties, which came into effect in 2002, are also called the internet treaties. They reflect aspects of the WIPO's stated objective to promote access for less developed countries to intellectual property information, and enhancement of their participation in global policy formulation in the new digital environment, especially its electric commerce component. Quite unlike the Patent Agenda, these two treaties have been touted as accommodating the interests of both hi-tech industries in developed countries with high stakes in the digital and internet-based technologies, and those of local communities in less developed countries whose traditional cultural and musical performances are easy targets for exploitation in the digital environment.[32]

The development agenda at the WIPO

WIPO's self-ingratiation with WTO/TRIPS' new vision of intellectual property (as evidenced by the Patent and Digital Agendas and the CDP) has opened, in a dramatic way, an intense intra-regime and counter-regime dynamic in the WIPO, and in the global governance of intellectual property in general. In their bid to reassert their collective interest in development and to push back the WIPO's fast eroding commitment to development pursuant to its status as a UN specialized agency, less developed countries have fought back by initiating and foisting a *new* development agenda on the WIPO. In 2004 Brazil and Argentina, with the subsequent but resounding support of 16 WIPO countries under the aegis of Friends of Development (FOD) (Yu 2007: 1451), proposed a comprehensive development agenda for the WIPO (de Beer 2009a; May 2006). As a forerunner of the official unfolding and subsequent adoption of the development agenda, the global NGO community and activists met in Geneva in the WIPO General Assembly to critically evaluate WIPO's role in intellectual property and development. This initiative culminated in the Geneva Declaration on the Future of WIPO.

The Declaration articulates the need for a reorientation of WIPO to promote development interests, and to re-engage WIPO with its status as a special agency of the UN. In a nutshell, the Geneva Declaration identified development as central to the future of WIPO. It notes that: "The functions of WIPO should not only be to promote efficient protection and harmonization of intellectual property laws, but to formally embrace the notions of balance." It urged WIPO to "work from the broader framework described in the 1974 agreement with the UN, and take a more balanced and realistic view of the social benefits and costs of intellectual property rights." The Declaration called for a "moratorium on new treaties and harmonization of standards that expand and strengthen monopolies and further restrict access to knowledge," while urging the WIPO to embrace the development agenda proposed by the governments of Brazil and Argentina. Accordingly, the Declaration provided much needed momentum for the enunciation and final adoption of the WIPO development agenda.

After three years of unsurprisingly heated deliberations and reluctance from the US, the European Union and Japan, in 2007 the WIPO General Assembly unanimously adopted 45 recommendations compressed into six thematic clusters, which now constitute the WIPO Development Agenda proper.[33] Santos was correct in observing that the contingency of history, indeed, breeds "the necessity to change it: victims don't just cry, they fight back" (Santos 2008: 248). The General Assembly charged a permanent Committee on Development and Intellectual Property (CDIP), among other things, to implement the Development Agenda at the WIPO.

The details of the WIPO Development Agenda have been discussed elsewhere (de Beer, 2009a; May 2006). For our purposes here, it is sufficient to underscore its significance for WIPO and for the future direction of intellectual property in global governance. First, in a way, the Development Agenda aggregates in a detailed but convoluted and overlapping manner, the developmental imperatives that historically constitute WIPO's Achilles' heel. The Development Agenda is a calculated response by less developed countries and other stakeholders to pitch the WIPO in a direction that plugs the development or public-regarding deficit in its modus operandi in the pre- and post-WTO/TRIPS era. According to Jeremy de Beer, the Development Agenda represents a significant "paradigm shift for IP policies in the twenty-first century" (de Beer 2009a: 2). For May (2006: 442) the agenda, "seeks to orient the WIPO towards a more developmental set of concerns . . . [and] to 'mainstream development' at the WIPO" in a constructive manner sensitive to the interests of less developed countries.

Already, the Development Agenda has prompted the WIPO to commence liaisons with relevant UN agencies and other stakeholders at the intersection between intellectual property and development. In this potential and emergent partnership, the relevant agencies would do well to be mindful of WIPO's poor score card in regard to development, and not allow deference to its technical expertise to undermine their ability to assist in plugging the development gap in the organization's modus operandi and ideological bias. Despite reservations over the juridical status of the Development Agenda (de Beer 2009a: 11) the complexity, depth, and flexibility of the agenda evinces the inevitability of "forum proliferation" and the imperative for forum coordination as the new reality of intellectual property in global governance at the WIPO and the WTO. As much as the Development

Agenda may have the status of soft law, the sincerity with which its implementation is pursued by developed and less developed countries alike will shape the future of progress, or lack thereof, in consensus building around the multiplicity of issues implicated in intellectual property in global governance. Describing the Development Agenda as arguably "the most significant [or strategic] IP matter [. . .] since the TRIPS Agreement [. . .]" de Beer (2009a: 19) rightly contends that:

> [i]implementation is the litmus test for the Development Agenda's success. To meaningfully implement the agenda will take foresight, creativity, and, perhaps, most of all perseverance [. . .] Only by pursuing practical, concrete strategies will the Development Agenda lead to results rather than rhetoric.

Second, more than any one issue, the failure of the WIPO diplomatic conferences in the 1980s, which were convened to review the Paris Convention, was instrumental to the regime shift in global intellectual property lawmaking that brought the WTO/TRIPS Agreement to the forefront. Paradoxically, 12 years after TRIPS, the WIPO's Patent Agenda, which aims at a harmonized global patent system and ostensibly to restore the WIPO into the confidences of developed countries, was catalytic of the resounding response from developing countries expressed in the 2007 WIPO Development Agenda. The comprehensive nature of the latter appears to have stalled further deliberations on the Patent Agenda in the WIPO, opening future initiatives on global intellectual property law and policymaking to a more holistic perspective in a way that deliberately incorporates the diverse issue linkages that continue to shape the global intellectual property debate since the advent of the TRIPS Agreement. It is instructive that the Geneva Declaration on the Future of WIPO called for a moratorium on new treaties and the harmonization of standards on intellectual property. This is an obvious reference to the WIPO Patent Agenda and other TRIPS-plus initiatives.

The holistic approach to intellectual property that underlies the Development Agenda requires a balanced consideration of intellectual property laws and policies as integral aspects of a more complex "information [and knowledge] ecosystem" (Yu 2005a: 1). It is striking that in its early text, "the development agenda made reference to the Doha Development Round of the WTO multilateral trade negotiations (a.k.a the Development Round)," thus "linking the Agenda to a wider range of proposals and actions that have 'all placed development at the heart of their concerns'" (May 2006: 441).[34]

Third, without a doubt, the WIPO Development Agenda is an important platform for tackling the crisis of equity into which the WIPO and the WTO/TRIPS Agreement plunged the global intellectual property system. Exploring the issue linkages that drive the extant intellectual property regime complex is critical to understanding not only that crisis of equity, but also the reality and role of regime proliferation in the global governance of intellectual property. Although the WTO and WIPO are pivotal to intellectual property in global governance, the crisis of equity in the global intellectual property system transcends WIPO and the WTO in regards to that concern. If anything, it requires the two organizations to reappraise their roles in light of the ubiquitous nature of intellectual property as a concept inherently critical to development and equity. Not many will doubt that in the new knowledge-based global economic order, intellectual property is central in "accounting for global inequalities and for framing progressive responses" thereto (el-Ojeili and Hayden 2006: 40). This accounting and framing is at the core of the development narrative and, perhaps, constitutes the most important aspect of the Development Agenda.

Fourth, Gervais, de Beer and others affirm that global intellectual property governance has reached a "calibration" phase (de Beer 2009a: 15; Chon 2006: 2831; Gervais 2007: iv). They agree that in this phase, the issue is not necessarily how much newer or stronger intellectual property regimes are required to be for economic growth, or how far we are prepared to push back on stronger intellectual property protection, but essentially, how intellectual property can be finetuned to respond to the prevailing contingencies of diverse stakeholders. For Dutfield and Suthersanen (2005), it is a matter of how to entrench differentiation as a principle of international intellectual property policy and lawmaking. Equity and the development imperative should be at the core of the calibration phase of intellectual property in global governance. A one-size-fits-all or self-serving coercive bilateralism, or surreptitious hard-edged TRIPS-plus tactics insensitive to the monumental impacts of intellectual property on less developed countries and on the most vulnerable in the new global knowledge economy, would be unacceptable. That is the message of the Development Agenda, whether or not it truly represents a paradigm shift or a touchstone for continued tension in intellectual property in global governance.

Last, and perhaps most important, the resurgence of the development discourse in the WIPO is, in part, indicative of the enduring relevance of WIPO as a venue for intellectual property policy and politics, given the continued development of new technologies, as evident in the conclusion of WCT, the WPPT, and the ongoing deliberations on the digital agenda. These developments implicate issues that are either not covered in the TRIPS Agreement, or concerning which the WTO is less competent to deal with. As well, ongoing deadlocks and testy debates at the WTO and the TRIPS Council demonstrate that progress on international intellectual property lawmaking will be hard to accomplish at the last two forums.[35] Along this line, May enthuses that "to a large extent the organization [i.e. the WIPO] has recovered from the threat of marginalization" at the onset of TRIPS and "has regained some measure of its previous influence and importance in the global governance of IPRs" (May 2007: 96, 35). He notes that WIPO has recorded a shift to a more focused manner in its operation in the global governance of intellectual property, thus leaving issues of enforcement to the WTO while "concentrating on socialization and norm-building" (May 2007: 35).

Entrenching and enforcing a development norm in global intellectual property governance is, perhaps, the most challenging task for the WIPO and the WTO. But as I demonstrate in the last chapter, it would require the intervention of emerging and regional powers to initiate and accomplish any meaningful change in that direction. Indeed, a combination of this turn of events in the WIPO and the WTO with the increased voices of leading middle income developing countries in global governance confirms reminds us of the observations of Kennedy, noted in the last chapter, that global governance is a dynamic process in which political, economic and legal pressures "unleash interests, change the balance of forces, and lead further to the reinvention of the governance scheme itself" (Kennedy 2008: 832). In the next chapter, I focus on the human rights question and the global public health crisis as key issue linkages and aspects of regime proliferation or overall regime complexity in the global governance dynamic in intellectual property law.

Notes

1   Through the Edison Light Company and Siemens Corporation, respectively.
2   Footnote omitted.
3   For example, Charles Dickens in 1842 expressed frustration over America's attitude to copyright in a letter to John Foster.
4   For a timeline from Berne and Paris (including key treaties and dates) up to the establishment of WIPO in 1970, see May 2007: 20–21.
5   Current (2010) membership of the WIPO is 184, while the current membership of the United Nations is 192.
6   In 2010 not much has changed in the composition of NGOs that participate in the WIPO processes. See Reichman 2009a.
7   See The Berne Convention, Stockholm, Act 1967: "Protocol Regarding Developing Countries."
8   The agreement between the UN and the WIPO, Online. Available online: http://wipo.int/treaties/en/agreement (accessed 20 November 2010).
9   Martin (2009) examines the uniqueness and the natural rights origin of that rule of priority in American patent jurisprudence in light of the anticipated change of the rule by Congress.
10   WIPO's substantive contractual obligations and rights are largely set out in Articles 1, 2, 5, 6, 7, 9, 10, and 17 of the agreement with the UN.
11   See Article 10.
12   Article 5.
13   Footnotes omitted. Musungu and Dutfield (2003: 19) make a neutral mention of this.
14   Musungu and Dutfield (2003) do not give the impression that there is dissonance between UNCTAD and WIPO in regard to this report. Rather, they indicate that at the time the agreement between WIPO and UN was being prepared, WIPO was undertaking this project as a joint study with UNCTAD.
15   The two UNCTAD reports, The Role of the Patents System in the Transfer of Technology to Developing Countries, UN Doc. TD/B/AC 1 1/19 (1974), and The Role of Trade Marks in Developing Countries, UN Doc. TD/C/C.6/A.C3/3 (1979), are both constructively critical of the international intellectual property system, especially in the area of technology transfer to less developed countries and their negative implication for their developmental aspiration. The reports call for a change in the system through, among other things, the removal of impediments and inherent abuses in the operation of the international intellectual property system.
16   Halbert's position is slightly different in that she points out that the incorporation of WIPO into the UN created a competition between two UN agencies with oversight regarding intellectual property. This concern was raised by UNESCO during the 1967 Stockholm Conference.
17   Citing Drahos 2002.
18   According to May and Sell (2006: 137), "[t]he pharmaceutical industry in the United States really came into its own during World War II."

19 Footnotes omitted.
20 Emphasis in original.
21 Quoting Kastriner 1991: 20.
22 Emphasis in original.
23 Footnotes omitted.
24 Article III(5) of the Agreement Establishing the World Trade Organization provides: "With a view to achieving greater coherence in global economic policy-making, the WTO shall cooperate as appropriate with the International Monetary Fund and the International Bank for Reconstruction and Development and its affiliated agencies."
25 Quoting Helfer 2004.
26 Drahos and Braithwaite (2004: 206) have analogized TRIPS to "a floor without a ceiling."
27 Discussing the WIPO Patent and Digital Agendas, WIPO's technical assistance programs, its institutional complicity and related activities that have collectively resulted in a TRIPS-plus intellectual property world order.
28 Cited in May 2006: 440.
29 This is still the case, despite developed countries' recourse to free trade agreement (FTA) bilateralism as a way around this and other subjects.
30 Given the ongoing nature of the negotiation of the draft of SPLT, except when they relate to facts, our remarks here are speculative and reflect general impressions from those negotiations.
31 An account of the progress of the negotiation on the draft of SPLT is available online: http://www.wipo.int/patent-law/en/harmonization.htm (accessed 20 November 2010).
32 However, the antecedents to these treaties cast doubt over their putative benefit for less developed countries. For example, the WCT faced domestic opposition in the United Sates before it made its way to Geneva as a forum-shopping strategy by its proponents. Also, the UK Commission on Intellectual Property, a respected organization with a development orientation to intellectual property, has expressed reservation over the benefit of these treaties to developing countries. Specifically, the Commission urges developing countries to resist pressure to deny them free to access materials on the Internet for education and research and other fair use purposes. Indeed, the negative impact of the WIPO Copyright Treaty on developing countries is generally perceived to outweigh any benefits claimed on its behalf. See, generally, Pistorius 2006. Even in the US, the legislation that implements the WIPO Copyright Treaty, the Digital Millennium Copyright Act (DMCA), is perceived to be overkill in several quarters.
33 For text of the Development Agenda, see WIPO online: http://www.wipo.int/ip-development/en/agenda/ (accessed 20 November 2010).
34 For some reason, the final text of the Development Agenda did not incorporate the reference to Doha. But in their entirety, the 45 recommendations and six clusters of the Development Agenda are deeply rooted in a broad approach to development that completely underscores the multifarious nature of issue linkages implicated in the contemporary discourse on intellectual property. Those issues transcend the direct jurisdictions of both WIPO and WTO/TRIPS.
35 Since the 1999 disruption of the WTO Ministerial Meeting by NGOs and a broad-based coalition of civil society organizations, there has been no let up by less developed countries and their diverse sympathizers in expressing lack of confidence in the WTO processes, especially in the TRIPS Council, leading to a series of stalemates at Ministerial Council meetings. Increasingly, the unpopularity of the WTO in less developed countries is resulting in a shift to utilize more temperate and conducive forums, such as the WIPO and other UN agencies, WHO and the CBD as platforms for pursuing their shared interests in the regulation of the knowledge economy.

Part II

4 Human rights in the new intellectual property dynamic

The last chapter noted that one of the effects of global governance in intellectual property is the reconfiguration of the governance scheme, as evident in the build-up to the emergence of the WIPO Development Agenda and its subsequent ramifications. The contestation that led to the reconfiguration indexes the overall dynamic of the international regime process at work. In a way, the reinvention is hardly deliberate. Rather, it is as much a consequence, as it is the context of the diverse issue linkages arising from the role of intellectual property in the global knowledge economy. Its offshoot is not only an escalation of asymmetry in the power relations between developed and less developed countries. It has also created a crisis of equity and a significant development gap between the two. In the next four chapters, I explore specific thematic issue linkages to the global intellectual property order and how they attract diverse actors and stakeholders who jostle and contest in the reinvention of the global governance scheme for intellectual property.

The focus of this chapter is the intellectual property issue linkage to human rights, global public health crises, and the global health inequity. The selection and framing of this issue linkage does not exhaust the complexity of the interaction between intellectual property and human rights. Given the gamut of human rights and intellectual property rights, the contours of their intersection transcend public health. They include, but are not limited to, the broader development narrative, specifically in sometimes overlapping contexts of technology transfer, education, and access to information; the digital divide; freedom of expression; privacy; cultural property; self-determination; democracy; food security; and the rights of indigenous peoples. Chapters 5, 6 and 7 focus on the last two subjects in our exploration of the intellectual property issue linkages and issue aggregations from a global governance perspective, rather than within a strict human rights paradigm.

The decision to discuss human rights and global public health crises in this chapter is essentially discretionary, but logical one. First, beyond its other negative impacts, the introduction of the TRIPS Agreement is associated with the freeze in access to essential drugs, resulting in the escalation of the global public health and human rights crises, especially in less developed countries (Eppich 2002; Gathii 2002; Mirabile 2002; Sell 2007; Watson 2009). Also, a global public health crisis is, perhaps, the primary site for the recent expression of interest by the UN human rights system in the relationship between intellectual property and human rights.

Last, beside the perceived role of pharmaceutical patents in impeding access to medicine for the benefit of needy populations, perhaps only a few other issues have provoked the same passion around global governance and the politics of intellectual property by diverse stakeholders.

Intellectual property and human rights

For too long, the nexus between intellectual property and human rights seemed impalpable to scholars and policy analysts. In seminal works on the subject, Helfer and Yu (Helfer 2003: 47; Yu 2007a: 1041) agree on the point of the following illuminating remark by the former:

> Human rights and intellectual property, two bodies of law that were once strangers, are now becoming increasingly intimate bedfellows. For decades the two subjects developed in virtual isolation from each other. But in the last few years, international standard setting activities have begun to map previously uncharted intersections between intellectual property law on the one hand and human rights law on the other.[1]

Helfer identifies the neglected rights of indigenous peoples in the international system and the emergence of the TRIPS Agreement as two factors responsible for facilitating new consciousness over the location of intellectual property in the human rights framework. In regard to the former, he notes that the UN's response to continued complaints by indigenous peoples over the need to have control of their diverse cultural heritage dates back to the 1980s, indeed, to the 1970s. Such responses led to the integration of the indigenous question into the UN human rights system (Kingsbury 2001; Oguamanam 2004a; Sanders 1998). Consequently, that action has yielded diverse receptive legal instruments, culminating in the UN Declaration on the Rights of Indigenous Peoples, adopted September 13, 2007. Although a non-binding instrument, that document reflects the sentiments in earlier regional and international instruments. Among other things, it comprehensively articulates the significance of intellectual property as a knowledge control mechanism in regards to indigenous human rights, self-determination and indigenous peoples' overall aspiration in the new knowledge society. Recent elaborations of the International Covenant on Economic, Social and Cultural Rights (ICESCR) by the Committee on Economic, Social and Cultural Rights continue to clear lingering doubts over the inclusion of indigenous knowledge, innovation and practices and their creators in the elaboration of human rights in international law (CESCR General Comments).[2]

The intersection of intellectual property and human rights implicates the interests of indigenous peoples as creators or innovators of scientific, literary, and artistic works, as well as their collective interest in their right to self-determination, to life, and to survival. Indigenous peoples and local communities of the enclave territories and elsewhere in less developed countries stand at the receiving end of the socioeconomic transformations of the new knowledge economic order. There is little doubt that the role of intellectual property in the new economic order, as explored in Chapter 3, has provoked diverse concerns, including those relating to human rights in indigenous circles, especially in the late 20th century. That period has opened up for scrutiny the history and normative assumptions of 500 years of colonial hierarchies of culture and power that have denied indigenous knowledge any intellectual content. This scrutiny has left indigenous and local communities determined to stake and reclaim their contributions to the global basket of knowledge (Arewa 2006a, 2006b; Oguamanam 2008a). A combination of factors, including the rise of innovation in bio- and digital technologies and in the life sciences, and the escalation of biopiracy and rapid expansion of intellectual property regimes, results in the enclosure of indigenous knowledge (Yu 2007b, 2007c).[3] These same developments provoke resistance to the enclosure. For a people whose relationship of dependence with their ecosystem is first nature and the basis for their knowledge and socioeconomic and cultural life (Brush and Stabinsky 1996; McManis 2007), intellectual property's role in knowledge enclosure is a fundamental human rights issue bordering on life and survival. For example, the recent interest of biotechnology in the genetic information of indigenous communities and the extension of intellectual property to human cell lines and the human DNA of isolated indigenous communities under the threat of extinction, raises serious human rights issues at individual and community levels (Amani and Coombe: 2005).

Similarly, the use of digital technological devices and other information, communication and multimedia resources, especially the internet platform to manipulate and exploit expressive culture and the intangible cultural heritage of indigenous communities results in the deprivation of scientific, literary and artistic production of indigenous peoples and communities as basic human rights recognized under the CESCR (Arewa 2006b; Wendland 2009). In addition, and perhaps more important, the reliance of biotechnology and life sciences on biological diversity and biological resources and the associated knowledge of indigenous and local communities implicates the dialectics of indigenous peoples' interest in intellectual property. On one hand, intellectual property represents a tool for indigenous empowerment; for the realization of their basic aspiration to use their biological resources and knowledge for their self-determination. On the other, there is a sceptical perception of intellectual property as a western device that undermines indigenous epistemological autonomy and compromises their right to self-determination (Agrawal 1999; Helfer: 2003; Oguamanam 2008b).[4] Thus, the debate over a governance modality for indigenous knowledge is a component of the global governance dynamic in intellectual property.

As already noted, the exploration of the indigenous question in international law, especially in the new knowledge economic order, is not only linked to the intersection between intellectual property and human rights; it also transcends that framework, as evidenced in the following chapters. In a way, indigenous knowledge is one important factor that has brought the UN human rights system into the global governance of intellectual property as an important actor. Besides the UN, international finance institutions such as the World Bank,[5] and various NGOs, indigenous peoples and knowledge advocates, have forged links between intellectual property and human rights in the context of indigenous peoples and knowledge.

The second reason for the location of intellectual property in the human rights framework, according to Helfer (2003), is the TRIPS Agreement. This comes from America's linking of intellectual property to trade, and the tightening of pre-TRIPS flexibilities in the international intellectual property regime that enabled states to adapt intellectual property to their national economic contingencies. The strengthening of intellectual property rights, especially the patents regime, in terms of their scope and enforcement under the TRIPS Agreement has been linked to the global public health crisis, especially in regard to the cost of, and access to, essential drugs in indigenous and local communities globally, and in regard to indigenous and local peoples' contributions to the process of pharmaceutical innovation in some cases (Heald 2003; Mgbeoji 2006; Oguamanam 2010).

Perhaps more than any other industrial sector, the expansion of the patent regime bears a direct relationship with the pharmaceutical industry (Mgbeoji 2006; Oguamanam 2010). That expansion is but an aspect of the overall expansion of intellectual property rights under the TRIPS Agreement to include new rights over computer programs, compilations of data, genes, plants and animal genetic resources, software algorithms, etc. The case for pharmaceutical patents is instructive for a few reasons. First, under the pre-TRIPS WIPO framework, many less developed countries did not sanction patents on pharmaceuticals because of strategic health and economic considerations. Also, they had a comparatively unfettered option to exercise the compulsory licensing provisions of the Paris Convention. At all points, they reserved the discretion to opt out of any WIPO-administered treaty provision that did not support access to generic drugs to tackle a national health challenge. All these liberties were constricted, for the most part, under TRIPS, which not only made pharmaceutical patents compulsory, but also circumscribed the option to use compulsory license.

The TRIPS Agreement bears a direct link with the globalization of pharmaceutical and medical markets, and the consequent undermining of the important contributions of mid-level economic blocs such as India, Brazil, Argentina, China, Mexico, Korea and Thailand in the supply of generic drugs for needy populations (Drahos and Braithwaite 2004). In terms of timing, the Uruguay Round of the Multilateral Trade Negotiations (MTN) on the General Agreement on Tariffs and Trade (GATT) started in 1986 and terminated in 1993. It resulted in the transformation of GATT. By all accounts, the US pharmaceutical interest group, led by the Pharmaceutical Research and Manufacturers of America (PhRMA), along with the top executives of that country's leading pharmaceutical corporations, are on record as the single largest most influential group behind the TRIPS Agreement (Drahos and Braithwaite 2003; Sell 2003). Given the export base of the pharmaceutical industry, its significance to the US economy makes it a favored industrial sector. PhRMA readily ingratiates itself with Washington politicians of all ideological shades and the transnational profile of its members makes the ability of "Big Pharma"[6] to influence pharmaceutical and medical policy globally unrivalled. By most, if not all accounts, from the less developed countries' perspective, the WTO/TRIPS-supervised globalization of pharmaceutical and allied markets has negatively impacted their citizens' right to health and, consequently, left a trail of tears and sorrows for the world's most vulnerable.

The WTO/TRIPS was essentially a strategic brainchild of the US, conceived and birthed at a time when America was determined to take advantage of its sole superpower status to impose its legal scheme and neoliberal market economic ideology on the world – and to take optimum advantage of its head start in bio- and digital technologies. Specifically, in the pharmaceutical sector, the 1980s (a.k.a the Reagan years) was a highpoint during the era of intellectual property triumphalism. It was a time when anti-trust laws were relaxed in the US to boost American global competitiveness (Sell 2004: 369). A weaker anti-trust regime has since paved the way for merger and acquisitions in key industries, notably, the pharmaceutical and allied industries. Pharmaceutical corporations capitalized on a weaker anti-trust regime to consolidate patent, brand and market monopolies. By leveraging and mopping up alternative processes, products and brands, this approach progressively eliminated competition in the industry, which was, hitherto, possible through competing patents and brands.

Another feature of the pharmaceutical industrial sector in the WTO/TRIPS era is its capitalization on the extension of patent to life sciences (Bagley 2003; Kelves and Berkowitz 2001; Knoppers 2000). Life sciences patents promote technological advances in basic biomedical sciences. This approach facilitates research convergences to create a research network culture that operates to expand scientific opportunities with a cumulative system benefit in pharmaceutical research and development (R&D) and drug production. For example, random screening is gradually giving way to a targeted and rational approach to drug discovery. Globalization and free trade continue to facilitate applications of biotechnology for bioprospecting mainly in indigenous and local communities for pharmaceutical compounds of economic value (Oguamanam 2008a). Today, instead of a scatter-shot approach, pharmaceutical companies increasingly rely on the traditional knowledge of indigenous and local communities to screen viable compounds. By some accounts, this tactic has improved the success rate in drug discovery by some 78% (Oguamanam 2004b: 140).

The TRIPS Agreement's expansion of patents into pharmaceuticals and the life sciences has led to an unprecedented growth of the scientific complex, resulting in a boost for the US-led global pharmaceutical industry. Coupled with the relaxation of the anti-trust regime, the US has set up a global pharmaceutical architecture designed for an emerging global market for health products and services, and controlled by it and a few other countries. The implication of a reinvigorated patent regime under TRIPS is a structural aspect of emerging global public health policy which, according to Sell (2004: 364, 370), confers economic power on life sciences industries, including the pharmaceutical industry, thereby escalating and prioritizing their influence in the making of that policy. According to Drahos and Braithwaite (2002: 221–2), this vision of a global intellectual property paradigm is a negative one designed for market domination by developed countries. Clear evidence is the unrelenting bid to circumscribe or constrict India's pharmaceutical export capacity pursuant to the TRIPS Agreement. According to them:

The acquisition of skills by newcomers disturbs roles and hierarchies. After India built a national drug industry it began exporting bulk drugs to places such as Canada. A developing country that has acquired skills threatened those at the top of an international hierarchy of pharmaceutical production – the US, Japan, Germany and the UK. Underneath the individualist ideology of intellectual property lies an agenda for underdevelopment, of maintaining an economic hierarchy in the world. Today's global intellectual property paradigm is all about protecting the knowledge and skills of the leaders of the pack.

(Drahos and Braithwaite 2002: 221–2)[7]

As we shall see later in this chapter, the pharmaceutical industrial sector has capitalized on this influence to optimize their market economic space with little regard for a balance with public regarding considerations, let alone the resulting human rights questions that their lopsided dominance raises. This strategy translates into an access freeze on essential drugs for needy populations, a jeopardization of their human right to "the highest attainable standard of physical and mental health" (International Covenant on Economic, Social and Cultural Rights, Article 12.1). The adverse health impacts of the HIV/AIDS pandemic in many less developed countries, especially in Africa, also highlighted the negative impact of the tightening of pharmaceutical patents by transnational pharmaceutical corporations supported by their home governments. This scenario provides the direct and ultimate reason for concrete policy elaboration, on an interventionist basis, to restructure the consequential incidents located at the juncture of intellectual property and human rights. The next section explores the juridical framing of this intersection.

Intellectual property and human rights: juridical framing

Notwithstanding the long period of separation or non-interaction between intellectual property and human rights, there are ample juridical grounds for their relationship both on conceptual and practical bases in the International Bill of Rights.[8] Without being exhaustive, the following provisions make a direct link between intellectual property and human rights at a basic level. The 1948 Universal Declaration of Human Rights (UDHR)[9], in Article 27 provides as follows:

1) Everyone has the right freely to participate in the cultural life of the community, to enjoy the arts and to share in scientific advancement and its benefits.
2) Everyone has the right to the protection of the moral and material interests resulting from any scientific, literary or artistic production of which he is the author.

Article 25.1 of the UDHR provides that "Everyone has the right to a standard of living adequate to the health of himself and his family, including clothing, housing and medical care and necessary social services." In giving stronger legal backing to that *declaration*, the 1966 ICESCR[10] provides, in Article 12.1 that state parties to the Covenant recognize "the right of everyone to the enjoyment of the highest attainable standard of physical and mental health." In 2000 the CESCR issued General Comment No. 14, which elaborates the interpretative scope for effective implementation of that right. In addition to the ICESCR, there are several other international instruments at both the core and periphery of human rights, including the 1965 International Covenant on the Elimination of All forms of Racial Discrimination,[11] the 1979 Convention on the Elimination of All Forms of Discrimination against Women,[12] and 1989 Covenant on the Rights of the Child.[13] But the ICESCR provision is, perhaps, the most authoritative textual grounding of the human right to health in the UN human rights system. Consequently, the UN Commission for Human Rights (UNCHR) and its successor body, the UN Human Rights Council, has rightly championed opposition to the perceived external conflict which the TRIPS Agreement and the WTO system posed for human rights.

The ICESCR builds on the above declaration, and imbues it with a more than a declaratory status. Article 15 provides:

1) The state Parties to the present Covenant recognize the right of every one:
   a) To take part in cultural life;
   b) To enjoy the benefits of scientific progress and its applications;
   c) To benefit from the protection of moral and material interests resulting from any scientific, literary, or artistic production of which he is the author.

From this, there is little doubt that at the international level, the intersection between human rights and intellectual property had occupied the attention of policymakers as far back as 1948. Accounts and references to the drafting histories of this text (Cullet 2007; Yu 2007a) indicate that policymakers were quite mindful of the implications of the intersection between human rights and intellectual property rights. However, according to Yu (2007c) the drafters' intentions have since remained elusive. This is precisely in regard to the extent or scope of the rights to the two categories of interests therein mentioned, namely, the moral and material interests of authors, on the one hand, and the omnibus category which speaks to the interest of the public to exploit and access the benefits of culture and scientific innovation, on the other. Clearly, these provisions echo the fundamental tensions that shape law and policy on intellectual property, i.e. balancing the need to adequately reward innovation with the need to accommodate public interest in access and overall dissemination of the benefits of innovation for the greater public good and the enrichment of the public domain. Because the textual provisions of the ICSECR are generally unclear, a clue to the interpretive implications of the provisions of Article 15 is found in General Comment No. 17 (CESCR General Comments). These are not considered binding, but they outline the nature of obligations and expectations from states parties regarding compliance with the ICSECR.

The overall impression is that the extant global intellectual property regime now supervised, for the most part, by the WTO and post-TRIPS WIPO caters to the interests of rights holders at the expense of public-regarding considerations (e.g. Musungu and Dutfield 2003). Some analysts suggest that the drafting history of the ICSECR indicates that it was not so intended. For example, Cullet (2007: 407) points out that subparagraph (c) of Article 15 of the ICSECR was not part of the original draft. Even when it was introduced, the objective was to protect authors from exploitation by publishers. Also, the placement of that subparagraph after (a) and (b) suggests, in a way, that the moral and material interest of authors would be moderated by the public-regarding considerations outlined in subparagraphs (a) and (b). And if this were not convincing enough, paragraphs 2–4 of Article 15 speak directly to public-regarding considerations by making references to "development and diffusion of science and culture," "freedom of scientific research and creative activity," and "international cooperation in scientific and cultural fields."

According to Cullet (2007: 408–9), though Article 15 of the ICSECR did not indicate how to strike the required balance between incentivizing innovation and the public's right of access thereto, "it provides a framework within which the development of science and culture is undertaken for the greater good of society while recognizing the need to provide specific incentive for authors [and other categories of creators] for this to happen." Overall, commentators seem to agree that the drafters of the ICESCR were inclined toward a weak regime of intellectual property as human rights (Chapman 2002a: 314; Torremans 2004: 9; Yu 2007a: 1070). In this regard, Lessig (2003: 775–7) counsels that the inbuilt qualifications on intellectual property point to the fact that they are lower in status in comparison to the weight of rights attaching to classical property.

As opposed to its intellectual property counterpart, the international human rights establishment is the initiator of the rapprochement between intellectual property and human rights (Cullet 2007: 414; Helfer 2003, 2007; Yu 2007a). Principal intellectual property regimes, such as the Paris and Berne Conventions and, lately, the WTO/TRIPS Agreement, do not directly accommodate human rights considerations in their texts. Although municipal intellectual property rights legislation incorporates a politically drawn balance in intellectual property policy, such as term limits and special public policy-driven exemptions, those balancing interventions are not necessarily considered from a human rights perspective. Indeed, in the US where the need is strongly felt to protect the rights of creators, it is directly entrenched in a constitutional provision.[14]

In elaborating the human rights ramifications of intellectual property, the UN Human Rights Commission decidedly adopts what Helfer and Yu (Helfer 2003, 2007; Yu 2007a) characterize as a conflict approach in contrast to a complementary or coexistence approach. According to them, a conflict approach to a human rights framework for intellectual property is one that perceives the two concepts as in conflict or at cross-purposes. A complementary approach is one that views the two subjects as mutually re-enforcing and complementary to one another's objectives. Under the latter approach, negotiation regarding the "appropriate scope of monopoly power that gives authors and inventors a sufficient incentive to create and innovate, while ensuring that the consuming public has adequate access to the fruits of their efforts" (Helfer 2003: 48) remains unresolved. When there is a perception that such a balance is overly skewed in favor of owners of intellectual property at the expense of the public, a conflict situation arises. So, the coexistence approach readily and almost always flips into a conflict situation.

The tension between a conflict and a coexistence approach constitutes part of the dynamic in the intersection between intellectual property and human rights. Yu (2007a: 1078) sums it up as follows:

> It is misleading to inquire whether human rights and intellectual property rights coexist or conflict with each other. Because of the overlapping human rights attributes, these two sets of rights both coexist and conflict with each other. A better, and more important, question is how we can alleviate the tension and resolve the conflict between human rights and the non-human-rights aspects of intellectual property protection.

Perhaps it is not as if the wealth of expertise within the UN human rights system is insensitive to the complementary nature of the relationship between intellectual property and human rights. Rather, the nascent and interventionist role of the UN human rights system is classified as a conflict approach (Helfer 2003; Yu 2007a). In a way, that interventionist role is a reactionary response to how the post-TRIPS pharmaceutical patent and continuing increase in bilateral TRIPS-plus agreements, for example, have strengthened the rights of holders at the expense of the needy public, especially in less developed countries. According to Cullet:

> [T]he links between human rights and the realization of human rights in developing countries exist with regard to a number of human rights. They are easily visible in the case of rights to food and to health. With regard to human right to health, the link has become apparent in the relationship between medical patents and the realization of the right to health, particularly in the context of the HIV/AIDS epidemics. This is due to the fact that a number of drugs used to alleviate HIV/AIDS are protected by patents. There is therefore, a direct link between patents, the price of drugs, and access to drugs. With regard to the right to food, there are links between patents in the field of genetic engineering, limitation of farmers' rights, and access to food.
>
> (Cullet 2007: 413–4)[15]

The UN human rights system's interest in intellectual property started effectively in 2000, the year the Sub-Commission on the Protection and Promotion of Human Rights adopted resolution 2000/7, "Intellectual Property and Human Rights." Since 2001, via the CESCR, the UN has engaged in interpretative efforts to flesh out aspects of the prescriptive details of the Covenant in relation to intellectual property and human rights.[16] That 2000 Resolution was quite critical of the TRIPS Agreement. It sets the tone for the negative perception of TRIPS in the UN human rights mechanism. In addition to instigating a flurry of activity within the UN human rights system, and inspiring human rights NGOs globally, that initiative drew global attention to the negative consequences of intellectual property on human rights, especially in regard to health. Through its work, the Commission and its former affiliated sub-commissions have called attention to the negative effects of globalization and the TRIPS Agreement, while promoting the primacy of human rights over intellectual property in situations of conflict. Specifically, the Commission's work has focused on the practical impacts of TRIPS and globalization in the specific human rights context of the plight of those with HIV/AIDS.

In advancing the burgeoning UN human rights agenda in intellectual property, the High Commissioner for Human Rights has expressed a strong interest in seeking an observer position at the WTO and to contribute in the review of TRIPS. In the WIPO, the UN High Commissioner for Human Rights, as well as the WHO and a host of NGOs now enjoy observer status at the WIPO-Intergovernmental Committee on Intellectual Property and Genetic Resources, Traditional Knowledge and Folklore (WIPO-IGC) (Helfer 2003: 60). As explained in Chapter 7, the WIPO-IGC was established in 2000 by the WIPO General Assembly to examine, among other things, several issues sensitive to less developed countries that were ignored by the TRIPS Agreement, especially the subject of traditional knowledge (Ogumanam 2006a). Given the holistic ambit of the WIPO Development Agenda as examined in the previous chapter, the activities of the IGC will be further re-enforced and, perhaps, better coordinated from the framework of the Development Agenda. The presence of the High Commissioner for Human Rights is probably the best guarantee that human rights issues will not be glossed over.

At present, there is an increased awareness in the international arena, especially in less developed countries, of the negative effects of TRIPS and the global intellectual property rights order on various aspects of human rights (Helfer and Austin 2011). Indeed, the expansion of intellectual property rights followed a gradual process in most developed countries over a long period without raising the urgency of its conflict with human rights. But with TRIPS, less developed countries were coerced, literarily overnight, into a stringent intellectual property regime that has exposed their vulnerabilities in vital areas, such as health and access to essential drugs, leaving in its wake dire human rights and public health crises.

Despite the links between intellectual property and human rights, the recent interventionist activities of the UN human rights system have failed to "provide a detailed textual analysis of human rights framework for intellectual property and how that framework interfaces with existing intellectual property protection standards in national and international law" (Helfer 2007: 987). Put differently, the form and pattern of the juridical boundary, as well as the juridical interface between intellectual property and human rights has yet to crystallize; they are evolving, and are posing strong conceptual challenges (Helfer 2008; Yu 2007d). However, for many in the less developed world, the impact of TRIPS is a lived reality; for them, it is a matter of "he who wears the shoes knows where it pinches." Their experience tells their stories much more than a textual analysis of the human rights framework for intellectual property could, as desirable as that certainly is. Nonetheless, a combination of legal and quasi-legal instruments, including the General Comments on the ICESCR and commissioned studies by the UN human rights system, leaves little doubt of the clear conflict between the effects of the TRIPS Agreement in relation to the continuing elaboration of human rights, especially under the relevant Articles of the ICESCR.

The reluctance to fully embrace the jurisprudential or textual basis of the human rights framework for intellectual property is, in part, not unconnected to the historical trajectory and continuing mindset that looks at the ICESCR as within the junior cadre of human rights, in comparison to the category of rights recognized under the 1966 International Covenant on Civil and Political Rights (ICCPR). In addition, the exhortatory character of the ICESCR text and the subjection of the implementation of its provisions to the economic contingencies of individual states, continue to undermine the status of those rights in human rights jurisprudence. With the end of the Cold War and America's consolidation of political and economic power on a global scale, its historical opposition and general reluctance to embrace the ICESCR is a setback for progressive development of human rights.

Indeed, 43 years after the fact, the US has not yet ratified the ICESCR (Sell 2004: 389). In part, this state of affairs accounts for the insensitivity or failure of the WTO framework and TRIPS Agreement to appreciate that the ICESCR constitutes core aspects of public-regarding considerations and, by extension, the developmental imperative for a balanced intellectual property framework at national and international levels. Ironically, more than anything else, this hard-edged market economic approach to intellectual property rights makes them a threat to human rights. The UN human rights system also shows that this situation is also the basis for resistance via counterhegemonic responses and complex regime forms that shape the extant global governance scheme for intellectual property. In the next section we focus on the WHO and the Doha Declaration on the TRIPS Agreement and Public Health (Doha 2001) and the role of newer actors in the intersection of intellectual property, the right to health and the overall global public health crises.

TRIPS on human rights trial: the Doha Declaration

Any lingering doubts over the jurisprudential grounding for, or the interface between human rights and existing intellectual property rights should by now be put to rest because of the 2001 Doha Declaration (Doha). Doha sought to moderate the TRIPS Agreement to be responsive to the development imperatives that it radically constrained. Doha is significant for a number of reasons. First, it was negotiated in the context of the so-called "Development Round" of the MTN under the auspices of the WTO. It is portrayed as marking "the beginning of a new era of negotiations, which can and should provide real and lasting opportunities for developing countries to participate in the multilateral trading system" (WTO 2002). Somehow, despite the stalled progress in the continuing negotiations of the Development Round, its existence is a tacit acknowledgement of the development deficit in the GATT administered by the WTO.

Second, although the Doha text reaffirmed the ability of the so-called flexibilities or "wiggle room" (Reichman 1998) in TRIPS to cater to public health crises in member states, Doha, in fact, directly acknowledged the negative impact of TRIPS and intellectual property on the price of drugs, access to essential medicine and, by logical consequence, the escalation of public health crises, especially in less developed countries. Hence, the need for an interventionist strategy neither rooted in, nor supported by, the text of TRIPS itself. To its credit, Doha was the basis for the first ever amendment of the TRIPS Agreement in 2005, specifically with the addition of a new Article 31, designed to ease the pre-existing compulsory license requirements in order to give effect to paragraph 6 of Doha (Abbot and Reichman 2007). That paragraph provides a special window for facilitating the export of drugs manufactured under a new regime of a negotiated compulsory license "to WTO Members with insufficient or no manufacturing capacity in the pharmaceutical sector" (Doha 2001).

Third, Doha has since provided a platform for domestic legislative revisions on intellectual property rights in some developed countries, notably Canada, Norway and Switzerland (WTO 2009)[17] to enable the exportation of HIV/AIDS drugs to countries in need under strict contractual terms. For example, pursuant to Doha and the post-Doha amendment to TRIPS, Canada amended its 1985 Patent Act, adding 20 new subsections under the title of "use of patents for international humanitarian purposes to address public health problems." Thereafter, Canada entered into a pact with Rwanda for the supply of HIV/AIDS drugs under the revised TRIPS regime pursuant to Doha. After a protracted bureaucratic tangle that caused the process to move at glacial pace, Rwanda received the first consignment of drugs from Canada under this scheme in the fall of 2008. Unfortunately, given the overlayered bureaucracy in the process, all parties to this pilot project are unwilling to continue with it unless the process is simplified.

The road to Doha was not smooth. The declaration emerged against the backdrop of the unflattering sentiments over the TRIPS-instigated access freeze on essential medicines in less developed countries, feelings that seemed to have peaked between the mid-1990s and early 2000s. In a way, the struggle leading to Doha received a boost from contemporaneous developments in South Africa. The South African government sought to redress, under its South African Medicines Act 1997, the unenviable profile it had as the nation with the highest number of HIV+ patients, globally. The Act sought to facilitate access in South Africa to much needed HIV/AIDS drugs by a number of means, including generic substitution of off-patent medicines and medicines imported and produced under compulsory licenses.[18] The Doha Declaration, which came in the wake of these developments in South Africa, resulted in a pushback by the US and its powerful pharmaceutical lobby. The lobby included several pharmaceutical corporations and other industrialized-country proponents of a strict application of TRIPS in regard to procuring HIV/AIDS drugs. In all, a total of 41 pharmaceutical companies formed a powerful coalition of intellectual property champions. In terms of their pushback, first, the South African Medicines Act came under strong opposition from the US for its perceived infraction of South Africa's obligation under TRIPS. Consequently in 1998, the coalition sued the Nelson Mandela-led South African government, challenging its decision to use compulsory licenses to provide badly needed HIV/AIDS drug regimens for that country's suffering poor (Drahos and Braithwaite 2004: 218; Gathii 2002). The imbroglio was later resolved politically (Barnes 2002: 932). However, it indexes the complex confluence of economic and political interests and influences that undergird the intellectual property system.

The tactical retreat by the US and its allies did not, otherwise, necessarily reflect any deep-seated recognition on their part of the human right to health, including access to essential drugs. In fact, they could not weather the negative public relations storm generated by their notorious opposition to South Africa, an attitude that had more than symbolic ramifications for the rest of the developing world. So they needed to quickly retreat, as the emotions their attitude generated in light of the health crisis in issue threatened to undermine their legitimacy and reputation as governments and institutions supposedly concerned with the health and welfare of people (Bloche 2002: 845). The loss of legitimacy and good moral standing would have been too high a price for them to pay, a price that might have shortchanged both the future of the TRIPS Agreement and business opportunities for the US Big Pharma and the other members of the coalition.

Indeed, Doha benefited from the momentum provided by the UN human rights system's principled and critical outlook on the TRIPS Agreement which started as early as 1998, three years before Doha. Without a doubt, the stance of the UN human rights system emboldened less developed countries in their insistence on both a progressive revision, and a search for a new interpretative space in regard to TRIPS in a manner responsive to public health crises in WTO member states. Despite the US-led developed countries' opposition to it, Doha was, after all, not about developing countries only. Interestingly, long before Doha, the US had used a compulsory license scheme to undermine German pharmaceutical companies in regard to the supply of much needed vaccines to allied forces during World War II (Dutfield 2009). In the wake of the anthrax attack in the US in 2001, that country and its northern neighbor, Canada, had threatened to use compulsory licenses to procure Ciprofloxacin, the brand-name drug made by Bayer to treat exposure to anthrax spores (Sell 2004: 329). Between the 1960s and 1980s, Canada used compulsory licensing to procure essential pharmaceuticals – a move that advantaged it in relation to the US and UK. The latter is known to also have used a compulsory license scheme in the 1970s (Yu 2007a: 1102) to advance its national interests.

The WHO's role in the intellectual property and human rights interface

In addition to the proactive contribution of the UN human rights system, a number of UN agencies and specialized bodies have also weighed in on the subject of the interface between intellectual property and the human right to health, with a focus on access to drugs and public health crises, especially in less developed countries. We concentrate here on the contributions of WHO on the subject not only because its mandate is directly related to health concerns, but also because, arguably and, indeed, for good reason, WHO's involvement in the exploration of the intersection between intellectual property and health is clearly more elaborate than that of any other UN agency or affiliate. In addition, WHO is strategically influencing the tenor of the emerging counter regime dynamics in response to the subsuming of human rights to health by the extant framework on global intellectual property (Sell 2007).

The WHO was founded in 1948. Its principal objective is to pursue the "attainment by all peoples of the highest possible level of health" (WHO Constitution, Article 1). As one of the foremost organs of the UN, WHO is the most authoritative global body entrusted with the overall subject of global public health policy and governance. To conduct its work, its enabling instrument gives it a very broad mandate. It includes powers to coordinate authority on international health work; to propose treaties, regulations, and to make recommendations on international health governance; to initiate, promote and conduct international health-related research; to determine and periodically revise international disease taxonomy, and generally to address issues relating to global public health; and overall, to promote international health related standards in regard to food, biological and pharmaceutical materials and related subjects (WHO Constitution, Article 2).

Following on the heels of the UN human rights system's initiatives on TRIPS, WHO has been proactive in condemning the negative impact of TRIPS, especially on pharmaceutical R&D and access to essential drugs to the needy (Sell 2002: 504–6, 2004: 389). Indeed, like the initiatives of the UN human rights system, pre-Doha deliberations by WHO member states and various public health interest NGOs at WHO forums incorporated the same issues that constituted the Doha agenda. Given the strong contributions of NGOs and developing countries in influencing the conduct of WHO affairs, a combination of WHO and UN human rights programs provided the significant momentum that resulted in Doha (Sell 2007: 48). Responding to the concerns expressed by global public health activists and such less developed countries as Brazil, South Africa and Zimbabwe on access to medicine and the need to implement the TRIPS Agreement, the World Health Assembly (WHA) – WHO's highest decision-making body – adopted Resolution WHA52.19 (1999) on a revised drug strategy that built on earlier similar resolutions. The 1999 Resolution requested "the WHO to examine the impact of the WTO on national drug policies and essential drugs and to make recommendations for collaborations between the WTO and WHO" (WHA52.19).

The WHO has strenuously worked on this task to provide expert and strategic support for many less developed countries on how best to navigate the TRIPS Agreement by exploiting its so-called inbuilt flexibilities in order to source essential drugs (Abbot 2002: 475; Sell 2007). In its work on this project, and in other regards including several Resolutions of the WHA[19] and WHO-issued policy guidelines,[20] the WHO endorses the viability of compulsory licensing and parallel importation schemes and a creative reading and exploitation of the so-called TRIPS flexibilities. Since the late 1990s, Big Pharma, the US and, to a lesser degree, the European Union have opposed WHO's drug strategy, a WHO policy document designed to assist less developed countries to fashion their health planning and health policy strategies. Essentially, this opposition stems from the perception that the document is largely influenced by NGOs and public health interest groups with an anti-free market approach to the procurement of essential drugs. In addition, through its policy papers and position statements, WHO affirms the negative impact of the TRIPS Agreement on public health, and is opposed to less developed countries entering into TRIPS-plus agreements that undermine their public health needs. This position is consistent with the CESCR's General Comment No. 14 in respect of Article 12 of the ICESCR (Right to the Highest Attainable Standard of Health) which provides in part that the "failure of the State to take into account its legal obligations regarding the right to health when entering into bilateral or multilateral agreements with other States, international organizations and other entities such as multinational corporations" (CESCR General Comment 14, para. 50) would constitute a violation of its obligation under Article 12 of the ICESCR.

The WHO makes an effort to encourage a broadbased, multi-stakeholder participation in its processes. This includes the involvement of pharmaceutical interest groups and diverse NGOs. Nonetheless, WHO is perceived to be much aligned with public health interest NGOs and less developed countries (Sell 2004, 2007). Despite America's pressures, including the occasional constriction or watering down of WHO's principled opposition to aspects of the TRIPS Agreement, and sometimes threats of withdrawal of financial support, WHO has maintained its core position that "access to essential drugs is a human right," and that "essential drugs are not simply another [trade] commodity" (WHO 2001a). It has been consistent in insisting on equitable access to the benefits of pharmaceutical R&D. Not surprisingly, America's relationship with WHO remains tense, fluctuating as circumstances dictate (Sell 2004, 2007: 72). Similarly, WHO's proactive defense of access to medicine in the era of TRIPS and the globalized medical landscape places it, in the perceptions of its opponents, at cross-purposes with the WTO and countries within the latter's institutional apparatus (Sell 2004: 391). Sell (2004: 397) bluntly notes that the WTO maintains a relationship of "overt antagonism" toward the WHO and the UN human rights system under the auspices of the United Nations High Commission on Human Rights (UNHCHR).

Despite the WTO's overt antagonism, WHO launched the Commission on Macroeconomics and Health (CMH) in January 2001. It charged the CMH with analyzing the impact of health on development, and to explore ways in which investment in health could promote economic growth (WHO 2001b, 2002). The 2002 Report of Working Group 2 of the CMH made a case "for a New Global Health Research Fund with an annual funding of US$1.5 billion by 2007 to spur scientific knowledge" vital to addressing "critical underinvestment in basic science, product development, and operational research regarding diseases that mainly hit the world's poor, especially tropical diseases such as malaria" (WHO 2002: xii). The WHO initiative is a clear response to the lopsided or negligent nature of global pharmaceutical R&D in regard to the drug needs of 90% of the global population and the extant global public health crises spurred by a combination of factors, including, notably, globalization, the TRIPS Agreement and the opposition of neoliberal economic forces.

Just before the CMH initiative, the UN signed the 2000 Millennium Declaration, setting out eight millennium development goals (MDG) for development and poverty eradication (UNDP 2000) to be achieved within a 15-year period (2000–2015). Five of these focus directly or indirectly on health inequality in regard to less developed countries. This is instructive, as it underscores the pivotal role of health in the global development or inequity index. Specifically, these five key MDGs highlight the targeted reduction, by 2015, of child mortality, improvement of maternal health, and combating HIV/AIDS, malaria and other tropical diseases that afflict the poor. The emphasis on the health of the poor and vulnerable in the MDGs reflects the general lack of access to healthcare delivery and essential medicines for the neediest of our world's population.

It serves the interests of some to argue that access to medicine is not a semantic or jurisprudential corollary to the right to health, or "that the problem is not patents [or intellectual property] but poverty" (Sell 2004: 373).[21] Access to medicine is a critical component of the right to health. Indeed, as we have demonstrated, there is ample juridical and philosophical basis to regard access to medicine as a human right (Risse 2008; WHO 2001) both on its own and as a derivative of the right to health. According to General Comment No. 14 on the ICESCR, one of the core or non-derogable state obligations under Article 12 is "[t]o provide essential drugs, as from time to time defined under the WHO Action Program on Essential Drugs; [t]o ensure equitable distribution of all health facilities, goods and services" (CESCR General Comments: paragraph 43 (d)(e)). To separate access to medicine from the right to health, as the pharmaceutical interest groups are inclined to do, is to argue a reduction to absurdity – one that can be reversed against them. It is as good as arguing that the pharmaceutical industrial complex is not part of the global health matrix; or that the right to safe drinking water can be guaranteed simultaneously with denying the "beneficiary" the physical ability to actually drink.

Intellectual property overreach: new actors in global health governance

From the tenor of the MDGs and the work of CHM, it is clear that the lopsidedness of pharmaceutical patents and the access freeze on essential drugs open the way for the burgeoning of new global public health governance and a funding regime aimed at addressing global health crises. That regime is being positioned as an alternative to the failed market economic model supervised by the WTO and the TRIPS Agreement. A scattered glance at samples of the global development and health inequity index underscores the urgency of the crises. El-Ojeili and Hayden (2006: 39–41) outline selected details of the general global inequity that characterizes the health outlook as between rich and poor countries:

> Life expectancy for those countries such as Japan, Sweden, Australia, France and the United States is above or close to 80 years of age, while it is less than 40 for people living in Rwanda, Zambia, Lesotho, Zimbabwe, and the Central African Republic. While GDP per capita in Norway, the US, Denmark,

Switzerland, and Ireland is above $30,000, it is below $1,000 for Ethiopia, Tanzania, Nigeria, Yemen, and the Democratic Republic of Congo. Norway, Australia, Sweden, the US, and Belgium, register as having none of their population living on less that $2 per day, while over 40 per cent of the population of Ecuador, Indonesia, Nicaragua, Egypt, Nigeria live on less than $2 per day. Relatedly, over 40 per cent of the population are undernourished in Angola, Tanzania, Haiti, Mozambique, and Tajikistan. The prevalence of HIV in Japan, New Zealand, Slovenia, Hong Kong, and Korea is less than 0.1 per cent of the population; in contrast, it is over 20 per cent in Swaziland, Botswana, South Africa, Namibia, and Lesotho. Cases of Malaria per 100, 000 of the population are negligible in the US, the UK, Japan, Netherlands, and Canada, while they reach over 20, 000 in Botswana Burundi, Zambia, Malawi and Guinea.

Similar or worse gaps in global inequity are posted by various development-oriented studies, even those commissioned by neoliberal institutions such as the World Bank and the Organization for Economic Cooperation and Development (OECD). This index is hardly off the mark in regard to the rates of literacy, technological diffusion, and access to telephones, computers and the internet. In terms of pharmaceutical supplies, less than 10% of global spending on health R&D is applied to diseases that mainly afflict the poorest 90% of the global population, a statistic analysts deride as the "10/90 [health] gap" (Oxfam 2008; Torreele et al. 2004; WHO 2006). According to a 2004 Médicins Sans Frontières' (MSF) study, "[o]f the 1393[22] new medicines marketed between 1975 and 1999, less than 1 per cent are destined to treat tropical diseases which are responsible for almost 10 per cent of the global disease burden" (Torreele et al. 2004: 6). Isabel Hilton points out that, "[o]f the thousands of new compounds drug companies have brought to the market in recent years, fewer than 1 per cent are for tropical diseases" (Hilton 2000). The MSF 2004 report also found that in 2000:

> [O]ver 17.7 million people died from communicable diseases and nutritional deficiencies, which represents one third of the total deaths in the world. The large majority of these people live in the third world countries. Some of these diseases could be preventable and/or curable with existing drugs but others have no treatment available.
>
> (Torreele et al. 2004: 8)

Overall, "R&D for neglected tropical diseases receives only $1 of every $100,000 spent worldwide on biomedical research and product development" (Oxfam 2008: 1). The average annual per capita health expenditure in sub-Saharan Africa is thought to be $6.00 whereas in all the OECD countries, that figure is well above $2000. In the US, it is over $3000 (OECD 2010). In some cases, the long-term treatment of an orphan disease sufferer in a developed country costs about $150,000 (Torreele et al. 2004: 8).[23] Such a disease incidence is an automatic death sentence for even the well off in less developed countries. While per capita health expenditure does not indicate system efficiency, these figures demonstrate the unattractiveness of less developed countries as viable target markets to drive pharmaceutical R&D.

These statistics may attract skepticism for one reason or another. However, literature on global public health is unequivocal regarding the misalignment of pharmaceutical R&D and the health needs of 90% of the global population (e.g. Abbot and Reichman 2007; Drahos and Mayne 2002; Lim 2001; Oriola 2009; Portman 2003). This trend calls into question the impact of patent-based pharmaceutical R&D on global health. The reason for the inequity is not necessarily the concentration of pharmaceutical corporations in the industrialized or developed countries, as our current globalized economic order has overridden any spatial barriers to trade. Rather, it is because the 10% has the ability to pay for the cost of new drugs, as compared to the neglected 90% (Oxfam 2008; Torreele et al. 2004). Patent is the guarantor of profitability for new R&D products. The priority of the pharmaceutical companies is to seek more efficient and effective ways of recouping their investment dollars within the shortest possible time (Pugatch 2004). Thus, a critical aim of pharmaceutical companies is to match need with affordability (Torreele et al. 2004). This mindset questions the value of a need when the needy can ill afford what they need (Oguamanam 2010). It also depicts an unfortunate separation between need and market (Drahos and Braithwaite 2002: 167– 8).

According to the Report of the WHO Working Group 2 of the CMH co-chaired by Richard G.A. Feachem and Jeffrey D. Sachs, the health needs of the poor in developing countries are "public goods, which are types of goods that markets undersupply because market-based incentives [e.g. intellectual property/patents] are not adequate" (WHO 2002). The authors argue that many global public goods must be provided by concerted international initiatives, "since national governments [especially of less developed countries], acting individually, lack the incentive to provide such efforts at sufficient level for global wellbeing" (WHO 2002).

Echoing the same sentiments from a more critical perspective than the Feachem and Sachs Report, Drahos and Braithwaite (2002) identify knowledge as a public good that must be accessible to all. They blame intellectual property for robbing "much knowledge of its public goods qualities" and creating avoidable scarcity in a manner that aggravates the needs of the world's poor. In their words, "when knowledge becomes a private good to be traded in the markets the demands of many paradoxically go unmet. Patent-based R&D is not responsive to demand, but to ability to pay" (Drahos and Braithwaite 2002: 167–8; Maskus and Reichman 2005). In making strategic commercial decisions regarding the direction of patent-based R&D, pharmaceutical companies undermine the interest and needs of an overwhelming percentage of the global population because of the artificial dichotomy between market and need. The Feachem and Sachs Report recommends an increase in public–private partnerships (PPPs) for "targeted opportunities such as vaccines for HIV/AIDS, TB and Malaria" (WHO 2002: xiii).

In addition to the CHM and other initiatives, the WHO, in 2003, pursuant to WHA56.27, inaugurated a Commission on Intellectual Property Rights,

Innovation and Public Health (CIPIH).[24] The Commission was charged with collecting data and proposals from relevant quarters and preparing an analysis of the intersections of intellectual property rights, innovation and public health (WHO 2006). More importantly, CIPIH's mandate included the incorporation of "the question of appropriate funding and incentive mechanisms for the creation of new medicines and other products against diseases that disproportionately affect developing countries" (WHA56.27). In its 2006 report (WHO 2006), CIPIH concluded that intellectual property's ability to promote innovation cannot be universally guaranteed. Rather, it is context specific. In less developed countries – where there is no market for profitable innovation – the impact of intellectual property is limited.

In line with the sentiments of the CMH, the CIPIH report acknowledged progress in the growth of "private–public partnerships and [research] funding from foundations and governments" (WHO 2006: xi). It also recognized a strong global awareness of the role of intellectual property in global health inequity, increased prospects of additional funding, and progress in science targeted at the problem. However, it argued that there is need for a synergistic approach by all partners and stakeholders to sustainably bridge the gap between pharmaceutical R&D and access to drugs for the world's poor. Following the CIPIH report, the WHO, at the direction of the WHA, established an Intergovernmental Working Group on Public Health, Innovation and Intellectual Property (IGWG) to prepare a global plan of action for pharmaceutical R&D targeting the health needs of less developed countries. The IGWG released a draft report in 2007 that was finalized and submitted in 2008 (WHA61.21).

Without a doubt, WHO's proactive position in interrogating intellectual property's interface with the human right to health exposes weaknesses in the neoliberal market economic model that drives the pharmaceutical patent system. It also has helped to advance the public goods argument in relation to the health needs of the world's most vulnerable, demonstrating the limits of the market economic model, an issue to which Stiglitz and others have consistently called attention (Maskus and Reichman 2004; Serra and Stiglitz 2008; Stiglitz 2006, 2008a). Overall, the WHO and the UN human rights system have created momentum for multiple collaborations that target neglected regions of the globe, including private–public partnerships in support of pharmaceutical R&D. This is evident in the proliferation of private foundations, NGOs and several civil society groups committed to tackling global health inequity and the burden of disease (Oriola 2009; Oxfam 2008). These groups have continued to forge new partnerships with diverse stakeholders, including relevant professional groups, big pharmaceutical corporations, universities and allied research institutes, and intergovernmental bodies, for funding support, logistics and collaborations.

Some of these non-market initiatives have a far broader scope in regard to their program of work or mandate; a number of them are disease specific in their orientation. It is beyond the scope of this book to discuss the operational and mandate details of these and other hybrid initiatives. A few samples from the private philanthropy/NGO portfolio include the Bill & Melinda Gates Foundation, the

William J. Clinton Foundation, the Wellcome Trust, the Global Network for Neglected Tropical Disease Control (GNNTDC), MSF, and Universities Allied for Essential Medicine (UAEM). Examples of other "high-profile global health initiatives" (Travis et al. 2004: 900) include the (US) Presidential Emergency Plan for AIDS Relief, the Global Alliance for Vaccines and Immunization, the Drugs for Neglected Diseases Initiative (DNDI), the Global Funds to Fight AIDS, TB and Malaria, Stop TB, and the Rollback Malaria Partnership. Needless to say, this list is only representative of a multitude of initiatives, groups and activities that seek a non-market or quasi-market approach to addressing global health inequity in order to fill the gap regarding access to public goods created, especially, by patent-driven pharmaceutical R&D.

Over the course of the two decades or so since the non-market initiatives serendipitously responded to the TRIPS-instigated escalation of the global health inequity and its attendant human rights crisis, their impact has been remarkable. They have pushed hope onto the horizon for many in the less developed world. Over the period, "investment in health research is greater than it has ever been" (Tallaksen 2005). Determining the most appropriate incentive strategy to undergird research in neglected diseases is a major challenge in a non-market context (Oriola 2009: 75–7; Oxfam 2008).[25] There is no dearth of literature exploring the pros and cons of the multitude of competing options (Oriola 2009: 75–7; Oxfam 2008). Here, I highlight a few pivotal preliminary concerns. First, conceptualizing an appropriate approach is critical. For instance, a clear distinction must be drawn between public–private partnership models and private–public partnership approaches. The former is not new. In the US, that is a Bayh-Dole Act approach that essentially "involves transferring of default patents from government to [private] parties with stronger incentives to license invention" (So et al. 2008). The latter is basically private sector driven, but relies strongly on public infrastructure for upstream delivery of the objectives of sponsoring institutions. In the global health context, global private–public partnerships (GPPPs) "are those collaborative relationships which transcend national boundaries and bring together at least three parties, among them a corporation (and/or industry association) and an intergovernmental organization so as to achieve a shared health-creating goal on the basis of a mutually agreed and explicitly defined division of labour" (Sell 2004: 371).[26]

Whether the operative model is public–private or private–public, there is usually a role for pharmaceutical proprietary interest holders.[27] Thus, if the non-market initiatives are to make any sustainable impact, they must find a strategy for collaboration with patent-driven pharmaceutical R&D concerns. Specifically, non-market initiatives must seek ways to use their goodwill and the incentives they provide to leverage and negotiate better intellectual property deals in regard to R&D schemes and the resulting products from the programs they sponsor. It must always be borne in mind that the imperative for non-market intervention arose from the failure or deficiencies of the patent-driven pharmaceutical R&D arrangement. The influence of Big Pharma in the global corridors of power, especially Washington, accounts in part for the strong clouds of suspicion that hang over their role in GPPPs, and perhaps, as evident in the critique of the Presidential

Emergency Plan on AIDS Relief.[28] The AIDS Relief program is being coordinated by the US Agency for International Development (USAID) under varied forms of partnership based essentially on a public–private framework, with pharmaceutical corporations exerting strong influences over their proprietary rights to brand name drugs sourced under the program. This undermines the imperative for cost efficiency and, consequently, threatens to compromise the reach of such a program.

The entrenchment of pharmaceutical companies in emerging patterns of GPPPs, coupled with their ad hoc donations of drugs, occasional concessions of their IPRs (for mitigating specific diseases and public health emergencies, or more appropriately targeted at responding to public outrage as a public relations management strategy), have led analysts to accuse pharmaceutical companies of having ulterior motives (Shah 2009). The visibility of these companies in GPPPs is perceived as designed "to discourage the use of compulsory license [and other independent initiatives] to facilitate access to essential medicines" (Buse et al. 2002: 55; Sell 2004: 371) by needy populations. In other words, pharmaceutical companies have the potential to infiltrate the GPPPs to ensure that Big Pharma's permanent interest in a market-driven approach to a global supply of drugs is not undermined in any significant way by those partnerships. It is in their interest to ensure that GPPPs' initiatives represent ad hoc and non-permanent interventions. That way, GPPPs will not pose a threat to the status quo in pharmaceutical R&D that unduly benefits drug companies at the expense of the majority of the global population in need of innovative and affordable drugs.

Given these and several other concerns raised in critiques of the non-market or quasi-market models, their sustainability as a permanent feature in global health governance may have to be supported through a global treaty or some other framework (Oguamanam 2010: 569; Pogge 2005: 167).[29] Patent-based pharmaceutical R&D is an integrated aspect of the global intellectual property matrix under the regime of the TRIPS Agreement, a regime that has woefully failed to cater to the health needs of the majority of the world's population. Those needs have been characterized as public goods outside the capacity of the intellectual property-based market economic model to make available to the extent and in the manner in which they are needed. This is why it is tenable to have an international treaty regime lay down the framework for a synergistic and effective operation of a multiplicity of prevailing non-market models in pharmaceutical R&D.

An exploration of the details of the envisaged treaty is beyond the focus of this book,[30] except to suggest that it needs to be an integral aspect of the global intellectual property and health governance regime. It must not only build on the sentiments of the Doha Declaration; it must be more elaborate in providing the legal basis for the viable operation of non-market mechanisms directed at rectifying the prevailing global health inequity. The need for such a treaty arises from the glaring failure of the intellectual property-based market model and the acknowledged imperative for global action to address the public good question in issue, an issue whose adverse impact on the survival of the larger segment of our world's population threatens the very basis of our civilization. The present legal landscape of pharmaceutical R&D accounts for this health inequity and the public goods crises it creates. To effectively tackle the latter and to build on the progress made by diverse non-market interventions requires a new treaty regime.

Intellectual property and human rights: contested jurisdiction

In their approaches to the interface between intellectual property and human rights, especially in the context of health, the UN human rights system and the WHO have called attention to the policy dilemma intrinsic to that node. Inherently, the attempt to resolve that dilemma invokes a revisionist debate and contestation over where to draw appropriate balancing lines among all the competing needs that surround intellectual property and knowledge governance, especially a balance between the private and public in respect to considerations regarding access to the benefits of innovation. Clearly, in their interventionist roles, the UN human rights system and the WHO have exposed the weaknesses in the present international intellectual property governance framework under the TRIPS Agreement. Because the latter is premised on the neoliberal economic framework, it supervises a narrowly focused global intellectual property vision in which the public-regarding and other balancing considerations are disregarded as a result of a faith-based adoration of the market system. This approach has been responsible for an escalation in the global north–south development or inequity index.

Increasingly, the focus on the interface between intellectual property and the human right to health is placed on the pharmaceutical sector. As the engine of health services delivery and general health promotion, that sector has benefited from recent advances in the basic sciences, biotechnology, life sciences, and networking in the research culture. Like health, pharmaceutical services delivery is strategic to the overall economic wellbeing of society. As an export-based and transnational industry, it is equally strategic for economic competitiveness among states. According to the UNDP, "governments gain leverage in the global economy on the coattails of their most powerful corporations, so they have a vested interest in their success. As a result industry has a tremendous interest in framing regulations" (Drahos and Braithwaite 2004; UNDP 2001: 116 [31]). Not surprisingly, the unity of interest between Big Pharma and the industrialized countries, especially the US, has created an alliance against the health and human right imperatives in less developed countries. This alliance constitutes the source of tension and pressure in the convergence of global intellectual property and public health governance.

Pressures to the contrary notwithstanding, the position of both the UN human rights system and that of the WHO support the primacy of human rights over intellectual property. In a way, this is symbolically articulated by the CESCR in its General Comment No. 17 on Article 15 of ICECSR where its states, in part, that "Human rights are fundamental, inalienable and universal entitlements belonging to individuals and, under certain circumstances, groups of individuals and communities [. . .] whereas intellectual property are first and foremost means by which States seek to provide incentives for inventiveness and creativity" (CESCR General Comment 17, para. 1).

The UN human rights system and WHO's interest in intellectual property rights have raised the stakes on the future of global governance in intellectual property. This is especially so if we give regard to their significant profiles in the UN structure. Added to that is the visibility of diverse NGOs and various multiple interest groups in the deliberations and activities of both the UN human rights system and the WHO. In a way, those two now constitute a critical part of the regime complex that marks the global governance of intellectual property. Their activities may not necessarily or directly give rise to any deliberate regime shifting or regime proliferation sponsored by the less developed countries, or even by their developed counterparts. Rather, they have provided the less developed countries a strong platform on which to challenge the brazen extension of a lopsided neoliberal economic regime to health and the consequential erosion of human rights.

The UN human rights system and the WHO interventionist roles in regard to intellectual property and human rights are logical extensions of their commitment to their constitutive mandates that are now clearly threatened by the trade-driven intellectual property expansionism. The constitutional roots of the UN human rights system and the commitment to human rights and health it shares with the WHO are the reasons these institutions have been tenacious in exposing the WTO's functioning to human rights scrutiny. Even though Big Pharma, their sponsors and other stakeholders have tended to downplay, if not totally undermine, the human rights argument to health and access to patented drugs, the UN human rights system and the WHO are unlikely targets for attempts to orchestrate a regime shifting strategy as regards the subjects of human rights and health.

Admittedly, the mandates of the UN human rights system and the WHO have no direct relevance to intellectual property. However, the two have an indissoluble stake in knowledge governance and, therefore, cannot be indifferent to the effect or impact of intellectual property on their mandates. Truly, the nature of the UN human rights system and the WHO's interest on intellectual property call into question what it actually means to say that an organization, such as WIPO or the WTO, has a special jurisdiction, mandate, or competence in regard to intellectual property matters. That claim is certainly in need of critical and urgent revision. Intellectual property issues are complex, and they transcend the competence or jurisdiction of a few organizations. This much is evident in the holistic approach adopted by the WIPO Development Agenda explored in the previous chapter.

Globalization and the great technological innovations of our time in the digital and biotechnological spheres have facilitated unprecedented extensions of intellectual property into hitherto unimaginable realms. Therefore, as observed, other institutions within and outside the UN framework "have important and legitimate interests in framing and evaluating the impact of intellectual property rules in their areas of competence" (Musungu 2005: 5). In this regard, one analyst rightly notes that "[c]ritical engagement is required from all the relevant UN agencies [. . .] to address the key challenges we face in governing the knowledge society in the 21st century [. . . and] the idea of specialization in the UN over intellectual property must be radically rethought" (Musungu 2005: 25).

The new global governance framework for intellectual property is characterized by issue linkages. As earlier noted, those issue linkages are translated into practical contestations in different ways. For instance, they assume the form of a counter regime or counter hegemonic response to TRIPS' neoliberal economic ideology. The nature of these issue linkages leads to an inescapable and self-evident conclusion. That is, intellectual property policymaking and expertise therein are hardly found in one disciplinary or policymaking concentration. Rather, they can be sought in diverse organizations dealing with many areas that are now the subject of interest or some form of intersection with intellectual property matters. Just as well, the vision of the trade-related aspects of intellectual property rights has, indeed, translated into trade and other related aspects of intellectual property rights – a state of affairs that may be described as a move from TRIPS to "ORIPS." According to Sisule Musungu (2005: 22):

> [f]rom a strategic standpoint, the WTO and TRIPS may have been a blessing in disguise. Because of TRIPS and the bluntness given to its rules [. . .] civil society has emerged to play a critical role in the debate on intellectual property and development. TRIPS issues also underpin the growing intra and inter-institutional dialogue at the multilateral level on intellectual property issues. The trade-related concept introduced by TRIPS has helped other institutions, especially within the UN such as WHO to make the [intellectual property] relatedness argument a basis of their work.)

Global governance in the intellectual property system is, to a significant degree, shaped by complex reactions and responses to the role of globalization, new technologies, and the WTO/TRIPS and the WIPO in the enclosure of developmental spaces and the escalation of margins of equity, especially in less developed countries. Such reactions are driven and influenced by diverse stakeholders in the intellectual property project, and manifest in diverse institutional or regime sites that characterize the regime complex in intellectual property. In the next chapter, we focus on another conceptual site of issue linkage that shapes the global governance of intellectual property, namely, the subject of agricultural biotechnology and food security.

Notes

1 See generally Helfer and Austin 2011.
2 Specifically, General Comment 17 describes Article 15 (1) (c) as guaranteeing "The right of everyone to benefit from the protection of the moral and material interests resulting from any scientific, literary or artistic production of which he is the author." General Comments are issued by the CESCR, which is an expert committee. These comments provide interpretive guidelines or insights to specific provisions of the ICESCR. Generally, like the ICESCR itself, they are written in exhortatory language and are not considered binding.
3 Yu distinguishes between two types of enclosure movement in the intellectual property arena. One refers to international intellectual property policy and lawmaking that result in scuttling the ability of developing countries to deploy intellectual property for

national policy objectives through the freezing up of social policy space for national intellectual property lawmaking. The other is more generic and refers to increasing intellectual property expansionism that has resulted in a radical shrinking of the public domain. On the latter concept of enclosure, see Boyle, J. (2003) "The Enclosure Movement and the Construction of the Public Domain," *Law and Contemporary Problems* 66: 33.

4 Helfer (2003: 54) notes that "when indigenous culture is analyzed from a human rights perspective, intellectual property rules are seen as one of the problems facing indigenous communities and – only perhaps – as part of a solution to those problems."

5 As evidence of what one analyst describes as the decline of the Washington Consensus, since 1982, the World Bank has responded to criticism of the negative impact of its project implementation programs on indigenous communities by issuing guidelines that seek to make the projects responsive to indigenous rights and developmental aspirations.

6 "Big Pharma" is a term both of derision and approval, that critics and proponents or supporters alike use in reference to the big, western-based, influential transnational pharmaceutical corporations.

7 But see Reichman 1998: 585, who suggests that the WTO appellate decision was an affirmation of sufficient wiggle room in the WTO for developing countries to pursue pro-competitive strategies while remaining TRIPs-compliant, and that the WTO has been consistent in supporting different national and international policies that do not necessarily endorse a harmonized global intellectual property order.

8 That is, the UDHR, ICESCR and the ICCPR.

9 Adopted by the General Assembly of the United Nations, 10 December 1948. Available online: http://www.un.org/en/documents/udhr/index.shtml#atop (accessed 23 November 2010).

10 Adopted by the General Assembly of the United Nations, 16 December 1966. Came into force January 3, 1976. Available online: http://www2.ohchr.org/english/law/cescr.htm (accessed 23 November 2010).

11 Adopted by the General Assembly of the United Nations, 21 December 1965. Came into force January 4, 1969. Available online: http://www2.ohchr.org/english/law/pdf/cerd.pdf (accessed 23 November 2010).

12 Adopted by the General Assembly of the United Nations, 18 December 1979. Came into force September 3, 1981. Available online: http://www2.ohchr.org/english/law/cedaw.htm (accessed 23 November 2010).

13 Adopted by the General Assembly of the United Nations, 20 November 1989. Came into force September 2, 1990. Available online: http://www2.ohchr.org/english/law/crc.htm (accessed 23 November 2010).

14 Article 1, section 8, clause 8 (the "copyright clause").

15 Footnotes omitted.

16 See ECOSOC, "Implementation of the Covenant on Economic, Social and Cultural Rights" ECOSOC Doc. E/C.12/2000/15, 9 October 2000. Available online: http://www.unhchr.ch/tbs/doc.nsf/898586b1dc7b4043c1256a450044f331/872a8f7775c98 23cc1256999005c3088/$FILE/G0044899.pdf (accessed 20 July 2009); see also CESCR General Comments 12, 13 and 17, on the rights to health, education and protection of moral and material interests resulting from scientific and/or artistic production.

17 The less developed countries that have implemented similar regulation include China, India, Philippines and Singapore. Canada is the only country that has logically translated paragraph 6 of Doha Declaration to provide pharmaceuticals to Rwanda in 2008. See WTO 2009.

18 The Act also endorsed parallel importation of brand name medicines, and establishing a pricing committee to implement a transparent drug-pricing regime.

19 See the WHO, Trade and Intellectual Property and Access to Medicines (detailing specific resolution of the WHA since 1996 on these subjects). Available online: http://www.who.int/medicines/areas/policy/globtrade/en/index.html (accessed 26 November 2010).
20 E.g. WHO 2001a.
21 The author credits this reasoning to industry-supported American thinktanks, such as American Enterprise Institute and the International Intellectual Property Institute (IIPI) (Sell: 2004: 373 and nn. 49–50).
22 The WHO's figure is 1400.
23 See n. 1 therein. This is the figure posted for a life-long treatment of Gaucher's disease with Alglucerase. "Orphan disease" is a reference to rare diseases that affect a relatively small number of people in developed countries and elsewhere. They enjoy special legal categorization in the US, as a result of which they are targets of special non-market incentives designed to support R&D for them. This is because R&D on orphan diseases would not be viable on strict market considerations.
24 See WHO 2006.
25 Oriola lists the major models to include advance market commitment, product-development partnerships, priority review vouchers, prizes, tax credits and orphan drug schemes.
26 Sell (2004) cites the Global Alliance for Vaccinations and Immunizations established by the Bill Gates Foundation in collaboration with WHO, UNICEF, World Bank and Merck Pharmaceuticals, as an example of GPPP.
27 Perhaps nowhere is this clearer than in the text of the IGWG's Draft Global Strategy, see WHO (2007), which identifies pharmaceutical companies as almost permanent collaborators in every conceivable program initiative.
28 The initiative is a US Government-led global interventionist outreach program initiated by President George W. Bush aimed at making AIDS treatment globally available to those in need, with emphasis on 15 developing countries. For details see the President's Emergency Plan for AIDS Relief, available at http://www.pepfar.gov/ (accessed 2 July 2009).
29 Pogge critically examines such alternative ways of incentivizing pharmaceutical research outside of TRIPS as differential pricing and compulsory licensing.
30 An effort to map the substance of such treaty has been made elsewhere. See Oguamanam 2010.
31 Cited in Musungu 2005: 8, n. 52; UNDP (2001) *Making New Technologies Work for Human Development: Human Development Report*, Oxford; New York: Oxford University Press.

5 Intellectual property and the political economics of agriculture

Professor Keith Aoki and Kennedy Luvai (2007: 36) have rightly noted that:

> Our global food supply depends on a broad and diverse, and genetically dynamic, base of plant genetic resources (PGRs) to adapt crops to changing local conditions, diseases, pests, and soils. However, during the twentieth century, PGRs have become the object of a variety of intellectual property laws that when instantiated on a global level through trade regimes, such as the Trade-Related Aspects of Intellectual Property (TRIPS), pose problems for conservation of genetic diversity [and, by extension, food security].

More pugnaciously, Peter Drahos and John Braithwaite (2002: 168) have warned that "[m]uch of what happens in the agricultural and health sectors of the developed and developing countries will end up depending on the bidding or charity of biogopolists as they make strategic commercial decisions on how to use intellectual property rights."

Clearly, agriculture and food security represent a critical site of intellectual property issue linkage. The discourse about food and agriculture invokes, inherently, a complex mix of diverse subjects within the broader political economics of agriculture and knowledge governance. These include, but are not limited to, conflicted epistemic narratives of the relationship between western scientific perceptions and traditional knowledge relating to agricultural practices and the oft conflicted environmental and ecological philosophies between the two knowledge systems. Also, the food and agricultural question goes to the power relations in the colonial division of labor during the period of conventional colonialism and continuing thereafter. Further, recent advances in biotechnology, especially agricultural biotechnology, and the aggressive extension of intellectual property to life sciences happen in the context of globalization in general, but specifically also in the globalization of the regulatory frameworks for intellectual property and trade. Further, agriculture and agricultural knowledge science and technology (AKST) constitutes a site of policy intersection in complex ways across open-ended fields including, for example, climate change, bioenergy, nutrition and public health to mention a few. These multifaceted transformations and intersections in agriculture, which appear to have climaxed, at least for now, in the contemporary phenomenon of genetic modification have implications for food security. As an integral aspect of the neoliberal economic regime, biotechnology, especially genetic engineering and intellectual property expansionism, are critical factors that shape food security in the 21st century.

Not surprisingly, the management of plant genetic resources for food and agriculture (PGRFA) is at the heart of complex regime tensions and various other contestations critical to exploring the global governance dynamic in intellectual property in the agricultural arena and its ramifications for food security (Andersen 2008; Shiva 1993). While mindful of various aspects of agricultural production, which include fisheries, marine products, forestry and primary forestry products, this chapter focuses on PGRFA both as a source of global food supply and, perhaps, as the most suitable subject for setting the stage in the exploration of the historic transitions in agricultural science and for taking stock of the complex global political economics and governance scheme for agriculture.

Agriculture: from a model of life to a mode of production

As an integral aspect of human civilization, agriculture has a modest origin. From hunting and gathering, pioneer farmers veered into crop domestication (Oguamanam 2007a: 260) some 10,000 years ago. This initiative started with a small number of crop varieties. Through careful selection of seeds or propagating materials and meticulous observation of the ecosystems or ecological dynamics and responses thereto, farmers were able to develop an initial handful of crop varieties into several (Oguamanam 2005: 60, 2007a: 260). Given the correlation of human diversity with biological diversity, including plant genetic diversity, about three-quarters of PGRFA are located in the global south and in indigenous and local communities elsewhere (Oguamanam 2006a: 23, 39–40). From the early history of agriculture, crop varieties were selected based on their adaptability to the vagaries of local ecological conditions while economic viability was a secondary consideration. By means of shrewd management, innovation, cultural practices of seed exchange and sharing of knowledge, there is today "an inconceivable wealth of crop diversity" comprising an estimated 7000 species of key food crops, each with distinct varieties estimated in the region of 100,000 (Andersen 2008: 1).[1] Humble in its beginning, agriculture is essentially an aspect of folk culture in all civilizations. "Indeed, more sophisticated or 'scientific' [including industrialized] approaches to agriculture that later distinguished the western industrial agricultural complex from traditional [or subsistence] agriculture practices have never been the folk tradition of the West" (Oguamanam 2007a: 260). Anthropologists agree that in addition to its inherent subjectivity, "scientific knowledge as we know it today owes its origin to the 18 and 19th century reconstitution and absorption of European folk knowledge and practices" (Oguamanam 2007a: 261).[2] That scientific knowledge is critical in the historical transitions in agricultural production.

In many traditional communities in the less developed world, agriculture is basically an ecological and cultural process for individual, family and broader social or communal subsistence. It constitutes the site for negotiating complex ecological and broader environmental relationships, "whereof the sanctity of life forms, the holism of the natural order and the compelling imperative for humanities humbler mediations and appreciation of its dependence on other life forces [and diversities thereof] is more of a lived reality than a theoretical postulate" (Battiste and Henderson 2000; Oguamanam 2007: 261). This traditional approach to agriculture encapsulates an important epistemological and environmental ideology or ethic that contrasts sharply with western science-driven techno-scientific transitions in agricultural production. Under traditional or subsistence agricultural methods, farmers rely mostly on careful observations of randomly occurring mutations in nature as the basis for their identification and selection of desired varieties or traits. This process involves limited intervention in the process of natural propagation. Nonetheless, that method of breeding results practically in the gradual homogenous recombination of plant genomes over a long period as the basis for the creation and nurturing of genetic diversity.

In contrast, in the west, the process of agricultural production gradually shifted from its historic subsistence and folk origins. It metamorphosed into an industrial and commercial endeavor through intense scientific activism. This happened, first, by more formal conventional breeding and hybridization processes, and, subsequently, through intensified R&D in genetic resources, fuelled by the discovery of recombinant DNA in the early 1970s (Krimsky and Wrubel 1996: 9; Oguamanam 2007b: 221–2). Given the limitations in the propagation potentials of seeds from hybrid varieties, profitable R&D focused on conventional plant breeding and forms of genetic manipulation in the context of PGRs. That effort has since climaxed into genetic engineering, also known as genetic modification.

In contrast to traditional subsistence agriculture, genetic engineering is a more direct or intrusive intervention in the biological propagation process at the heart of agricultural biotechnology (i.e. the application of biotechnology in the agricultural context). Agricultural biotechnology is a subset of broader biotechnology, which, simply, is the instrumental deployment of microorganisms to accomplish diverse tasks (Mehta and Gair 2001: 241). Genetic engineering "involves the applications of molecular genetics or biological processes in agriculture [or other life sciences] through the selection of natural strains (gene splicing) associated with desirable traits and other molecular or scientific devices for the manipulation of plants and animal life forms" (Oguamanam 2007b: 222). In a way, genetic engineering amounts to direct alteration of the genetic code of living organisms through the insertion of novel genetic materials into cells for the purpose of influencing the propagating characteristics of the organisms. It targets, isolates and generally manipulates genes associated with specific traits, controlling their use, expression, or suppression within and across organisms to achieve preferred results (Bains 2003; Lee 1996: 280). In the context of genetic engineering, "plants and animals are molecular lots and bundles of genetic information" (Oguamanam 2007a: 263). In this respect, the control of agricultural production lies literarily in the control of information and consequently intellectual property rights. Genetic engineering and agricultural biotechnology have opened new frontiers in agricultural revolution.

They have shifted "agriculture from land-based farming and opened it up to trans-disciplinary convergences in therapeutics, pharmaceuticals, chemicals, and marketing in the complex political economics of globalization. According to Krimsky and Wrubel, 'agriculture, once a model of life, has [now] become a mode of production'" (Oguamanam 2007b: 222).[3]

Before the advent of techno-scientific interventions in agricultural production, including hybridization, R&D in agricultural production was essentially undertaken by the public sector through science in the public interest (Kesan 2000). Knowledge relating to plant genetic resources was readily shared within the scientific community. There was little fuss about proprietary claims over genetic resources. Indeed, as recently as the 1980s, PGRs were considered the common heritage of mankind, an open resource that everyone could exploit (Aoki and Luvai 2007). Historically, however, intellectual property, especially patent, conferred exclusive rights to creators of mechanical or technical inventions and did not extend to living materials such as plants or plant varieties or to innovations in life sciences as a process (Mgbeoji and Allen 2003). All these were to radically change as a result of the new industry interest and their stake in formal scientific entrepreneurial plant breeding and the burgeoning of biotechnology (Kesan 2000).

Hi-tech advances in plant breeding through both conventional methods and more recent agricultural biotechnology processes are the basis for entrepreneurial plant breeding. For more than 125 years, when entrepreneurial breeding in PGRs took hold (Srinivasan and Thirtle 2002: 161), the question of the profitability of that exercise, as well as the viability of the public sector's continued financing of R&D in PGRs, became the two defining issues for the future of management of PGRs. In regard to the first question, the self-propagating nature of seeds undermines the profitability of entrepreneurial dealings in PGRs. Self-propagation in seeds is fundamentally at cross-purposes with the private sector's proprietary interest in the control of seeds. Also, the exclusion of life forms or genetic materials from the ambit of intellectual property remained an obstacle to a viable private sector interest in entrepreneurial plant breeding. Along these lines Srinivisan and Thirtle (2002: 161) observe that "[t]he vast discrepancy between the benefits that could be appropriated privately by the breeder and the total social benefits [inherent in the self-reproducing nature and agronomic value of seed] implied that the market mechanism would fail to produce a socially desirable level of investment or effort in plant breeding."

In regard to the second question, the advent of entrepreneurial plant breeding correlated to a consistent decline in public sector investment in R&D in PGRs, a trend consistent with the neoliberal economic ideology of shrinking public sector involvement in the provision of critical social assets. Consequently, there was a great opportunity for private entrepreneurial plant breeding. But its profitability could only be realized through strategic exploitation of the historically malleable character of the intellectual property system to secure a tight regime of private proprietary control of PGRs.

A combination of diverse historical, political and economic factors, coupled with intense ideological undercurrents promoted a regime constellation around intellectual property in PGRs. Expectedly, no country had the clout and power, none had a greater head start in plant breeding and biotechnology, and, overall, no country was better positioned than the US to champion a radical extension of intellectual property in PGRs. With regard to timing, the impact of this significant shift in intellectual property resonates in the context of the political economics of agriculture in the post-war global food crisis and on the backdrop of the neoliberal economic forces of globalization. The post-war intervention in the global food supply facilitated convergences of American-led transnational agro-allied corporations and an opening of a new export market for agricultural exports (Gonzalez 2004). It also supervised the incorporation of less developed countries into the global agricultural market. As we shall see later, this transition not only compromised the diversity in the global stock of PGRFA but also it weakened the economic strength and epistemic identity of traditional practitioners of subsistence agriculture in less developed countries. In the next section, we explore in a quasi-chronological order the regime constellations undergirding the extension of intellectual property to PGRs and its implications for food security.

Intellectual property in agriculture

While some locate the extension of intellectual property regimes to PGRs in the 1980s (Aoki and Luvai 2008), perhaps a better and more convenient starting point for our purpose is in the 1930s. In 1930 the US enacted it first Plant Variety Protection Act (PPA). That country provides a natural anchor for the discourse of intellectual property pertaining to PGRs at the global level for several reasons, a couple of which warrant mentioning at this point. In comparison to Europe and the rest of the industrialized world, the US had a head start in scientific plant breeding. Also, the same is true in regard to biotechnology. The US' stakes in these critical fields were part of the reason it championed the most revolutionary review of intellectual property jurisprudence at a global level in ways that brought its municipal intellectual property standard to the global stage via the TRIPS Agreement. The latter, we have noted, is a strategic economic and legal instrument under the new WTO to shape America's vision of neoliberal economic order in a post-Cold War epoch.

Given the historic reluctance of patent jurisprudence to extend to life sciences, at domestic and international levels a *sui generis* regime of protection applied to PGR-related innovation; hence the PPA in the US. The PPA predated similar legislation in Europe, which dates back to the 1940s. In fact, the initial European reluctance to extend intellectual property protection to PGRs and life forms as a whole could not be sustained, partly as a result of pressure from European corporate interests eager to remain competitive with their American counterparts, which were successful largely through the courts (Mgbeoji 2006: 123–4). The 1930 PPA owed its life to the horticultural industry lobby. It applied to innovations relating to asexually reproducing plants. It was revised in 1970 via the Plant Variety Protection Act (PVPA), which extended protection to sexually reproducing plants to incorporate perhaps the world's most stable crop sets such as rice, maize, oats, wheat, beans, peas, etc. The PVPA created a regime of plant breeders' rights (PBRs), which reflects the state of R&D in PGRs at that time. At the international level, in 1961 most industrialized countries had formed an elite club of industrialized plant breeders under the aegis of the Geneva-based International Union for the Protection of New Varieties of Plants, better known by its French acronym, UPOV.[4] The UPOV was perhaps the first major attempt to address, at a multilateral level, the obstacles posed by divergent national regimes on PGRs in industrialized countries. For this reason, as a regulatory harmonization initiative, it is premised on national treatment principles.

Since their coming into effect, there has been an increased frequency in the revisions of both UPOV and other domestic plant variety protection laws, especially in the US. This trend is indicative of the tensions between traditional and subsistence farmers and emergent transnational seed corporations seeking to control not only the seed market, but, most importantly, the propagating character of seed. For example, the inclusion of sexually reproducing plants in the 1970 PVPA was, in part, an attempt to harmonize it with the UPOV. Consistently, all the revisions were progressive attempts to impose limits on the rights of users or buyers of protected seed in order to facilitate breeders' profitable trade in proprietary varieties. For instance, to date, the UPOV has undergone three revisions: in 1972, 1978 and 1991. Members retain the right to limit or upgrade their membership in relation to any of the three versions of the UPOV. With each revision, previous accommodation of the farmers' interest to save seeds and reuse them for propagation purposes under the concept variously characterized as "farmers' exemption," "farmers' rights," or "farmers' privileges" were whittled down. The same is true of rights previously extended to the use of PGRs by researchers (Goss 1996).

The cumulative effect of these revisions is reflected in the 1991 version of the UPOV. Under those revisions, breeders' rights trump whatever concessions are granted to farmers; those rights are now extended to all species and all circumstances for reproduction of seeds of protected varieties by farmers and other dealers in PGRs. The farmers' exemption is no longer guaranteed. Instead, member states of the UPOV have the option to provide and determine the extent of farmers' privileges or exemptions in their national laws. Consequently, "'in almost the whole of Europe, farmers' privileges [or exemptions howsoever called] no longer exist except in the case of small farmers,' whereas all other farmers are required to pay royalties to PBRs holders for the use of farm-saved seeds associated with a protected breed" (Oguamanam 2005: 62).[5] In the US, farmers' sale of farm-saved proprietary seed commonly known as brown bagging, which was permissible under the 1970 PVPA, was circumscribed by a spate of judicial decisions sponsored by seed corporations in the early 1980s.[6] This practically brought the domestic PGR regime in the US earlier to the level of 1991 UPOV. In addition to circumscribing the farmers' and researchers' exemption, the 1991 revisions of the UPOV increased the term of PBRs to 20 years.

In essence, these revisions in the UPOV PBRs regime meant that the PBRs laws in most UPOV member states are now as close to those of utility patents[7] as can be. For instance, the radical circumscribing of third-party or farmers' interests in proprietary seed varieties strengthens the PBRs holders in an exclusive fashion akin to those of a patentee. Also, the 20-year term of PBRs is consistent with the patent regime. Further, criteria for the protection of new plant varieties under the PBR regime include novelty, distinctiveness, uniformity and stability. These technical prescriptions bring PBRs close to a more exacting patent regime. It excludes traditional farmers' dealings in PGRs, which, as we have noted, is premised on careful selections of accidental occurring mutations in nature which is often devoid of precision or uniformity in the resulting propagating materials. For all practical purposes, the *sui generis* nature of intellectual property in relation to PGRs is only theoretical. Via the UPOV and various plant variety protection (PVP) regimes in many industrialized countries, intellectual property has, in effect, been fully been extended to PGRs.

From this analysis, it is clear that the tension in the intellectual property regime in PGRs is between two major interest blocks. They are, on the one hand, represented mostly by transnational seed companies and their industrialized state sponsors, and, on the other hand, by traditional or smallholder subsistence farmers in both developed and less developed countries. The first category consists of vested interests in AKST, i.e. those steeped in hi-tech agricultural production. They are the dominant rights holders in agricultural innovation. The second represent the interests of traditional or subsistence farmers. Their involvement in agricultural innovation happens mainly outside the narrow box of western science and is central to sustainability of diversity in PGRs. The relationship between these two interests in the governance of PGRs has been characterized as a tension between the intellectual property rights regime, on the one hand, and equity and conservation regimes in PGRs (Aoki and Luvai 2007), on the other. Under that characterization, so far, the equity and conservation regimes are represented by the concept of farmers' or researchers' exemptions. In a way, the relationship also encapsulates the tension between proprietary rights holders in PGRs and the forces of mono-culture, and the broader interest in epistemic plurality in agricultural production and diversity in PGRs. Before exploring the ramifications of these tensions for food security, the next section sketches, in a more global perspective, how those tensions unfold in the global governance regime on PGRFA with a focus on the FAO and other regime constellation pertaining to proprietary control of PGRs.

Global governance regime on PGRFA

The Food and Agriculture Organization (FAO)

The Food and Agriculture Organization (FAO) is the UN specialized agency that "leads international efforts to defeat hunger" (FAO 2010). Created in 1945, the same year as the UN, the FAO was critical in the international initiative to address post-war global hunger. According to its constitution, the FAO's functions span the provision of technical, scientific, educational, and research support with the aim of improving conservation of natural resources, global nutrition, food and agricultural practices, and the overall marketing and distribution of food and agricultural products (FAO Constitution, Article I). The FAO functions to influence national and international action toward "the adoption of international policies with respect to agricultural commodity arrangements" (FAO Constitution, Article 1(2) (f)). Perhaps more importantly, the FAO is putatively a neutral forum where both less developed and developed nations interact to negotiate and debate policies pertaining to agriculture, food production and global hunger. In this regard, the FAO has been described as "a flashpoint of conflict between developed countries of the northern hemisphere and the developing countries of the southern hemisphere regarding appropriation, exploitation, and proper legal treatment of PGRs" (Aoki and Luvai 2007: 40).

The conflict between developed and less developed countries on PGRs is driven by a number of interrelated factors. The first is a shared concern over global genetic erosion and the depletion of PGRFA. In the past century, losses of varieties of several major crops are estimated at 80 to 90% by some accounts (Andersen 2008: 4). While some blame this interminable trend on industrial agricultural practices, others point to anti-conservation practices in indigenous and local communities in the less developed world (Oguamanam 2006a: 55; Shiva 1993). The second reason for the north–south conflict over PGRs is the suspicion of the underlying motives of industrialized countries for establishing *ex situ* publicly held gene banks for the conservation of a bulk of the world's priciest genetic resources, most of which were from the global south under the Consultative Group on International Agricultural Research (CGIAR) (Mgbeoji 2006; Shiva 1993).

Consultative Group on International Agricultural Research (CGIAR)

CGIAR is a private and public sector initiative[8] that dates back to 1970s. It provides a vehicle under the FAO and CGIAR-constitutive International Agricultural Research Centers (IARCs) for the management, use and access to samples of PGRs for agricultural research, including plant breeding and other useful endeavors. It describes itself as a strategic partnership, whose 64 members support 15 international centers (IARCs), working in collaboration with hundreds of government and civil society organizations, as well as private businesses around the world. CGIAR members include 21 developing and 26 industrialized countries, four co-sponsors[9] as well as 13 other international organizations (CGIAR 2009).[10]

In regard to the suspicion surrounding CGIAR, there is continued skepticism in less developed countries over the role of the World Bank as CGIAR's chief sponsor and in regard to the unresolved issue of intellectual property arising from dealings in genetic materials in CGIAR and in other public gene banks (Shiva 1993).[11] Also, there is an impression in some quarters that CGIAR[12] and other public gene banks were perspicaciously set up by industrialized countries not necessarily as a conservation strategy but as a way to ensure control and a continued flow of the south's genetic resources to the north, which could not be guaranteed in the *post-colonial* era. According to Mgbeoji (2006), CGIAR's origin is rooted, in part, in the Rockefeller Foundation, the Ford Foundation and the US' joint interest in a program of agricultural development for Latin America with a specific focus on Mexico. This alliance was to subsequently spawn the IARCs in the south that constituted the CGIAR federation. It was a program hardly devoid of political and economic benefit. Echoing sentiments expressed by William Lesser (1997), Mgbeoji (2006: 106) writes that:

> [T]he Rockefeller-Ford initiative displayed profound business acumen in that it realized that the imminent demise of colonialism and the consequential loss of colonial apparatus for funnelling plant germplasm from the South to the North. Hence, a new mechanism [like the CGIAR] for appropriating plant life forms was imperative if the crucially important transfer of plant germplasm was to continue unhindered.

In some way, this is a plausible contention because with "the decline of the empire system [. . .] governments lacked the military presence and legal authority to compel [the new] sovereign nations to yield valuable germplasm" (Lesser 1997: 99). After all, under the colonial arrangement, the funneling of genetic resources was a brazen and, some would argue, "legitimate" activity that required no protocol whatsoever given that colonial outposts of the south were practical extensions of empire. Under this theory, the formal end of colonialism necessitated the creation of a platform for legitimate funneling of less developed countries' genetic resources by hitherto colonial interests. Rather than assuage the suspicions of the south, the nature of the management of PGRFA in CGIAR *ex situ* seed banks aggravated those concerns. While the *ex situ* seeds banks were set up as a public good pursuant to the principle of common heritage of mankind (CHM), it became a target of appropriation by those with scientific knowhow. As I have noted previously:

> Taking advantage of prevailing intellectual property regimes in their various countries, as well as the UPOV, seed breeding and allied agro-tech corporations in the North . . . continued to exploit publicly held PGRs as well as those in CGIAR *ex situ* seed banks obtaining intellectual property rights, especially PBRs. They are able to effectively exclude natural and original suppliers of those PGRs from benefiting from the resulting innovation. . . . In the supplying communities, there was virtually no mechanism for protecting farmers' valuable knowledge or for rewarding their contributions in the generation of important PGRs which are the mainstay of modern entrepreneurial agricultural biotechnology.
>
> (Oguamanam 2006b: 282)

Importance of diversity in PGRs

The proponents of PBRs and the extension of intellectual property to PGRA tend to narrowly focus on exploiting the benefit of their hi-tech scientific innovations. Hardly do they give regard to the fact that plant breeding and other sophisticated dealings in PGRs via agricultural biotechnology do not happen in vacuum. As Aoki and Luvai (2007: 36) have noted, "[o]ur global food supply depends on a broad and diverse, and genetically dynamic base of plant genetic resources (PGRs)." Such diversity corresponds with the human and ecological diversity prevalent in the indigenous and local communities of farmers in the global south and elsewhere who work to "adapt crops to changing local conditions, diseases, pests, and soils" (Aoki and Luvai 2007: 36). According to Andersen (2008: 3), "plant genetic diversity is decisive to the breeding of food crops and it is thus one of the central conditions for food security throughout the world." Traditional farmers' fields are laboratories of genetic revolution that are critical to sustaining plant genetic diversity without which modern plant breeding and agricultural biotechnology could not be viable. For example, a number of disruptions in agro-economic activities that resulted in regional or national hunger crises of historic proportion, including the potato and corn blight, coffee and wheat rust, cotton epidemics, brown spot disease (rice), etc., were contained by tapping into crop genetic diversity from elsewhere, especially those from traditional agrarian communities in far flung places (Andersen 2008: 3; Shiva 1993: 73; cf. Gonzalez 2004: 438).[13] The short point is that modern plant breeding is critically dependent on the diversity of PGRFA. Traditional and subsistence agricultural activities in indigenous and local communities represent a unique epistemic approach to agriculture which is intricately linked to the sustainability of industrial agriculture. Ironically, the extension of intellectual property claims to PGRs has historically been insensitive to the equity and conservation imperatives directly represented by traditional, or so-called local farmers, especially in the developing world. This time of historic depletion in the global stock of PGRFA is also a period for the burgeoning of agricultural biotechnology and convergences of the western agro-industrial complex, thus forcing less developed countries to push back, staking their claims and interest for a more equitable management of PGRFA.

Regime constellation and knowledge governance on PGRs

The International Undertaking on Plant Genetic Resources (IUPGR)

The FAO was the forum used by less developed countries to protest their perceived shortchange in access and the use of PGRs in the CGIAR *ex situ* gene banks. Joined by a number of NGOs, this initiative by less developed countries paid off when the 1983 FAO Conference passed Resolution 8/83 on the International Undertaking on Plant Genetic Resources (IUPGR) and Resolution 9/83 setting up the Commission on Plant Genetic Resources (CPGR). The CPGR became the principal forum for international negotiations on PGRs. Its mandate was later tailored specifically to food and agricultural genetic resources, resulting in a name change to the Commission on Plant Genetic Resources for Food and Agriculture (CPGRFA). Given the vehement opposition of the US and other industrialized countries to the IUPGR and the CPGR (Aoki and Luvai 2007), it is not surprising that IUPGR remained, in terms of its legal status and effect, a non-binding instrument. Similarly, the CPGR was largely circumscribed. In order to discharge its mandate, it operated carefully so as not to further alienate the interests of the US and its industrialized allies. As discussed later, this was the tone of the Keystone Dialogue as expressed in the results of FAO Conference of 1989, which radically modified the IUPGR. The IUPGR makes at least two significant contributions to the contestation over the intersection of intellectual property or proprietary control and management of PGRs, on the one hand, the imperatives for equity, on the other. First, it restates that free access to PGRs for innovation is premised on what it calls "the universally accepted principle that plant genetic resources are a heritage of mankind and consequently should be available without restriction" (IUPGR, Article 1). Second, it endorses the concept of "farmers' rights" in very ambiguous terms as "rights arising from past, present and future contributions of farmers in conserving, improving and making available plant genetic resources particularly those in the centers of origin" (IUPGR, Article 1).

Clearly, these two specific concepts promoted by the IUPGR were antithetical to the *raison d'être* of the UPOV, which, in a nutshell, is the promotion of private ownership of PGR innovation and logically, the restriction of free access by means of intellectual property-like barriers, specifically PBRs. In responding to America's pressure to undermine the IUPGR, the 1989 FAO Conference readily found a superficial quick fix to the problem. It agreed to three compromise interpretive resolutions on the relationship between PBR and IUPGR, the notion of common heritage, and farmers' rights, to complement the final text of the IUPGR. Aoki and Luvai outline the import of these interpretive interventions, also called the Keystone Dialogues, as follows:

> First, the Keystone Dialogues came to a rough consensus on the point that plants protected by plant variety protection rights would *not* be considered freely appropriable – a recognition by developing countries of the validity of intellectual property rights in plant varieties. Second, the parties agreed that "common heritage," or free accessibility to and the appropriation of, farmers' landraces located in the developing countries by developed countries did not mean that access was free of charge. This agreement considered that it might be possible and desirable to design arrangements whereby plant breeders would be obligated to pay for PGRs collected within a country's territory. Finally [as we have noted above] the parties adverted to the vague idea of Farmers' Rights. However, these rights were left undefined.
>
> (2007: 42)[14]

Even though the Keystone Dialogues represented an apparent victory for the US and its allies, they had at least two important symbolic ramifications. First, the dialogues prepared the ground for a paradigm shift in less developed countries via subsequent international regimes. The shift is a move away from considering PGRs as a common heritage to PGRs as a subject matter of ownership within the sovereign rights of specific countries. This is evident in the Convention on Biological Diversity (CBD), to which we will turn shortly. Second, the results also demonstrate the weakness of the IUPGR, especially in regard to farmers' rights. This failure to achieve a strong farmers' rights framework helped to keep the pressure on less developed countries to search for a stronger juridical framework for the accommodation of an equitable mechanism in the exploitation of PGRs, especially those in *ex situ* CGAIR seed banks. That resolve paid off in the 2001 FAO International Treaty on Plant Genetic Resources for Food and Agriculture (ITPGRFA) explored later. However, there is skepticism over the extent to which the ITPGRFA actually advanced farmers' rights beyond what the IUPGRs accomplished.

To undermine farmers' rights, the Keystone Dialogues provide that the UPOV's PBRs regime is not incompatible with the IUPGRs. It also overrode the idea of unrestricted access to PGRs in the IUPGR and allowed states to impose minimum restrictions on the free exchange of seeds in order to make those countries comply with their existing national and international obligations. Clearly, those obligations arise pursuant to national PVP laws and the UPOV. As we have noted, those national and international regimes are akin to utility patent protection for innovation on PGRs. Finally, even though the IUPGRs established a mandatory international fund to promote conservation and the equitable use of genetic resources, an initiative that squarely and specifically includes farmers' rights, it yielded no encouraging results. In 1996, via its Global Plan of Action, the FAO attempted to implement farmers' rights pursuant to the International Undertaking, but did not succeed. This was, in part, because developed countries did not identify with the initiative; and moreover, contributions to the fund were optional (Aoki and Luvai 2007: 52–3). In essence, for most of the member nations of the UPOV, the IUPGR was a mere motion without movement, as it was only a non-binding undertaking. As we will see later, not much progress has been made by the subsequent FAO initiative in 2001 via the ITPGRFA.

The Convention on Biological Diversity (CBD)

Almost 10 years after the IUPGR, "PGRs went from being considered 'common heritage of mankind' in the early 1980s to being considered sovereign national property by the turn of the century" (Aoki and Luvai 2007: 37). Interestingly, this dramatic turn of events happened neither in the context of a direct regime of intellectual property nor in the one for the governance of PGRFA. Rather, it happened in the context of environmental conservation under the auspices of the CBD. The entrance of the CBD as part of the regime constellation and as a layer of the regime complexity in knowledge governance around PGRs is instructive for appreciating the nuanced character of the intellectual property discourse in global governance. We begin by exploring the few distinctions and correlations between the CBD regime and the previous regimes we have discussed, i.e. the UPOV and the FAO (IUPGR). A detailed analysis of the interaction between CBD and diverse international agricultural-related regimes has been competently undertaken elsewhere (Andersen 2008: 173–211) and is outside the scope of the present analysis.

The CBD is an important part of what has been described as the Rio package of international environmental instruments. It resulted from the 1992 United

Nations Conference on the Environment and Development (UNCED) held in Rio de Janeiro, Brazil. The objectives of the CBD as outlined in Article 1 are:

> [T]he conservation of biological diversity, the sustainable use of its components and the fair and equitable sharing of the benefits arising out of the utilization of genetic resources, including by appropriate access to genetic resources and by appropriate transfer of relevant technologies, taking into account all rights over those resources and to technologies, and by appropriate funding.

This loaded provision, along with Article 8(j) (on traditional knowledge), is the pivot around which almost all the remaining 41 Articles in the CBD text revolve. Along with the preambles, they provide the basis for distinguishing as well as reconciling the CBD with various other regimes in the governance of PGRs. In terms of distinction, the CBD does not deal squarely with PGRFAs, but it adopts a holistic perspective on genetic resources. It is basically an environmental conservation text promoting the core norms of conservation, sustainable use and equitable access to the benefits of genetic resources via benefit sharing as incentives for environmental conservation. It also promotes, perhaps more proactively, the recognition of the role of traditional knowledge in the conservation of genetic resources, and encourages domestic policies and legal measures towards the realization of its objectives. Also, the CBD endorses the principle of the sovereign right of states to their own natural resources (Articles 15, 3) and implicitly discounts the notion of genetic resources as the common heritage of mankind. Finally, it makes a peripheral reference to the relevance of intellectual property only to the extent that intellectual property protection is supportive of, and does not run counter to, the convention's objectives (Article 16(5)).

These core objectives of the CBD readily distinguish it from the rest of the regimes we have discussed. However, except for UPOV, the distinctions are perhaps more matters of degree and emphasis. Indeed, there is ample room for an overall synergy in the core expectations from those regimes and the CBD. First, the exception in regard to UPOV is at least three-pronged. The UPOV is reward focused on a specific or *sui generis* regime of intellectual property, namely PBRs. Whereas the CBD takes on the entire intellectual property rights regime, albeit peripherally, but makes them subservient to the objectives of conservation. UPOV is indifferent to considerations of equity, including access and benefits sharing and the role of traditional knowledge and traditional farming communities in the generation of the diversity of PGRs vital to a sustainable innovation in plant breeding and other hi-tech activities. Finally, the UPOV was, naturally, a friendly forum for developed countries, while the historic accounts of the making of the CBD and its continued program of work implicate it as a site for counter-regime momentum for less developed countries and their supporting NGOs to challenge the neoliberal ideological and hegemonic agenda of both the UPOV and the TRIPS Agreement in overall global knowledge governance. It is noteworthy and equally symbolic that the US has yet to ratify the CBD.

In regard to convergences, even though the CBD makes no provision pertaining to farmers' rights, its norms of conservation, equitable access, benefit sharing and recognition of traditional knowledge dovetail with the *raison d'être* for farmers' rights under the IUPGR. Also, the CBD's focus on conservation and recognition of the role of traditional knowledge aligns closely with the undergirding objectives for farmers' rights in regard to PGRFA under the IUPGR. A liberal conceptualization of farmers' rights and the role of traditional knowledge in supporting sustainable innovation in industrial plant breeding and agricultural biotechnology in general readily provide the paradigm for a synergistic appraisal of the inbuilt equitable consideration in the CBD and the equitable imperatives of the farmers' rights debate. Thus, even though the CBD is an environmental regime, it adopts a holistic approach to the environment that encompasses PGRFA. It is an approach in which equitable considerations are central to knowledge governance over genetic resources. Along these lines, Andersen observes that:

> Whereas the IU [IUPGR] emerged from an agricultural rationale, the point of departure for the CBD was nature conservation. This means that the IU and the [later] ITPGRFA are basically agricultural agreements, whereas the CBD is an environmental convention that takes into account sustainable development – in terms of requirements for sustainable use of resources and for fair and equitable sharing of the benefits from such use.
>
> (Andersen 2008: 180)

Despite the largely reconcilable nature of the IUPGR and the CBD, they differ on an important ideological point. While the former supports the idea of PGRs as the common heritage of mankind, the CBD affirms a paradigm shift in the developing world's embrace of the notion of PGRs as sovereign property. This overly schismatic ideological approach needed an urgent mediatory initiative to reconcile the two regimes.

The International Treaty on Plant Genetic Resources for Food and Agriculture (ITPGRFA)

That initiative came in 2001 when more than 100 member states of the UN signed the International Treaty on Plant Genetic Resources for Food and Agriculture (ITPGRFA). The objectives of the treaty mirror those of the CBD: "conservation and sustainable use of plant genetic resources for food and agriculture and the fair and equitable sharing of the benefits arising from their use, in harmony with the Convention on Biological Diversity, for sustainable agriculture and food security" (Article 1). The treaty accomplished three core relevant objectives for our purposes. First, it supersedes the IUPGR, rejects the notion of common heritage and reconciles the FAO approach to PGRs with the CBD, endorsing PGRs as a sovereign property. Second, it associates the protection of farmers' rights with the protection of "traditional knowledge relevant to plant genetic resources for food and agriculture" (Article 9.2(a)). Third, instead of the CBD approach of encouraging a national or bilateral access regime, it establishes a multilateral system (MLS) of open access and exchange of a select category of PGRs from *ex situ* seed banks devoid of intellectual property claims. Finally, the ITPGRFA also provides for farmers' rights in the exact same vague language as the IUPGRs.

From a regime perspective, it is important to indicate that the ITPGRFA came into being and effect in 2001 and 2004, respectively. That period falls within the implementation phase of the CBD. Consequently, the ITPGRFA has given rise to a dichotomous regime over PGRs. Analysts argue that while the FAO/ITPGRFA deals with only the limited categories of PGRs in the publicly held *ex situ* seed banks, the CBD would apply only to such PGRs falling outside those seed banks and/or those acquired after the CBD (Andersen 2008: 188) under bilateral arrangements. In the latter context, the applicable law would be CBD-inspired access and benefit-sharing legislation within the national regimes of participating countries.

A couple of issues constitute sticking points over the effectiveness of the ITPGRFA regarding the equity and conservation objectives of its sponsors. First, its attempt to create a regime of open access to PGRs in *ex situ* banks remains inchoate or at best very weak. For example, Article 12.3(d) bars claims to intellectual property rights on PGRFA "or their genetic parts or components." By implication, this suggests that PGRFA include their "genetic parts and components" and, that being so, "genes and genetic materials isolated or purified from the common pool could not be subject of exclusive claims under intellectual property rights" (Oguamanam 2006a: 296). However, the US and Japan, leading a pack of other industrialized countries, opposed that provision. They realized that it could be a major victory for less developed countries and other public interest and farmers' rights advocates in their desire to rid PGRs, in publicly held seed banks, of intellectual property claims. To soothe that tension, albeit motivated by self-interest, the European Union proposed a compromise addition, which bars claims to intellectual property rights on PGRFA only if they are "in the form received from the Multilateral System," so that any tinkering, via genetic modification and/or other high- or low-tech intervention, may well take the PGR away from the original form in which it was received from the MLS and thus make it subject of a legitimate intellectual property claim.

Helfer argues that "the critical question is whether the act of extracting a gene is, in itself, a sufficient alteration to the seed's genetic material so that the extracted gene is no longer 'in the form' received from the multilateral system" (Helfer 2002: para. 2.3.2.3). There is no agreement among analysts as to the appropriate interpretation of Article 12.3(d) of the ITPGRFA (Andersen 2008; Aoki and Luvai 2007; Helfer 2002). On the basis of the negotiation history of the ITPGRFA, that provision is considered a victory for industrialized countries. Nonetheless its interpretive inchoateness opens a difficult but interesting opportunity for intervention by the governing body of the treaty to clarify the practical import of that provision.

Recently, a similar situation arose in regard to the text of the 2010 Nagoya Protocol on Access and Benefit Sharing (ABS)[15] to the CBD. While many less developed countries celebrate a victory by claiming that the genetic resources derivatives are clearly subject of ABS under the new Protocol,[16] others claim that the extent to which the protocol covers derivatives is far from clear and, is at best, open to interpretation. While the protocol text in Article 2(c) and 2(e) has elaborate definitions of "utilization of genetic resources" and "derivative," Article 3 (on the scope of the Protocol) is silent on its application to derivatives. Rather, it specifies that the Protocol applies to genetic resources "within the scope of Article 15" of the CBD and "to the benefits arising from the utilization of such resources."

According the International Centre for Trade and Sustainable Development (ICTSD), even though there is no agreement between developed and less developed countries in regard to whether Article 15 of the CBD covers derivatives, the Protocol's reference to benefits arising from the utilization of such resources could be interpreted to include them. The importance of including derivatives in ABS for developing countries stems, in part, from the fact that "90 percent of all biopiracy is related to derivatives – 'naturally occurring biochemical compounds resulting from genetic expression of metabolism of biological or genetic resources' – rather than actual genetic resources capable of reproduction" (ICTSD 2010).

The other sticking point over the effectiveness of the ITPGRFA relates to its provision on farmers' rights, which, as I have noted, is stated in the exact same words as the IUPGRs. Even though the ITPGRFA is an internationally binding instrument, its provision on farmers' rights is of doubtful effect. The ITPGRFA did little to strengthen or improve the juridical status of farmers' rights from their status under the IUPGRs. While elaborating on farmers' rights on less precise terms and language, it subjects the core of those rights, namely farmers' rights to use, share or exchange traditional or improved proprietary farm-saved seeds, to the discretions of the national laws of member states (Article 9.3;[17] Aoki and Luvai 2007: 53–4). Because of the focus of farmers' rights on PGRs in publicly held *ex situ* seed banks, other plant breeders operating outside that system are unfettered in regard to their private proprietary or intellectual property rights over improvements on PGRs. Overall, the commitment to farmers' rights is weakened in so far as it is to be moderated in accordance with the needs and priorities of member states and subject to their national legislation and pre-existing international agreements or obligations of member states (Article 9.2; preamble para. 10).

Clearly, the national interests and priorities of most industrialized countries do not favor farmers' rights, as evident in their confidence in the UPOV and its continued calibration of PBRs and support for intellectual property expansionism into the realm of life forms. Neither do their existing obligations under multilateral agreements, including the TRIPS Agreement, to which we turn shortly. Consequently, the extent to which farmers' rights under Article 9 of the ITPGRFA and the entire treaty framework constitute a counter-balancing regime to private ownership or intellectual property over PGRs is "at best doubtful or at worse unfeasible" (Oguamanam 2006a: 295).

The TRIPS Agreement on PGRs

Despite having no material differences from utility patents, the PBR provisions in the UPOV and various pieces of PVP legislation in the US, Europe and the rest of the industrialized world have the status of *sui generis* forms of intellectual property. Technically or formally speaking, they are not conventional intellectual property regimes like patents. As noted in the previous chapter, the US-led global extension of the scope of intellectual property to life forms builds largely from the domestic sentiment as expressed in 1980 by Chief Justice Warren Burger in *Diamond v. Chakrabarty* that "Congress intended statutory [patent] subject matter to 'include anything under the sun that is made by man'" (309). Not surprisingly, Article 27(1) of the TRIPS Agreement provides in part that "patents shall be available for *any inventions*, whether products or processes, *in all fields of technology*."[18] In regard to PGRs, Article 27(3)(b) of TRIPS provides, in part, that "[m]embers shall provide for the protection of plant varieties either by patents or by an effective *sui generis* system or by any combination thereof."

By this provision, as part of the WTO neoliberal economic and legal regulatory structure, TRIPS directly extends patent protection to the realm of PGRs, albeit allowing member states the option to exclude "plants and animals" from patentability (Article 27(2)(b)). The implications of the WTO's interventions in the broader political economics of agriculture for food security will engage us shortly. Now, it suffices to mention that Article 27(3)(b) of TRIPS has far reaching consequences. First, it unequivocally brings PGRs within the patent regime. Second, it allows for a regime of multiple and overlapping protections for innovations in PGRs. Third, given the correlation of signing on to TRIPS with membership in the WTO, TRIPS' provisions on PGRs open the door for the calibration of states' obligations relating to PBRs under the UPOV to a far bigger and stronger forum. Not only does that mean that many more states, including those outside the UPOV, are held to a higher standard of PBRs protection, those states also have an option to protect innovation in PBRs by patent and other contrived devices. Fourth, TRIPS' provisions on PGRs are subject to the enforcement powers of the WTO dispute resolution mechanism.

Finally, the option to protect innovations in PGRs by *sui generis* methods has resulted in an ambiguous state of affairs. While it is feasible that a *sui generis* option could mirror the UPOV framework, its details remain uncertain, as it will depend on the UPOV version to which a state subscribes. For instance, under the 1978 UPOV, there is ample room for farmers, breeders and researchers to use protected materials. Those opportunities are radically circumscribed under the 1991 revisions. For many developed countries the TRIPS' standard of *sui generis* protection for PGRs, even though unspecified, should be the standard of the 1991 UPOV which is a tighter regime, close to the protection afforded by utility patents. For good reason, this approach does not find favor with less developed countries. While developed countries, especially the US, have made compliance with the UPOV standard and UPOV membership an aspect of its TRIPS-plus bilateral trade agreements, most less developed countries would prefer a regime of PVP protection that gives robust latitude for farmers' rights and other public regarding considerations.

In sum, TRIPS' intervention marks a formal and the most authoritative regime of protection for PGRs in international intellectual property jurisprudence, far above the UPOV standard. TRIPS effectively strengthens, even escalates, the use of intellectual property to undermine less developed countries and various other stakeholders' interests in equitable knowledge governance over PGRs. Not surprisingly, this state of affairs provides the impetus for regime shifting, mainly by those countries through post-TRIPS initiatives such as the implementations of the CBD, for example, via the 2002 Bonn Guidelines on Access to Genetic Resources and Fair and Equitable Sharing of the Benefit Arising from their Utilization. The latter instrument provided the basis for the recently negotiated 2010 Nagoya ABS Protocol to the CBD, and its provisions reflect the sentiments of the FAO framework treaty, the ITPGRFA inaugurated in 2001.

It must be noted that even though the TRIPS' negotiations predate those of the CBD, the latter was adopted long before the adoption of TRIPS.[19] In a way, having lost the intellectual property struggle in the WTO, less developed countries found the CBD and FAO veritable forums to press their cause for equitable sharing of benefits of PGRs. However, by the time the text of TRIPS was finalized, its overall provisions, especially its silence on traditional knowledge and farmers' rights, appeared to have eroded the progress less developed countries made in the CBD. This turn of events necessitated, in part, the attempt at regime convergence between the CBD and the FAO's ITPGRFA. As we have seen, these regimes diverge in some respects, especially regarding the conflict between the FAO/ITPGRFA's multilateral system of access and CBD's bilateral or national access and benefit-sharing regime. Nonetheless, they reaffirm the imperatives for equity in the context of many critical paradigms including access and benefits sharing, conservation objectives and the values of traditional knowledge and farmers' rights pertaining to PGRs. Collectively, they represent an attempt to moderate intellectual property expansionism by equitable and public-regarding considerations vital to sustainable dealings with PGRs and by logical implication to food security.

For their part, both the WTO/TRIPS and the CBD have been mindful of real or perceived conflicts between themselves and have strategically engaged each other in some form of rapprochement or another. TRIPS' indifference to traditional knowledge and benefit sharing thus far in its implementation has resulted in pressure from less developed countries, which is being diffused at the moment through different strategies. Presently, these two issues continue to traverse the CBD via its Conference of Parties (COP) and the TRIPS Council in a contest of wit between developed and less developed countries regarding which forum best serves their interest. Presently the WIPO, via its Intergovernmental Commission on Traditional Knowledge Genetic Resources and Folklore (IGC), is the forum for dealing with CBD and post-TRIPS questions around traditional knowledge. By the same token, the WIPO, where negotiations have stalled on the Substantive Patent Law Treaty, mentioned in Chapter 3, is the forum for exploring knowledge governance and reward mechanisms regarding PGRFA (Arezzo 2007). The choice of the WIPO for deliberations on PGRFA appears to be a natural option, one on which neither developed nor developing countries appear to have much, if any, choice. Under the TRIPS Agreement, the provisions of Article 27(3)(b) will be due for review four years after the WTO agreement comes into force. As noted in Chapter 3, the serial stalemate in the TRIPS Council over the revisions of the TRIPS Agreement since the failed 1999 TRIPS Ministerial Conference in Seattle leaves the WIPO as literarily a fallback forum. Interestingly, as I also noted in Chapter 3, the enunciation of a Development Agenda by less developed countries led by Brazil and Argentina and the Friends of Development (FOD) adopts a holistic approach to development in a manner that practically puts on hold ongoing negotiations at the WIPO, especially those concerning the Patent Agenda.

Appraising the nature of regime constellation on PGRs

From this brief *tour de monde* a few conclusions logically follow. First, unlike the intersection between intellectual property and health and human rights, the nexus between intellectual property or knowledge governance and PGRs is not a subject matter of latter-day consciousness. From the outset, at the global level, intellectual property has been directly implicated in the issue of the equitable management (or lack thereof) and control of PGRs and innovations in the agricultural sector. However, as in health and human rights, awareness of the role of intellectual property has only been bolstered by technological advances, in this case relating to industrial plant breeding and other forms of agricultural biotechnology. Third, in the realm of PGRs, there is perhaps a more complex regime constellation and far more regime overlap than we saw in health and human rights discourse. The governance of PGRs is partly supervised by the UN Environmental Program (UNEP), which is the umbrella organization for the CBD and its operations, and the FAO, including the various treaty and non-treaty instruments associated therewith and diverse institutional interests and emergent forms of private public partnership (PPP) – explored later. In addition, other multilateral forums include the UPOV and the WTO/TRIPS Agreement. In one way or another and some-times to an overlapping degree, these actors explore myriad issues around conservation and the sustainable use of PGRs/PGRFA, access and benefit sharing thereto, the role of traditional knowledge, intellectual property and the concept of farmers' rights, and funding mechanisms pertaining to PGRFA management, etc.

In part, aside from the cross-cutting nature of issues revolving around PGRs and PGRFA, the volume of regime constellation and regime overlap in the governance of PGRs is attributable to the fact of the concurrence in the timeline for the negotiation and implementation phases of the various operative treaties and international instruments. Consequently, in the PGR arena, putting aside the obvious cases, the pattern of regime patronage is hardly crystal clear; what is obvious is the ability of less developed and developed countries to rotate their interests on contingent bases while taking advantage of developments in other regimes or forums to realign those interests. In this regard, we saw how less developed countries, not able to make headway on the CHM principle, made a radical switch to the notion of PGRs as sovereign property. Similarly, developed countries have gradually put a soft pedal on the notion of free and unconditional access to PGRs. Also, we have seen how developed countries used the Keystone Dialogues to push back the potential impact of the IUPGRFA and how they have consistently watered down moves toward a juridical calibration of farmers' rights. However, when all is said and done, in the context of PGRFA, the pendulum clearly swings in favor of the developed countries' bid to use a neoliberal market agenda in the governance of PGRFA. In the next section, I explore the implications of this for food security.

The food security imperative

The concept of food security is arguably novel. Given the interdisciplinary appeal and conceptual vagueness of the subject, there is at the moment no authoritative legal articulation of the concept. However, dedicated researchers on food security and development studies within the broader social sciences provide important insights. There are, to date, 200 definitions of food security (Scoones 2002). All the definitions emphasize a broad range of technical and policy issues pertaining to food security from different analytical perspectives (Oguamanam 2007b: 230). The FAO notes that the concept is in continuing evolution, but posits that food security is achieved "when all people at all times, have physical and economic access to sufficient, safe and nutritious food to meet their dietary needs and food preferences for an active and healthy life" (FAO 1996).[20] Other definitions of food security directly or indirectly embrace all factors in the FAO definition while emphasizing the elements of personal or cultural acceptability or availability of food within the context of self-respect or human dignity of peoples (Stevens et al. 2000: 2).[21]

In this context, according to the framework of the Centre for Studies in Food Security at Ryerson University, Canada, the five components of food security are: availability (sufficient food for all peoples at all times); accessibility (physical and economic access to food at all times); adequacy (nutritious and safe foods produced in the context of environmental sustainability); acceptability (food that is culturally acceptable, produced and accessed in ways that give regard to human dignity, rights or self-respect); agency (food obtained in the context of policies and process, including actors that facilitate the achievement of all other elements of food security) (Centre for Studies in Food Security 2010).

From the references to nutrition and safety, it is quite clear that food safety – which I do not directly address here – is a component of food security. The dichotomy between food security and food production as well as the complicity of political, economic and legal factors in undermining food security has received prominent treatment in the work of Nobel Laureate in economics, Amartya Sen (1982: 45). Sen espouses an entitlement-based approach to food security at the household level, i.e. the ability to control access to or ownership of food within the framework of chains of entitlement relationships that legitimizes one ownership claim by reference to another. This involves three layers of entitlements: production based (domestic food production capacity); trade based (ability to earn foreign exchange to import food); transfer based (ability to access food aid). In extrapolating the household level food security analysis to the national level, Carmen Gonzalez avers that "a food-secure state is one that can produce, purchase, or obtain as aid the food necessary to satisfy the needs of its population" (2004: 430).[22] Following Sen's pioneering works and other subsequent literature, analysts have agreed that food security is not addressed by increased food production, but can only be fixed by addressing a combination of various factors. Not the least of such factors are economic inequities, distributional distortions, epistemic marginalization, technological asymmetry, intellectual property expansionism, the historical colonial division of labor and other multifarious dynamics implicated in the global political economics of agriculture, to mention a few.

Despite increased food production due to the unprecedented convergence of technologies in agricultural and allied sectors, 852 million people worldwide are undernourished. An estimated 815 million of this number are in less developed countries. "Progress in hunger reduction has slowed in recent years, and the number of undernourished people is growing in most of the developing world. Rampant hunger and malnutrition impair the economic performance of individuals, and entire nations" (Gonzalez 2004: 420) with dire political and economic consequences that strike at the root of global stability. At a time of great technological breakthroughs in genetic modification and agricultural biotechnology why has the global food security index remained depressing? Opening up discussion around this question warrants a step back in time.

The colonial division of labor and economic specialization

Our current global trading system has its roots in "the colonial division of labor that relegated the colonized periphery to the production of primary agricultural products for the benefit of the [industrialized and industrializing] colonial 'core'" (Gonzalez 2004: 423). The degree of crop or general agricultural diversity in many colonial outposts or so-called present-day less developed countries was dictated by the needs of the colonial establishments. Through the application of the theory of economic specialization, the colonial core limited less developed countries to producing only such cash crops over which they had a comparative advantage. This practice resulted in the diversion of prime agricultural land from food to cash crop production for export. Also, it made revenues from less developed countries susceptible to the volatile global agricultural market (Gonzalez 2004: 423). Apart from concentrating agricultural land ownership on indigenous elites and consequently providing for the displacement of many poor agrarian smallholder farming households, economic specialization was a major threat to the diversity of PGRFA guaranteed under traditional or subsistent agricultural practices (Shiva 1993). According to Gonzalez (2004: 438), "[f]rom environmental [and indeed agrobiodiversity and sustainability] standpoint[s], the chief legacy of colonialism was the displacement of local biodiversity by monocultures in order to provide raw materials for distant, affluent markets." In this situation, "[u]niformity as a pattern of [agricultural] production becomes inevitable only in the context of control and profitability" (Shiva 1993: 71) that marks the transitions in agricultural production from the colonial era to the contemporary epoch of the formal end of colonialism.

The green revolution and industrial agriculture

In addition to the colonial division of labor, the attempt to mitigate the post-war global food shortages through a program of intervention called the green revolution (GR) was critical in the escalation of food insecurity in less developed countries. The GR was an initiative of Mexico- and the Philippines-based international crop-breeding institutions, with the support of the US and its two traditional charities, the Rockefeller and Ford Foundations (Mgbeoji 2006: 106; Shiva 1993: 66). The initiative was putatively aimed at increasing the output or yield of basic food crops in order to stem the tide of post-war global hunger between the 1940s and the 1960s. Many analysts agree that the GR actually delivered in regard to its core objectives and succeeded to a significant degree in boosting global food production and in tackling global hunger (Conway 1997: 44–5; Gonzalez 2004: 441). The most critical issue was the social cost of that initiative as it relates to the environment, less developed countries and sustainable agriculture.

In terms of timing, the GR came at a time when the US was beginning to exert its economic influence on the rest of the globe, especially less developed countries. One of the hallmarks of the GR was the chemicalization of agricultural production through the use of high-input agricultural supplements, notably synthetic fertilizers and pesticides. This happened in the post-war epoch, a time of rapid expansion of the US chemical industries and its subsequent entry into seed production and the resulting convergences between the chemical and agro-allied industries. These corporations were important and self-interested actors in the introduction of the much criticized high-input and high-yield varieties (HYVs)[23] of major food crops into less developed countries. In addition to introducing newer crops such as wheat that threatened to dilute crop diversity and food choices in many less developed countries, US corporations set out to entrench their major food crops into the agricultural systems of less developed countries under the GR, sometimes through food aid, with the hope of creating offshore markets for their costly high-input agricultural supplements. For instance, in 1954 the US Congress passed Public Law 480, known as the Agricultural Trade Development Assistance Act, as the foundation for the expansion of US agricultural exports. In 1961, President John F. Kennedy renamed the Act "Food for Peace" and implemented it as the legal framework for using food as instrument of diplomacy to court the friendship of less developed countries in the Cold War era (USAID 2009).[24] The Act is credited with facilitating the establishment of a foothold for US agricultural and allied corporations in new foreign markets (Gonzalez 2004: 436).

The attractions of the HYVs not only undermined the use of slow-yielding but genetically diverse PGRFA in developing countries, it also marked the introduction of industrialized agriculture to the less developed world. This trend has at least two glaring structural consequences. First, it resulted in the systemic displacement and disempowerment of smallholder rural agrarian farmers through land reforms that favored an elitist and corporate agricultural class that not only secured loans from banks easily but also catered to the needs of the overseas agricultural and industrial markets. Second, it brought about a regime of monoculture that concentrated on genetically uniform but fragile HYVs that depended on agrochemicals to thrive. In this regard, again, Gonzalez (2004: 441) captures the consensus shared by critics of GR – its failure "to solve the problem of world hunger because it focused on improving the supply of food without addressing the issue of equitable distribution of food and food-producing resources." For Shiva (1993), the GR supervised the destruction of diversity and the erosion of the indigenous or alternative ecological worldview through the creation of uniformity that left many in less developed countries vulnerable and dependent on external input and external control of their food resources.

From the structural adjustment program to the WTO and its agreement on agriculture

It was under this climate of structural inequity that the so-called developing countries became part of the global political economics of agriculture and trade. Clearly, the more things seemed to have changed the more they remained the same. The colonial division of labor remained entrenched at the end of formal colonialism in the 1960s and was actually intensified by the entrance of the US and its championing of a neoliberal economic order in the global economic equation. In the 1980s, under US supervision, the Bretton Woods System (BWS) prescribed the Structural Adjustment Program (SAP) both to service existing developing world debts and as a condition to securing new loans to pave the way out of the latter's debt crisis. The SAP led to a radical recalibration of economic specialization whereof most less developed countries intensified the export of their key economic crops and natural resources to a secure competitive balance of trade. This was done through the export of major cash crops in a monocultural fashion. In many developing countries, including Brazil, India, Pakistan, the Cameroons and the Philippines to mention a few, the expansion of export for natural resources accounted for a decline in the diversity of PGRFA, habitat and species (Oguamanam 2006a: 56; Wood et al. 2000: 66). Rooted in the neoliberal economic mantra, the SAP required a radical cutback in government provisions of social services. Governments were required to focus attention on maximizing export to pay foreign debts, to eliminate agricultural subsidies, to privatize public institutions and to adopt a faith-based approach to the fetishism of market forces in order to deliver an economic miracle.

That faith-based reliance on market forces reached a new phase and highpoint on a global scale with the conclusion in the 1990s of the Uruguay Round of Multilateral Trade Negotiations (MTN) that brought about the WTO. Specifically, one of the agreements in the WTO package is the Agreement on Agriculture (AoA). Ironically, while the AoA putatively aimed at correcting and preventing restrictions and distortions towards an equitable level playing field in world agricultural markets (AoA, Preamble 2–3), it exacerbated the asymmetry and market inequality in the global trade in agriculture. Developed countries have continued to exploit the loopholes in the WTO system to undermine their commitment to open their markets to the less developed world's agricultural produce (Gonzalez 2002: 440–46, 2004: 460). Pursuant to the SAP, the bulk of less developed countries curtailed tariffs and other trade barriers. Under the AoA, insofar as they had not used export subsidies in the past, less developed countries were not allowed to use them, whereas developed counties were allowed to retain such agricultural export subsidies on the condition that they reduce them gradually in the future. For the most part, the AoA did not tamper with the use of existing, large-scale domestic subsidies on agricultural products in the US and the European Union (EU). This resulted in an increase in the level of agricultural subsidies in most developed countries following the AoA. Professor Gonzalez (2002, 2004: 460) characterizes the effect of AoA on developing countries as the institutionalization of inequities, "by requiring market openness in developing countries while permitting protectionist policies in the industrialized world."

Also, even among developed countries, the WTO system allows neoliberal free market considerations to trump concerns over the environmental impact of agricultural biotechnology, specifically genetically modified organisms (GMOs), in ways that weaken alternative agricultural practices. For instance, the WTO Agreement on the Application of Sanitary and Phytosanitry Measures (SPS Agreement) narrowly permits states to adopt trade restrictive measures to check overall health concerns relating to human, animal and plant life on the basis of strict scientific evidence and principle insofar as such measures would not constitute a disguised restriction on international trade (SPS Agreement, Articles 2 and 3). So far, the environmental and health impact of GMOs are inchoate and will so remain over time. Under the precautionary principle of the international environmental law as articulated in Article 15 of the 1992 Rio Declaration on the Environment and Development[25] and affirmed in the CBD's 2000 Cartagena Protocol on Biosafety,[26] "where there are threats of serious and irreversible damage," full scientific certainty is not required as a condition precedent to take or impose remedial action, which could include trade restrictions. The EU's prudent (albeit politically motivated) disposition toward the invocation of the precautionary principle in the regulation of GMOs has since constituted a flash point of tension at the WTO between the EU and other WTO states, especially the US, Canada and Argentina. Jointly, this trio grows 80% of the world's GMOs[27] and they consider the EU's precautionary approach to GMOs an obstacle to free trade contrary to the WTO.

Some WTO panel decisions on the SPS Agreement[28] relating to the approval and marketing of biotechnology products, including the US-Canada victory over the EU's ban on certain beef growth hormones are quite instructive in many respects (Choudry 2004: 47–9). First, they symbolize a regime clash between the CBD as an environmental regime and the WTO as a trade regime. Second, they are indicative of the US's determination to use the WTO as a form of trade police to force the products of agricultural biotechnology down the throat of the rest of the globe. Third, the impact of those decisions transcends "trans-Atlantic muscle flexing" between the US and Europe (Oguamanam 2007b: 242); rather, they send cold chills down the spine of less developed countries as "a violation of a people's right to make appropriate choices about their food and how it is grown" (Tokar 2006), which is crucial for food security. The practical implication is that if Europe can be made to "bow", no less developed country has the political and economic muscle to resist GMOs no matter how benign or legitimate their reason. The beef hormone decision has been described as "a precedent for using the WTO to attack all kinds of domestic regulations based on health concerns, which are viewed as barriers to trade" (Choudry 2004: 48). Current WTO food safety standards are based on the Codex Alimentarius Commission model. The Codex Alimentarius was jointly established in 1963 and is co-administered by the FAO and the WHO. Its objectives include developing and coordinating food and food safety standards at international governmental and NGO levels, and to ensure fair trade practices relating to food. The Codex model has found favor in US agribusiness and agro-biotechnology policy circles (Oguamanam 2007b: 241). That constituency favors a narrow, trade-driven approach to food safety, with little regard to precautionary principles and other environmental risk issues, not to mention food security in developing countries.

Food security on a downward plunge to food insecurity

The recent unleashing of neoliberal economic strategies in the globalizations of markets for PGRFA and in the control of technological innovations in food production has not improved the global food security index for a number of reasons. First, a combination of policy and judicial decisions around the control of food and agricultural biotechnology indicate the stifling of alternative forms of agricultural production, especially those falling within the smallholder, subsistence, traditional and organic farming communities (Oguamanam 2007a).[29] As we have noted, this trend has led to the supplanting of diversity and, by implication, the sustainability of PGRFA, with a monocultural regime (Shiva: 1993). It is therefore hardly surprising that despite historic progress in agricultural biotechnology, the global stock of agricultural food crops has yet to diversify from the few economically viable ones such as rice, peas, potatoes, wheat, maize, sorghum, millet, canola, etc.

Increasingly, even recent attempts to incorporate PGRFA from less developed countries into genetic modification technologies have only fuelled the practice of biopiracy – the unidirectional appropriation of those resources and associated knowledge by the western agro-industrial and allied complex. India, Ethiopia, Nigeria, South Africa, Madagascar, Mexico and many other centers of biodiversity have become sites of protest over the appropriation of crucial PGRs for food, agriculture and medicinal applications from western-based interests (Arewa 2006a, 2006b; Mgbeoji 2006). In some ways, the extremely limited progress on farmers' rights, and the recent unprecedented wave of the unidirectional transfer of PGRs and associated knowledge from indigenous and local communities via the process of biopiracy, account for a radical shift by less developed countries from a CHM approach to PGRs to sovereign property.

Second, the process of appropriation of PGRs and associated knowledge is legitimized by the TRIPS-led global intellectual property order. As noted already, Article 27 of TRIPS extends patents to all fields of technology provided they are new, involve an inventive step and are capable of industrial application. In a way, this requirement restates the standard of industrial or scientific uniformity for innovation in plant varieties under the UPOV's PBRs regime. A combination of these standard requirements for innovation in PGRs alienates the incremental and communal process of dealings and improvements common to traditional farming practices in indigenous and local communities. This strikes at the roots of the debate over the incompatibility of conventional intellectual property with traditional knowledge forms, which I broach in the next two chapters. Thus, in addition to neoliberal industrial agriculture's structural erosion of the diversity of PGRFA, the contributions of indigenous and local communities steeped in traditional and subsistence agricultural practices are excluded in the conventional reward scheme.

Third, by compromising the diversity both in PGRFA and in the epistemic approaches to agricultural production, the combination of intellectual property and a neoliberal trade-based framework for agricultural production and trade undercut the three key aspects of the entitlement-based approach to food security. For instance, as we have noted, the attraction of HYVs and other GM food crops makes the labor-intensive but sustainable means of production of traditional landraces less appealing. A combination of changing and adverse ecological conditions and the progressive displacement of smallholder and subsistence agrarian communities since colonial times have resulted in a downward plunge in domestic food production in less developed countries. Clearly related to this is the failure of the trade-based approach to food security. As I have noted, the SAP and the WTO's inequitable AoA undermine the ability of less developed countries to earn foreign exchange to import food. From the colonially entrenched division of labor to the contemporary distortions in the world trading systems, the exportation of raw materials by less developed countries pursuant to economic specialization has not attracted a fair exchange deal, not to mention a balance of trade in relation to their import of finished products from industrialized countries (Gonzalez 2002, 2004). Today, most of the global food supply is gradually turning around GMOs and 80% of GMOs produced globally are from three industrialized countries – a statistic that is sure to change.[30] Finally, in regard to transfer-based entitlement, less developed countries are increasingly targets of food aid and agricultural assistance under the current global trading system, especially when it is convenient for industrialized countries. Often this happens in the form of "food dumps" for food aid in order to optimize the benefits of the WTO scheme while getting around its anti-dumping regulations when domestic agricultural subsidies have resulted in excess produce that cannot be absorbed by the domestic market.

Overall, the current neoliberal economic framework for knowledge governance and trade in agriculture undermines the five elements of food security enunciated above. First, analysts agree that even though industrial agriculture has resulted in increased food production, less food is available or physically accessible to the world's neediest peoples. Second, concerns about the safety and nutritional quality of food still remain and are hardly addressed by a strict recourse to industrial agriculture or market fetishism. Even when industrial agriculture holds positive prospects, they do not readily translate to the needy. For instance, the WHO maintains that malnutrition, especially in less developed countries, "is the greatest single risk factor contributing to the global burden of disease." (Labonte et al. 2004). Indeed, "worldwide, malnutrition affects one in three people and each of its major forms dwarfs most other diseases globally" (WHO 2010). Biotechnological intervention is helpful for the production of functional food or "nutraceuticals"[31] by various means, including "biofortification."[32] However, because of intellectual property rights, many in less developed countries cannot access these real or potential benefits of genetic engineering or agricultural biotechnology.

Food security for less developed countries as a public good

Unlike access to essential drugs, where the failure of the neoliberal market model opened opportunities for PPP intervention, the key global food and agricultural governance institutions, at least by their mission statements and often overlapping mandates, are largely driven by public-regarding considerations in tackling hunger, food safety, nutrition and associated public health challenges in less developed countries. In his recent seminal study (2009), Shaw identifies five such institutions (some of which I discussed earlier) at the core of global food and agricultural interventions. They are the FAO, the World Bank, through its Agricultural and Rural Development (ARD) Department and several other indirect interventions, the International Fund for Agricultural Development (IFAD), the UN World Food Program (WFP) and the CGIAR. The mission statements of these organizations, as they relate to the subjects of food and agriculture, are directed at the eradication of hunger and poverty, and at achieving sustainable food security, especially among the rural poor on a global scale. Shaw sums it up in this way, "[t]he five institutions share a number of common features. They all work for and with food. They all seek to end hunger and to alleviate poverty. They all subscribe to contributing to the achievement of the MDGs [millennium development goals]. And, to a large extent, they share common members" (2009: 214).

In Shaw's analysis, for the most part, the history, evolution and general thrust of these institutional interventions are premised on the use of food and agricultural development as a form of crisis intervention in one form or another. Consequently, the association of food and agriculture with the alleviation of poverty and hunger at the global level has long been an entrenched aspect of the international development apparatus. Recently, that conceptual framework has provided a platform in all of these institutions for the advancement of the decade-long MDGs of the UN. Indeed, the eradication of hunger and poverty is intricately linked to the overall attainment of MDGs and takes on the form of global public goods.

Despite the public interest orientation of the mission and mandates of key global food and agricultural institutions, their ability to sustain that focus is under considerable threat at all fronts and for a variety of reasons. First, technological interventions and the increased mechanization of agricultural production, for example, through the application of transgenic techniques and other forms of biotechnologies, as well as globalization dynamics, have provided veritable opportunities for new actors and stakeholders, necessitating shifts in state interests and priorities. For example, "the biggest structural change is using food crops to produce bio-fuels," in addition to concerns surrounding the intersection of food aid and international trade (Shaw 2009: 203). Second, the marked reduction of public funding of food and agricultural research at the wake of industrialized agricultural resulted in private transnational corporate entities in chemical, biotechnology and agro-allied concerns taking up the gauntlet at the expense of public science (Evenson et al. 2002).

Third, as an extension of the second point, there have been recent paradigmatic shifts in intellectual property jurisprudence at both national and global level. Those shifts have capitalized on the malleability of the intellectual property scheme to now fully accommodate innovations in PGRFA to protect private sector investment. Consequently, agricultural production and innovation has become a site of creeping privatization and proprietary control via the market economic matrix and intellectual property rights in a way that is likely to exacerbate rather than mitigate hunger and poverty, especially in traditional and subsistence agricultural communities mostly in less developed countries.

The key global food and agricultural institutions are not immune from the complex neoliberal economic framework for knowledge governance in food and agricultural production, innovation and trade, which we examined earlier. Not surprisingly, tension exists between the developmental and equitable fundamentals of their mandate as they navigate and strive to accommodate the role of industry, other actors and nation states, especially those with a head start in agricultural biotechnology and who are determined to profit there through proprietary and market control. For example, even when the mandate of an institution like the UN WFP is essentially directed at emergency food relief, WFP's resource problem is described as "serious, many-sided and complex" (Shaw 2009: 201).

The flow of food aid to the UN WFP reflects an interesting dynamic. It increases when global food prices are low and decreases when they are high, making it difficult for needy countries to access food aid at critical times. Perhaps more instructively, there is mutual self-interest reflected in the timing and type of food commodities food secure countries donate to the WFP. As part of this trend, the US not only ties its food aid to its surplus agricultural production, it also requires that 75% of such food aid to be shipped in its vessels at rates that are "significantly above the international level" (Shaw 2009: 201). A recent study of the US food aid program observes that "rising business and transportation costs contributed to a 43 percent decline in the average volume [of food aid] delivered over the past five years" (Shaw 2009: 201).

Strategic partnerships for food security

So far, these global food and agricultural institutions are involved in a number of strategic partnerships, including forms of PPP with all manner of stakeholders in the food and agricultural sector. Indeed, all five core global food and agricultural institutions are sustained by diverse partnerships with the private sector and various other stakeholders in agriculture innovation and production. Elaboration on the details of such partnerships is outside the scope of this book, except to mention that such an approach is consistent with the situation in global public health we explored in the previous chapter.

An example of this strategic partnership in the food and agricultural context is the HarvestPlus initiative. In 2004, through the HarvestPlus program, the CGIAR developed what it calls a micronutrient challenge project. HarvestPlus is "a global alliance of research institutions and implementing agencies coming together to breed and disseminate crops with nutritive value" (Sasson 2005: 14) aimed at global malnourished populations, especially in less developed countries. One of the attractions of this initiative is its focus on the conventional breeding of nutrient-dense crops that can be adapted to local growing environments or those that are common as a traditional staple of the target population. Despite lingering concerns about intellectual property, the initiative has continued to attract donations and support from diverse sources, including the Bill and Melinda Gates Foundation, the US Department of Agriculture, the Syngenta Foundation for Sustainable Agriculture, and the World Bank.[33]

In addition to engaging in pragmatic partnerships, to effectively sustain their developmental mandate, global food and agricultural institutions require strong inter-institutional cooperation and coordination. In the long run, such a relationship could result in a reflective self-assessment toward a more efficient and less duplicative governance structure. In the meantime, it would enable them to harness their comparative advantages and to better understand and participate in shaping the nature of the appropriate interaction between the development imperative of food and agriculture on the one hand, and the underlying role of market forces and stakeholders in the proprietary control of agricultural innovation and market on the other. This form of collaboration has been envisaged in the form of a global partnership program similar to the trends emerging in the global public health arena (Shaw 2009: 215).

That analogy is relevant and instructive. But it falls short of recognizing the complicated nature of the intersection between food and agricultural, and development. A recent report arising from a World Bank-initiated multi-stakeholder sponsored International Assessment of Agricultural Science and Technology (IAASTD) suggests that agricultural development transcends technological interventions and requires factoring in environmental and social cost benefit that condition for healthy agro-ecological practices (IAASTD 2009). Also, the report underscores the complexity, diversity and intersecting nature of agriculture and AKST in relation to eight convenient cross-cutting sectoral clusters, namely: bioenergy, biotechnology, climate change, human health, natural resources management, trade and markets, traditional and local knowledge community-based innovations, and women in agriculture (IAASTD 2009: 3). In addition, the report recognizes that agricultural development must essentially provide support for traditional lifestyles and cater to the livelihoods of the hungry and poor in the context of food and nutritional security. In essence, global food and agricultural institutions must engage with technological and market interests in agricultural production in a complex negotiation of a food and agricultural development outlook that reflects an understanding of both the role and the limits of technology and the complex interests and interactions embedded in food and agricultural production.

Thus, the key challenge for global food and agricultural institutions is to attain and sustain the essential development imperative at a time of increased neoliberal economic activism in the governance of knowledge and innovation for proprietary control of food and agricultural production. To the extent that these institutions are not in and of themselves directly involved in food and agricultural production, a strategic engagement with downstream private actors would constitute an inevitable dynamic in the global fights against poverty and hunger, especially in the MDGs framework. The role of food and agriculture in the eradication of hunger and poverty and the attainment of food and nutritional security for the world's poor takes the status of global public good. Thus far, market forces, technological interventions and intellectual property rights may have contributed to increased global food production. But that has happened at the price of equity, access and a high social and environmental cost that leaves a significant part of the global population vulnerable to unmitigated hunger and malnourishment, food and ecological insecurity and ravaging poverty.

Strategic partnerships aimed at addressing global food security must accommodate the epistemological question in agricultural production. The accommodation of epistemic pluralism beyond the techno-scientific emphasis of industrial agriculture caters to the cultural element of food security, which diverges from the interests of the western industrial agricultural complex. The foisting of the products of industrial agriculture globally, especially GM foods, as potentially the largest source of global food supply, not only undermines cultural acceptability, also, it distorts the role of agency in food security. The convergences and transformations since the 1960s of the American-led transnational chemical and allied corporations, lately including biotechnology concerns, have constituted them into key agencies that influence global agricultural policy and process. These actors have continued to wield influence, supervising the erosion of the role of traditional and subsistence smallholder, and increasingly landless, farming communities in indigenous and local communities. The last are not only the bedrock for diversity and sustainability of PGRFA but also of culturally epistemic milieu for food production and traditional knowledge generation. Peoples' food choices are socioculturally determined as an extension of their culture and identity and general belief systems and ecological worldviews (Oguamanam 2007a: 261; Pascalev 2003: 588).

In the globalized market for agriculture, corporate stakeholders in industrial agricultural production and their industrialized state sponsors use intellectual property and the neoliberal global trading system to entrench a homogenous food culture. For example, the US Food for Peace initiative and the failure of the WTO to address the historic inequity in global agricultural trade via the AoA have led to state of affairs in which dealings in traditional landraces in less developed countries are hardly viable locally, let alone internationally. From this state of affairs, a culture of dependence has arisen, making many indigenous and local communities in less developed countries helpless and hapless targets for food aid and food dumping in circumstances that compromise their human dignity/rights, cultural identity, self-determination and national security.

As we have noted, interests are rotated on values in the global governance equation, especially from the neoliberal economic and knowledge governance prism where the overriding value is economic. Consequently, we have a status quo in which traditional or other agro-epistemic forms are marginalized by hi-tech industrial agriculture to the point of extinction (Oguamanam 2007a). Also, it is a status quo that reflects the misalignment of progress in food and agricultural production with food security in less developed countries. It is a state of affairs that serves the interests of developed countries in the battle for the control of food. As we have noted, that battle involves multiple actors with overlapping interests within a mélange of regime interactions and the globalization of markets in agricultural innovation and production. In terms of its character, the struggle is economic, geopolitical, environmental, strategic, and perhaps more importantly, epistemic. On that note, in the next chapter we explore the concept of indigenous/traditional knowledge as a pivotal basis for a few other intellectual property issue aggregations or multiple issue linkages within the global governance dynamic.

Notes

1 Footnote omitted. These estimates are official figures from the FAO.
2 Citing Ellen, R., Parkes, P. and Bicker, A. (2000) *Indigenous Environmental Knowledge and Its Transformations: Critical Anthropological Perspectives*, Amsterdam: Harwood Academic.
3 Quoting Krimsky and Wrubel 1996: 213.
4 *L'Union internationale pour la protection des obtentions végétales*.
5 Quoting Srinivasan and Thirtle 2002: 164, footnote omitted.
6 For example, the Fifth Circuit of the Court of Appeals in *Delta and Pineland Company v. Peoples Gin* Co. 964 F. 2d 1012 (5th Cir 1983) ruled against farmers' selling of farm-saved proprietary seeds through intermediaries. The court held that the major rationale for the PVPA of 1970 was to mitigate profiteering on proprietary seeds at the expense of holders of PBRs. Similar sentiments were echoed in *Asgrow v. Winterboer* 11 S Ct 788 (1995).
7 Utility patents are the most common patents. They apply to inventions that are new or those that constitute functional improvement to existing inventions and include product, machine, process or composition of matter. Often, utility patents are contrasted from design patents, which deal with inventions in the realm of ornamental design, shape, or general configurations with decorative or stylish appearance or appeal.
8 The co-sponsors of CGIAR include the FAO, the World Bank and the UN Development Program. According to the CGIAR 2009 figure, the US, Canada, UK and the European Commission rank in that order as the top developed country/regional funders of the CGIAR, whereas India and China lead other less developed

countries in their funding support for the organization. See http://www.cgiar.org/who/members/funding.html (accessed 7 November 2010).

9   They are the FAO, the International Fund for Agricultural Development (IFAD), the United Nations Development Programme (UNDP), and the World Bank.

10 Available online: http://www.cgiar.org/who/index.html (accessed 14 December 2010).

11 According to Shiva (1993: 154), "two-thirds of all seeds collected in gene banks are in industrial countries or are stored in international research centres [elsewhere] controlled by Northern countries and the World Bank."

12 In fact, the CGIAR and its affiliated IARCs control only 10% of PGRs in *ex situ* seed banks.

13 Gonzalez suggests that, ironically, farmers "resorted to using dangerous agrochemicals that endanger human health and the environment" in order to "mitigate the vulnerability of large-scale genetically uniform crops, which was the legacy of colonialism, namely the displacement of local biodiversity by monocultures."

14 Footnotes omitted.

15 See the text of the Nagoya Protocol adopted at the COP-10, Nagoya, Japan, available online: http://www.cbd.int/abs/doc/protocol/nagoya-protocol-en.pdf (accessed 25 May 2011).

16 See for example the Hindu National News Report (31 October 2010) "Nagoya Protocol, a Big Victory for India." Available online: http://www.thehindu.com/news/national/article859977.ece (accessed 8 November 2010).

17 It provides: "Nothing in this Article shall be interpreted as to limit any rights that farmers have to save, use or exchange and sell farm-saved seed/propagating material, *subject to national law as appropriate*" (emphasis added).

18 Emphasis added.

19 Negotiations toward the TRIPS Agreement started in the late 1987, concluded in 1994 and the agreement came into effect in 1995, whereas negotiations toward the CBD started in 1988, were concluded in 1992 and the agreement came into effect in 1993.

20 Cited in Oguamanam 2007b: 230 and n. 73.

21 See also Canadian Dietetic Association, (1994) "Hunger and Food Security in Canada, Official position of the Canadian Dietetic Association" Agriculture and Human Values 11: 97-98; Centre for Studies in Food Security, Ryerson University, "Food Security Defined." Available online: http://www.ryerson.ca/foodsecurity/ (accessed 8 November 2010).

22 Writing on the corollary between food security at household and national levels; see also Stevens et al. (2000: 18).

23 Shiva (1993: 39) argues that the term HYV is not a neutral observational term, but one "determined by the theory and paradigm of the Green Revolution [. . .] [a]nd [its] meaning is not easily and directly translatable for comparison with the agricultural and indigenous farming systems for a number of reasons."

24 The History of America's Food Aid. Available online: http://www.usaid.gov/our_work/humanitarian_assistance/ffp/50th/history.html (accessed 14 December 2010).

25 Principle 15 of the Rio Declaration on the Environment and Development, U.N. Doc.A/Conf.151/26/Rev.1 (13 June 1992), 31 I.L.M. 874, 879 states: "Where there are threats of serious or irreversible damage, lack of full scientific certainly shall not be used as a reason for postponing cost-effective measures to prevent environmental degradation."

26 For text of the Cartagena Protocol on Biosafety to the Convention on Biological Diversity, see: http://bch.cbd.int/protocol/text/ (accessed 8 November 2010). Article 1 provides: "In accordance with the precautionary approach contained in Principle 15 of the Rio Declaration on Environment and Development, the objective of this Protocol is to contribute to ensuring an adequate level of protection in the field of the safe transfer, handling and use of living modified organisms resulting from modern biotechnology that may have adverse effects on the conservation and sustainable use of

biological diversity, taking also into account risks to human health, and specifically focusing on trans-boundary movements."

27 If we add China and South Africa to the pack, these five countries produce 99% of the world's GMOs (Gonzalez 2004: 450).

28 In 1996 the US requested consultations with the European Commission seeking to challenge the EC's ban on the import of meat and meat products treated with any of the six listed growth hormones pursuit to the SPS agreement. Canada, Australia, New Zealand and Norway joined the complaint as third parties. Both the Panel and Appellate Body found for the complainants. The Appellate Body Report is titled *EC Measures Concerning Meat and Meat Products (Hormones)*, WT/DS26/AB/R (16 January 1998). In 2006 a WTO Panel decided on the US, Canada and Argentina's challenge on Europe's de facto five-year freeze on the approval of GM crop varieties as contained in the Panel Report, *European Communities – Measures Affecting the Approval and Marketing of Biotech Products*, WT/DS291/R, WT/DS292/R (29 September 2006). Other countries, including Australia, Brazil, Chile, Colombia, India, Mexico, New Zealand and Peru joined the US in this complaint.

29 In Canada, examples of such decisions include: *Monsanto Canada Inc. v. Schmeiser*, [2004] S.C.R. 902; *Hoffman and Ors. v. Monsanto Canada Inc. and Bayer CropScience Inc.*, 2005 SKQB 225; 264 SASK R. 1.

30 With progress in scientific and biotechnology research and overall economic progress in the BRICS (Brazil, Russia, India, China and South Africa) countries, notably Brazil, India and China, the leadership of leading industrialized countries in agricultural biotechnology and production of GMO food are sure to be eroded by these emerging economic powers.

31 This term is in reference to "the potential of food to provide health benefits." See Ryan-Harshman 1997: 845 at 847.

32 This is in reference to the use of agro-biotechnology techniques to fortify food products to improve their nutritional quality.

33 See: http://www.harvestplus.org/content/donors (accessed 14 December 2010).

Part III

6 Traditional/indigenous knowledge in the global governance of intellectual property

Recent technological transformations in bio- and digital technologies are supervised, in terms of control and benefit allocation, by intellectual property rights. For the most part, intellectual property is increasingly perceived as a vehicle for the inequitable allocation of rights over knowledge, often at the expense of indigenous or local knowledge forms and their holders. Consequently, intellectual property has become a touchstone for diverse issue linkages, as explored in preceding chapters. In virtually all those issue linkages – human rights, global health crises, food security, biodiversity and the environment, etc. – the subjects of traditional/indigenous knowledge (T/IK) and its custodians are implicated. In a way, T/IK does not, in itself, constitute a single issue linkage to intellectual property, for example, in the way food security does. But the interaction or tension between intellectual property and T/IK and the dialectical approach of local knowledge stakeholders to intellectual property, shape the outcome of virtually all the diverse issue linkages implicated in the dynamics of intellectual property and global governance.

TK and intellectual property: history and tension

Understanding the tensions between T/IK and intellectual property and how they play out in the global governance discourse, does not lend itself to easy conceptual mapping. Before I articulate the reasons for this, I will briefly outline aspects of that tension in some limited historic context.

Knowledge and culture are two fused, albeit elusive, phenomena. One thrives in the agency of the other. Early modern conceptions of culture and knowledge were based on progressive accounts of human development (Ivison 2002). In the conventional renditions of those accounts, Europeans were at the peak of the cultural ladder, while non-western peoples were located on its lowest rung. Consequently, it was not uncommon to depict the "West's *other*" (Darian-Smith and Fitzpatrick 1999) in derogatory terms to underscore the superiority of the European cultural outlook and to justify European political domination in all its colorations, including, particularly, colonialism and its ideological baggage. Indeed, in some quarters, colonialism was Europe's self-assumed messianic and benevolent project designed to bring civilization to those perceived to be on the fringe of human civilization at the God-forsaken ends of the world (Mgbeoji 2007; Oguamanam 2004a). Emboldened by the mindset of its cultural (racial) superiority, 19th-century Europe treated indigenous and other non-western cultures and local knowledge practices in a derogatory fashion and within a framework of entrenched hierarchies of culture and power. Elsewhere it has been observed that:

> These power dynamics were serviced by imperial and colonial structures that facilitated the appropriation of the economic values in local knowledge of colonized peoples, for instance through colonial division of labor. The uncivilized European other were depicted as incapable of intellectual engagement or output in their dealings with the natural resources around them. That claim took the appearance of an evident truth with the advent of industrial revolution. The accounts of various regimes of intellectual property rights trace the phenomena to Europe, understandably without any mention of knowledge protection regimes in other civilizations. Intellectual property and, in some cases, classic property regimes in the colonies were extensions of what existed in the colonial powers [. . .] indigenous territories were *terra nullius*, and when a people were colonized, their natural resources, knowledge systems and ways of life were not exempt. Because indigenous peoples operated outside the market economy, their economic system was perceived as inefficient and in urgent need of abrogation and substitution with a civilized economic model.
> (Oguamanam 2008a: 33–4)[1]

It is hardly surprising that early attempts at forging an international intellectual property framework via the Paris and Berne Conventions of 1883 and 1886 were exclusively conducted by colonial powers without the involvement of indigenous and local communities. For one thing, only states can be parties to treaties in international law. And most indigenous peoples and other communities of T/IK stakeholders in both the non-enclave territories (i.e. where colonial settlers withdrew following independence) and the enclave territories (i.e. where the colonial settlers did not withdraw) either did not have state agencies at all or, where they existed, they were extensions of the colonial power and did not represent the interests of their own.[2] The evolution of those key treaties re-enforced the exclusion of T/IK and its diverse custodians and, indeed, representatives of the vast majority of the world's population from the intellectual property negotiation table (Arewa 2006a; Bently 2005; Sherman and Bently 1999). It was only following their independence at the end of World War II that a majority of former colonies began to place indigenous and local knowledge-sensitive subject matters on the global intellectual property agenda.

For the most part, some of the issues, such as "folklore," diverged from the strategic interests of the colonial and industrialized powers in intellectual property. In 1971 India championed the revision of the Berne Convention to accommodate the protection of folklore by member states (Bentley 2005; Oguamanam 2008a). After independence, less developed countries and other indigenous knowledge stakeholders have continued to pressure the international intellectual property system for an equitable policy space capable of accommodating and rewarding alternative knowledge frameworks within and outside that system. Nonetheless, they entered into the debate fundamentally underprivileged and have since confronted an epistemic gulf or intellectual property order in which T/IK forms and the socioeconomic and political contexts of their production are in a state of continuing negotiation, and are unraveling.

We can surmise, then, that historically, T/IK and indigenous interests have had an inherent relationship of conflict and tension with the intellectual property system. As discussed in previous chapters, that ongoing tension has translated into the present constellating regime dynamics of intellectual property in global governance. In a way, this tense relationship between intellectual property and T/IK is readily traced to Europe's self-location at the pinnacle of cultural hierarchies and its positioning of non-European, indigenous and multifarious others at the bottom of that pinnacle. Similarly, it is also premised on Europe's evaluation of the worth of different cultural and knowledge systems and their sense of civilization in relation to European values (Ivison 2002). Succinctly expressed, "[t]his historical interplay of hierarchies of culture and power, especially in the colonial and post-colonial [even neo-colonial] projects, has inadvertently made the legal and policy treatment of local knowledge a flashpoint of tension and resistance and one that irresistibly conditions for a revisionist history of colonial relations" (Oguamanam 2008a: 34).

Beyond colonial relations, the distribution of rights accruing from new technological advancements, particularly in bio- and digital technologies, and within the complex regime interactions in which T/IK is implicated, have placed the latter at the center of the global governance dynamic in intellectual property. To properly unravel the intricate configurations in which the knowledge of indigenous and local communities has evolved in the narrative of intellectual property in global governance, we begin by sketching the unique conceptual challenges that bestride the notion of T/IK. Those conceptual challenges are critical for weighing the measure of progress or traction T/IK and its stakeholders are able or unable to muster as contenders in the governance dynamics of the extant global knowledge economy.

T/IK: a conceptual challenge

First, as both concept and phenomenon, T/IK is not readily amenable to definitional or analytical precision. T/IK or similar constructs designed to demarcate knowledge systems are a convenient attempt to juxtapose alternative knowledge frameworks with the so-called dominant western science which, as discussed in the last section, is privileged by the hierarchies of culture and power. The attempts are inherently loaded with a number of questionable and inconclusive presumptions. Some of these presumptions are the form, content, context and the general philosophical outlook of these knowledge forms, on the one hand, and, on the other, their assigned or presumed contrasting character, such as universalism/localism, objectivity/subjectivity, formalism/informality, and embededness/disembededness, features that are perceived to undergird their general orientation and, to some extent, the process of their production (Dutfield 2001; Johnson 1990; Oguamanam 2006a).

Few would disagree that these classificatory approaches are bereft of analytical rigor and have been largely discredited in anthropological and sociology of knowledge circles (Brown 1998). In addition, as we will see later, because of globalization's facilitation of cross-cultural exchanges, there has been an increase in knowledge creolization, cultural hybridism and cosmopolitanism, developments that are viewed as hallmarks of postmodernism. Consequently, contemporary anthropology and sociology of science back away from vehement markings of knowledge and cultural boundaries. For example, anthropologist Michael Brown (1998: 96) contends that knowledge or "culture is not a bounded static entity [as the notion of indigenous knowledge may suggest] but a constantly negotiated process." In the postmodern environment, he argues, "the processual nature of culture gives rise to creative mixing (creolization) or invention of traditions," hence, there seems to be no clear-cut or rigorous spatial and temporal boundaries for the demarcation of culture and knowledge (Oguamanam 2008a).

Second, the analytical and conceptual morass bedeviling T/IK is further confounded by the multiplicity of competing phrases (each with intricate nuances) that jostle for attention in the narratives of alternative knowledge. For instance, writings on the subject fluctuate between a purposeful and irresolute use of prefixes such as "indigenous," "traditional," "aboriginal," "native," "tribal," "local," etc., to qualify knowledge. A purposeful preference of a specific term or prefix is often informed by some critical subtleties or nuances that have important political ramifications, such as in regard to the narrowness or broadness of categories of rights claimants to knowledge. In this respect, "indigenous knowledge," *stricto sensu* has been associated with the knowledge and cultural traditions of the inchoate categories recognized as indigenous peoples in international law (Ellen and Harris 2000; WIPO 2001), while traditional knowledge is depicted as more inclusive of other right holders or claimants, especially those who operate outside the western scientific and free market economy, whether recognized as indigenous or not (Arewa 2006a).

Yet the more neutral and non-literal category, "local knowledge," represents a compromise and an attempt to avoid the unsustainable dichotomization of knowledge stakeholders. For these reasons, it is customary for literature on the subject to devote a significant amount of space and time not only to clarifying or distinguishing these competing terms, but also to justifying analysts' preferences of specific prefixes (Oguamanam 2008a: 35). At policy and lawmaking levels, relevant institutions have continued to grapple with this clarity gap. As discussed later, for the World Intellectual Property Organization (WIPO), indigenous knowledge is a form of TK, but not all TK is indigenous. For the Convention on Biological Diversity (CBD), the issue is resolved by a consistent and complementary reference to the knowledge of indigenous and "local communities" in its text as an attempt to accommodate a broad range of other indistinguishable or hard-to-distinguish stakeholders.

In spite of that and, as we will see later, TK, *stricto sensu*, is also distinguished from other categories of T/IK, especially those in the expressive realm often referred to as traditional cultural expressions or expressions of folklore (TCE/EoF). The emphasis here is on TK and practices not only as a sociocultural form integral to dealings with the physical and cultural environments of indigenous and local communities, but also as the creative adoption, management or response to their ecological and general environmental challenges (WIPO 2001: 25, 2003). In this strict sense, the focus is on the applied forms of TK that are dominated by dealings in genetic resources or in the intertwining of the latter with TK (Taubman and Leistner 2008: 69). This notion of genetic resources as a dominant site for the practice and production of TK, *stricto sensu*, informs the CBD's focus on the role of TK in the conservation of biological diversity. WIPO-IGC's ongoing work has consolidated the idea of a conceptual distinction between TK in relation to dealings with genetic resources as compared to TK in the realm of expressive culture or folklore.

Aside from the tendency to demarcate or distinguish forms of TK along lines of differing emphases, a preference for or rejection of specific terms of reference to the knowledge forms of indigenous and local communities is also part of the resistance narrative indicating the disdain in which such knowledge forms are held under colonial hierarchies of culture and power. For instance, T/IK was perceived as frozen in time and lacking in dynamism, as a process and practice associated with the "folk" tradition of cultures and peoples or savages in static societies functioning mainly on the fringe of humanity. The ceremonies, rituals and "pagan" religious practices – including their rich traditional contexts – as part of the holistic sociocultural process for the production of knowledge by indigenous and local communities were dismissed as barbaric exercises in fetishism and superstition, lacking any rational basis on which to be taken seriously. It was not uncommon that T/IK and associated cultural practices and the languages that carried them constituted a composite target sought to be dislodged by exercises of colonial political and administrative authority in concert with their ecclesiastical allies.

In the postcolonial arena, however, T/IK stakeholders have rejected the derogatory depiction of their knowledge systems and the underlying social processes driving that depiction. In this endeavor, "indigenous," "native," "traditional," or "folk," and other prefixes to knowledge are being reclaimed by the diverse stakeholders to whom such references directly or indirectly apply. For some, these references do not qualify the knowledge system itself but the nature of the communal and social processes in which the knowledge is generated. In this sort of epistemic semiotics, alternative and sometimes overlapping terms are often deployed in an interchangeable but less coherent manner. One thing, however, is clear: "indigenous knowledge" or "traditional knowledge," terms deliberately deployed interchangeably in this book, signify resistance to and contestation over the epistemic racism underlying the colonial rendition of the sociocultural process for the production of knowledge in once-colonized societies. Although T/IK has thus far been used interchangeably, it is a widely held view that TK encompasses indigenous knowledge. Therefore, henceforth, for analytical convenience, reference will be made to TK except where it is necessary to distinguish the latter from indigenous knowledge.

So far, ongoing attempts to redefine and reclaim TK have yielded modest results. It is increasingly common when reference is made to various and competing depictions of local knowledge to dissociate same, by way of caveat, from the negative and derogatory tenor of the colonial accounts. Similarly, in international policy and lawmaking, there has been a progressive incorporation of more politically sensitive and, sometimes, neutral language in the discourse of TK. This is evident in a number of now familiar, even if complementary references, including TCEs/EoF, cultural property, cultural heritage (including tangible and intangible aspects), and knowledge of indigenous and local communities within the elaborate, even if emergent jurisprudence of cultural rights.

Third, the open-ended nature of the subject matters taken within the ambit of TK is a feature of its conceptual complexity. For example, on a fairly broad or holistic level, TK constitutes an aspect of ecological management and environmental stewardship, sustainable development, economic empowerment, self-determination, human rights, property rights, culture, arts, craft, music, songs, dance, and diverse creative repertoire; religion, lifestyle and innumerable aspects of social processes that undergird a people's overall worldview. As we will see later, the indefinite and unwieldy scope of TK is a source of enormous frustration in terms of grappling with the regime overlap and regime complexity around it. As noted, this unwieldy scope accounts for the emergent policy and analytical strategy in which TK, *stricto sensu*, is demarcated from TCES/EoF. Therefore, how to coordinate and harmonize law and policy across the complex regime landscape for TK is one of the challenges that the latter poses for intellectual property in global governance. Specifically, the unmanageable framework of TK is critical to what WIPO[3] characterizes as the "gap analysis" between it and intellectual property.

The gap question is the fourth aspect of the conceptual problems associated with TK. Gervais (2009: 556) refers to this gap as those "areas where current intellectual property norms leave traditional knowledge holders in the dark." He argues that the normative debate over how international law should deal with TK is "situated at the confluence of intellectual property law, cultural studies, ethnology and anthropology" (2009: 552). In addition to the fundamental but over-rehearsed arguments regarding the unfitness of TK to come under conventional intellectual property (Mgbeoji 2001; Oguamanam 2004b), a critical aspect of the gap analysis is rooted in the absence of appreciation for the intellectual and creative ingenuities inherent in the cultural, ethnological and anthropological schemes that undergird the knowledge of indigenous and local communities.

When TK is rightly construed as an integral part of cultural, ethnological and anthropological schemes, it is hard to see how conventional intellectual property could be made ethnologically neutral in order to adapt it to the demands of TK as a gap-fixing measure. Or, in the formulation of Gervais (2009: 552), gap analysis involves infusing relativism from the ethnographic scheme of TK into extant intellectual property norms. He thinks the major task is how to accomplish this without endangering the foundations of the intellectual property system. However the task he envisages could, as well, endanger the foundation of TK and its associated sociocultural processes.

Many commentators on the intersection of TK and intellectual property agree that because of its cultural and ethnological orientation, there are aspects of TK, such as sacralization or sacred knowledge, that are not created with commercial exploitation in mind (Binkert 2006: 151; Gervais 1999: 555).[4] According to Rosemary Coombe, "the protection of indigenous knowledge cannot be reduced to an issue [of intellectual property rights] because it is more fundamentally tied to the marginalization, exploitation, and operation of indigenous and local communities embodying traditional life styles and the failure to recognize their basic rights as human peoples" (2009: 233). Toshiyuki Kono (2009: 17) also observes that:

> While individual specimens of traditional crafts and performance may be protected by intellectual property laws when they satisfy general requirements for copyrightability or registration, in many cases, intangible cultural heritage, including traditional ecological, agricultural, medicinal knowledge and traditional cultural expressions, go beyond the scope of intellectual property protection. Collective knowledge, ideas, innovations, creativity, traditional cultural expressions, practices and other social processes of numerous communities worldwide go beyond the concerns of intellectual property laws.

Fifth, as already evident, the bulk of the conceptual problems for TK revolve around its relationship with intellectual property. Given the broader compass of TK and the narrow economic focus of intellectual property, for many custodians of TK, intellectual property poses a serious dilemma. On the one hand, some local knowledge stakeholders think that intellectual property can potentially serve the ends of economic empowerment. On the other, it represents a threat to cultural survival, since intellectual property tends to weigh culture and knowledge on an economic scale of values (Farley 1997). Even then, any practical results of the fusion of intellectual property with TK would be contingent on the form of TK in issue and several other indeterminable context-dependent and variable factors.

This is why it is tenable to observe that, "indigenous and local communities [. . .] have a complex relationship with the intellectual property system. From suspicion to trepidation, they engage the system reluctantly, often proactively, and like the 'dialectics of the colonized mind,' indigenous peoples' attitude toward intellectual property reflects both admiration, and disaffection or resistance," (Oguamanam 2008b: 490).[5] Illustrating this trend, Madhavi Sunder (2006: 297–8) notes that the custodians of indigenous knowledge "focus simultaneously on a defensive [or passive] intellectual property rights policy, [for example, supporting] limiting rights in the context of essential medicines, and an offensive intellectual property policy, seeking to expand intellectual property protection for "poor people's knowledge" through mechanisms to protect biological diversity, traditional knowledge and geographical indications."[6]

The sixth conceptual challenge engaged by the TK phenomenon centers on the global diversity of its stakeholders and their variegated and often diverging perspectives on the overarching objective for TK protection. The vast majority of less developed countries, such as India, Brazil, China, most of Africa and elsewhere, have tended to pursue the issue of protecting TK in the international arena as a matter, firstly, of economic and political leverage (Coombe 2001; Oguamanam 2004c). In doing this, they deploy the agency of the state on behalf of the custodians of TK while masking any dissonance between the two. For the most part, these states have been more proactive and far more willing than indigenous peoples of the enclave territories to explore ways to fix the gaps between intellectual property and TK for economic and political benefits.

By way of contrast, because of the longstanding disunity of purpose between indigenous peoples and the state in the enclave territories, the agency and legitimacy of the state in indigenous issues is fiercely contested. Given the severe threat to the cultural survival and the sustainability of the traditional lifestyles of these communities, they have tended to approach the indigenous knowledge struggle outside state agency. They have done so by approaching the issue as an overarching matter of human rights, self-determination, solidarity, cultural identity and cultural survival taking priority over economic considerations. In this regard, indigenous peoples of the enclave territories are likely to be selective, carry a sense of suspicion and trepidation, and be generally more critical of the impact of intellectual property on their cultural heritage than their counterparts in less developed countries. The majority of the latter do not perceive their cultural traditions as under palpable threat, in part because there is no dominant colonial settler culture in those countries.

Another issue that complicates the conceptual difficulty around TK relates to ownership or devolution of rights to genetic resources between national governments and indigenous and local communities. In many national and international legal regimes, genetic resources are vested in the state (rather than in indigenous or local community custodians) as an integral part of their sovereign rights.[7] The same is true in regard to the right to make laws and policies on TK and related matters.[8] However, the intricate and overlapping relationship of dependence between genetic resources and TK does not mean that the sovereign right of a state over genetic resources overlaps with the TK of indigenous and local communities. Indigenous and local communities' relationship with their genetic resources and their TK predates the colonial Westphalian states into which indigenous peoples and local communities are presently coopted. In addition to the ambiguity over the state ownership of genetic resources, and indigenous and local communities' claims to TK associated therewith, another potential area of conceptual challenge is the use of international human rights as the normative framework for validating TK and TCEs/EoF. For example, as indicated in the next chapter, the UNESCO Convention on the Protection and Safeguarding of the Intangible Cultural Heritage (ICH) recognizes only ICH forms that are compatible with existing international human rights instruments,[9] in a manner that presumes that the age-long debate over the universalism of human rights across cultures and civilizations is settled.

In sum, the complex global diversity of TK communities and the political contexts in which they presently operate reflects their diverse colonial historical experiences. Consequently, there are divergent objectives and priorities for the protection of TK and the overarching expectations that flow from this, particularly in regard to its interface with intellectual property. Along with other issues highlighted in this section, the global diversity of TK custodians and stakeholders, and their diverging priorities, as well as the overall dilemma that intellectual property poses for TK, are at the center of the complex conceptual morass and frustration embedded in the notion of T/IK. The present dissection of some of the factors that undergird the quagmire is, of course, selective. But the factors discussed provide the backdrop for exploring and understanding the theme of global governance at the intersection of TK and intellectual property rights. The next section examines the underlying factors providing the context for the attention that TK enjoys as an integral aspect of the dynamics of the global knowledge economy.

TK as a factor in the global knowledge economy

The postmodernist perspective

The rise to pre-eminence of TK in the new knowledge economy results from the interaction of a number of theoretical and practical triggers. On the theoretical plank, the resurgence of indigenous peoples' movements and the value of their knowledge systems, in a way, are rooted in the postmodern outlook of the 20th century. As a reaction to, or a rejection of the erstwhile dominant modernism that held sway in the colonial project through the reification of scientific truth and objectivity, unity, cultural hegemony and exclusion, uniformity and authority, postmodernism projects the value of difference, subjectivity, relativism, social context, alterity and skepticism in the understanding of, and dealing with phenomena.[10]

As a symbolic depiction of this trend, Kuhn's much cited seminal work (1962) challenged the objectivity of "western science" and explored its deployment of consensus among leading experts to foist a "paradigm shift" as the basis of scientific advancement. Kuhn and others (e.g. Derrida, Foucault, Heidegger) in their works opened up a postmodern critical introspection on science and other conventional concepts and conceptualizations in philosophical circles. They did this especially within the emergent critical sociology of science, and deconstructed a number of traditional presumptions and the uncritical privileging of western science over alternative knowledge systems. Essentially, postmodernism's demystification of science identifies the latter as a cultural process not radically different from other indigenous or alternative knowledge systems. In no small measure, this approach warranted a revisionist approach to the colonial or modernist derogation of traditional epistemic systems.

Postmodernism rejects the notion of a universal or objective truth, of a global cultural narrative and of a vehement division across so-called rationally demarked categories. Instead, postmodernism erected the philosophical structures of a critical transdisciplinary orientation willing to rethink primordial prejudices in the humanities, including arts, culture, and diverse other disciplines, not the least of which are human and power relations, law and anthropology. For instance, as already noted, postmodern anthropology rejected strict demarcations of knowledge systems along indigenous versus western scientific categories or subcategories.

The International Bill of Rights

The postmodern orientation has made its imprints in the international lawmaking process, seemingly by both design and chance. For example, a major overhaul of the international legal process in the post-World War II era, reflected in the Charter of the United Nations, was the renegotiation, or perhaps more appropriately, a whittling down of the influence of the Westphalian state as the hitherto unquestioned arbiter and basis for participation in the international process. This shift emerged in the wake of the horrors perpetrated by Nazi Germany in the war and resulted in the global enthronement of the human rights of peoples, *qua* people, and the empowerment of non-state actors in the global constitutive process (Oguamanam 2004a). According Nunes (1995: 528):

> [T]he starting point of the Peace of the United Nations, as opposed to the peace of Westphalia, which was essentially centred on the nation-state, is the constitutive instrument known as the United Nations Charter, and it speaks of, "We the Peoples . . ." Actually, the U.N. Charter speaks of the rights that accrue to the peoples prior to the organization of the nation-state which is party to the Charter as an international agreement or treaty.

In addition to the United Nations Charter, key instruments of the then emergent global order, notably the Universal Declaration of Human Rights, 1948, the International Covenant on Civil and Political Rights (ICCPR), the International Covenant on Economic, Social and Cultural Rights (ICESCR), both of 1966 (collectively, the International Bill of Rights) were, to a large extent, products of postmodern legal thinking. Largely, they provide the framework for entrenching religious freedom and tolerance, diversity, multiculturalism, and self-determination of peoples; protection of the rights of minorities, including indigenous peoples; and for the preservation and enjoyment of cultural heritage. Generally, the UN Charter encourages "meaningful levels and forms of non-state participation in [its] deliberative process, for example, by permitting the affiliation of non-governmental organizations (NGOs) with the Economic and Social Council" (Oguamanam 2004a: 360–1).

Analysts of the evolution of indigenous peoples and indigenous knowledge in the contemporary global constitutive process (e.g. Barsh 1986; Kingsbury 2001; Sanders 1983; Wiessner 1999) agree that indigenous peoples and their sympathizers have capitalized on the post-war international legal landscape to advance their cause. They have confronted the international process as well-organized pressure groups seeking to redeem the promises contained in the International Bill of Rights. As well, they have penetrated the international system by helping to shape both hard and soft law regimes for further elaboration of their rights. So far, the results of these endeavors demonstrate the pivotal nature of indigenous knowledge in relation to virtually all other issues that touch on the political, economic and sociocultural welfare of indigenous and local communities.

For example, Article 27(1) of the Universal Declaration of Human Rights, 1948, provides that "[e]*veryone* has the right to freely participate in the cultural life of the *community*, to enjoy the arts and to share in scientific advancement and its benefits".[11] In accordance with postmodern thinking, this provision gives a nuanced, neutral conception of science, deploying it "as a synonym of knowledge as well as a cultural process. It provides an authoritative protection for knowledge in relation to both indigenous peoples and other generators of, and sites for the generation of knowledge (communities), both within and outside the colonial state" (Oguamanam 2004c: 207).

Similarly, Article 27 of the ICCPR provides: "In those States in which ethnic, religious and linguistic minorities exist, persons belonging to such minorities shall not be denied the right, in community with other members of their group, to enjoy their culture, to profess and practice their religion, or to use their own language." Though there is no direct reference to "indigenous knowledge" here, the reference to culture and its components, such as language and religion, sufficiently incorporates indigenous knowledge. Second, though the Article is silent on indigenous peoples, its reference to minorities, in a way, includes indigenous peoples, albeit inconclusively because "minority rights" is hardly a synonym for indigenous peoples' rights in international law. Perhaps more importantly, the United Nations Human Rights Committee has traditionally opted for an elastic interpretation of the provision by extending its guarantee to indigenous peoples (Kingsbury 2001).

In sum, one of the palpable effects of post-modern thinking in international law is the willingness to vest rights on people as entities on their own outside the stranglehold of the hitherto super sovereign nation-state. This evinces a willingness to recognize and legitimize the cultural rights of peoples, to acknowledge cultural pluralism, and to concede a nuanced acceptance of the relevance of the democratic process in knowledge generation across cultures and peoples. The foregoing basic references to the International Bill of Rights capture the general post-modern thrust of these documents which frame the issue of indigenous knowledge as one of human and cultural rights and as an aspect of self-determination.

In addition, the willingness of the new post war international legal order to accommodate non-state actors in the UN process has an empowering effect, which indigenous peoples and their friends have tenaciously capitalized upon, prompting an analyst to admit: "[t]he [indigenous] Indian way of life has not merely survived; it is back as the foundation of a strong identity, which has forced itself to the top of the international agenda. . . . Indigenous peoples have re-entered the arena of power. . . . [T]hey have become recognized actors in the world constitutive process" (Wiessner 1999: 58).

The International Labour Organization

A detailed account of how indigenous peoples have re-entered the arena of power has been provided elsewhere (e.g. Kingsbury 2001; Oguamanam 2004a, 2004c;

Sanders 1983; Wiessner 1999). However, a singular development in the international lawmaking process that represented a morale booster for this transformation must be noted. This was courtesy of a shift in the orientation of the International Labour Organization (ILO), the first major world body to address indigenous concerns, especially in regard to the exploitation of indigenous peoples as the labor pool for colonial industries. The ILO's interest in indigenous issues predates the modern era of international lawmaking, which may be conveniently dated with the founding of the UN. The policy approach of the ILO was essentially based on the trusteeship doctrine pursuant to which the ILO Indigenous and Tribal Peoples Convention No. 107 of 1957 adopted the principles of integration and assimilation of indigenous peoples into the dominant colonial culture. It was not too long before the wave of post-modernism in the late 20th century pushed for a radical rethinking of the policies of assimilation, culminating in their total abandonment, and in a radical expansion of the ILO mandate beyond its focus on the exploitation of indigenous labor, toward a new institutional and international legal initiative dealing with virtually all aspects of indigenous concerns.

The ILO Convention No. 107 of 1957 was replaced with the Indigenous and Tribal Peoples Convention No. 169 of 1989, which revised the policy of assimilation but opted to preserve indigenous cultural identity within the framework of limited self-determination pursuant to the International Bill of Rights. The symbolic ramifications of the new orientation at the ILO have been articulated elsewhere to include:

> set[ting] an agenda for subsequent elaboration of the indigenous question [as evident] in the initiatives' basic theme, which was the "right of indigenous peoples to live and develop by their own designs as distinct communities" [and as] a "part of a larger body of developments that can be understood as giving rise to a new customary international law with the same normative thrust".
>
> (Oguamanam 2004a: 364–5)[12]

From UNWGIP to DRIPS

These progressive developments at the ILO did not happen in isolation from other events in the international norm-setting process concerning indigenous peoples and their knowledge systems, especially in the late 20th century. For instance, in 1971, the UN through its Economic and Social Council (ECOSOC), commissioned a study on the problem of discrimination against indigenous populations. The resulting report, known mostly as the Cobo Report,[13] recommended setting up a UN Working Group on Indigenous Populations (UNWGIP), which was accepted by the UN Human Rights Commission. The UNWGIP was established in 1982 with a mandate to review issues concerning indigenous peoples from a global perspective with a view to the evolution of a common normative international standard for addressing them. Instructively, the UNWGIP mandate included the study of treaties between indigenous peoples and colonial states, and the investigation of the concept of indigenous, cultural and intellectual property rights (Anaya 1996; Barsh 1986; Daes 1998).

Ten years after its inauguration, the UNWGIP issued a Draft Declaration on the Rights of Indigenous Peoples in 1993.[14] The document represented a very bold, comprehensive and authoritative articulation of "indigenous claims, including but not limited to, the core categories of cultural protection in all its ramifications, rights to economic and social welfare, self-determination, political empowerment, ancestral lands, and territories and treaty commitments by colonial powers" (Oguamanam 2004c: 201–2; see also Kingsbury 2001). Directly relevant to our present purpose, the subject of indigenous knowledge is a pivotal feature of the entire text of the declaration. Because of the political intrigues at work regarding the sensitive nature of the issues addressed in the Draft Declaration, the document remained, literally, in limbo within the UN review process and bureaucracy for nearly 15 years before it was adopted as an official declaration of the United Nations General Assembly in 2007 as the Declaration on the Rights of Indigenous Peoples (DRIPS). In the meantime, the UN established a Permanent Forum on Indigenous Issues within its ECOSOC to act in an advisory capacity regarding economic and social development, culture, the environment and human rights of indigenous peoples.

Chroniclers of the evolution of indigenous peoples and indigenous knowledge in the international law and policy arena agree that the UNWGIP was one of the most elaborate human rights processes at the UN (Burger 1996; Daes 1998; Moses 2000; Wiessner 1999). This is in regard not only to the impressive attendance, but also in terms of the participation of diverse stakeholders. Also, analysts agree that the process that gave birth to DRIPS was perhaps one of the most legitimate of the UN processes. Among others, it involved a massive mobilization of indigenous stakeholders across the globe and created an environment in which they participated freely outside the paternalistic stranglehold of colonial states. The integrity of the process could only have been facilitated by the postmodern thrust of international law, which provided opportunity for non-state actors to influence the process of international normative development.

Indigenous peoples' tenacity

The resurgence of indigenous peoples' issues at the center of what Wiessner calls the world constitutive process is owed largely to the tenacity of indigenous peoples' leadership, especially in enclave territories such as Argentina, Australia, Canada, Europe, New Zealand, and the US (Wiessner 1999). It is, therefore, hardly surprising that the comparatively small population of "indigenous peoples" in relation to their colonized counterparts elsewhere notwithstanding, "indigenous knowledge" as the knowledge of "indigenous peoples" gained a prominence that placed it at par with, if not over, traditional knowledge, which applied to far broader knowledge categories and stakeholders. Through national and international mobilization and networks, indigenous peoples galvanized global consciousness of their plight and drew attention to the increasing threat to their cultural survival (Coombe 2001).

They won the sympathies of friends and allies in the non- and intergovernmental communities and variegated civil society groups in colonial capitals and elsewhere. They were later to incorporate their counterparts in the non-enclave territories or less developed countries. In part, this new solidarity is facilitated by the technological infrastructure of globalization through the deployment of the internet platform. This facilitated an elaborate networking culture that assisted in focusing attention on the issue of indigenous or local knowledge as a site for solidarity among the world's colonized peoples (Oguamanam 2004c). Through this emergent strategic alliance, indigenous people have been able, in the words of Coombe, to form new "networks of advocates and activists" that have coalesced into formidable and organized "pressure groups on governments and United Nations bodies [where they] insist upon a new understanding of justice, equity, and accountability" in the international intellectual property system (Coombe 2001: 278; Oguamanam 2004b).

The international environmental regime

Compared to the International Bill of Rights, the progressive recognition of indigenous peoples and omnibus "local communities" and their knowledge systems as part of the postmodern orientation of new international lawmaking is more palpable in the international environmental law regime. Since the early 1990s, the protection of indigenous and local knowledge has been recognized as received wisdom in international environmental law and policy. Specifically, virtually all the hard and soft law instruments arising from the 1992 Rio Earth Summit,[15] including the Rio Declaration on Environment and Development[16] (e.g. Principle 22), Agenda 21[17] (e.g. Chapter Six), the Convention on Biological Diversity (e.g. Article 8(j)), the Statement of Forest Principles[18] (e.g. Articles 5, 12(d)) are unequivocal on the role of indigenous and local knowledge in promoting sustainable environment and development.

It is instructive that while the UN Draft Declaration on the Rights of Indigenous People was issued in 1993, the processes that led to it date back to the 1970s. Similarly, the 1992 Earth Summit, which had its foundation in the 1972 Declaration of the United Nations Conference on the Human Environment (UNCHE), held in Stockholm, laid the foundation for modern international environmental law (Brunnée 2009). The overarching principles of the Stockholm Declaration have been amplified via the 1992 Earth Summit and subsequent legal, policy and regulatory instruments. In regard to indigenous peoples and indigenous knowledge, the 2007 DRIPS, in several provisions, poignantly articulates the contemporary international consensus on indigenous knowledge. For example, Article 31 states:

> Indigenous peoples have the right to maintain, control, protect and develop their cultural heritage, traditional knowledge and traditional cultural expressions, as well as the manifestations of their sciences, technologies and cultures, including human and genetic resources, seeds, medicines, knowledge of the properties of fauna and flora, oral traditions, literatures, designs, sports and

traditional games, and visual and performing arts. They also have the right to maintain, control, protect and develop their intellectual property over such cultural heritage, traditional knowledge and traditional cultural expressions.

From a practical perspective, this links indigenous knowledge (from a gamut of cultural, ethnological and anthropological perspectives) with intellectual property. It reflects a strategy of looking into both indigenous environmental related knowledge, and diverse traditional cultural and creative practices through which international environmental law and the cultural rights movements have coopted indigenous knowledge or TK into the policy cliché of environmental sustainability or sustainable development in general (Hodgson 2002; Kono 2009). Given the encompassing nature of culture and the environment, this approach has helped in no small measure to focus attention on indigenous or traditional agricultural and medicinal practices, biodiversity and general conservation in the new knowledge economy, which is depicted by the new focus on TK *stricto sensu*.

Bio- and digital technologies

By extension, the last observation reflects, in part, the contemporary transition in the life sciences and the emergence of modern biotechnology. The transition has supervised a focus on the deployment of global biological or ecological resources (e.g. animal, human, plant, marine and forest genetic materials) and associated TK for innovations in health, agriculture, drug production and other industrial applications. Indigenous and local communities are repositories or traditional custodians of more than 70% of our precious global biological resources and associated local knowledge (Oguamanam 2006a: 23). The symbiotic relationship between modern biotechnology, biodiversity and biological resources and ensuing biopiracy or allegations thereof, has helped in no small measure to draw attention to TK in the emergent knowledge economy.

Another practical development that has facilitated the drawing of TK into prominence and contention is the computer-driven digital revolution. As observed elsewhere, "[b]y facilitating the generation, processing, diffusion, manipulation of sensitive information on biological resources, digital technology is intertwined with biotechnology and facilitates the transfer of local biodiversity-related knowledge to Western industrial and scientific complexes" (Oguamanam 2008a: 31). In its real and exaggerated renditions, this technology-propelled trend of biopiracy is a contentious, even if complementary, feature of the global knowledge economic order. It is not only in the biotechnology and genetic resources context that digital or new information technologies have thrown TK and cultural practices into contention. As discussed in the next chapter, in the realm of cultural property, including tangible and intangible cultural heritage and other forms of cultural expression, new technologies have had a dialectical outcome in regard to TCE/EoF as a complementary aspect of TK.

The context of globalization and global governance

The open-ended scope of TK is evident in the extremely complex and overlapping operative international regime environments in which its intersection with intellectual property is being negotiated. In the simplest of terms, that negotiation takes the non-deliberate but practical form of the exploration being carried out under "gap analysis" from diverse perspectives with a view to forge some accommodation of the conflicted interests of a broad range of stakeholders. This attempt, a critical aspect of global governance, is facilitated in large measure by diverse stakeholders taking advantage of multiple regimes and forums, and, where necessary, deploying counter-regime platforms and other resistance strategies.

We have noted that postmodernism created the enabling philosophical and legal environment for the resurgence of TK. Frederick Jameson, a prominent American theorist and the author of the notable work *Postmodernism or, the Cultural Logic of Late Capitalism* (1991), has associated postmodernism with the pivotal logic of "late capitalism," i.e. capitalism's post-war phase, which, to some extent, corresponds with contemporary globalization. The connection between postmodernism and late capitalism (globalization) seems palpable. Postmodernism's opening of the philosophical space for alterity, diversity, difference, context and relativism, and its rejection of a global cultural narrative provides fillip for an unprecedented interaction between the local and the global as shifting and indeterminate status in a continual state of negotiation (Santos 2006). In this context, TK and the social processes necessary for its production have been opened up to western science, its traditionally privileged comparator, in a mutually influencing tussle through knowledge creolization and cultural hybridism mostly facilitated by globalization.

Globalization and its technological infrastructures create an enabling environment for a dynamic interaction and negotiation between the local and the global through the opening up of markets, liberalization of choices, a "cultivation of taste for the exotic," and facilitation of access to knowledge forms (especially TK and its associated practices) and to cultural goods and services. The easy flow and exchange of information across increasingly blurring epistemic boundaries breeds a resistance to the emergent cultural cosmopolitanism through the persistent claim of entitlement to cultural spaces, especially by indigenous and traditional communities. The persistence and resurgence of indigenous or local knowledge in an increasingly cosmopolitan, epistemic and cultural landscape is part of the unsuspecting logic or dialectics of globalization.

Without question, "the processual emergence of a cosmopolitan cultural and epistemic order is an affirmation of the existence and, to some large degree, the vibrancy of insular cultural locale that is critical in sustaining our postmodern [cosmopolitan] cultural world" (Oguamanam 2008a: 44; see also Hannerz 1990; Kymlicka 1989; Santos 1995). For this reason, the manner in which TK is negotiated within the dynamics of the global governance of intellectual property poses a crucial challenge to how the prevailing crisis of equity in the global knowledge economy is resolved. As we will see shortly, that negotiation assumes multiple dimensions within and, sometimes, outside the intellectual property framework, and manifests in multiple forms as aspects of gap-fixing measures, *sui generis* jurisprudence, protection, safeguarding, access and benefit sharing, etc.

The next section maps the international regime landscape for the global governance dynamic at the intersection of TK and intellectual property. Already, our focus in the last two chapters on intellectual property issue linkages to public health, agriculture and food security, implicates aspects of TK, especially those dealing with genetic resources or what we generally refer to as traditional bio-cultural knowledge and its relevant regimes. Presently, we need to outline the international regime framework on genetic resources as they relate to the negotiation of indigenous ecological or biocultural knowledge. This focus on TK and its relation to genetic resources reflects the emerging distinction between TK *stricto sensu* and TCE/EoF. The rest of the present chapter focuses on TK, *stricto sensu*, as distinguished from TCEs/EoF. Before then, a word about the inchoate nature of the dichotomization of TK is in order.

Bifurcation of TK and TCEs/EoF

Save for analytical convenience, it is hard to sustain a distinction between TK *stricto sensu* and TCEs/EoF or even the concept of ICH. For instance, in practice and application, the bulk of TK is intangible experience associated with dealings with the tangible. In this regard, the WIPO-IGC notes that though TK is distinguished from traditional cultural expressions, "[s]ome forms of protecting TCEs will have the indirect effect of also protecting TK – for instance, in the protection of recordings of traditional songs and narratives that are used to maintain or pass TK within a community, or handicrafts that embody distinctive TK methods or knowhow" (WIPO 2009a: Annex I, 8). As the saying goes, there is no folk without folklore. There is no knowledge without the sociocultural process or tradition for its production. Virtually all forms and manifestations of TK are aspects of cultural expression, while TK itself thrives in both the tangible and the intangible.

However, the dichotomy between TK and its other aspects, such as TCEs or ICH is rooted in the emphasis of early international jurisprudence on cultural rights as it relates to the protection of mainly its tangible aspects, i.e. those having physical or material existence (Kono 2008: 10), as opposed to the multivalent intangible sociocultural processes integral to the production of various forms of TK.

The unsustainable nature of that distinction is evident in the overlapping ways in which TK, TCEs or ICH feature in multiple regimes. Graham Dutfield has rightly noted that "the most substantial negotiations [on indigenous or traditional knowledge] seem now to be those taking place at WIPO." This is in direct reference to the IGC, where "a set of draft provisions on the protection of traditional knowledge and traditional cultural expression" are being hammered out (Dutfield 2006b: 10). It is striking that this most substantial negotiation adopts a converging approach to TK and TCEs. According to WIPO, the IGC is "a forum for international policy debate and [for the] development of legal mechanisms and practical tools concerning the protection of traditional knowledge and TCEs (folklore) against misappropriation and misuse, and the intellectual property access of benefit-sharing in genetic resources" (Yu 2008c: 437, n. 24). One of the precursor initiatives to the WIPO IGC, the 2001 WIPO Fact Finding Mission (FFM) report adopts an inclusive concept of TK. It sees it as an integral aspect of cultural heritage encompassing "tradition-based literary, artistic or scientific works; performances; inventions; scientific discoveries; designs; marks; names and symbols; undisclosed information; and, all other tradition-based innovations and creations resulting from intellectual activity in the industrial, scientific, literary or artistic fields" (WIPO 2001: 25).

In elaborating core principles and guidelines for the protection of TK, the WIPO-IGC takes care not to preclude any potential subject matter by adopting an inclusive definition (Coombe 2009: 259), as follows:

> [T]he content or substance of knowledge that is the result of traditional activity and insight in a traditional context, and includes the know-how, skills, innovations, practices and learning that form part of traditional systems, and knowledge that is embodied in the traditional lifestyle of a community or people, or is contained or codified knowledge systems passed between generations. It is not limited to any specific technical field, and *may include agricultural, environmental and medicinal knowledge, and knowledge associated with genetic resources.*
>
> (IGC 2004: Annex I, B3 s. 2, 6)[19]

The reference to agricultural, environmental and medicinal knowledge and the open-ended "knowledge associated with genetic resources" represent easily distinguishable sites for the concentration of several traditional knowledge categories, subcategories and practices. Traversing food, agricultural, ecological/biodiversity, environmental, and medicinal and other forms, indigenous and local communities' dealings with genetic resources constitute critical sites for TK's intersection with intellectual property.[20] Not surprisingly, with the advent of modern biotechnology and increasing concerns about biopiracy, TK associated with genetic resources has received much attention. To a large but hardly exhaustive extent, those forms of TK are also the target of the regime concentration easily distinguishable from those regimes that focus on TCEs and, in some ways, ICH, which is explored in the next chapter.

International legal framework for TK *stricto sensu*

As noted in Chapter 1, the symbiotic relationship between genetic resources and biotechnology as a technology of appropriation (especially in its interaction with digital technologies) often targets the genetic, or perhaps more appropriately, biological resources in indigenous and local communities and associated TK. This predatory aspect of the global knowledge economy is re-enforced by intellectual property rights, and provides the entry point for exploring legal and policy schemes for the protection of TK relating to genetic resources or traditional biocultural knowledge in different regimes. Graham Dutfield identifies the key regimes in that field as follows:

TK is being debated at the international level in various intergovernmental forums and processes. These include the Conference of the Parties (COP) to the Convention on Biological Diversity (CBD), the World Intellectual Property Organization (WIPO) and the World Trade Organization. Sometimes, the negotiations focus specifically on TK protection, whether positive or negative, or else TK is discussed in the context of a wider negotiation, such as the WTO's review of the implementation of Article 27.3(b) of the Agreement on Trade-related Aspects of Intellectual Property Rights (TRIPS) or the COP and its subsidiary working groups' elaboration of an International Regime of Access and Benefit Sharing.

Other forums that supervise activities relating to the TK of genetic resources include the United Nations Permanent Forum on Indigenous Issues,[21] the Food and Agriculture Organization of the United Nations,[22] the World Health Organization, the United Nations Conference on Trade and Development (UNCTAD),[23] and the CBD. In addition, the WIPO-IGC Draft Gap Analysis on TK has also identified a comprehensive list of instruments dealing directly or indirectly with various aspects of TK. They include: the TRIPS Agreement, the Patent Cooperation Treaty, International Patent Classification, the Paris Convention on the Protection of Industrial Property, the Madrid Agreement and Protocol, the Lisbon Agreement on Protection of Appellations of Origin, the Berne Convention for the Protection of Literary and Artistic Works, the Hague Agreement Concerning International Deposit of Industrial Designs, the WIPO Performances and Phonograms Treaty, the United Nations Convention to Combat Desertification and the Interlaken Declaration on Animal Genetic Resources. Some details of the continuing debates and policy actions in these forums and instruments have been provided in the preceding chapters and in WIPO (2009).[24] Here, we are interested in gauging the underlying tension and in appraising the nature and pattern of the emerging outcome from the debates as they shape the global governance landscape for intellectual property.

In terms of tension, Peter Yu rightly points out that "intellectual property protection is a form of protection for the 'haves.' Those who have interests in the system are eager to protect what they have, while those who do not are likely to find the laws counterintuitive, annoying and socially pernicious" (Yu 2003: 402, 2008c: 451). Because of the wealth of global genetic resources within their national boundaries or within their traditional ecological domains, the less developed countries and various indigenous peoples have championed the development of a protection regime not only for those resources, but also the TK associated with them. They are open to exploring this protection regime within and outside the intellectual property system. However, for most developed countries, attempts to create an equitable and accountable regime for the use of genetic resources of indigenous and local communities are mostly perceived as an irritation. Their preferred approach is that both genetic resources and associated TK are the common heritage of mankind and are available in the public domain, justifying no barriers to access.

As noted in Chapter 5, there is now, however, a template shift regarding the ownership of genetic resources. Instead of being presumed to be common heritage, genetic resources are now affirmatively vested in the sovereign state within which they are located.[25] It remains open how that ownership will be exercised as between the state and its indigenous and local communities. Similarly, there is complex, ongoing jurisprudential, policy, and customary legal and general cultural analysis of whether TK is amenable to "ownership," and if so, who the appropriate claimants may be, whether traditional communities, indigenous peoples, or individuals within various socio-cultural contexts (Anderson 2009).

From the Bonn 2002 Guidelines to the 2010 Nagoya Protocol on ABS

Through its Bonn Guidelines and various programs of work, the CBD has encouraged a proliferation of access and equitable benefit-sharing (ABS) laws and regulations in regard to genetic resources and associated TK. The Guidelines are intended to provide guidance for developing legislative, administrative and policy measures on ABS and incidental contractual schemes. It contains many provisions on dealing with intellectual property rights, most notably disclosing the country of origin of genetic resources in applications for intellectual property rights (Dutfield 2006b: 11).

In advancing the underlying objectives of ABS, Switzerland championed an initiative to amend the Patent Cooperation Treaty (PCT) Regulations to require the disclosure of genetic resources and TK used in patent applications. The concept of the disclosure of genetic resources and TK now feature in the WIPO Patent Agenda, not only through PCT, but also in deliberations regarding the Substantive Patent Law Treaty, the Patent Law Treaty and, perhaps most importantly, in the WIPO-IGC (Arezzo 2007; Musungu and Dutfield 2003). As an idea with broad development ramifications and as an important aspect of the protection of TK, the issue of disclosure of origin would most certainly be subsumed within the WIPO Development Agenda, though it is one of its critical elements at the implementation stage.[26] Meanwhile, the subject of disclosure of the source or origin of genetic resources and associated TK has continued to feature in the various aspects of the WTO's programs, including the Committee on Trade and Environment (CTE) and the TRIPS Council. It is noteworthy that segments of less developed countries have pressed for the amendment of the TRIPS Agreement. They propose the addition of Article 29bis to require disclosure of the origins of biological resources and traditional knowledge implicated in an invention that is the subject of a patent application. Finally, recent revisions of the International Patent Classification now extend its coverage to specific traditional medicinal preparations, including compounds from traditional herbal medicines, as a strategy of defense and protection for TK against biopiracy.

In terms of results, there has already been tremendous regional and national policy and legislative initiatives on ABS in regard to the intersection of intellectual property rights with TK. These include the Andean Community of Nations

Common Regime of Access to Genetic Resources 1996; the African Union Model Law on Rights of Local Communities, Farmers and Breeders 2003; and the Central American Agreement on ABS 2008. Also, ideas for the ASEAN Framework Agreement on Access to Biological Resources and for a Regional Framework on ABS in the Himalayan Region are presently being explored. At national levels, there are to date almost 100 country-specific legislative initiatives and policy initiatives on ABS regarding genetic resources. To underscore the complexity and breadth of indigenous knowledge in the context of genetic resources, those legislative and policy schemes traverse general environmental, biodiversity, biotechnology and biodiscovery/bioprospecting strategies. They also include legislation on farmers' rights, traditional medicine, wildlife resource conservation, plant genetic resources and indigenous peoples' rights (GRAIN 2010; Oguamanam 2011).

For the most part, the laws and regulations on ABS are structured along the lines of the CBD Guidelines on ABS. They provide for the ethics and practice of prior informed consent (PIC) regarding access and use of genetic resources and the deployment of standard material transfer agreements to govern the transfer of specific genetic material between provider and user entities. Also, the guidelines provide for disclosure of the source and origin of genetic resources and TK in patent applications and for the accommodation of contractual schemes for technology transfer and for patent royalty-sharing arrangements on mutually agreed terms – all aimed to support equitable ABS. Despite the different levels of entrenchment – at national, regional and international levels – there has yet to be a binding agreement to adjust extant international intellectual property jurisprudence to the dictates of ABS. Even the recently concluded Nagoya Protocol fails to *directly* require the disclosure of source or origin of genetic resources and associated TK as part of the ABS process.[27]

Less than a year after the issuance of the CBD Bonn Guidelines on ABS, at the 2002 World Summit on Sustainable Development (WSSD) in Johannesburg, a coalition of 15 of the most biologically diverse countries in the world (Bolivia, Brazil, China, Costa Rica, Colombia, Ecuador, India, Indonesia, Kenya, Mexico, Malaysia, Peru, the Philippines, South Africa and Venezuela,) pressed for a binding international regime on ABS. Two years earlier, during the negotiation of the Bonn Guidelines, the idea of a legally binding protocol on ABS was eschewed to avoid "unnecessary distractions and prolonged negotiations" that were sure to ensue (Chambers 2003). But the WSSD approved the commencement of negotiations for a binding ABS regime "within the framework of the Convention on Biological Diversity, bearing in mind the Bonn Guidelines, an international treaty regime to promote and safeguard fair and equitable sharing of benefits arising out of the utilization of genetic resources" (Dutfield 2006b: 13). Since then, that process has continued to unfold at CBD COP, which is sanctioned by the UN General Assembly as the main forum to coordinate the evolution of such a regime. After almost six years of talks at the CBD Working Group on ABS, which have been informed by developments at other forums, such as the IGC and the WTO (the TRIPS Council, the CTE), the 193 member states of the CBD agreed to a binding Protocol on ABS at the 10th COP held in Nagoya, Japan.[28]

In the immediate aftermath of the Protocol, reviews of what it accomplished or failed to accomplish are mixed. As far back as 2006, Graham Dutfield reflected on the expectations from the anticipated ABS Protocol, wondering "what the regime will look like in terms of its form, its provisions, and the extent to which they will be legally binding and enforceable." In particular:

> It is unclear how far it will deal with TK. It is possible that it would merely reiterate the CBD provisions on TK without deviating much from the extant language. On the other hand, the International Regime could go beyond CBD's language on TK and clarify and strengthen the rather vague and undeniably weak legal obligations placed on governments by Article 8(j).
>
> (Dutfield 2006b: 14)

In regard to TK and other issues, the Nagoya Protocol came very close to confirming Dutfield's projection in most respects. Its language has been described as a "masterpiece of ambiguity" (ICTSD 2010). Already, we have discussed its ambiguous treatment of derivatives. Not only did the Protocol adopt the generally loose and exhortatory language of the CBD, it leaves open to interpretation whether its provisions are retroactive in regard to genetic resources, associated TK and related information already in the hands of "biogopolists" and in the public domain. In terms of obvious gaps in the Protocol text, few would underestimate the need to make provision on the role of technology, for example, in regard to the idea of digital libraries for storing and managing information relating to plant genomes in bioprospecting, biopiracy and transference of TK into the public domain. The Nagoya Protocol is silent on this important issue.

The Protocol is also silent in regard to the knotty issue of disclosure of source or origin of genetic resources and associated TK. However, it makes elaborate implementation provisions, albeit in ambiguous language, conferring discretion on parties to take "appropriate," "effective," "proportionate" measures, including the establishment of "effective check points" to ensure compliance with ABS. The actual extent or scope of such measures is open to interpretation. Whether they would include disclosure of source or origin of genetic resources in patent application remain to be seen.

On a more positive note, one of the important contributions of the Protocol is its creation of a multilateral benefit-sharing mechanism in regard to genetic resources and associated TK "in trans-boundary situations or for which it is not possible to grant or obtain prior informed consent" (Article 10). This was the fruit of a hard-fought intervention by Japan, the host of the 10th COP, as part of its trouble-shooting determination to ensure that the Nagoya summit did not collapse. The Protocol broke new ground by providing for an expedited ABS scheme to tackle "present and imminent emergencies that threaten or damage human, animal or plant health" (Article 8b). Analysts see a direct relevance in this provision to negotiations at the WHO over whether countries could be obligated to share and be compensated for sharing "genetic material relating to human pathogen (such as the avian flu)" (ICTSD 2010).

As expected, the Protocol recognizes pre-existing schemes for ABS to the extent that they are not contrary to the objectives of biodiversity conservation and the Protocol. It makes ambiguous provision in regard to its relationship with "other international instruments relevant to the Protocol," in effect, enjoining that "due regard should be paid to useful and relevant ongoing work or practices under such international instruments and relevant international organizations" (Article 4(3)). Article 31 of the Protocol provides for a periodic assessment and review process to evaluate the Protocol's effectiveness, which would include the evaluation of the Protocol "in the light of developments in other international organizations, inter alia, WIPO" (ICTSD 2010). Thus, it follows that though the relationship between the Nagoya Protocol, the WIPO-IGC, the TRIPS Council and the WIPO Patent Agenda, especially in regard to the subject of disclosure of source or origin of genetic resources is left ambiguous in the text of the Protocol, there is an implicit recognition that recourse could be had to those other instruments in those areas where the Protocol is silent. Thus, the Protocol is not the exclusive instrument on ABS, and its provisions would have to be viewed alongside other instruments.

Despite its generally ambiguous language and reiteration of weak obligations prescribed under the CBD, the Protocol not only has affirmed the established principles of the Bonn Guidelines, but also has moved closer to stronger recognition of indigenous and local communities as holders of TK, even though it falls short of the standard anticipated in the DRIPS.[29] Notably, it provides for the recognition of the customary laws of indigenous and local communities in regard to PIC and overall ABS procedures, even though it also subjects that provision to national legislation. According to one commentator, given the anticipated delay by less developed countries to set up effective and functional national ABS regimes, this form of subjection of ABS and PIC to national legislation, "threatens to undermine effective implementation of the Protocol, rendering TK something only really recognized at the discretion of governments" (Robinson and Tobin 2010). The Protocol has created elaborate enforcement or implementation provisions[30] for ABS, including the management of transboundary TK and genetic resources. Yet it missed the opportunity to move TK outside the limiting matrix of the CBD which associates it with genetic resources, instead of the more appropriate association with biological resources.[31]

At a glance, the Nagoya Protocol affirms the accuracy of Dutfield's predictive assessment and reflection quoted earlier. Other reactions to the Protocol underscore its significance as a milestone – an important "starting point," but no more. However, its prospect as a viable anti-biopiracy instrument will depend on its implementation. And because the language of the Protocol is mostly weak and ambiguous, a lot will depend not only in the genuine commitment of parties to effectively leverage their discretion to domesticate the Protocol, but also on the outcome of relevant ongoing negotiations in other venues, especially those identified here. In addition, the role of non-parties to the CBD (and of course the Protocol), in particular the US is also crucial for the future success of the Protocol. This fact is recognized in the text of the Protocol.[32] Indeed, delegates to Nagoya were faced with a clear choice: to abandon six years of hard negotiations or to trade compromises to produce a Protocol text that only a few are likely to view – in ICTSD's characterization – as anything more than a masterpiece of ambiguity.

Summation of the state of progress

To their credit, less developed countries and the world's indigenous peoples and their allies have prevailed in placing TK on the front burner of the new knowledge economy. They have done so, in part, by exploiting the value of their genetic resources and knowledge to pressure the extant intellectual property jurisprudence. That pressure, which is galvanized in multiple and overlapping regimes, constitutes part of the global governance dynamic in the intellectual property system. It has resulted in ongoing attempts to re-evaluate the perceived equity gap at the intersection of intellectual property and biotechnology that has occasioned an uneven distribution of the benefits of new technologies, especially biotechnology. This trend is associated with the phenomenon of biopiracy, that is, the unidirectional transfer of genetic resources and related innovations to developed countries usually at the expense of the custodians of local biocultural knowledge (Mgbeoji 2006).

It is instructive that most of these responsive strides are more evident in national and regional efforts by less developed countries that constitute genetic resources "haves." In contrast, there is an apparent reluctance on the part of developed countries that are genetic resources "have-nots" to embrace, at national and international levels, a new thinking on intellectual property's intersection with biotechnology and TK.[33] At various forums where the intersection of intellectual property and TK is negotiated, most developed countries are disinterested (if not reluctant) participants. Although the Nagoya Protocol is silent on intellectual property and on TK in the textual articulation of its objectives in Article 1, it essentially recognizes the association of TK with genetic resources as an important basis for ABS. Hence, for many less developed countries, despite their occasional bluff during the Nagoya negotiations, a failure would have been a bitter setback for them and a victory, of sorts, for developed countries.

Consequently, it would now be imprudent to underestimate the influence of less developed countries and indigenous and local communities in shaping the global constitutive process. So far, they have been instrumental in opening the TRIPS Agreement to development scrutiny, as evident in the Doha Declaration on TRIPS and Public Health and its aftermath. They have exploited the CBD processes, advancing the international accommodation of indigenous biocultural knowledge, as evident in the emergent jurisprudence on ABS – they have advanced their cause in the milestone represented by the Nagoya Protocol to the CBD. Recently, they have pushed a Development Agenda onto WIPO that has the potential to shift issues of development from the periphery to the core of several strategic regimes and institutions.

Similarly, opposition to these advances from the developed countries is real and has manifested in various arguments designed to counteract progress toward opening up intellectual property jurisprudence to scrutiny. Often, the opposition takes the form of regime politics. Developed countries deflated initial pressure from their less developed counterparts to amend the TRIPS Agreement to accommodate protection of TK so that its illegal exploitation could be subjected to a strong TRIPS sanctions regime and the latter's enforcement mechanism. Many developed countries were inclined to re-channel issues around TK to the then newly established WIPO-IGC, envisaged as a forum for debate with a prolonged and doubtful potential for concrete outcomes. However, in retrospect, given the impact of the WIPO-IGC so far and the potential of its continued work, that expectation may have been unrealized.

Developed countries have not hidden their discomfort with the CBD and its processes, which are perceived as having emboldened indigenous and local traditional communities and genetic resource provider countries. Also, inevitable regime proliferation as an inherent feature of the multifaceted character of TK has left less developed countries weaker. Stronger states benefit from regime proliferation or forum shifting in relation to weaker ones (Braithwaite and Drahos 2000; Helfer 2004; Krasner 1983; Yu 2007b: 16).[34] Commenting on the developed countries' preference for regime proliferation in the recently concluded negotiation on the Nagoya Protocol, Chee Y. Ling of the Third World Network observes that "[f]or many years developed countries have been resistant to the calls of developing countries for a single legally binding international agreement to deal with access and benefit sharing. Their preferences ranged from voluntary guidelines to an 'international regime' comprising legally binding and non-legally binding instruments (but not a single agreement)" (Ling 2010).[35] While that approach has merit given the complex nature of subject matters implicated in ABS, not many disagree that the strategy of "'forum management' in relation to genetic resources issues and TK protection might be more effective than indulging in forum shopping" (Dutfield 2006b: vii).

Finally, the lack of a global consensus over the adoption of disclosure of origin rules, or its more practical version, "proof of legal acquisition"[36] of genetic materials, into intellectual property jurisprudence is owed to strategic opposition by developed countries. In the politics of ABS, intellectual property and indigenous knowledge, developed countries are inclined to have ABS regulated by specific national governments.[37] But the asymmetric power relations between national governments and their indigenous communities, on the one hand, and less developed country providers and developed country users of genetic resources, on the other, cast a cloud over the prospect that a national regime alone would be able to optimize the interests of indigenous and local communities and provider countries. It is instructive that the Nagoya Protocol preserved several years of individual countries' national experiences on ABS, including existing contractual arrangements insofar as they do not run counter to the CBD's and the Nagoya Protocol's objectives.[38] Yet the Protocol came about because of the imperative for an international instrument that provides a stronger global legal framework for binding ABS.

Beyond the aforementioned highlights of the politics of ABS, developed countries and users of genetic resources have several other counter arguments that are not necessarily lacking in merit or driven by an intention to undermine the ABS movement. Some of the arguments are often canvassed at international forums; others are advanced elsewhere by the multifarious defendants of developed and industrialized countries' positions on the issues at stake. First, the subject of equitable ABS is generally perceived as an irritation and an imposition of an accountability regime on the biotechnology industrial complex in regard to their dealings with genetic resources. Most developed countries, notably the US and Japan, oppose the disclosure of origin as imposing an undue burden on the patent system. They argue that the patent system is not designed to address concerns about equity, and that disclosure of origin could constrain research and innovation.

Second, arguments are often made regarding the practical hurdle of resolving disputes over "source" and/or "origin" of genetic resources or TK, which may or may not be mutually exclusive. Determining the origin or source of genetic resources, as well as associated TK, is, for many practical purposes, an inexact science. A third closely related argument is that given the multiplicity of claimants to TK, and the nuanced and subtle distinctions between one form of knowledge and the other, especially in relation to translation into biotechnological innovation for patent application, it is hard to know who should be entitled to benefit. Arezzo (2007), Brown (1998) and Yu (2008c) collectively affirm these sentiments. Yu captures them as follows:

> [D]etecting the use of genetic resources can be difficult, time consuming, and technology intensive. Researchers may also "find that a bioactive ingredient has a medical use different from that suggested by the original collectors"; such varied use "is by no means unusual because traditional plant remedies may be effective within the framework of a society's own understanding and yet fail the efficacy standard of Western medicine."
>
> (Yu 2008c: 465)[39]

A classic illustration of this point is the subtlety in the association of a specific plant genetic resource, such as the Hoodia cactus, with appetite suppression in indigenous circles and the subsequent application of the same insight to transform Hoodia cactus into an anti-obesity compound via scientific or pharmacological research by second comers. Although the relationship between appetite suppression and obesity may seem obvious after the fact, it is not necessarily so before the fact, especially in the context of two different epistemological experiences or platforms. One knowledge form may pave the way or lift the other onto a breakthrough and, yet, technically, the result could be justified as a standalone innovation. The Nagoya Protocol does not seem to have a direct solution for this situation its innovation provision for dealing with genetic resources in transboundary situation notwithstanding.[40] Indeed, it is hardly a straightforward exercise to determine what is meant by or, what is the scope of TK associated with, "genetic resources."

Fourth, rightly or wrongly, the uncritical cooptation of genetic resources and TK into the intellectual property framework has the potential to exclude or restrict access to valuable knowledge forms against not only second comers, but also holders of TK. Such a state of affairs could shrink the public domain, accelerating its enclosure and ultimately stifling innovation in traditional and other contexts. While the basis on which most genetic resources and associated TK are considered to be within the public domain in intellectual property jurisprudence remains questionable, a wholesale and uncritical immersion of TK forms into private proprietary realms can also be equally damaging to their sustainability. This raises age-old concerns about the need to rethink or stem the tide of propertization of culture, cultural elements, shared symbols and heritage (Brown 1998; Coombe 1991, 1998).

Fifth, opponents of a progressive regime of access maintain that, often, the contributions of TK and the value of genetic resources to biotechnology and other industrial endeavors are exaggerated and romanticized. Since the 1970s, scientists have continued to advance the science of gene manipulation. In 2010 – some 40 years later – they announced the creation of a synthetic cell, albeit not from scratch (Callaway 2010). However, this re-enforces the promise of synthetic and combinational chemistry, genomic, proteomic devices and RNA inferences, which, they argue, provide a more viable pathway to drug discovery than "enthno-bio-prospecting" or natural products-driven research. Finally, the oft unrivalled "cultural, intellectual and jurisprudential diversity" of indigenous peoples and local communities present an intimidating, even insurmountable, challenge to a global harmonized regime for protection of T/IK in diverse contexts.

All these arguments are tenable and have merit. But they are hardly conclusive and are easily assailed by counterarguments. However, they underscore the tenor and character of the tensions undergirding contemporary debate and policy elaborations within the multifaceted regimes at the intersection of TK *strictu sensu* in the global governance of intellectual property. In the next chapter, we explore that intersection with a focus on TCEs/EoF and ICH, and within the broader rubric of cultural heritage analysis.

Notes

1 References omitted.
2 "Enclave territories" refers to colonies from where the European settlers did not withdraw, such as Canada, Australia and most of the South American continent. "Non-enclave territories" refers to the majority of present-day less developed countries in Africa, the Indian sub continent, parts of Asia and elsewhere, where colonialism formally ended with settler withdrawal and formal proclamation of independence.
3 See WIPO (2008).
4 Binkert argues that some traditional knowledge is held as sacred and that for holders of such knowledge, "financial reward is not an incentive for seeking [IP] protection."
5 Footnote omitted.
6 Footnote omitted.
7 See Articles 3 and 15 of the CBD.
8 See Article 1(h) of the UNESCO Convention on the Protection and Promotion of Diversity of Cultural Expressions, 20 October 2005. 2440 UNTS. Available online: http://unesdoc.unesco.org/images/0014/001429/142919e.pdf (accessed 15 December 2010); see also Articles 11 and 12 of the Convention for the Safeguarding of the Intangible Cultural Heritage, 17 October 2003. 2368 UNTS 3. Available online: http://unesdoc.unesco.org/images/0013/001325/132540e.pdf (accessed 15 December 2010).
9 See Article 1 of the ICH Convention.

10 It must be mentioned that even during the colonial period, pockets of secular and religious thinkers, notably two Spanish Catholic clerics of the Dominican Order, Francisco Vitoria and Bartolome de las Casas, questioned the colonial mistreatment of indigenous peoples and affirmed in their works the essential humanity of Indians. See Anghie, A. (1996) "Francisco Vitoria and the Colonial Origins of International Law," *Social and Legal Studies* 5: 321; see also Sanders (1983).

11 Emphasis added.

12 Quoting Anaya 1996: 49–50 and Wiessner 1999: 100.

13 Named after its author, Ecuadorian diplomat Jose Martinez Cobo. The Cobo Report itself owes its existence to a little known 1970 UN interim report on racial discrimination written by Augusto Willensen Diaz, which acknowledged that the concept of racial discrimination did not fully capture the gamut of issues relating to indigenous peoples, and insisted that indigenous peoples' issues should have a place in the agenda of the UN, a vision that was realised through the Cobo Report and its aftermath.

14 This draft version of the Declaration is available online: http://www.unhchr.ch/huridocda/huridoca.nsf/%28Symbol%29/E.CN.4.SUB.2.RES.1994.45.en (accessed 15 December 2010).

15 Also known as the United Nations Conference on Environment and Development (UNCED).

16 Available online: http://www.unep.org/Documents.Multilingual/Default.asp?document id= 78&articleid=1163 (accessed 15 December 2010).

17 Available online: http://www.unep.org/Documents.Multilingual/Default.asp?document id=52 (accessed 15 December 2010).

18 Officially titled: Non-legally binding authoritative statement of the principles of global consensus on the management, conservation and sustainable development of all types of forests, UN Doc A/CONF.151/26 (Vol. III) (14 August 1992). Available online: http://www.un.org/documents/ga/conf151/aconf15126-3annex3.htm (accessed 15 December 2010).

19 Emphasis added; see also WIPO 2009: Annex I, 4.

20 These are part of the list of specific examples of TK in WIPO 2009: Annex I, 5.

21 The Forum has continued to play an advisory role in regard to the Economic and Social Council on indigenous peoples' issues. Increasingly, the subject of indigenous knowledge as a critical development issue, assumes pivotal status in the UNPFII's agenda.

22 The FAO operates in respect of TK especially through the implementation of the International Treaty on Plant Genetic Resources for Food and Agriculture, which provides the framework for implementation of domestic legislation for the protection of farmers' rights and the conservation of biological diversity.

23 UNCTAD has aligned with the various initiatives of the CBD, the WIPO and the WTO-TRIPS Council. Its Commission on Trade in Goods and Services is active in the promotion of fair and equitable sharing of the benefits of TK and the strengthening of TK holders through globally sanctioned forms of *sui generis* systems for the protection of traditional knowledge. As part of its Traditional Medicine Strategy, the WHO encourages cooperation with the WIPO and UNCTAD "to support countries in developing their capacities to protect knowledge or traditional medicine and medicinal plants (Coombe 2009: 253, n. 39).

24 In regard to instruments and institutional dealings with TCEs, see also the earlier version of the Gap Analysis (WIPO 2008).

25 See Articles 3, 15(1) of the CBD. For similar provisions, see Article 11 of ICH Convention and Articles 1(h), 2(2) of the Cultural Diversity Convention.

26 The IGC in its revised Draft Gap Analysis (WIPO 2009a), notes that the protection of TK includes both physical protection and their further development, arguing that further development falls within both WIPO's general and IGC specific mandates to warrant a link with WIPO's Development Agenda.

27 It is tenable that the language and general provisions of the Protocol, such as references to taking "appropriate" and "effective" measures, do not exclude such discretionary measures regarding, for example, disclosure of source/origin of genetic resources and associated traditional knowledge.

28 The Protocol came into effect in February 2011.

29 For example, while Article 31 of DRIPS affirms indigenous communities' rights of ownership and control of their knowledge, most of the text of the Protocol subjects indigenous ability to exercise those rights to the discretionary legislative authority of states.

30 E.g. Articles 8, 10, 11, 13, 14, 17, 29 and 31.

31 Association of TK with genetic resources is quite limited to the extent that TK mainly thrives with indigenous and local communities' engagements with ecological and biological resources, a reality that is not fully captured by the concept of genetic resources.

32 Article 24.

33 In the realm of genetic resources, the distinction between "haves" and "have-nots," corresponding to providers and users, is not sustainable, as it is hardly rigorous for a number of reasons. For example, key developing countries, such as China, Brazil, India and South Africa, are not only providers of genetic resources, they are also increasingly becoming key users of those resources because of the rise in their national competences in biotechnology. Also, as biotechnology focuses on genetic resources other than plants and animals, such as marine genetic resources, countries hitherto perceived to be bio-resource "have-nots," such as Canada, may become bio-resource "haves."

34 Yu argues that while Helfer insists that forum shifting is a strategy employed by both weak and strong states, Drahos and Braithwaite are convinced that "only the powerful and well resourced states" indulge in the game.

35 At the Cali meeting of the CBD Ad Hoc Open-ended Working Group on ABS, Canada insisted that the idea of an international regime is one that includes existing international legal instruments and processes relating to ABS and other relevant international agreements and protocols that may be hammered out in the future.

36 Dutfield (2006b: xi) argues that "[p]roof of legal acquisition seems to have promise as an effective measure in terms of encouraging equitable processes and outcomes to the economic benefit of both providers and users," since much TK and many genetic resources may be learned or acquired without any physical presence in the countries of origin or source.

37 Because developed countries tend to capitalize on regime proliferation, which has potential for contradictory outcomes, it is hard to make any general claim regarding their preferred strategy on any given issue, or to assume that there is always a deliberate strategy. In the diplomatic world of international negotiations, interests often are rotated and negotiated on values that are often less than permanent. For example, Ling (2010: 3) observes in regard to the negotiations on an ABS Protocol that "developed countries want internationally binding standards to secure access [to genetic resources], while developing countries say that access is a matter of national legislation and the primary objective of the protocol is benefits sharing to correct past and continuing injustice."

38 Article 1.

39 Footnote omitted.

40 Articles 10 and 11.

7 Traditional cultural expressions, expressions of folklore, and tangible and intangible cultural heritage

As part of indigenous and local communities' attempts at cultural reclamation, they denounce the conventional focus of discourses and policies on traditional knowledge (TK), which emphasize tangible and physical renditions of culture, including cultural relics. They press for the constructive inclusion of other open-ended cultural categories referred to variously as folklore, or expressions of folklore (EoF), traditional cultural expressions (TCEs), intangible cultural heritage (ICH), expressive culture, etc., into international law relating to TK. In so doing, indigenous and local communities and other stakeholders are able to influence the international lawmaking process to accommodate a more expansive outlook on their knowledge forms beyond the commercial or merchantable undertone of the prevailing emphasis on cultural monuments or relics of cultural significance.

The renewed interest in expressive aspects of culture assists in entrenching the essentially inchoate bifurcation of the knowledge of indigenous and local communities. On the one hand is TK *stricto sensu* which, as we saw in the previous chapter, focuses on those TK forms relating to genetic or biological resources. On the other is TCEs, the focus of the present chapter. The previous chapter demonstrates that the increased limelight on traditional biocultural knowledge is enhanced, in part, as a consequence of the advent of modern biotechnology. To some degree that trend is correlated with regard to developments in the realm of TCEs/EoF. Akin to the role of biotechnology in shining the light on traditional biocultural knowledge or TK *stricto sensu*, recent developments regarding TCEs/EoF and ICH are exacerbated or enhanced by their interaction with digital technology. As will shortly become clearer, pursuant to the long historical evolution of TCEs/EoF and intellectual property, recent developments demonstrate, in more elaborate ways, the intricate regime dynamics that mediate these complex subjects as a constitutive and important feature of the global governance of intellectual property.

The significance of expressive culture relies, in part, on the fact that:

> TK [in a general sense] is not simply a collection of intangible [or tangible] items or features *simpliciter*; rather, it is the integration of these features into a cultural system: past, present, and future; secular, or religious; useful or aesthetic; generally known or observed selectively (such as, for example, secret

ritual) within the community. It is not static knowledge. Creativity and innovation is continuing and current.

(Howel and Ripley 2009: 225)

Lending her support to the significance of folklore or TCEs as important complements of TK, Coombe notes: "If TK [i.e. *stricto sensu*] is most commonly used to refer to knowledge, innovations and practices associated with properties and qualities of the environment [e.g. traditional biocultural knowledge relating to genetic resources], the category of folklore [or TCEs] applies to a wider range of traditional cultural forms" (Coombe 2009: 260). The inclusion of such a wider range of traditional cultural forms has progressively shaped the evolution of the nascent field of cultural property and its broader and more recent transformation, i.e. cultural heritage law, to accommodate both the tangible and intangible aspects of culture. Cultural heritage encompasses cultural property and, transcends the narrow juridical confines of the latter to incorporate a bundle of rights and complex relationships that revolve around physical and non-physical expressions of culture. Under this matrix, cultural property, as an aspect of cultural heritage, "embodies a far more complex system of relationships" (al Attar et al. 2009: 319), hence it is being subsumed into the idea of cultural heritage. As Erica-Irene Daes has noted, "[f]or indigenous peoples, heritage is a bundle of relationships, rather than a bundle of economic rights" (1993: para 26; Harding 1999: 303), with which intellectual property rights are primarily concerned.

Those relationships include sophisticated limits on alienability of rights, issues of communality and sacredness, aspects of sociocultural values, etc., outside the narrow economic logic of intellectual property rights. The accommodation of a vast range of traditional cultural forms, including "language, literature, music, dance, songs, mythology, rituals, customs, handicrafts, architecture, and other arts, etc.," (UNESCO 1989) under cultural property and cultural heritage has a significant conceptual ramification. Among other considerations, it makes it easy to link TK in its broad construct with the sociocultural identity of its custodians as aspects of their self-determination, human rights and cultural survival, perhaps in a manner that complements similar linkages in the context of traditional biocultural knowledge and practices.

The elasticity of the expressive aspects of culture in their various overlapping depictions reflect nuanced but important shifts in the regime dynamics at the intersection of TK and intellectual property in global governance. As a clear extension of the intricate bundles of sociocultural relationships of indigenous peoples and traditional communities, expressive culture and several forms of indigenous cultural heritage transcend intellectual property rights. As such, the trade frameworks, represented by the WTO and the TRIPS Agreement and, in some ways, the WIPO, constitute equivocal regimes for the protection of expressive culture. Consequently, in regard to the latter, there is a marked shift toward UNESCO, the principal UN agency with a direct mandate on cultural matters.

However, given the symbiotic relationship between culture and knowledge, UNESCO and its counterpart, WIPO, have historically maintained a sometimes tense partnership and, usually, share overlapping jurisdictions over the intersections of their mandates on the governance of culture and knowledge. In addition to WIPO (already identified in previous chapters), other international regimes or institutions, such as the CBD, FAO, WHO, UNCTAD and UNDP, are involved in the genetic resources realm of TK. It is a mark of the innate difficulty or frustration over the fragmentation or bifurcation of TK that such regimes and institutions are also actors in shaping the law and policy regarding the wider range of indigenous cultural rights and heritage, including, of course, aspects of TCEs or expressive culture. As actors, they contribute to the horizontal regime interactions that straddle TK in the global governance of intellectual property. WIPO has long been involved with UNESCO in matters bordering on their intersecting mandates as easily exemplified through various programs, notably (for our present purposes) the joint 1982 WIPO-UNESCO Model Provisions for National Law on the Protection of Expressions of Folklore Against Illicit Exploitation and other Prejudicial Actions (the Model Provisions),[1] to which we shall return later. In the meantime, before evaluating the contemporary regime constellation over TCEs/ EoF and aspects of tangible/intangible traditional cultural heritage, a selective historical perspective on the treatment of cultural property or tangible objects of cultural heritage would be helpful.

Historical privileging of tangible cultural heritage

Similar to the case of intellectual property, early international instruments relevant to cultural property and related rights were concluded at a time when the present-day less developed countries and many of the world's indigenous peoples were fully under colonialism and did not participate in negotiating them. In addition to this legitimacy deficit, the instruments tended to construe cultural property or objects of cultural heritage as tangible and scripted, as opposed to intangible or unscripted. Although not directly dealing with cultural property, two instruments that came out of the Hague Peace Conferences, namely, Conventions II and IV (1899 and 1907, respectively) on the Regulations Concerning the Laws and Customs of Wars on Land, represent an important example of this trend.[2] Both Conventions (at Article 56) prohibit the seizure, destruction and deliberate damage to institutions, historic monuments, works of arts and science. They prescribe (at Article 27) restraint in the siege and bombardment of buildings, including those dedicated to religion, arts, science, etc. (Kono 2009: 10, 11).

Without regard to the impact of conflict on intangible culture and the social processes for the latter's production, similar instruments, including the fairly recent ones negotiated under the auspices of UNESCO, focus on the protection of artefacts and cultural sites during armed conflict and in peace time. These newer instruments, which are discussed later in this chapter, include the Convention for the Protection of Cultural Property in the Event of Armed Conflict (1954 Hague Convention) and the Convention on the Means of Prohibiting and Preventing the Illicit Import, Export, and Transfer of Ownership of Cultural Property, 1970.

With the exception of Haiti, Liberia and Ethiopia none of the present less developed countries was independent when the first sets of Hague Conventions were negotiated. Striking, but hardly surprising, none of the colonial powers that negotiated the treaties in the late 19th and early 20th centuries considered addressing colonialism's impact in order to call attention to its devastating effects, which included the plunder of all forms of cultural property, the disruption and outright destruction of relationships and undergirding social processes of knowledge and cultural production in indigenous and various colonized traditional societies. Nonetheless, colonialism is, perhaps, the greatest historic assault on indigenous cultural heritage, tangible and intangible. Its impact on expressive or forms of intangible culture derives mostly from colonialism's radical truncation and disruption of the processes of sociocultural cohesion vital to the production of knowledge among the colonized peoples. For example, in Canada, colonialism supervised a systematic suppression of native languages through the infamous Canada Indian residential school program (Annett 2001; Monture 1990).

Similar to the early Hague Peace Treaties, two fairly recent but important treaties, the Convention on the Means of Prohibiting and Preventing the Illicit Import, Export and Transfer of Ownership of Cultural Property (1970), and the Convention for the Protection of the World Cultural and Natural Heritage (1972) (or the World Heritage Convention), on balance, emphasize physical aspects of cultural heritage – the latter Convention more so than the former.[3] Specifically, the World Heritage Convention limits its scope to the protection of tangible or physical cultural symbols, such as buildings, monuments and sacred sites of cultural significance under the heads of natural features, geological and physiographical formation and natural sites (Articles 1 and 2). It totally neglects immaterial or intangible aspects of culture. This omission creates a wide gulf between TK and international law, inadvertently triggering a counter-regime response as this opens up the struggle to protect folklore or expressive culture and other forms of intangible cultural heritage through different institutional forums within the international lawmaking process.

Blurry boundaries of convenience: tangible and intangible culture

For the avoidance of doubt, the focus of these instruments on physical or tangible aspects of cultural heritage is not misplaced. What is worrisome is any approach that tends to perpetuate the impression that there is a clear-cut boundary between tangible and intangible cultural heritage (Oguamanam 2009c: 361). The blurry line between the two is borne out by the fact that, like the chicken-and-egg riddle, in the complex process of creativity, the tangible is often inspired by the intangible, and vice versa. Put slightly differently, "intangible cultural heritage is manifested in tangible forms" (van Zanten 2004: 39). Moreover, in terms of protection, "materials that are considered tangible cultural heritage can also be protected as intangible cultural heritage" (Yu 2008c: 444). Some go as far as suggesting that demarcating the tangible from the intangible is an artificial exercise with a doubtful practical value, as it makes little sense. In this regard, it is relevant to note that "among many local and indigenous communities, particular land, mountains, volcanoes, caves and other tangible physical features are endowed by intangible meanings that are thought to be inherently tied to their physicality" (Kurin 2004: 70). Similarly:

> [T]he knowledge base of an indigenous and local community flows naturally from the inherent intellectual process in their dynamic relationships with natural phenomena, ecological forces, the environment, cultural properties or artefacts and other natural and artificial creations and objects. Knowledge is generated through constant interaction between these entities. In indigenous circles, there is a unity of purpose between the creator or maker of a thing and the process of creation, and the resulting object. Knowledge is generated through constant interaction between these entities. Every object is a domain of knowledge in a holistic order; the tangible is fused with the intangible and vice versa.
>
> (Oguamanam 2009c: 361)

Reservations over the dichotomization of tangible and intangible heritage do not necessarily change or render nugatory the emphases of some treaty texts on either tangible or intangible cultural heritage. As an important and empirically manifest facet of TK, the protection of tangible or physical cultural symbols, including natural heritage sites, are crucial for global cultural diversity and socio-cultural development and sustainability. Physical or material cultural heritage, in both their human creative and natural manifestations, are jewels of human civilization and embodiments of invaluable information in need of safeguarding. Traditionally, along with human-made cultural relics, natural heritage, in its various forms, including natural features, physical, biological, geological and physiographical formations, constitute the fulcrum of tangible cultural heritage.

Natural heritage is naturally occurring physical, biological or other formations with outstanding universal appeal in regard to science, conservation, aesthetic and other indeterminable considerations.[4] Unlike their human-made counterparts or movable cultural relics, for the most part, the bulk of natural heritage is immovable. Far from being objects of human creativity, they are sites of limited human creative intervention. However, they inspire various forms of human creativity and related endeavors. The largely immovable nature and low profile of natural heritage in the human creative enterprise makes the issue of their protection or safeguarding, mainly a matter of illicit commercial transaction and other forms of exploitation and, consequently, less contentious, at least, from the intellectual property point of view.

Besides natural heritage, other forms of movable physical cultural heritage, or what Peter Yu refers to by the open-ended term, "cultural relics," raise similar but distinct tensions at the intersection of TK and intellectual property rights within the discourse of the global governance of intellectual property. Distinct because "at first glance, cultural relics and intellectual property are protected differently . . . [and]

[d]ue to the tangible nature of cultural relics, cultural patrimony laws tend to focus on retention, repatriation, preservation, and authentication" (Yu 2008c: 446–7). Because developing or less developed countries are generally considered rich in cultural relics, they are cultural relic "haves." As source nations for cultural relics, they have a vested interest in their protection, more so than their developed nation counterparts' interest in unhindered access to them. As Yu (2008c: 451) notes:

> Those who argue for weaker protection of cultural relics – or for a broader view of world cultural heritage – are often those who do not have a lot of protectable treasures within their country. Those who argue for stronger protection, by contrast, are likely those who have objects worth protecting in their country.[5]

In terms of similarity, the tension raised by tangible cultural relics at the intersection of TK and intellectual property rights is easily compared to the role of biopiracy in the flow of genetic resources from less developed and developing countries, which we explored in the last and earlier chapters. Like biopiracy, illicit trade in cultural relics constitutes a substantive pathway for the unidirectional movement of cultural treasures from the "have" nations to the "have-nots," a trend that contributes to the crisis of equity in the global knowledge economy. Unlike most cases of cultural appropriation, the flow of cultural relics from source nations is exacerbated, perhaps, less by intellectual property and more by globalization's invigoration of the intense appetite and market for the exotic through new networks of culture facilitated by the technologies of globalization. Again, Yu provides a cogent assessment of the global trend in the one-way traffic of movable tangible cultural heritage or cultural relics, tying it with different kinds of organized criminal enterprise of contemporary global concern. Quoting Patty Gerstenblith and INTERPOL, Yu (2008c: 451–2) writes:

> [R]ecent revelations concerning the functioning of the art market and the acquisition of antiquities with unknown origins now demonstrate that the looting of archeological sites is a well-organized big business motivated primarily by profit. One would even make an argument that the problem of illicit trade in cultural relics far exceeds that in pirated and counterfeit goods [. . .] INTERPOL estimates the value of the illicit trade in art and artefacts worldwide each year at $5 billion – only the illegal markets in drugs and arms are larger.[6]

Consequently, it is questions of authentication, repatriation and preservation that mainly characterize the nature of dealings with cultural relics, even as their unidirectional transfer via illicit trade is not only enhanced by technologies of globalization, but also exacerbated by globalization's cultivation of trade and appetites for the exotic.

Thus, the vehement demarcation of tangible and intangible cultural property yields a disjointed and unpredictable outlook on the interaction between TK and intellectual property in the global governance analysis. Not the least of the reasons for this is the fact that such demarcation may be inevitable as it helps us to understand the different or specific legal and policy questions, which do not necessarily overlap. This is why it is not surprising that a recent, more progressive approach emphasizes the fusion of the tangible and intangible in the bundle of social processes and relationships that undergird the production of knowledge and culture in indigenous and local communities. This approach provides for a more robust appreciation of the intersection between TK and intellectual property in global governance. As already noted, it embraces the idea of cultural heritage over cultural property. In a way, it helps to redirect attention to the longstanding conceptual struggle around folklore, EoF or TCEs, and creates space to spotlight the importance without necessarily undermining the practical limitations of a holistic outlook on cultural heritage.

Resisting exclusion: TCEs/EoF in global intellectual property policy

By now, it is clear that TCEs/EoF have many manifestations, the immaterial forms, for example, verbal, musical, dance, acrobatics, physical art, and the material ones, such as carvings, textiles, drawings and physical expressions of creativity. Unfortunately, because of the cultural hierarchies of power that characterize intellectual property's relationship with TK, folklore is traditionally excluded from the corpus of conventional intellectual property. Consequently, diverse forms of expressive culture in indigenous and local communities are open to enclosure and appropriation by external interests or second comers. Ironically, by transforming, decontextualizing and manipulating TCEs/EoF to suit their narrow economic or mercantile ends, second comers or those that have the wherewithal to make such transformations are able to consolidate their proprietary enclosure of them by means of new technologies and intellectual property rights without regard to other sensitivities such as the sacred, religious and deep sociocultural roots and symbolisms associated thereto.

The failure of the conventional intellectual property system to accommodate folklore spurred the less developed countries to initiate the 1967 Stockholm Diplomatic Conference for the revision of the Berne Convention to allow for the possibility of granting protection to expressions of folklore. Even so, it has been mainly under the auspices of WIPO and UNESCO that efforts aimed at finding an appropriate modality for the intellectual property aspects of folklore has remained a permanent feature of the global governance of culture and knowledge. The foundation for the current wave of such efforts appears to have been laid following the World Forum on Folklore in 1997, a product of the collaboration between WIPO and UNESCO. In part, the forum was organized in response to the 1989 UNESCO recommendation for the safeguarding of traditional culture and folklore, and generally pursuant to the longstanding imperative for a viable international framework to protect traditional culture and folklore.[7] According to Denhez (1997), the importance of the search for such a framework, which predates

UNESCO, is premised on the realization that "the growing threat of ethnocentrism to world peace, makes the international conservation, exchange and appreciation of intangible heritage more important to international and intercultural under-standing . . . [and] that these expressions of traditional culture and folklore play a significant role in the overall UNESCO objective of a 'culture of peace.'"

As folklore "haves," the majority of less developed countries have shown strong commitment, at national and international levels, to a pragmatic solution to the intellectual property protection of folklore. However, their developed country counterparts – rightly or wrongly perceived as folklore "have-nots" – consistently stall on this matter. Also, while the less developed countries seek a *sui generis* approach to folklore, many in developed countries favor resolving the question within the conventional but unaccommodating intellectual property framework (WIPO 1998). Simply, at the core of the difficulty straddling TCEs/EoF and intellectual property are the putative communal character and the perceived lack of individual originality of folkloric creations, which contrast sharply with the individual originality and author-centric focus of copyright. This conceptual deadlock, the gap question between TCEs/EoF and copyright, is a critical aspect of the intersection between TK and intellectual property in global governance, especially as it relates to expressive culture or ICH.

In 1982 a Committee of Governmental Experts jointly convened by WIPO and UNESCO adopted the Model Provisions. This provided a template on which creative domestic legislative or regulatory regimes could advance the protection of folklore in accordance with the contingencies or experiences of specific national systems. Shunned and disdained by developed countries, the Model Provisions could not move the folklore initiative toward a stronger and wider international or global regime. At regional and national levels among less developed countries, this template was patronized for the protection of complex and diverse artistic heritages under the banner of folklore.

Despite the Model Provisions' widespread impact on the domestic laws of some less developed countries, the international community has, since 1982, remained reluctant to embrace the idea of an international legal regime for the protection of folklore. The debate continues, but has been sporadic, being engaged at opportune turns, occasionally through WIPO, UNESCO, and various UN agencies. For instance, in the wake of the development of new technologies, it took mere pressure from a powerful bloc of right owners and allied industry interests for the majority of developed countries to agree to a responsive adjustment of international copy-right law to accommodate the internet-based delivery of copyrighted work via the 1996 WIPO Copyright Treaty (WCT) and the WIPO Performances and Phonograms Treaty (WPPT). Spirited resistance from less developed countries resulted in the semblance of balance and the no-victor-no-vanquished outcome reflected in these instruments.

Aside from rethinking the concept of fixation for the purpose of copyright, the WPPT adopts an industry-serving definition of "performers" that reluctantly includes an oblique reference to those engaged in the expressions of folklore. Accordingly, performers are defined as "actors, singers, musicians, dancers, and other persons who act, sing, deliver, declaim, play in, interpret, or otherwise perform literary or artistic works or expressions of folklore" (Article 1). Contrasted with the lack of concrete outcome after several decades of international legal engagements over protecting folklore or expressions of folklore and its latter-day rendition, TCEs, the short time and space within which this twin set of so-called WIPO internet treaties were negotiated leads one to, at least, a couple of conclusions. First, less developed countries and indigenous and local communities' lack of political clout is one of the main reasons there is slow progress in tackling the challenge which folklore poses for intellectual property. Second, and perhaps more important, developed countries are reluctant to make a genuine and realistic commitment to address the gap question between intellectual property and folklore.

The WIPO-IGC

Meanwhile, the latest incarnation of the debate for an elaborate international legal regime for the protection of TCEs/EoF has come about through the more broadened work of the WIPO Intergovernmental Committee on Intellectual Property and Genetic Resources, Traditional Knowledge and Expressions of Folklore (WIPO-IGC). Apparently obvious from its self-descriptive title, the Committee represents the tension between a holistic and bifurcated or fragmented approach to TK (i.e. in regard to genetic resources) and TCE/EoF (i.e. in regard to expressive culture). In historical context, the WIPO-IGC is an extension of WIPO's late 1990s' initiative under the then Global Intellectual Property Issues Division (GIPID). The GIPID itself was a strategic institutional response by WIPO to adjust to both the biotechnology-driven imperative to protect genetic resources and associated TK, and pressures from less developed countries eager to cash in on the promise of the Convention on Biological Diversity (CBD), especially in regard to its provisions dealing with TK.

GIPID's objectives included positioning WIPO "to identify and respond to the new challenges for the intellectual property system of globalization and rapid technological change" (Coombe 2009: 257; Dutfield 2001: 273). The core global intellectual property issues identified and championed by GIPID included TK innovations and the protection of folklore. The highpoint of its tenure was perhaps the result of its 1998–1999 global fact-finding missions (WIPO 2001) which it commissioned to examine the intellectual property needs and expectations of TK holders. Published in April 2001, the study, which has since provided the hub for policy direction on TK at the WIPO and elsewhere, adopts a comprehensive view of TK in its diverse domains, including expressions of folklore. It concludes that:

> From WIPO's perspective, "expressions of folklore" are a subset of and included within the notion "traditional knowledge." "Traditional Knowledge" is, in turn, a subset of the broader concept of "heritage." "Indigenous Knowledge," being the traditional knowledge of "indigenous peoples," is also a subset of "traditional knowledge." As some expressions of folklore are created by indigenous persons,

there is an overlap between expressions of folklore and indigenous knowledge, both of which are forms of traditional knowledge.

(WIPO 2001: 26)

In the previous chapter, we highlighted the conceptual quagmire in the semiotics, and even semantics, around T/IK. Nonetheless, it is worth noting that WIPO's adoption of a literal approach to indigenous knowledge may be misleading or, at best, just convenient. But the essence of this remark in regard to the bounded and inextricable nature of TK in relation to its other multivalent and sometimes competing depictions, which often take a diversionary dimension in analysis, should not be lost. The WIPO fact-finding mission was a fieldwork initiative based on very broad consultations with TK holders in 10 regions of the world.[8] The term "TK holders" is used by WIPO in reference "to all persons who create, originate, develop and practice traditional knowledge in a traditional setting and context." WIPO goes a step further to clarify that "[i]ndigenous communities, peoples and nations are traditional knowledge holders, but not all traditional knowledge holders are indigenous" (WIPO 2001: 26).

The inclusive and legitimate manner in which the fact-finding process was conducted helped WIPO in no small measure to reclaim its dwindling influence on TK in general, while opening a new chapter of interaction between WIPO and TK holders. Rosemary Coombe suggests that "it was the consequence of these [GIPID fact-finding] consultations that the concerns of indigenous peoples entered into WIPO's sense of its mandate and indigenous delegations began to participate in its international deliberations" (Coombe 2009: 257). Following pressures from less developed countries to seek redress in the WTO for the TRIPS Agreement's omission of TK in its text, the opportunity came for WIPO when the developed countries deflated such pressure by channeling issues relating to TK to the WIPO (Dutfield 2006b; Oguamanam 2006a).

GIPID's transformation into the IGC then came when, in 2000, before the release of the report of the fact-finding mission, the Twenty-Sixth General Assembly of the WIPO Member States established the IGC. The latter was designed as a forum for WIPO member states to explore three agenda items, namely, access to genetic resources and benefit sharing, protection of TK, innovations and creativity, and protection of expressions of folklore (Oguamanam 2006a: 212). Since its inception, the WIPO-IGC appears to have been mindful of the circumstances of its evolution and the complex regime intersections implicated in its mandate, especially in relation to the CBD, UNESCO, FAO, etc. As a necessity, rather than a choice in the pursuit of its mandate, the WIPO-IGC strives to collaborate with these and other relevant institutions and organizations. Understandably it adopts a consolidated and complementary outlook on TK and TCEs.

As expected, the WIPO-IGC has risen above the initial opposition and censorship of the US which barred its predecessor (the GIPID) from engaging in norm-setting or treaty-making activities on the subject of TK (Halewood 1999: 986).[9] Like the CBD's COP, in addition to influencing several national regimes on various aspects of TK, 10 years after it was established, the WIPO-IGC has raised and continues to revise key elaborate working documents, including those articulating the objectives and principles underling the protection of TCEs/EoF and TK. Others include Draft Provisions for the Protection of Traditional Cultural Expression/Folklore (TCEs), Draft Provisions for the Protection of Traditional Knowledge (TK) Against Misappropriation and Misuse, Revised List of Options for the Protection of Genetic Resources, the Draft Gap Analysis on the Protection of Traditional Knowledge, and the Draft Gap Analysis on the Protection of Traditional Cultural Expression. Consistent with the tradition of the GIPID, the WIPO insists that the IGC "draft provisions draw on a wide range of community, national and regional experiences, and have been developed over several years by and in consultation with member states, indigenous peoples and other traditional and cultural communities, civil society organizations and a range of other interested parties" (WIPO 2010a). WIPO justifies the presentation of the draft in two instruments, one dealing with TCES, another with TK, as a response to:

> [T]he choice made in many cases to address distinctly the specific legal and policy questions raised by these two areas. However, the draft materials are prepared in the understanding that for many communities these are closely related, even integral, aspects of respect for and protection of their cultural and intellectual heritage. The two sets of draft provisions are therefore complementary and closely coordinated. Taken together, they do form an holistic approach to protection. This reflects existing practice at the international and national levels. Some jurisdictions protect both TCEs and TK in a single instrument. Others use a range of laws and instruments to address the two areas distinctly. Some laws also address specific aspects of these two areas, such as biodiversity-related TK or indigenous arts and crafts. The draft objectives and principles acknowledge those diverse choices and facilitate a holistic approach.
>
> (WIPO 2010a)

Mindful of the norm-setting recommendations of the WIPO Development Agenda, the Thirty-Eighth Session of the WIPO General Assembly renewed the IGC's mandate for the 2010–2011 budgetary biennium to continue its work and undertake "text-based negotiations with the objective of reaching agreement on a text of an international legal instrument which will ensure the effective protection of genetic resources, TK and TCEs" (WIPO 2009a: Annex II), building on work already done by the committee.[10]

A notable transformation in the character of the current developments is a forced shift from developed countries' censorship of a norm-setting approach that would result in a binding treaty on TK and related matters. This pressure has also created a notable paradigm shift in the self-serving arguments by developed countries since 1967 that effective protection of folklore must emanate from the national initiative of individual countries (WIPO 1998), a position that scuttled the potential global impact of the Model Provisions and similar initiatives on folklore. Like the protection of cultural relics, so it is with TCEs and TK (relating to genetic resources), namely, that "it is no longer possible to rely on national measures alone, [and that] global solutions are increasingly needed" (Yu 2008c: 451).

UNESCO

A full picture of the growing international law and policy program on TCEs emerges when we match WIPO's recent but growing interest in the area alongside the equally recent, even simultaneous activities on cultural heritage at UNESCO. In 2003 delegates to UNESCO from 190 countries adopted the United Nations Convention for the Safeguarding of Intangible Cultural Heritage (ICH Convention), which came into effect in 2006. The general objectives of the Convention include safeguarding, ensuring respect, and promoting awareness and international cooperation regarding ICH of communities, groups and individuals. In Article 1, the Convention defines ICH in an elaborate way, highlighting aspects of the features and processes of its production as follows:

> [T]he practices, representations, expressions, knowledge, skills – as well as the instruments, objects, artefacts and cultural spaces associated therewith – that communities, groups and, in some cases, individuals recognize as part of their cultural heritage. This intangible cultural heritage, transmitted from genera-tion to generation, is constantly recreated by communities and groups in response to their environment, their interaction with nature and their history, and provides them with a sense of identity and continuity, thus promoting respect for cultural diversity and human creativity. For the purposes of this Convention, consideration will be given solely to such intangible cultural heritage as is compatible with existing international human rights instruments, as well as with the requirements of mutual respect among communities, groups and individuals, and of sustainable development.

In addition to this detailed definition, in Article 2, the ICH Convention identifies four principal sites for the manifestation of ICH: oral traditions and expressions, including language; performing arts, social practices, rituals and festive events; knowledge and practices relating to nature and the universe, and knowhow associated with traditional craftsmanship.

The ICH Convention reflects the progressive effort aimed at using TCEs or folkloric aspects of TK both to complement existing regimes on cultural heritage and to underscore the sociocultural relationships, aspects of cultural identity, sustainable development and self-determination implicated in cultural heritage. Although the Convention is fairly recent, it evolved over three decades: 1970s– 2000. The build-up to the Convention can be linked to the time of drafting and the period following the adoption of the 1972 World Heritage Convention where the need was felt, and various actions were taken toward the protection of ICH in the wake of the apparent neglect of the intangible aspect of cultural heritage by the then new convention (Kono 2009: 11).[11] Essentially, the ICH Convention is a crystallization of the earlier attempts, mainly through soft laws,[12] to plug the gap in the emphasis of prior international legal initiatives on cultural rights on tangible cultural relics or heritage. According to one commentator, "[s]ince its adoption, cultural heritage no longer remains associated to physical works [. . .] but also with songs, oral epics, and poems, woodcarvings and other traditional cultural expressions and practices" (Kono 2009: 12).

Strategically, the ICH Convention focuses more on the preservation and sustainability of communities, peoples and social processes that generate and sustain intangible culture,[13] rather than the economic processes, exemplified by intellectual property rights, that often devalue and ultimately commercialize ICH. As will become clearer later, the focus of the ICH Convention has implications for the dialectical relationship that TK and its holders or custodians have with modern intellectual property rights. In Article 2(2), the Convention defines safeguarding as: "[M]easures aimed at ensuring the viability of the intangible cultural heritage, including the identification, *documentation, research, preservation, protection, promotion, enhancement, transmission,* particularly through formal and non-formal education, as well as the revitalization of the various aspects of such heritage".[14] We shall return to this point later.

Two years after the ICH Convention, the UN concluded another treaty with significant consequence for ICH under the auspices of UNESCO. In 2005 the UNESCO General Conference adopted the Convention on the Protection and Promotion of Diversity of Cultural Expressions (the Cultural Diversity Convention or CDC), which came into force in 2007. The CDC builds, in part, on the 2001 UNESCO Universal Declaration on Cultural Diversity (UDCD). Both the UDCD and the CDC regard culture "as the set of distinctive spiritual, material, intellectual, and emotional features of a society or a social group and [. . .] encompasses, in addition to art and literature, lifestyles, ways of living together, values systems, traditional beliefs" (UDCD: Preamble, para 5).[15] According to the UNESCO, the rationale for the CDC issues from UNESCO's mandate in regard to the promotion of "fruitful diversity of cultures" and a "free flow of ideas in word and image" (UNESCO 2007: 2).

In terms of their text and overall objectives, more than the ICH Convention, the CDC and UDCD – the latter inherently more so – are essentially aspirational in their outlook. The CDC is said to be "more interested in providing a platform for nurturing a long-term dialogue than achieving [any] short term results" (Mezey 2007: 2013; Yu 2008c: 435). A summation of the objectives of the two instruments points to the promotion and optimization of the value of the diversity of cultural expressions, especially in less developed countries, and sustainable conditions for cultural interaction and exchange, as well as equitable transmission of the benefits of cultural diversity in an atmosphere of respect and solidarity among peoples and cultures globally.[16] In spirit and letter, the two instruments and the ICH Convention recognize the sovereign rights of states in regard to making laws and policies for the promotion of the diversity of cultural expressions within their jurisdictions.[17]

In contrast to the aspirational tone of the CDC and the UDCD, the ICH Convention is more pragmatic. It draws developments in UNECSCO closer to the more practical tenor of the works of the CBD (in regard to ABS) and WIPO-IGC (in regard to TCEs, TK and genetic resources) in terms of shifting the character of the debates and policies around TCEs and ICH toward norm- or standard-setting outcomes. In reference to the ICH Convention, UNESCO enthuses that following the commitment of state parties to take steps to safeguard their intangible heritage and to establish one or more inventories of ICH in concert with relevant communities and groups, the CDC completes UNESCO'S standard-setting initiative "to preserve the intangible heritage and aims to safeguard oral traditions and expressions thereof (including language as a vehicle for the intangible heritage), performing arts, social practices, rituals and festive events, knowledge and practices concerning nature and the universe, as well as know-how linked to traditional crafts" (UNESCO 2006).

Linking expressive culture to sustainable development

Another important overarching feature of the recent legislative and policy instruments at UNESCO (as epitomized by the ICH Convention, CDC and UDCD) is the link the instruments have made between ICH and sustainable development and their adoption of a shared understanding of ICH as the "main-spring of cultural diversity and a guarantee of sustainable development" (ICH Convention: Preamble para 2).[18] Without mincing words, the CDC makes reference to "the need to incorporate culture as a strategic element in national and international development policies, as well as in international development co-operation, in taking into account also the United Nations Millennium Declaration (2000) with its special emphasis on poverty eradication" (CDC, Preamble para 6). The emphatic linking of ICH with sustainable development strikes a chord with the new thinking in the global governance of intellectual property. As earlier noted, by virtue of this new thinking, less developed countries have confronted WIPO with the imperative for a Development Agenda which includes sustainable development within the broader matrix of development discourse.

Collectively, the recent initiatives at UNESCO provide a platform for advancing the culture of solidarity, healthy exchange, sustenance and the optimization of a rich diversity of global cultural expressions. In the shared visions that undergird the three instruments in review, these broad objectives are to be attained within a framework in which the promotion of cultural diversity is complementary to the goals of cultural, economic and sustainable development. Not surprisingly, all the instruments make references to a free flow of ideas; constant exchanges, diffusion, and interactions between cultures; and the deployment of diverse media to facilitate the flourishing of cultures within societies in cognizance of the principles of equitable access, openness, balance and sustainable development.[19]

The globalization factor

At UNESCO, these fairly new initiatives around ICH occur within the context of the dialectics of globalization and the latter's amorphous relationship with new technologies and in the context of prevailing apprehensions over the rapid decline of ICH and the need to stem that tide. Specifically, the ICH Convention is necessitated in part by the recognition that:

> [T]he process of globalization and social transformation, alongside the conditions they create for renewed dialogue among communities, also give rise as does the phenomenon of intolerance, to grave threats of deterioration, disappearance, and destruction of the intangible cultural heritage, in particular owing to a lack of resources for safeguarding such heritage.
>
> (ICH Convention, Preamble para 4)

Similarly, part of the reason for the adoption of the CDC is the recognition that "while the processes of globalization, which have been facilitated by the rapid development of information and communication technologies, afford unprecedented conditions for enhanced interaction between cultures, they also represent a challenge for cultural diversity, namely in view of the risks of imbalances between the rich and poor countries" (CDC, Preamble para 19). Still, on the same point, the UDCD is justified, in part, as an act of recognition that: "[T]he process of globalization, facilitated by the same rapid development of new information and communication technologies, though representing a challenge for cultural diversity, creates the conditions for renewed dialogue among cultures and civilizations" (UDCD, Preamble para 9).

There is little doubt that "throughout the world, intangible cultural heritage is threatened with decline, even with extinction" (UNESCO 2006, para. 7). There is also little doubt that the forces of globalization, including new technologies, present both a challenge and opportunity for the safeguarding of ICH. Similarly, not many will doubt that a wider diffusion of culture is critical to the sustainability of cultural diversity. However, because intellectual property or, indeed, knowledge and cultural protection are about stakeholders, a form of protection for the "haves" (Yu 2003: 402, 2008c: 451), the pressure for the protection of ICH is coming mainly from less developed countries. Writing in reference to cultural relics, Yu notes that it is "no surprise that source nations make up the majority of the membership of the UNESCO Convention on the Means of Prohibiting and Preventing Illicit Import, Export and Transfer of Ownership of Cultural Property" (Yu 2008c: 451). Similarly, on a more general note, less developed countries and indigenous and local knowledge stakeholders tend to assume activist roles in the overall work of the UNESCO, as it is the special United Nations agency with a direct mandate on the promotion and protection of culture. The UNESCO has since remained the hub for international law and policy on culture. To date, it takes credit for seven key "binding international legal instruments focusing on four areas of creative diversity and endeavours, namely cultural and natural heritage, movable cultural property, intangible cultural heritage and contemporary creativity" (UNESCO 2007: 3),[20] which were concluded under its auspices.

The context for the appropriation of TCE/EoF

Delegates to international negotiations are often reminded that "protection of expressions of traditional culture is not supposed to be a 'South–North' issue since each nation has cherished traditions with corresponding cultural expressions" (Ficsor 2005). The push to safeguard ICH and to promote cultural diversity is consequently presented as a win–win for "haves" and "have-nots." But that is more of an aspirational ideal than the present reality in which cultural diffusion between "haves" and "have-nots" remains mainly in disequilibrium at best, or is unidirectional, at worst.

Like biological diversity, the majority of the world's cultural diversity is an integral aspect of the complex and constitutive diversities prevalent in less developed countries and in indigenous and local communities. Whether in regard to cultural relics or ICH, the traffic of cultural property flows from "haves" to "have-nots." Never has there been such intensity in the flow of that traffic as in the manner exacerbated by globalization and its companion technologies, by which the capacity of the "have-nots" for cultural appropriation has been strengthened. As evident in the preambles of recent UNESCO treaties and non-treaty instruments, including the ICH Convention, the CDC and the UDCD, it is hardly surprising that current global apprehensions over cultural extinction and the alarm over the prevalence of categories of ICH in need of urgent safeguarding, target or spotlight the declining cultural treasures of the most vulnerable indigenous and local communities. Not much concern arises in regard to the cultural treasures of the developed world. The rapid uptake and transfer of the cultural treasures of indigenous and local communities through globalization's technologies of appropriation and transformation, notably, bio- and digital technologies, is at the core of these threats of extinction.

The subtext for the new movement toward the protection of cultural diversity implicates the control of new digital technologies and, by extension, intellectual property rights. The developed countries' quest for access to ICH and cultural diversities of the less developed world has extended the logic of equitable access, openness and balance to the cultural property realm. The safeguarding measures identified by ICH are also appropriation measures. As indicated earlier, they include *documentation, research, preservation, protection, promotion, enhancement* and *transmission*. Without question, these measures are effectively advanced by digitization, or by digital technologies and their complementary internet platforms.

For instance, in virtually all domains and processes of knowledge and cultural production, cultural preservation and cultural custodianship, digital technology as a technology of collection, recording, documentation, research, manipulation and transformation and information management, remains indispensable. However, when digital technology and digital media are deployed in the arena of hitherto unscripted TCEs/EoF and various forms of ICH and tangible cultural creations, the degree of ownership of the intellectual content of both the original creations and the resulting transformations becomes a hotly contested subject matter. In that contest, the holders of TCEs/EoF are fundamentally disadvantaged. This is not only because the *raison d'être* for the protection or safeguarding of TCEs/EoF and aspects of ICH transcend the narrow commercial logic of intellectual property, but also because technology's role in the fixation of expressive culture involves a process of alteration or manipulation that moves the latter to another sphere of creativity or transformation in which TK is held in contempt and in juridical disdain or disadvantage. Wend Wendland (2009: 80) captures the problem in the following observation:

> The ethnographic collections of museums and other institutions often include invaluable, even unique record of ancient traditions, lost languages and community histories which are integral to indigenous people's identity and continuity. Yet the intellectual content of such materials is often not owned by indigenous peoples but rather by the people who "made" the film, sound recording, photographs and manuscripts.

While new technologies, including digitization and other applications, have immense potential for the preservation of valuable TK in many ways that were not possible in the past, their attraction as "very valuable processes of preserving traditional cultural expressions can trigger concerns about their lack of legal protection against misappropriation and misuse" (Wendland 2009: 80). Without a doubt, the objectives of the emergent regime for the global preservation of ICH, especially via the 2003 ICH Convention, can be advanced by new technologies.

Yet, rampant occurrences of cultural appropriation, for example, in "ethnomusicology" or the application of technological recording devices for the uptake of traditional or folkloric music or other renditions for commercial purposes – "ethnographic recording" – as symbolized in the cases of the Ami "Song of Joy," "Return to Innocence,"[21] Deep Forest, and "Where Have All the Flowers Gone?", like those in traditional medicine and agriculture, such as turmeric, neem, ayahausca, enola bean, cow pea, etc., demonstrate the dialectical role of technology in regard to TK. The Ami "Song of Joy" involved a sample recording of a live performance that included the voices of members of the Ami, Taiwan's largest indigenous people. The recording was made by a French cultural organization, which then licensed the sample to ethno-techno artist, Enigma, whose song "Return to Innocence," included the licensed Ami folk sample. The song was a major commercial success that sold over five million copies and was licensed for use in the 1996 Atlanta Olympics (Arewa 2006b: 177; McLeod 2001). It took a lawsuit and an out-of-court settlement deal, before the defendant recording companies were able to formally thank the Ami, to acknowledge their contribution, and undertook to give them credit in the future releases of the "Return to Innocence." The defendants also established a foundation with the settlement proceeds.

Deep Forest also involved the use of technology to appropriate samples of indigenous peoples' musical art in a commercial recording by second comers. Deep Forest, the eponymous debut album of a French ethno-techno group, sold more than two million copies, was nominated for a Grammy and was listed top on the album chart of its time. Essentially, Deep Forest "was a techno-house dance rhythm album created in 1992 that fused digital samples from Ghana, the Solomon Islands, and African pygmies" (Arewa 2006b: 177). Despite being a commercial success, there was no evidence that any benefit arising from the commercialization of the folk songs extended to the local musicians sampled.

Finally, "Where Have All the Flowers Gone?" by America's renowned folksinger, Pete Seeger, was inspired by Russian folk song, "Koloda Duda." Unlike the case of the Ami "Song of Joy" and the Deep Forest album, "Koloda Duda" "had been recorded and made publicly available for safeguarding and promotional purposes, and it was therefore accessible to composers and performers such as Seeger. Seeger has since arranged for some royalties from the song to go to the national folk song archives in the Moscow library" (Wendland 2009: 82). Similar experience trailed Zulu music legend, Linda Solomon, whose leading album, "Mbube,"[22] reflects an unparalleled originality and creative fusion of ancient Zulu music tradition and performances with sprinkling of modernity, convention and individual talent. Mbube is said to be the first African music recording to sell up to 100,000 albums (Broughton et al. 2006: 358). Mbube went on to become a musical genre the origin of which is credited to Solomon. Through its several adaptations worldwide, the Mbube melody became a pivotal spinoff of hugely successful musical and performances portfolio. Notably, Pete Seeger's American folk group, the Weavers, reworked Mbube into the hit song, "Wimoweh". The latter's adaptation in the song "The Lion Sleeps Tonight" and several others have remained the stuff of several successful movies and musicals (Wassel 2009). Meanwhile, Linda Solomon died poor and was the least to benefit from a musical and creative revolution he authored until some recent out-of-court settlement between his estate and a music company regarding rights to "The Lion Sleeps Tonight" (Dean 2006). In other sites of traditional creativity, such as handicraft, Ghana's experience with its traditional Kente cloth is instructive. Traditionally made Kente textile design is a national symbol of that West African country's unique traditional handicraft, legendary creativity and cultural heritage. Unfortunately, Kente designs are now mass produced globally, especially in Asia and US often with the use of state-of-the-art technologies resulting in Ghana's potential loss of control over its sacred traditional heritage (Asmah 2008).

Beyond ethnomusicology, there is no dearth of incidence of technological interventions in the transformation of various folkloric and non-folkloric creations: stories, sounds, carvings, ceremonial materials relating to indigenous peoples, sacred and non-sacred communal creations of ritual and non-ritual significance, etc. These technological interventions enhance the delivery of the world's diverse cultural richness by way of various digital and related media. They have proved useful for educational, promotional and various purposes that advance the goals of cultural diffusion, preservation and safeguarding. However, these earlier examples from ethnomusicology demonstrate the up- and downsides of new technologies for the appropriation and safeguarding of TCEs/EoF.

For example, "Return to Innocence" and Deep Forest demonstrate the ease with which technology supervises cultural appropriation. This trend is further aggravated by the largely ad hoc unregulated, opportunistic (albeit democratic) forms of amateurish user-driven creativity via contemporary social networking media, such as YouTube and Facebook. A snap of a button on a digital camera, or a few minutes' video clip of hitherto unscripted or undocumented cultural experience, can set off contestation on a global scale as to the ownership of accidentally created cultural treasures via, sometimes, overlapping horizontal interactions of digital media among equally diverse participants, stakeholders and even ordinary enthusiastic witnesses to cultural transformation. Contrariwise, Seeger's experience with "Where Have All the Flowers Gone?" highlights the potentially beneficial role of technology for safeguarding ICH and for the promotion of cultural diffusion in a balanced and mutually beneficial context.

The deployment of new technologies by museums and other cultural institutions, including researchers and private individuals, especially those involved in the reconfiguration and (re)adaptation of ICH through, for example, the ethnographic recording of oral culture, including traditional music and other forms of cultural expressions, has provided immense opportunity for appropriation and reinterpretation of TK, even its desecration. Yu notes that "[w]hile globalization, the digital revolution and increasing commodification of information have enriched the lives of many traditional communities, these factors have equally threatened these communities by allowing for instantaneous distribution of knowledge and materials that are sacred or intended to be kept secret" (Yu 2008c: 455).

The complicity of digital technologies and the internet as technologies of globalization in the appropriation of culture has also yielded a transformation in "[t]echnological, political, legal and socio-cultural landscape within which cultural institutions, communities and other stakeholders operate" (Wendland 2009: 85). According to Wendland, contestation around the role of these technologies has led to changes in the dynamics of the relationship between museums and other institutional repositories of culture and the communities, allowing the latter to exert control on how they are represented, and the former to play the humbler role of custodians as opposed to owners of cultural properties. This may not be quite as settled as it sounds. Rather, there is a realization that technology's role in (re-) negotiating the stakes around the cultural transformations of the globalization era is enhanced by intellectual property to serve the ends of the appropriation of TK. Consequently, it is urgent to strike a balance in the marriage of technology and intellectual property to accommodate the objective of safeguarding expressions of folklore and ICH.

TCEs and other forms of ICH represent a problematic site for negotiating the dialectics of intellectual property rights at the intersection of technology and local knowledge. For instance, while most expressive culture or expressions of folklore, such as songs, incantations, stories, folk riddles, "sayings of the wise," etc., are treated under intellectual property law as falling within the public domain, recording or other forms of technology-induced fixation of those creations gives rise to intellectual property claims by people making the recording or other acts of fixation. A renewed focus on culture, ICH and on cultural diversity in the postmodern legal and policy environment has turned ICH into profitable assets, especially in light of new technological interventions. But that has yet to translate into visible benefits to indigenous and local custodians or holders of ICH. Cultural industries, services and goods have continued to grow, accounting for between 4 and 6% of the global gross national product. In the US, the cultural goods trade for 2002 got to the US$60 billion mark and will continue to increase. However, less developed countries are only able to lay claim to less than 1% of the world export of cultural goods (Wendland 2009: 86).

The interplay between intellectual property and technology in the context of TCEs/EoF and other forms of ICH is more likely to lead to the appropriation of TCEs/EoF than to its safeguarding. In addition, in the digital era, the ease of increase in the derivative uses of expressive culture, such as traditional songs, dance, performance and stories are easily facilitated by intellectual property. In order to realize the objectives of the new international regimes to protect and safeguard expressive culture and other forms of ICH, TK holders must be surefooted stakeholders in both the intellectual property and technological processes implicated in the transformations of culture in the new knowledge economy.

Safeguarding TCEs and intellectual property protection

Most of the emphasis of recent initiatives at UNESCO on expressions of folklore and diverse forms of ICH appear to focus on the issues of safeguarding, preservation, conservation, dissemination, diffusion, access, etc., with a view to optimizing the benefits of global cultural diversity. For the most part, these objectives turn on the social processes and overall environment for the production of knowledge, including expressive culture and other integral aspects of the cultural practices of peoples and communities. Also, safeguarding is concerned with preserving cultural practices, including cultural symbols or relics; it is not necessarily limited to the associated intellectual exercise or content generated and engaged in the process of cultural production.

Simultaneously, many holders of TCE/EoF and various forms of ICH are interested in intellectual property protection of their traditional cultural heritage. The essence of such protection is to vest stakeholders with the necessary legal powers, including those of exclusion, and the determination of the terms of access for second comers, with the aim to optimize the exploitation of their traditional creative endeavors. Put differently, "[i]intellectual property rights are temporary privileges over intellectual creations and other intangible goods, such as literary works, music, songs, inventions [. . . they] determine who holds exclusive rights to commercial exploitation of such expressions of ideas or other results of human and intellectual and creative labour" (Kono 2009: 11–12). Thus, the safeguarding of expressive culture and ICH is hardly the same thing as intellectual property protection. However, intellectual property protection is a significant aspect of the mutually reinforcing processes of safeguarding and preserving cultural heritage. Economically empowering holders of TK by intellectual property is perhaps one of the best guarantees for the sustainability of the knowledge and cultural production process and, ultimately, their preservation.

Nonetheless, the mutually supporting roles of intellectual property protection and the safeguarding of expressive culture are hardly absolute. In many indigenous cultures, the pure economic focus of intellectual property is antithetical to other more lofty objectives of TK and associated cultural practices. Also, in many indigenous and local communities where the process of knowledge generation is essentially communal, intellectual property signifies the privatization of knowledge in the public domain, a trend that, some argue, is potentially counterproductive to the communal processes of innovation, creativity and the free exchange of knowledge and information. Finally, under conventional intellectual property, most forms of TCEs are considered part of the public domain and are open to appropriation by all comers.

The foregoing qualifications of the mutually reinforcing relationship between the safeguarding of ICH, and intellectual property protection, do not undermine the significance of intellectual property for indigenous and local community stakeholders in regard to TCEs/EoF and ICH. One of the ramifications of the ICH Convention is that the international community has demonstrated a willingness to go beyond well-founded reservations in some circles over the feasibility of documentation and other forms of fixation of culture, especially folkloric or expressive culture. The conceptual and practical objections to documentation as a form of fixation notwithstanding (Oguamanam 2009c: 370–2; Yu 2008c: 467), it is a safeguarding measure of choice that had found favor at regional and national levels even before the ICH came into effect. Not many would dispute the centrality of documentation as a safeguarding measure on its own exclusive merit, but also as one that is pivotal to other safeguarding measures identified in Article 2.3 of the ICH Convention.[23] Many indigenous and local communities and less developed countries have bought into the idea of the documentation of ICH as a pragmatic defensive strategy against the appropriation of ICH and traditional biocultural knowledge and resources through the intellectual property process.

Unfortunately, despite providing for documentation and various safeguarding devices with capacities for fixation, the ICH Convention is silent on how intellectual property rights that arise from the various safeguarding measures are negotiated. It only makes a passing reference to intellectual property under Article 3(b) thus: "Nothing in this Convention may be interpreted as: affecting the rights and obligations of State Parties deriving from any international instrument relating to intellectual property rights or to the use of biological and ecological resources to which they are parties." In essence, despite the lofty ideals enunciated in the preamble to the ICH Convention, the instrument failed to address or, at least, provide a direction on the critical question regarding intellectual property rights over the results of various safeguarding measures. The lack of a specific or an elaborate provision on how to manage intellectual property rights arising from several safeguarding measures, especially inventorying and documentation, listed in the ICH Convention is a fundamental flaw and a missed opportunity. It can be argued that the Convention is not an intellectual property instrument. Yet it is an important instrument to create a practical and effective link between the safeguarding measures sanctioned under it and the potential intellectual property rights resulting therefrom.

The complex research processes dealing with TCEs involve myriad disciplines and innumerable players. All of them are stakeholders with varying degrees of interest in the intellectual property rights attached to the processes and their results. For instance libraries, archives, museums, other cultural institutions, and researchers from diverse disciplinary backgrounds, including photography, anthropology, medical geography, and lately information technology, are active players in both the safeguarding and the appropriation of TCEs of indigenous and local communities. Often in these activities, sacred and non-sacred information are obtained by unauthorized, or even authorized, persons or professionals at individual levels, or through these institutions in circumstances that leave oblique the terms under which the information are obtained. Further, dealings with vital information, or diverse forms of cultural expressions, also involve some forms of translation, transformation, transmission, adaptation via digital and various other media. In these murky waters of complex institutional and disciplinary interactions and convergences, holders of TK, especially TCEs, are at the crossroads of numerous dynamic initiatives for documentation and digitization, including, of course, corresponding intellectual property ramifications for their ICH in which multiple stakeholders are implicated.

A proactive role for indigenous and local communities

In order to effectively realize the objectives of the new international legal and policy schemes on TCEs and ICH, indigenous and local communities must be active players in the processes of complying with the safeguarding measures, especially those relating to documentation and the deployment of the technologies utilized for it. In so doing, they would consolidate their stakes in the intellectual property rights that rise from effectuating any such safeguarding measures. For too long, indigenous and local communities and their knowledge and cultural systems, have been objects of curiosity and research, some of them bordering on the predatory:

> Indigenous materials were often collected by non-Indigenous researchers in the absence of informed consent of Indigenous communities; the informational content of the collections might be sacred or confidential and subject to restricted use under customary laws; the legal status of such materials under intellectual property law is often unclear [. . .] while there is a lack of information available to Indigenous peoples regarding the existence and location of collection items relating to themselves, Indigenous peoples and communities have a growing interest in being directly involved in recording, presenting and representing their own cultures.
>
> (Wendland 2009: 85)[24]

Active involvement of indigenous and local communities in these forms of safeguarding measures would help their cause in mitigating the inequities of the global knowledge economy in many ways. First, indigenous and local community involvement, for example, in the documentation of TCEs and other forms of their ICH, would transform them from being historical objects of study by second comers, into partners assuming the responsibility to introduce and educate others regarding their culture, knowledge and worldviews. Second, they would be in a position to negotiate the general terms of use, access and the nature of uses permissible for some aspects of TCEs and ICH.

Third, the idea of negotiating terms of use is important given that the sacred aspects of TCEs and ICH transcend some considerations, especially commercial ones, which inform second comers' interests in TCEs and ICH. Closely related to the previous point is that when indigenous and local communities are actively involved in the safeguarding process, they would be in a position to renegotiate the boundaries of the public domain which has been arbitrarily drawn by the conventional intellectual property regime. Most forms of TCE, ICH and cultural practices hitherto perceived as within the public domain would surely come under closer scrutiny with the involvement of indigenous and local communities in the implementation of safeguarding measures. Fourth, if indigenous peoples were effective participants in these measures, they would naturally be in an enhanced position to monitor the location, uses or applications of their cultural treasures in order to ensure compliance with appropriate terms.[25] Finally, the involvement of indigenous and local communities in safeguarding measures, especially those that result in fixation, would enhance their claims to resulting intellectual property, or to being stakeholders in them.

In sum, the active engagement of indigenous and local communities in the safeguarding process requires their exposure, through capacity building,[26] to the various technological arenas, especially the digital and related forms of information technologies associated with operationalizing the measures. As well, the active role of indigenous and local community stakeholders would provide them the opportunity to contribute to policymaking in the relevant research ethics in cognizance of the need for cultural sensitivity in regard to such issues as sacrelization that are not directly recognized under conventional intellectual property.

We have already noted that the CDC, the UDCD and the ICH Convention recognize the rights of states in regard to making laws and policies on TCEs, ICH and other forms of cultural treasures within their jurisdiction. Similarly, the CBD vests member states with the sovereign right to genetic resources within their national boundaries. On the strength of these provisions, and led by India via its traditional knowledge digital library (TKDL) project, many national governments and regional organizations are now directly involved in the documentation and/or digitization of tangible TCEs and ICH. Further, we noted in Chapter 6 that the UN Declaration on the Rights of Indigenous Peoples vests them with the right to control their TK including, of course, TCEs/EoF. Although the latter is a declaration of the UN General Assembly and does not create a binding legal obligation, other instruments and policy documents regarding indigenous peoples interests sanction the involvement of indigenous and local communities in decisions that directly or indirectly affect their cultural identity, including their right to self-determination and sustainable development.

For example, the ICH Convention commits state parties to ensuring the participation of communities and groups that create, maintain, and transmit specific ICH in the establishment of inventories of a group's ICH (ICH Convention, Article 15). Nonetheless, the implication of vesting rights in TCEs, ICH and other forms of cultural treasure on nation states rather than directly in indigenous and local communities is that the latter's growing interest in being directly involved in recording, presenting and representing their own cultures is open to negotiation with nation states with whom, in most cases, they do not necessarily share common interests.

On the surface, vesting states with sovereign rights over genetic resources and other tangible natural and cultural heritage or relics in their territories seems logical. It becomes complicated when we recognize that the boundary between tangible and intangible culture is blurry, more so when regard is given to the fact that the bulk of the creative endeavors that result in identifiable TCEs/EoF and other forms of ICH are extensions of indigenous and local communities' sociocultural identity. An additional complication is that the territorial sovereignty being exercised by some states over indigenous territories and, by extension, over indigenous genetic and natural resources, arose from lingering historical controversies over colonial usurpations of indigenous ancestral territories under questionable treaties and other inchoate political arrangements.

TCEs/EoF: emerging modalities for safeguarding and protecting intellectual property

Obstacles in the way of indigenous and local communities notwithstanding, there is notable and ongoing progress in diverse, including unexpected arenas, for negotiating and streamlining modalities for safeguarding TCEs/EoF and ICH and the issues of intellectual property associated with them. As a matter of research ethics and corporate best practices, most research and cultural industry practitioners at institutional, individual or group levels are inclined to address concerns over access, safeguarding and intellectual property incidental to their dealings with traditional cultural heritage. With the continued increase in internet-enhanced networked surveillance by NGOs, IGOs and other groups that focus on equitable and respectful dealing in cultural heritage and intellectual property, few cultural industry practitioners, artists or motion picture and recording industries are willing to deliberately risk the damning public relations backlash that would be generated by their exploitation of indigenous and local communities, as exemplified by the reaction to Deep Forest and "Return to Innocence."

Similarly, many cultural institutions, such as museums, libraries, archives and relevant professional bodies like the International Council of Museums and the Society for Ethnomusicology, have now "developed valuable intellectual property related codes, protocols, policies and standard agreements relating to the safeguarding of, access to, ownership of and control over cultural heritage" (Wendland 2009: 90). In addition to the more elaborate work of the WIPO-IGC, these and related initiatives have attracted WIPO's interest, as evident in a number of that organization's directly related engagements on the issues of safeguarding, access, control and intellectual property regarding cultural heritage.

For example, WIPO has commissioned experts to conduct surveys of existing resources, practices and protocols and standard agreements relating to the safeguarding of, access to, ownership of and control over cultural heritage. So far, work on this project covers developments in South America, the South Pacific, Bulgaria, France and India.[27] This project is integral to the WIPO-commissioned case studies that have since generated a complementary database comprising examples of codes, guides, policies, protocols and standard agreements relating to the recording, digitization and dissemination of ICH, with an emphasis on intellectual property issues.[28] These two WIPO initiatives aim at the identification and promotion of best practices for negotiating intellectual property and safeguarding measures that advance the objectives of balance and equity in dealings connected to cultural heritage.

Both the survey and database programs are part of the broader WIPO initiative that come under the title of the Creative Heritage Project for Strategic Management of Intellectual Property Rights and Interests (CHP), the goal of which is to generate and audit resources for developing best practices in dealing with cultural heritage. Aside from encouraging and often sponsoring workshops on digital and other preservation devices for cultural heritage and incidental intellectual property rights, to date, the WIPO CHP has generated important policy documents, capacity building, and training and practical guidelines covering the intersection of safeguarding and intellectual property issues over aspects of cultural heritage in specific contexts or dealings, such as traditional handicrafts, intellectual property management by museums, libraries and archives, and intellectual property management relating to art festivals, and community cultural documentation.

One important aspect of the CHP is WIPO's involvement in capacity building which targets indigenous and local communities under the cultural community documentation initiative. To this end, WIPO has established a hands-on training program for indigenous and local communities and museum staff of less developed countries in partnership with two American institutions, the American Folklife Centre (AFC) and the Centre for Documentary Studies (CDS). According to WIPO's Director and the Acting Head of WIPO's Traditional Knowledge Division, Wend Wendland: "[T]his program will provide communities and museum staff with hands-on training in documentary techniques and archival skills necessary for effective community-based cultural conservation. Staff from WIPO will provide intellectual property training and WIPO will provide the community with a basic kit of audio and video equipment for its own use after the training" (Wendland 2009: 88). In December 2010 WIPO released CHP's commissioned study titled, "Intellectual Property and Safeguarding of Traditional Cultures: Issues and Practical Options for Museums and Libraries." According to its authors, the publication draws on information from WIPO commissioned surveys worldwide and builds on preceding works and prior body of publications[29] designed to illuminate "legal and ethical IP questions that arise for cultural institutions, especially with a focus on collections comprising intangible cultural heritage and traditional cultural expressions" (Torsen and Anderson 2010: 6).

Primarily, WIPO focuses on the promotion of intellectual property. Specifically, Wendland (2009: 95) avers that "WIPO's work on traditional cultural expressions is concerned with the protection of traditional cultural expressions, as intellectual properties." As such, WIPO's apparent engagement in the downstream side of access, ownership and control of cultural heritage requires a more critical scrutiny so that it does not unduly advance only the intellectual property aspects of cultural heritage at the expense of the complex issues implicated in indigenous and local communities' interest in their cultural heritage, especially their expressive culture. Given the new vista on development at WIPO, courtesy of the Development Agenda, the organization's commendable involvement in this downstream endeavor presents an opportunity for collaboration with UNESCO and other relevant agencies to explore issues of access, safeguarding, ownership and the control of cultural heritage from a more holistic and balanced point of view.

The importance of WIPO's new interest in safeguarding ICH notwithstanding, most of the initiatives under the CHP and related endeavors are voluntary. They neither derive their life from a binding legal regime, nor have any legal sting. As mentioned earlier, through its IGC (specifically the current negotiation over a treaty text or concrete rules), WIPO has come close to creating a binding legal, albeit *sui generis*, instrument to protect the cultural expressions and folklores of indigenous and local communities. As further noted earlier, the current negotiations at the WIPO-IGC date back to the fact-finding initiatives of the late 1990s. The negotiations have evolved through a process that synthesizes existing law and policy developments on TCEs/EoF, TK and other forms of ICH across diverse jurisdictions. Aside from being review driven, the WIPO-IGC process involves intense multi-stakeholder consultations and the participation of indigenous and local communities, and has helped in exposing the "messy" conceptual challenge around TCEs/EoF[30] and TK *stricto sensu*. At the same time, it is illuminating obstacles that have stood in the way of formulating definitive and comprehensive law and policy on the subjects.

First, the WIPO-IGC has articulated the policy objectives, the general as well as the core principles to undergird the protection of both TCEs/EoF and TK as discernable from national, regional and international practices. Taken together, the objectives and principles marry the main goals of the ICH Convention and the CDC. Generally, they indicate the fused or complementary nature of TK *stricto sensu* and TCEs. Essentially, the objectives and principles revolve around value recognition, promotion of respect, advancement of conservation, safeguarding, preservation and ethics, anti-appropriation measures that preclude unauthorized intellectual property claims, community empowerment, support for traditional innovation systems, and customary laws dealing with traditional innovations. Others include promotion of fair and equitable access via prior informed consent, transparency and certainty of procedures and protocols for balanced cultural exchanges, and advancement of cultural diversity. Second, the WIPO-IGC has outlined, through the Draft Gap Analysis, the obligations, provisions and pre-existing international framework in regard to the protection of TK and TCEs/EoF, the gaps existing in relation to it, and offering some direction on how they could be tackled.[31]

Third, the WIPO-IGC has helped, in no little measure, in setting the boundary for law and policy over an inherently complex subject by identifying the lists of issues in need of determination. They include: the definition of EoF/TK that merits protection; the beneficiaries of such protection; the objectives of the protection (economic/moral); the duration of protection; gaps in the existing intellectual property regimes that require fixing; the nature of illegal activities involving dealings in EoF/TK and their appropriate sanctions; the intersection of national and international regulation; and the proper approach to dealing with foreign TCEs/EoF and TK rights holders or beneficiaries. In very general terms, these lists of issues have since shaped by the deliberations in the WIPO-IGC, and have formed the structure of the WIPO-IGC Draft Provisions on TCEs and TK.[32] Pending the outcome of the ongoing negotiation of a treaty text, the objectives and principles, the lists of issues for determination, and the suggested ways forward arising from the gap analysis are hardly binding. However, because they build on existing best practices, and because they resulted from a process of intense consultation, solicitation of comments, and continued refinements pursuant to feedback, they have provided much needed guidance for the development of law and policy at various national, regional and international levels.

Without understating the different emphases in the texts of the WIPO-IGC Draft Provisions on TCE/EoF and its counterpart document on TK, here, we identify a few common features of the two texts that evolved from the preceding negotiations and which characterize the work of the committee. The common features assist to enhance clarity and forge consensus on hitherto more challenging issues; as well, they underscore the messy, complex and even elusive idea of a common juridical framework for the governance of TCEs/EoF and TK, and aspects of ICH within and outside the intellectual property mode. As explained later, those challenges continue to assail the ongoing negotiation of a "final" treaty text for TCEs/EoF and TK.

First, the two documents reflect the importance of the intersection of TCEs/EoF and TK, and the complementary nature of intellectual property protection and issues of promotion and the safeguarding of TCEs and TK as a matter requiring a holistic policy approach. Consequently the IGC notes that:

> From an IP point of view, which has been the main focus of the work of the Committee, the protection or otherwise of TK forms an integral part of policies concerning the promotion of creativity and innovation, community development and grass-roots knowledge-based commercial activity when this is chosen by communities to form part of their sustainable social and economic development. However, the protection of TK touches also upon other important policy areas. These include the safeguarding and preservation of diverse knowledge systems and the intellectual and cultural heritage of communities; conservation of the components of biodiversity and associated TK and mechanisms for prior informed consent and equitable benefit-sharing; respect

for the rights, interests and claims of indigenous peoples and traditional communities; access to knowledge and scope of the "public domain"; addressing the challenges of multiculturalism; and, the promotion of cultural diversity and the distinctive character of values and beliefs of diverse knowledge systems. As many Committee participants have pointed out, the protection of TK also need to be complementary to and mutually supportive of protection of TCEs as part of an overall holistic approach.

(WIPO 2006a: para. 15)

Second, as per the logic of the foregoing observation, the WIPO-IGC recognizes that its institutional interest in TCEs and, of course, TK is not exclusive. From the outset, the WIPO-IGC mandate required that its deliberations and outcomes be mindful of activities in other forums and not be prejudicial to the pre-existing commitments of states in the areas of TCEs/EoF and TK. Indeed, the WIPO-IGC draft objectives and principles regarding TCEs/EoF and TK were influenced by, and have since influenced regional, national and international efforts for safeguarding TCEs and TK. As opposed to being a one-stop rendezvous for law and policy on TCEs/EoF and TK, the WIPO-ICG notes:

> Indeed, an holistic approach to protection of TCEs/EoF within this broader international context entails recognizing and complementing legal instruments and policy approaches in cognate policy areas such as the UNESCO International Convention for the Protection and Promotion of the Diversity of Cultural Heritage, 2003 and the UNESCO Convention for the Protection and Promotion of Diversity of Cultural Expressions, 2005, and work in other forums such as the United Nations Permanent Forum on Indigenous Issues and the Working Group on Indigenous Populations of the Human Rights Council.
>
> (WIPO 2006b: para. 17)[33]

In regard to TK, the WIPO-IGC makes a similar observation:

> Indeed an holistic approach to protection of TK within this broader international context may entail recognizing and complementing legal instruments and policy approaches in cognate policy areas, such as the recognition, preservation and protection of biodiversity-related TK under the Convention on Biological Diversity, the recognition of farmers' rights and the regime for plant genetic resources under the FAO International Treaty on Plant Genetic Resources for Food and Agriculture, the protection of traditional and local knowledge under the United Nations Convention to Combat Desertification, and work in other forums such as the United Nations Permanent Forum on Indigenous Populations of the Commission on Human Rights.
>
> (WIPO 2006a: para. 17)[34]

Third, the WIPO-IGC attempts to bring some clarity to the issues of intellectual property rights of indigenous and local communities in regard to documentation, recording and other safeguarding measures. We earlier noted that this issue was not addressed by the UNESCO ICH Convention. In this regard, proposed Article 7 of WIPO's Draft Provision on TCEs/EoF requires indigenous people and community and traditional and other cultural communities, who so desire, to notify or register with the designated authority "specific traditional cultural expressions/expressions of folklore [of particular cultural or spiritual significance or value for which a level of protection is sought]" (WIPO 2010b: Article 7). That Article further provides:

> To the extent that such registration or notification may involve the recording or other fixation of the traditional cultural expressions/expressions of folklore concerned, <u>any intellectual property rights in such recording or fixation should vest in or be assigned to the relevant</u> [community] <u>indigenous peoples and communities or traditional and other cultural communities</u>.
> (WIPO 2010b: Article 7(2)(a))[35]

While the draft provisions on TK seem to be silent on this point (WIPO 2010c), a combined reading of several of its provisions, especially proposed Articles 5, 6(1) and 11(2) suggests otherwise. Article 5 pointedly provides that indigenous and traditional communities, or as the case may be, recognized individuals within those communities, should be the beneficiaries of the protection of traditional knowledge. Article 6(1) provides that "The benefits of traditional knowledge to which its holders or custodians are entitled include fair and equitable sharing of the benefits arising out of the [commercial or industrial] use of traditional knowledge" (WIPO 2010c: Article 6). Article 11(2) adds, in part, that "relevant national authorities may maintain registers or other records of traditional knowledge, where appropriate and subject to relevant policies, laws and procedures, and needs and aspirations of traditional knowledge holders" (WIPO 2010c: Article 11).

Fourth, overall, the WIPO-IGC draft provisions recognize other forms of protection beyond intellectual property, the latter being only one of several options for the protection and safeguarding of TCEs/EoF and TK. The draft provisions encourage complementary and non-duplicative efforts in the application of the various options. Consequently, Article 2 of the draft provision on TK (WIPO 2010c) identifies a range of legal measures to protect TK against misappropriation and misuse, including *sui generis* law on TK, intellectual property laws, unfair competition and unjust enrichment laws, laws of contract and civil liability (torts liability for compensation), criminal law, laws dealing with indigenous peoples' interests, fisheries and environmental protection laws and legal regimes on access and benefit sharing, or any combination of these legal categories.

Similarly, Article 10 of the draft provision on TCEs/EoF (WIPO 2010b) provides that the text of the draft provisions on the protection of TCEs/EoF does not constitute a substitute for, but complements the protections "applicable to traditional cultural expressions/expressions of folklore and [derivatives] [adaptations] thereof under intellectual property laws, laws and programs for the safeguarding, preservation and promotion of cultural heritage, and other legal and non-legal measures available for the protection and preservation of traditional cultural expressions/expressions of folklore" (WIPO 2010b: Article 10).[36]

Fifth, both in relation to TCEs/ToF and TK, the WIPO-IGC draft provisions recognize that a one-size-fits-all approach to protection and safeguarding is practically unfeasible. Rather, through the principles of flexibility, comprehensiveness, and the recognition of the nature and characteristics of TK and expressive culture, it endorses the deployment of a variety of malleable legal mechanisms to accomplish the ultimate objectives of protection and safeguarding. The IGC notes that "experience with TCEs/EoF protection has shown that it is unlikely that any single 'one-size-fits-all' or 'universal' international template will be found to protect TCEs comprehensively in a manner that suits the national priorities, legal and cultural environment, and need of traditional communities in all countries" (WIPO 2006b: Annex, 8, 2010a).

In regard to TK, WIPO-IGC notes the need to deploy a wide variety of legal mechanisms for protection that:

> should respect the diversity of traditional knowledge held by different peoples and communities in different sectors, should acknowledge differences in national circumstances and the legal context and heritage of national jurisdictions, and should allow sufficient flexibility.
>
> (WIPO 2006a: Annex, 10, 2010c: Annex, 12–13)

In similar ways throughout its deliberations and via the texts of its various documents, the WIPO-IGC clearly recognizes the importance of customary and traditional practices and jurisprudence in regard to, among other things, playing a role in benefit sharing and, as may be applicable, providing the basis for determining the eligibility of TK for protection and for entitlement to the benefits of protection.[37] In addition, the proposed draft of Article 5(1) (a), (2) on TCEs/EoF provides for the recognition of customary laws and practices in the implementation of measures to protect TCEs/EoF (WIPO 2006b, 2010b). In specific reference to the latter, which applies *mutatis mutandis* to TK, the WIPO-IGC remarks that the draft provisions are "broad and inclusive, and intended, while establishing that misappropriation and misuse of TCEs/EoF would be unlawful, to give maximum flexibility to national and regional authorities and communities in relation to which precise legal mechanisms may be used to achieve or implement the provisions at the national and or regional levels" (WIPO 2006b: Annex, 8, 2010b: Annex, 9).

Sixth, both the draft provisions on TCEs/EoF and TK seek to entrench a balance "between the rights and interests of those that develop, preserve and sustain TCEs/EoF, and of those who use and benefit from them" (WIPO 2010b: Annex, 8) through, among other measures, the reification of the principles of equitable access and benefit sharing, disclosure of origin, and prior informed consent in regard to TCEs/EoF and TK. Consequently, the draft text on TCEs/EoF make elaborate provisions in Article 3 to endorse the application of these principles to mediate diverse policy objectives undergirding the protection of TCEs/EoF to achieve balance among the relevant objectives. Similarly, Article 6 of the draft text regarding TK emphasizes that fair and equitable benefit sharing, including non-monetary options, is a fundamental entitlement of the holders or custodians of TK, in addition to respectful recognition and acknowledgement of their contribution and the availability of legal means "to provide remedies for [traditional knowledge] holders in cases where the [fair] direct and equitable sharing of benefits [. . .] has not occurred, or where knowledge holders were not recognized" by third parties (WIPO 2010c: Article 6(4)).

Finally, other sundry issues make it obvious from a combined reading of the draft provisions on TCEs/EoF and TK, that the WIPO- IGC is not open to prescribing formalities to regulate protection. For example, Article 11(1) of WIPO (2010c) provides that "[e]ligibility for protection of traditional knowledge against acts of misappropriation or misuse should not require any formalities." Article 7(1) of WIPO (2010b) provides, in part, that TCEs/EoF become eligible for protection at the moment of creation, and such protection "should not be subject to any formality." In addition to endorsing documentation and other safeguarding measures, these instruments are also unequivocal in their preference for simplicity, certainty and transparency of the procedures for safeguarding and protecting TCEs/EoF and TK, and as a matter of consistency, in regard to the adoption of appropriate transitional measures to align existing or parallel regimes at regional and international levels to the general framework of the draft provisions.[38]

Uncritical excitement and uninformed skepticism

In a nutshell, these represent the key features of the emerging international instruments on safeguarding and protecting TCEs/EoF under the auspices of the WIPO-IGC. Both reservation and optimism over the potential of the WIPO-IGC process to result in a binding treaty on TCEs/EoF and TK remain measured. A critical reading of the WIPO-IGC processes and the tenor of the contributions to the deliberations by diverse categories of participants demonstrates incredible courage and the resolve of WIPO member states to engage in no-holds-barred negotiations on the subject of TCEs/EoF and TK. So far, the outcome has been illuminating in regard to the intricate policy and legal issues that converge at the intersection of TCEs/EoF and TK, on the one hand, and intellectual property and various competing options for their safeguarding and protection, on the other. The coalescence of stakeholders with diverse interests seeking to achieve consensus while trading compromises at the WIPO-IGC deliberations demonstrate the unique, if not pivotal, role of TK subject matter(s) in the global governance of intellectual property rights.

The WIPO-IGC has committed the current textual negotiation (based on the draft provisions) of prospective treaties on TCEs and TK into the hands of an Inter-sessional Working Group (IWG). Priority is accorded in the ongoing negotiations to TCEs considered to be the most mature of the three WIPO-IGC-mandated subjects. Recently, however, the IGC transmitted the draft articles on TK and other relevant documents on genetic resources to IWG, setting the stage for working groups on TK and GRs to emerge in the very near future.[39] Delegation to the IWG is limited to one independent expert per member[40] state to support and facilitate the IGC's negotiations by providing legal and technical advice and analysis. In addition to the member state experts, indigenous experts and NGOs also participate in the informal drafting and deliberations at the IWG level. The IWG is divided into several specialized working groups, each tasked to draft a specific article. As the WIPO has explained, in the operation of the process thus far, "[e]xperts from around the world worked side by side, debating and drafting together. The groups came up with further revised versions of all the articles [11 in all], which were presented to and discussed by the IWG as a whole" (WIPO 2010d) in a compilation text. The WIPO-IGC has so far capitalized on the specific expertise of IWGs and the relatively small size of the meeting to achieve efficiency in these "final" textual negotiations.

Even in the expert-driven informal drafting sessions, there has been disagreement in many areas. The experts have not yet agreed on an acceptable definition of the beneficiaries and managers of the rights to TCEs (WIPO 2010d).[41] While many argue that TCE protection should benefit indigenous peoples and local communities, experts of the African Group want TCE protection to target "peoples and communities, for example, indigenous peoples, local communities, cultural communities and/or nations" (Mara 2010). This state of affairs reflects the increased representation made in the previous deliberations on the draft provisions in regard to the entitlement of "nations," as opposed to indigenous and local communities exclusively to TCEs, and the idea of national folklore or a national claim to rights in TK.[42]

Also, there is no agreement in regard to the management of access and administration of prior informed consent. While some experts believe that beneficiaries should manage their own rights directly, as far as practicable, during a July 2010 WIPO-IGC meeting, a delegate from South Africa insisted that "'We don't want those who wish to have access [to TCEs] to go directly to the communities involved' without first going through relevant national authorities" (Mara 2010). These disagreements regarding the beneficiaries of TCEs and the administration of rights echo the diverse political realities and objectives that underlie the protection of TK among the various stakeholders we discussed in earlier chapters.

Another issue among the many in contention is the duration of protection. While indigenous and some state experts make a case for an indefinite term of protection for TCEs given their unique nature as distinguished from conventional forms of intellectual property such as copyright, others like Belgium want a fixed term of protection. The US recognizes that some forms of TCEs are suitable to indefinite protection while some are not. Also subject to continuing debate are: the management of rights for indigenous or local communities in TCEs when such communities not only have many distinct groups but are also found to cross national borders;[43] the relationship between the customary laws of indigenous and local communities in regard to national laws; the form of sanctions for violation of rights over TCEs; the relationship between *sui generis* systems of protection of TCEs and the conventional intellectual property regime, etc. In summing up her impression of the state of progress on the extant IGC textual negotiations, Mara (2010) notes that in spite of progress in the IGC:

> [I]t is clear that creating a *sui generis* system for the protection of these areas of knowledge is not going to be a simple process. As attending delegates worked to refine the text, disagreements were revealed on several of the articles in the form of different options, comments to the text, and questions on the state of play of protection and related institutions.

The compilation text of the IWG's informal drafts has since been discussed in plenary sessions of the IWG. Along with delegates' comments and suggestions on the text, the compilation was presented, at the end of 2010, to the WIPO-IGC which decided to set up an open-ended group to streamline the provision on TCEs for further deliberations in 2011.[44] Without dampening optimism over the IWG stage of the WIPO-IGC process, it is quite clear that if, with the advantage of monumental background materials accumulated from more than a decade of negotiations, independent experts are unable to reach definitive agreements, the WIPO-IGC – fundamentally a political body – would have an even greater challenge coming to definitive agreement on a final text. Despite the optimism and the present momentum over the imminence of the text of an eventual international legal instrument on the protection of TCEs/EoF, it seems that a wait-and-see attitude would be more realistic to adopt. But the recent emergence of the Nagoya Protocol – in spite of mixed reactions that have so far welcomed it – provide reason for hope in regard to a WIPO-IGC treaty text on TK. There is apparently no basis for uncritical excitement or enthusiasm over the prospect of (a) treaty text(s) on the three mandate items of the WIPO-IGC. However, progress so far, even in the absence of a formal treaty document, does not justify resigning in despair or indulging in uninformed skepticism. If anything, more than a decade of work by the WIPO-IGC has resulted in a far-reaching understanding of the complexity of the global juridical framework on TCEs/EoF and TK.

Summary

This chapter has demonstrated that, unlike in the preceding chapters, T/IK does not constitute a single issue linkage to the discourse on global governance of intellectual property. Rather, the subject of the knowledge of indigenous and local communities implicates multiple issue linkages in all those areas that have direct or indirect relationships with the various forms of TK, including food, agriculture, medicine, genetic resources, biodiversity, environmental stewardship, cultural relics, diverse forms of ICH, etc. Perhaps, more important, the notion of T/IK demonstrates a conceptual morass that has been complicated by the colonial hierarchies of culture and power that found conventional intellectual property jurisprudence. Consequently, not only does T/IK provide a big tent for diverse issue linkages in the global governance of intellectual property, it also exposes the tensions and gaps in intellectual property jurisprudence that have supervised many centuries of excluding the knowledge of indigenous and local communities from the international intellectual property lawmaking process.

A combination of diverse factors – many historical, some empirical, others theoretical and many defying any analytical categorization – have since "conspired" to induce the emergence of TK as a factor in the extant global knowledge economy. Specifically, modern biotechnology and information and communication technologies demonstrate an intricate connection between the revolutions they embody and the forces of globalization. The outcome is the emergence of a more dynamic and process-oriented evolution of knowledge and culture with an increasing cosmopolitan outlook that is now an integral aspect of postmodernism. However, because TK has remained, at worst, outside or, at best, within the margins of the intellectual property system, the new technological revolutions constitute a threat to it, even as they hold a promise for the safeguarding, integration and empowerment of TK in the new knowledge economy.

As a feature of the global governance process, TK thus becomes the site for resistance via diverse strategies, including regime proliferation, counter-regime assertion and various forms of reclamation of the epistemic integrity of local knowledge. This resistance intensified in light of the glaring omission or non-recognition of TK in the major intellectual property treaty designed to order the emergent knowledge economy, the TRIPS Agreement. In virtually all spheres of international law and policymaking processes, including hard and soft law regimes, diverse categories of stakeholders continue to pressure the international system as to the imperative to promote, protect and safeguard TK for various reasons within and beyond the commercial fundamentals of the intellectual property system. Given the more accommodating nature of the new international lawmaking process following the birth of the UN, many actors, including states, NGOs and representatives of indigenous and local communities maintain the pressure on the international system to accord appropriate and equitable protection to TK.

Because of the inextricable relationship between knowledge and culture and their open-ended scope, especially in the new knowledge economy, contemporary initiatives aimed at addressing the equity gap surrounding protection for TK in the new global knowledge governance system have increased in multiple forums, notably WIPO, UNESCO, CBD and virtually all other UN agencies at their different deliberative levels.

Some major outcomes of the initiatives include, first, greater consciousness of the inadequacy of the conventional intellectual property platform to address objectives for the protection of TK and the resulting need for an open-ended *sui generis* framework to emerge for the purpose. A second outcome is that as desirable as a holistic outlook on TK may be, the categorization of the constitutive knowledge forms into specific but inchoate distinctions, such as TK *stricto sensu*, and TCEs/EoF, has clearly evolved as a tool of legal, policy, and analytical convenience and necessity that obfuscates the labyrinthine character of the phenomenon encompassed within TK. Third, although the distinctions have shaped the pattern of regime dynamics at the intersection of TK and the global governance of intellectual property, the work of WIPO-IGC demonstrates a convergence of objectives that could be harnessed to protect and safeguard the various forms of TK in multiple forums.

Fourth, it is tempting, and, indeed, may be logical, to conclude that the consequence of the last observation is that forum shopping may give way to the reality of forum management for parties and stakeholders who are genuinely committed to effective protection and safeguarding of TK forms. As it stands, forum proliferation appears to be an inherent necessity due to the elusive and indeterminate scope of TK. Fifth, discourses on local knowledge in the context of the global governance of intellectual property implicate biological and digital technologies as tools of globalization and of the appropriation of all forms of TK. This singular fact showcases how the interplay of the new technologies and intellectual property present a remarkable dialectical challenge to the security of the interests of TK holders.

Sixth, clearly, no-one is any longer under the illusion that a universal regime for the protection and safeguarding of TK or TCEs is feasible. So far, what can be realistically expected is a forging of consensus on a workable framework for such a goal, leaving details to be worked out at appropriate levels. Finally, the modest success achieved thus far in the long-drawn political and historical struggle over protecting TK shows the value of a deliberately flexible deliberative approach to seeking solutions for the problem. For instance, the WIPO-IGC, where the most substantial negotiations are presently being conducted, reflects a delicate blend of a bottom-up and top-down models that build on existing best practices at national, regional and international levels, with ample room to accommodate customary protocols, understandings, laws and practices of indigenous and local communities.

The WIPO-IGC provides possibly the most comprehensive, even audacious, effort to tackle the perpetually elusive challenge of resolving governance and distributive justice concerns regarding TCEs and TK at a global level. Because of its accomplishments and influence at national and regional levels, expectations are high regarding its ultimate outcome as work advances toward drafting a treaty text. Fears are well founded that the struggle to forge a consensus at the IWG level may implode when the more political WIPO-IGC sits to consider the informal draft of the text. Clearly, this is a critical phase, a moment for a reality check that would task the sincerity of many, especially from the developed countries, who continue to participate in the work of the WIPO-IGC. Any success at this stage would also vindicate, if not pleasantly confound many skeptical minds in the less developed countries and in the ranks of indigenous and local communities. These groups continue to be skeptical of the sincerity of the developed countries to channel the initial attempts and the pressure of the less developed countries from the WTO as the appropriate forum to fix the gap in TRIPS' treatment of TK, to a little known (and, indeed, seemingly non-existent) forum, the WIPO-IGC. Here, Graham Dutfield's observation, which echoes Peter Yu's (2003: 402, 2008c: 450–1), theory of "haves and have-nots" is most cogent:

> For several developed countries, there is little for them to gain economically from a legal regime on TK or TCEs. Consequently, they are not interested in

participating positively in negotiations targeted at such an outcome even if they agree that the IGC to continue to exist [sic]. There are exceptions to this general [sic] observations. Some European countries that wish to maintain good relations with developing country governments are willing to go much further than say, the United States. On the other [hand], developing countries are rather becoming negative about the IGC. They suspect two things. First, that they can never get an international treaty on TK that they seek through the IGC. Second, that the committee's very existence serves as a justification for the developed country opponents to actively keep the subjects of TK and ABS out of negotiations on intellectual property at the WTO and other WIPO forums using the argument that these are matters exclusively for IGC to deal with.

(Dutfield 2006b: 18–19)

This last observation remains even more relevant at this stage in the WIPO-IGC's work. While not many skeptics believed that the committee's work would reach the present level, the same may not be easily said of the current work of the CBD on the Nagoya ABS Protocol, which contains basic elements of the WIPO-IGC draft currently under negotiation. However, whether the WIPO-IGC sanctions a treaty (or more than one) on its three mandated areas and, if so, whether the substance of such a treaty, not to mention its practical implementation, would constitute a core development to assist in understanding the longstanding and ongoing political, legal and historical struggle over TK protection, is unknown. That understanding will become more significant to appraise the intersection of TK generally with the new technologies of globalization, and the complicity of intellectual property rights in global governance.

Notes

1 Available online: http://unesdoc.unesco.org/images/0006/000637/063799eb.pdf (accessed 16 December 2010).
2 The two versions of the Convention differ slightly and do not have same memberships. The subsequent Convention modifies the earlier one in some respects and omits the section dealing with the treatment of belligerents and the care of the wounded in neutral countries (the subject matter of the separately concluded Convention V). Available online: http://www.icrc.org/ihl.nsf/INTRO?OpenView (accessed 16 December 2010).
3 The 1970 Convention has an elaborate and elastic definition of cultural property at Article 1 that includes physical components such as engravings, sculptures, paintings, prints, lithographs, antiquities, products of archeological excavation as well as open-ended categories on the border of the material and non-material, such as archived sound, objects of ethnological interest and properties of importance for history, pre-history, art and science.
4 See Article 2 of the World Cultural Heritage Convention, 1972.
5 This claim may be a little oversimplified. In reality, those who may be identified as not having a lot of protectable treasures within their borders are more likely to be those who have historically had a longer regime of protection/safeguarding of their cultural heritage, for example, through a written tradition, technological advantage and socio-economic and historic frameworks that enabled the optimization of the benefit of their cultural treasures. These are nations more likely to be on the forefront of the quest for

the exotic by focusing on "less explored" climes to awaken them to a new and predatory system of valuing and dealing with cultural treasures.

6 Footnotes omitted.
7 Held in Phuket, Thailand, 8–10 April 1997, the Forum marked an important turning point in recent initiatives on TCEs/EoF at WIPO and UNESCO. See WIPO-UNESCO World Forum on the Protection of Folklore.
8 The South Pacific, Eastern and Southern Africa, South Asia, North America, Central America, West Africa, Arab countries, South America (Peru), South America (Bolivia) and the Caribbean Region.
9 Halewood notes that America's support for the fact-finding mission and the GIPID's initiative of the WIPO was premised on an understanding that the project would not pursue a norm-setting agenda or give rise to treaty or recommendations.
10 Specifically, by such instruments as the Protection of Traditional Cultural Expression/Expressions of Folklore: Revised Objectives and Principles, WIPO Doc WIPO/GRTKF/IC/9/4 (9 January 2006); Protection of Traditional Knowledge: Revised Objectives and Principles, WIPO Doc WIPO/GRTKF/IC/9/5 (6 January 2006); and Genetic Resources: List of Options [for protection], WIPO Doc WIPO/GRTKF/11/8A (3 June 2007).
11 For some insight into several initiatives preceding the birth of the ICH Convention, see Kono (2009) at 11; see also UNESCO (2003) "Brief History of the Convention for Safeguarding of Intangible Cultural Heritage." Available online: http://portal.unesco.org/culture/en/ev.php-URL_ID=29915&URL_DO=DO_TOPIC&URL_SECTION=201.html (accessed 16 December 2010).
12 E.g. the 1989 UNESCO Recommendation for the Safeguarding of Traditional Culture and Folklore, the 1994 Living Human Treasures Programme of UNESCO, which encouraged the transmission of intangible culture to younger generations, and the 1997/98 UNESCO Programme for the Proclamation of Masterpieces of the Oral and Intangible Heritage of Humanity, an initiative that creates international distinction through a listing system that identifies, shares, celebrates and encourages the safeguarding of select ICH.
13 The importance of this approach is underscored by the fact that, while some physical or material expressions of culture, such as genetic resources or natural monuments may be vested in the sovereign state (e.g. Articles 3, 15 of the CBD), communities and bearers of tradition have inalienable rights to their intangible cultural heritage.
14 Emphasis added.
15 See also Article 2(1) of the ICH Convention for its definition of "ICH."
16 See Article 1(a)–(i) of the CDC; see also preamble to the UDCD.
17 See Article 1(h) of the CDC; see also Articles 11 and 12 of the ICH Convention.
18 See also para. 3 of the CDC, which refers to cultural diversity as "a mainspring for sustainable development for communities and peoples and nations."
19 See generally the preambles to the ICH Convention, the CDC and the UDCD. See specifically Article 2 (5)–(8) of the CDC on the Convention's Guiding Principles.
20 These are: the Universal Copyright Convention, the Convention for the Protection of Cultural property in the Event of Armed Conflict, the Convention on the Means of Prohibiting and Preventing the Illicit Import, Export and Transfer of Ownership of Cultural Property, the Convention Concerning the Protection of World Cultural and Natural Heritage, the Convention on the Protection of Underwater Cultural Heritage, the Convention for the Safeguarding of the Intangible Cultural Heritage, the Convention on the Protection and Promotion of the Diversity of Cultural Expressions.
21 Also, often referred to as "Return of Innocence" in literature.
22 Mbube in Zulu means Lion.
23 Under the title of "Other Safeguarding Measures," Article 13(d)(ii) provides for establishing documentation institutions for the intangible cultural heritage and facilitating access to them.

24 Footnotes omitted.
25 With its elaborate provisions in regard to monitoring the utilization of genetic resources, compliance with mutually agreed terms, model contractual clauses, codes of conduct, best practices, etc. (Articles 13–16), the Nagoya Protocol represents a guide in this consideration.
26 Again, the Nagoya Protocol's provisions in Articles 17 and 18 on awareness raising and capacity building represent an important guide in this regard.
27 See WIPO, "Surveys of Existing Practices, Protocols and Policies." Available online: http://www.wipo.int/tk/en/culturalheritage/surveys.html (accessed 16 December 2010).
28 See WIPO, "Database of Existing Codes, Guidelines and Practices." Available online: http://www.wipo.int/tk/en/databases/creative_heritage/ (accessed 16 December 2010).
29 For, example, they cite Rina Pantalony, WIPO Guide on Managing Intellectual Property for Museums, 2008. Available online: http://www.wipo.int/copyright/en/museums_ip/guide.html (accessed 21 December 2010) and WIPO Surveys. Available online: http://www.wipo.int/tk/en/folklore/culturalheritage/ surveys.html (accessed 21 December 2010).
30 These terms are used interchangeably throughout the work of the WIPO-IGC.
31 See World Intellectual Property Organization (2009b), The Protection of Traditional Cultural Expressions: Revised Gap Analysis, WIPO Doc WIPO/GRTKF/IC/13/5(b) Rev (11 October 2009). Geneva: WIPO. Available online: http://www.wipo.int/edocs/mdocs/tk/en/wipo.../wipo_grtkf_ic_17_ inf_2.doc (accessed 15 December 2010).
32 For instance, WIPO (2010b) contains a total of 11 articles in proposed substantive provisions: (1) Subject Matter of Protection; (2) Beneficiaries; (3) Acts of Misappropriation and Misuse; (4) Management of Rights; (5) Exceptions and Limitations; (6) Terms of Protection; (7) Formalities; (8) Sanctions, Remedies and Exercise of Right; (9) Transitional Measures; (10) Relationship with IP Protection and Other forms of Protection, Preservation and Promotion; and (11) International and Regional Protection. Similarly, WIPO (2010c) has 14 articles in its proposed substantive provisions: (1) Protection Against Misappropriation; (2) Legal Form of Protection; (3) General Scope of Subject Matter; (4) Eligibility of Protection; (5) Beneficiaries of Protection; (6) Fair and Equitable Benefit-Sharing and Recognition of Knowledge Holders; (7) Prior Informed Consent; (8) Exceptions and Limitations; (9) Duration of Protection; (10) Transitional Measures; (11) Formalities; (12) Consistency with General Legal Framework; (13) Administration and Enforcement of Protection; and (14) International and Regional Protection.
33 See also WIPO (2010b).
34 See also WIPO (2010c).
35 Underlining in original.
36 Footnote omitted.
37 See WIPO 2010c: Articles 4(iii), 5 and 6(5).
38 See generally WIPO (2010b: Articles 9, 11, 2010c: 10, 11(1), 12, 14).
39 See WIPO (2008) The Protection of Traditional Knowledge: Draft Gap Analysis: Revision, WIPO Doc WIPO/GRTKF/IC/13/5(b) Rev. Available online: http://www.wipo.int/edocs/mdocs/tk/en/wipo_grtkf_ic_13/wipo_grtkf_ic_13_5_b_rev.pdf (accessed 21 December 2010).
40 Nominated experts are supposed to be independent subject area experts recognized on their individual capacity and not under obligation to argue in support of their countries' political interests.
41 See Articles 2 and 4 of the compilation text (WIPO 2010d).
42 For example, WIPO (2010b: Article 2): "Measures for the protection of national traditional cultural expressions/expressions of folklore should be for the benefit of the

indigenous peoples <u>and communities, individual groups, families, tribes, nations</u> and traditional and other cultural communities <u>or the nation/or the countries, to which a traditional cultural expression/expression of folklore is specific</u>" (underlining in original, footnotes omitted). The Moroccan delegation argued that a nation owned its own folklore, i.e. "national" folklore; however, it did not advance a case for "national" TCEs nor was any mention is made of such (WIPO 2010b: n 59).

43 The Nagoya Protocol provides a clue on this under Article 11, which provides for transboundary cooperation by parties with overlapping interests in trans-boundary genetic resources and associated traditional knowledge.

44 See WIPO Press Release, "IGC Makes Significant Progress, Sets Stage for Working Groups on GRs and TK". Available online: http://www.wipo.int/pressroom/articles/2010/article_0051.html (accessed 21 December 2010).

8 Managing intellectual property in global governance

Reconfiguring the governance scheme

A global intellectual property order at a crossroads

The present global intellectual property order is at a crossroads (Yu 2009), rocked on several fronts by crises of equity, imbalances of stakeholder interests, and reckless insensitivity to social welfare, including public and development-regarding considerations. In its gradual but phased evolution from the national, through the bilateral, to the international and current global stage, intellectual property law and policymaking has, for the most part, been dominated by developed countries and their industrial and information establishments, or the various rights-owning stakeholders within them. The narrative of intellectual property in global governance reveals deep-seated tensions between producers or owners and users of intellectual property – an overly broad, though convenient categorization that hardly aligns neatly with the complex dynamics, interests and actors involved. Nonetheless, in essence, intellectual property in global governance easily reduces to an interlocked series of conflicted binary relationships between, inter alia, developed and less developed countries; private and public good; private and public domain; monopoly and competition; development and underdevelopment agenda.

Some rightly disclaim the inflammatory, sometimes unquestioned, and even unhelpful use of these binary terms (Yu 2009: 7). But only a few analytical approaches to the issue capture and underscore the extent of the imbalance, which the current global intellectual property order continues to sustain. Concomitantly, only a few approaches also underscore the urgent need for a critical reconfiguration of the global governance scheme in regard to intellectual property. For more than two centuries, developed countries have sustained a "maximalists' stranglehold on intellectual property lawmaking exercises, which aims mainly to preserve 'knowledge cartel's comparative advantage in existing technological outputs at the expense of future innovation requiring more subtle forms of nurture" (Reichman 2009b: 1165). The outcome of the maximalist approach, which reached an unprecedented height with the coming into force of the TRIPS Agreement and its practical consequences, is an increased awareness on the part of the global public as to the significance of intellectual property rights. The adjunct to this development has been an escalation in the linkages between and among the issue areas discussed extensively in this book, on the one hand, and intellectual property rights with its associated regime complexity, on the other.

We saw that the maximalist approach to global intellectual property protection has been advanced through a harmonization strategy pursued under a one-size-fits-all regime outlook. Undoubtedly, there are some cosmetic attempts to create flexibilities or so-called wriggle rooms in the TRIPS Agreement and in various trade regimes to modify the stricture of this regime. However, these flexible accommodations are quite nuanced. In particular, TRIPS has a phased implementation time line directed at "developing" or "least developed" countries that was designed to accommodate the extraordinary challenges required in those jurisdictions to make them TRIPS compliant. As well, although the Doha Declaration elaborated TRIPS' "development" content, only a few would quarrel with the impression that TRIPS was overkill and, that in operation, its so-called flexibilities are actually inflexible (Stiglitz 2008a: 1717). Similarly, not many would dispute the suggestion that, as the gold standard of the new global intellectual property order, TRIPS has left in its wake a sobering list of negative outcomes for many in less developed countries (Reichman 2000).

It is in terms of those negative outcomes that TRIPS interacts with other relevant peripheral regimes that now constitute part of the global governance landscape for intellectual property. As we have seen, that interaction implicates diverse issue linkages and issue aggregation in regard to intellectual property. The categories of intellectual property issue linkages are open ended, but those explored in this book include human rights, public health and access to pharmaceuticals, political economics of agriculture, food security, and traditional knowledge including in regard to genetic resources, expressive culture and cultural heritage. When examined in the context of new technological revolutions of bio- and digital technologies and their complex interaction with globalization and global governance and the undergirding regimes at the intersection of these issue linkages, the negative outcomes become palpable.

In a way, intellectual property has the potential to advance public-regarding considerations in the areas of all the issue linkages discussed in this book. But the reality is that given the maximalist approach to intellectual property championed by the technology-exporting countries, the impact of intellectual property rights in those areas, at least in regard to less developed countries is, for the most part, negative. From access to medicine, to food security, information and biotechnology innovations, and broader human rights considerations including those arising in the context of traditional knowledge, the interaction of intellectual property with the forces of globalization and global governance do not reflect equitable distributional outcomes.

Modest progress

As we have seen, the search for fair distributional outcomes regarding the benefits of innovation is at the core of the complex regime dynamics that now characterize intellectual property in global governance. For the avoidance of doubt, it is not as if the continuing upward ratcheting of international intellectual property norms has gone unchallenged. Many countries from the less developed world – especially those in the high and middle income group and their sympathizers, multivalent stakeholders including indigenous and local communities, their supporters, diverse NGOs, IGOS, civil society groups and categories of sub-state actors – have continued to push for a more balanced global intellectual property order in different and opportune forums. Their efforts in these regards take the appearance of nuanced forms of counter-regime, or counter-harmonization movement. The most recent manifestation of these initiatives is symbolized in the new development agenda adopted by WIPO in 2007.

In various other forums, the pressure for a balanced global intellectual property order is sometimes couched in the overlapping language of development, empowerment, access to knowledge, distributional equity, social welfare or adjustment of social costs, public good, public-regarding consideration, and similar other characterizations. Significant strides have already been recorded in the burgeoning elaboration of intellectual property rights from a human rights perspective (Chapman 2002b; Cullet 2007; Helfer 2003, 2007, 2008; Helfer and Austin 2011; Yu 2007a, 2007d), including the intellectual property rights of indigenous peoples and local communities in the context of various forms of traditional knowledge, and as regards expressive culture and cultural heritage. Specifically in this issue area, developed countries' hegemony over intellectual property norms and their relentless inclination to ratchet them up are increasingly confronted by counterbalancing arguments from the less developed states.

In regards to global health, the public good argument has garnered traction by virtue of the activities of the WHO and emergent public–private actors in the sector. In agriculture and food security, despite its current weakness across regimes, the case for farmers' rights remains a counterbalancing challenge to the anti-competitive stranglehold of transnational agricultural and allied chemical corporate monopolies that have capitalized on the privatization of genetic resources in public gene banks. Also, as with health, the public good argument is now advanced and translated in the activities of FAO and allied institutions, especially through forms of public–private partnership in CGIAR'S federating IARCs.

So it is in regard to traditional biocultural knowledge where, through a form of silent revolution at the CBD, there has emerged a new Protocol on Access and Benefit Sharing over genetic resources and associated traditional knowledge, however imperfect. Similarly, from its modest and unsuspecting origins, the WIPO-IGC mapped the complex jurisprudential landscape in regard to the protection of traditional knowledge, genetic resources and folklore. Presently, as noted in Chapter 7, the WIPO-IGC is on the verge of concluding negotiations on a treaty text on its mandate subjects. Finally, recent policy and international lawmaking development under the auspices of the UNESCO demonstrate bold initiatives to advance protection and safeguarding of cultural heritage, and to promote cultural diversity and cultural exchange for sustainable development. In addition to these international developments, domestic legal regimes, especially at national and regional levels among many countries of the south, continue to adjust, reflecting the height of progress so far made in the various areas.

Steps forward and steps back

The foregoing developments continue to evolve; in fact, they hardly constitute a dent in or a counterforce to the unprecedented degree to which intellectual property expansionism has been entrenched. What appears to have been accomplished remains inchoate, especially in light of the continuing strategic implementation of bilateral and, sometimes, multilateral or regional free trade agreements with TRIPS plus components, particularly by the US through its divide-and-conquer politics. Indeed, despite the significant or, more appropriately, symbolic, strides that have been made in the areas of traditional knowledge such as via the Convention on Biological Diversity, the US has not yet become a party to it. In addition, the loose language of its text, and that of the recent Nagoya Protocol on ABS, cast serious doubts on how seriously states may take their obligations under them.

As noted, the CBD, WIPO, WTO, UNESCO, FAO-ITPGRFA, WHO and several other regimes, institutions, forums and instruments constitute part of the intellectual property regime complex, subsuming intellectual property in global governance to the dynamics of regime politics. The importance of regime proliferation as a counterbalancing force to the hard-edged approach to intellectual property under TRIPS cannot be discounted. At the same time, we are reminded that when regimes proliferate, for many reasons, stronger states benefit the most. In part, this trend in regime proliferation is a consequence of the diversity of issues linked to intellectual property. As well, it is an incidence of intellectual property's ubiquitous presence and impact in virtually all sectors of the new knowledge economic order. But regime proliferation is not an efficient way to find workable solutions to the distributional inequity and increasing development gaps engendered by the current dynamic of intellectual property in global governance.

What is urgently needed for intellectual property in the 21st century is a more efficient regime and forum management approach to reconfigure the current global governance scheme in intellectual property. Such an approach should be sensitive to the diversity and open-ended nature of issue linkages, and to the imperative for an effective way of mainstreaming development considerations into intellectual property policy and lawmaking.

In addition to the negative effects of regime proliferation on the ability of less developed countries to stem the tide of the maximalist approach to intellectual property, overall, pressures exerted by the less developed countries to induce a rethinking of the normative approach to intellectual property have failed to yield desired results. Self-serving changes that have only helped to accentuate continuity in current global intellectual property protection arrangements are readily secured by developed countries that wield coercive political clout. Development-oriented changes that touch on the aspirations of less developed counties are often considered too burdensome on established intellectual property norms. This view is often asserted with little or no regard to the historical malleability of intellectual property norms and their susceptibility to political influences.

For example, opposition by developed countries led by the US and Japan, sometimes with mixed signals from the EU, has ensured that progress remains elusive under the WIPO Patent Agenda, the TRIPS Council and even the Nagoya ABS Protocol, on the desire of the less developed countries to incorporate disclosure of source or origin of genetic resources and, where applicable, associated traditional knowledge, in relevant patent applications as an aspect of patent jurisprudence. This contrasts sharply with the rapidity with which the US and its allies secured a pair of the post-TRIPS WIPO internet treaties in 1996 to attune copyright jurisprudence to the vagaries of the internet. Similar is the consistent lowering of the patent threshold regarding biotechnology-related inventions, especially around genes and, overall, the pattern of extension of intellectual property to platform science and innovations, including digital data sets. Yet traditional knowledge forms, including those in the biocultural context and in expressive culture remain problematic in their relation to intellectual property because of the "gap question." Consequently, traditional knowledge forms remain perennial outliers to intellectual property norms and jurisprudence. Rightly or wrongly, they are conveniently treated under the rubric of the legally inchoate secondary rights category depicted as *sui generis*.

Intellectual property overreach: the dangers of a boomerang effect

As noted, the consistent addiction of developed countries and their strong industry lobby to an unbalanced optimization of intellectual property rights has left the global intellectual property order in a jurisprudential mess. Without question, less developed countries' economies and their vulnerable populations are at the receiving end of the distributional disequilibrium regarding access to knowledge and public goods in this unbalanced global intellectual property system. However, that is only part of the story. Continued calibration of intellectual property rights to their maximum in a bid to sustain the knowledge hegemony of a few countries in the new knowledge economy, has the potential to implode or flip over and to scuttle the pace of innovation even in those countries. As Reichman reminds and warns us:

> [E]fforts [e.g. through the TRIPS Agreement] to rig a regime for short-term advantages may turn out, in the medium and long-term, to boomerang against those who pressed hardest for its adoption . . . by reaching for high levels of international [intellectual property] protection (that could not change in response to less favourable domestic circumstances), technology-exporting countries risked fostering conditions that could erode their technological superiority and resulting terms of trade over time.
>
> (2009b: 1119,[1] also 1989: 891)

This self-destructive potential or counterproductive scenario could upset the extant "knowledge cartel" and throw up new actors from high and middle income developing countries, especially those currently characterized to be at the "crossover point" (Yu 2009: 10–11). At this juncture, a radically abbreviated but critical perspective on the real and potential impact of maximum intellectual property protection and expansion which technology-exporting developed countries have foisted on the rest of the world via TRIPS and other measures is in order. This would assist to underscore the real dangers of the extant intellectual property overreach and what it forebodes for the future of intellectual property in global governance.

In light of recent advances in bio- and digital technologies and the TRIPS Agreement, the indiscriminate extension of intellectual property protection to all manner of innovation shows that the global intellectual property system is designed to mirror the domestic regimes of developed countries. As in the US, to some extent in the European Union, and in most OECD countries, intellectual property now extends to everything under the sun that is made by man. The consequence of this overly permissive approach, especially in the bio- and digital technology arenas, is the escalation of patents based on a much lower non-obviousness standard, and the undermining of the idea expression dichotomy in copyright jurisprudence. In the biotech and software fields, this trend encourages a lousy and inefficient innovation culture in which big transnational corporations with strong capital and global factor endowments, invest their resources in fencing off competition through the creation of patent thickets and copyright cartels. The resulting situation is that the controllers of innovation are those who have learned how to "game" the domestic and global intellectual property system with a view to perpetuating their monopoly, as opposed to those who make truly meaningful innovation.

These questionable captains of innovation thrive in creating a "mounting thickets of rights that impede both technological progress and research" (Reichman 2009b: 1132). As well, they escalate intellectual property litigation costs and, most importantly, they corrupt and subvert the intellectual property system by turning it into an anti-competition instrument. In this subverted intellectual property order, among others, genetic materials, software and digital data sets, have become theatres of intense innovation intrigue or overlapping patents and copyrights patronized by rent-seeking entities interested in erecting barriers to entry.

These forms of intellectual property fence making do not only obstruct the rise of cumulative and sequential innovations. They also ignore the all important distinction between platform or basic science, research, information and technology and their applied or practical translations, not to mention cultural and ethical questions (Bagely 2003; Kevles and Berkowitz 2001; Mgbeoji and Allen 2003). Unlike platform or basic science, the practical or functional technological applications constitute a composite all important site of truly nonobvious innovation deserving of sound intellectual protection. In order to ensure qualitative innovation, access to basic or platform science and innovation is critical. But when intellectual property is, unfortunately, nested in the platform arena, it distorts and disrupts technological and scientific progress and excludes medium level and even institutional interests, especially those that are publicly funded and others that have less factor endowment, to operate in this increasingly perverted global intellectual property process.

Already in this book, I touched on the real and potential social costs of global intellectual property being at a crossroads, especially in regard to public health, access to essential medicines, food security and agricultural innovation, human rights and indigenous peoples' self-determination. As part of the litany of social cost partly induced by the current regime of intellectual property governance, a new scientific research culture is emerging. Presently, this research culture is transitioning from the customary knowledge sharing ethos, to one driven by a code of secrecy and suspicion within the scientific community (Downie and Herder 2007; Oguamanam 2010). This emergent culture is fundamentally not suited to tackle or optimize the exponential possibilities and the promise of networked collaboration in R&D in the wake of advances made in bio- and digital technologies (Oguamanam 2010; Reichman 2009b: 1151). It is evident that developed countries have shunned those promises. They prefer to deploy intellectual property in tolling platform information and critical data vital for a cost effective, fair and efficient and integrated optimization of bio- and digital technologies through cumulative and sequential innovation.

Having maxed or stretched intellectual property to its limits, they have turned to technology to erect "thickets of rights" via technology protection measures, including terminator and similar technologies, and forms of digital rights management to undermine public-regarding aspects of intellectual property rights (Burk 2002; Sheets 2000; Vaidhyanathan 2003). Capturing these sentiments, Reichman (2009b: 1152) notes that "successful special interest lobbying at both the national and international levels has overprotected existing knowledge goods at the expense of the public domain, while compromising digitally empowered scientific research opportunities with little regard for the social costs and burdens imposed on future creation and innovation."

As part of the social cost or the "boomerang effect" of a lopsided global intellectual property regime, access to knowledge in diverse public-regarding contexts is now fiercely contested. For example, there is now a radical enclosure of public science space, a tolling of access to publicly funded research, a pullback on intellectual property exemptions in regard to scientific research, educational applications, and technological surveillance or constriction of public libraries as centers for knowledge dissemination. Another aspect of the festering social cost of an intellectual property system out of joint with the public interest is the weakening of small and medium scale entities, such as genetic drug manufacturers.

In most industrial sectors, these entities are naturally positioned to make cumulative and sequential innovation from publicly accessible platform science, information and technologies. They are pivotal catalysts in the downstream translation of innovation and in the advancement of distributional justice in regard to innovation. However, in the bio- and digital technology arenas, such critical arteries in the innovation physiology have increasingly become victims of the choking or blocking effects of the proliferation of low standard patents designed to shut them out from the present anti-competitive and slothful innovation environment.

With the weaknesses in the smart-by-half politics of intellectual property and innovation governance, the ability of major technology-exporting countries to sustain their leadership in innovation should not be taken for granted. Consistently, these so-called knowledge cartels have increased the premium on intellectual property by a combination of upward calibration of rights and unmitigated expansion of the scope and sphere of intellectual property application. In their attempt to coopt the rest of the world into a harmonized global intellectual property order, they initiated a one-size-fits-all approach, and erected a global intellectual property floor without a ceiling. Since the coming into effect of the TRIPS Agreement, upward seems to be the only direction intellectual property protection could point, no matter the situation. But this claim must be countered by a radical call for a "ceiling approach" to intellectual property (Kur 2009) as unconventional as that may seem.

In fact, the present stage of intellectual property overreach has incrementally shown that its structurally defective floor-without-ceiling edifice is no longer safe, neither is it able to sustain the innovation leadership of the present crop of technology-exporting countries. In both bio- and digital technology arenas, intellectual property has been deployed to muzzle creativity, to toll the public domain, to erect barriers to entry and to choke competition. Increasingly, intellectual property is being subverted to reward only those who have the necessary factor endowment to mortgage platform information and basic knowledge as a strategy to stifle cumulative and sequential innovation and, in this way, perpetuate an unsustainable slothful culture of innovation.

Intellectual property overreach: alarms in critical constituencies

Like the poorly configured national intellectual property systems in some of the leading developed countries that championed the current global intellectual property order, such as the US, Japan, and countries of the European Union, the current global system has important implications. In the less developed countries, it has generated consistent tensions. In the developed countries themselves, it elicits concerns in critical constituencies (e.g. Boyle 2003; Drahos 2005; EPO 2007; Gay 2002; Heller 2008; Jaffe and Lerner 2005; Kemp 2010; Lessig 2004; Meyers: 2006; So et al. 2008). For instance, research communities are worried about the privatization of publicly funded research, especially by universities, and the erosion of the sharing norms or ethics of public science. As well, the protection of scientific databases and the role of overlapping foundational patents in clustering a wide ambit of interlinked sites of innovation around frontier science (Kumar and Rai 2007)[2] is a major source of worry for policymakers.

The European Commission is presently concerned about how to enhance unhindered dissemination of knowledge and innovation, especially research outcomes, scientific information and educational resources as a strategy to contain the threat to public science posed by the extant intellectual property culture in the European Union (EC 2008; Reichman 2009b: 1152–3). Also, concerns about the widening digital divide and access to knowledge and information between technologically endowed and less developed countries continues to engage stakeholders involved in the promotion of the information society (WSIS 2003, 2005; Yu 2005b, 2008a: 2). In the US, the current intellectual property overreach continues to elicit strong public debates and notable objections to its unmitigated social costs (Crews 2005; Kemp 2010; Meyers 2006). Recent signals from the US show a willingness by both the judiciary and Congress to attenuate the present addiction to the proliferation of patents on the basis of a lower non-obviousness standard (Heller 2008: 65–6; Reichman 2009b: 1128).

In the current era of bio- and digital revolution, perhaps only a few things signify the disquiet over a failing global intellectual property order in the leading industrialized countries, than does the popularity of open access ideology, A2K movements and the concept of scientific commons. Open access, including creative commons movements, have not only successfully evolved in theory and application; they are generally presented as viable alternatives to address the deficient distributional outcomes of the global intellectual property system in a manner that strikes at the core issue of access to information and knowledge. Not only do these open-access or creative-commons initiatives underscore the role of intellectual property in negotiating or structuring social relations (Sunder 2006: 288), they also serve as catalysts for networked innovation to advance individual and collective creativity of all sorts. The legendary success of Wikipedia, various open-source operating systems (Reichman 2009b: 1148), and the liberalization of collaborative information generation and sharing, especially through the activities of second generation social network sites and other creative commons platforms within and across geopolitical borders, have continued to fostered the open access culture. Also, they have induced an increased attraction to apply the model of networked innovations that attempt to bypass intellectual property bottlenecks or, where possible, minimize their social cost for optimal distributional outcomes (Benkler 2006; Gay 2002; Shaver 2008).

From followers to leaders: emerging and regional powers

Despite the concerns of critical constituencies within and outside the leading technology-exporting countries over the negative effects of perpetuating maximum norms of intellectual property, it would be naive to expect that the desired change will come voluntarily, let alone quickly from the same quarters that have rigged and led the global intellectual property regime to its present crisis point. Regimes take time to form, and when they do, they assume a life of their own. But things do not look as hopeless as they seem. One of the lessons from our exploration of intellectual property in global governance is the presence of resistance, by way of counter-regimes or "cross-currents" as permanent features of both globalization and global governance. For example, typical of trends in globalization and global governance, the birth of TRIPS and its induction of a harmonized global intellectual property order was, perhaps, the single most pivotal development responsible for eliciting different forms of resistance to the new intellectual property order. In this regard, different institutions, instruments, NGOs, IGOs, sub-state actors and multifarious stakeholders – hitherto outliers in the normative discourses on intellectual property – easily became sites or agents for critical exploration of intellectual property issue linkages and for the elaboration of the development imperative.

So far, modest strides have been made, at least, to open up and intensify conversation, for example, on traditional knowledge-related rights including farmers' rights, traditional cultural expressions, ABS, intellectual property intersection with public health and human rights, and the safeguarding and protection of intangible cultural heritage and cultural diversity. These advances do not only reflect increased global awareness of the critical importance and ubiquity of intellectual property. They demonstrate as well the realization that intellectual property is fundamentally an interdisciplinary subject matter and the target of multiple control mechanisms outside the ambit of a single or few governance institutions as previously thought.

The new way of understanding intellectual property and the stakes involved in its governance is empowering rather than intimidating, especially for those at the receiving end of the presently subverted and poorly configured global intellectual property order. It is on this backdrop that the less developed countries and their global sympathizers, (which transcend geopolitical and economic borderlines) under the leadership of Brazil and Argentina, successfully pushed for the adoption of a *new* Development Agenda at the WIPO in 2007. Although the Development Agenda is presently taking baby steps on its implementation journey, and though its future remains uncertain (de Beer 2009b), for the purpose of this treatise, its symbolism is what matters.

In terms of significance, first, the Development Agenda reflects an acknowledgement that the ongoing harmonization of global intellectual property rules weighs abysmally poor on the development scale and, as such, it is in need of salvaging. Second, although it has a very weak legal grounding, that fact should not be over-advertised. The process that resulted in the Development Agenda is legitimately robust, perhaps even more so than the one that yielded the TRIPS Agreement. Further, given the diversity of interest and actors that pushed for the Development Agenda the latter itself reflects the non-hierarchical or non-conventional nature of actors, instruments and processes that forge control mechanisms in global governance.

Third, and, perhaps most important, the Development Agenda symbolizes the real and potential ability of less developed countries, led by those increasingly described as emerging or regional powers, to influence a new vision for a global intellectual order through rethinking the present governance scheme or its reconfiguration. Last, the Development Agenda demonstrates, in accordance with David Kennedy's thesis (discussed in Chapter 2), a reification of global governance in action; it objectifies "a dynamic process in which political and economic arrangements unleash interests, [attempt to] change the balance of forces, and lead to further re-invention of the governance scheme itself" (2008: 832).

The ability of less developed countries to actually change the balance of forces and to reconfigure the direction and governance scheme of the global intellectual property process is an idea that holds great hope for many analysts (e.g. Reichman 2009b; Yu 2008a, 2008b, 2009) as a way out of a global intellectual property system at a crossroads. In a 2008 study commissioned by the Centre for International Governance Innovation (CIGI) titled *Building Intellectual Property Coalition for Development* (IPC4D), Peter Yu writes:

> The adoption of a Development Agenda [. . .] has provided less developed countries with a rare and unprecedented opportunity to reshape the international intellectual property system in a way that would better advance their interests. However, if these countries are to succeed, they need to take advantage of the current momentum, coordinate better and with other countries and nongovernmental organizations, and more actively share with others their experience and best practices.
>
> (Yu 2008a: 3)[3]

The potential of less developed countries to shape the future of the global intellectual property is not necessarily limited to addressing the development question for their own interest only. Indeed, learning from the mistakes of the major technology-exporting countries or knowledge cartels is also critical, and provides a window of opportunity for them to change the direction of the present global intellectual property order for the benefit also of the developed countries in the long run. However, a pro-development approach, broadly understood, takes aim at most of the wrong elements of that order. Under its broad construct, development becomes a touchstone to rally various open-ended intellectual property issue linkages, including those identified in previous chapters. To this extent, it provides a malleable framework for a holistic and critical outlook on the global intellectual property order.

For instance, depending on one's conceptual approach, all 45 of the recommended proposals adopted in the Development Agenda, even if overlapping, are comprehensive enough to accommodate most of the problematic or challenging issues highlighted by the present crisis besetting the global intellectual property. The six different issue clusters into which they can be reduced – technical assistance and capacity building; norm setting, flexibilities, public policy and public domain; technology transfer, information and communication technologies and access to knowledge; assessment, evaluation, and impact studies; institutional matters, including mandate and governance; and, last, the omnibus "other issues" – combine to give a clear sense of the issue compass compressed under the Development Agenda.

Pushing the development agenda: the benefits of a coalition imperative

According to Yu, the different but non-exclusive forms or platforms that the Intellectual Property Coalition for Development (IPC4D) could take include the formation of blocs, alliances, regional integration and miscellaneous cooperative arrangements by less developed countries. He proposes four different coordination strategies for the development and implementation of IPC4D. They are: Building of south–south alliances, engagement in north–south cooperation, a joint or collaborative strategy for effective participation in the WTO dispute settlement process, and the development and patronage of regional development forums for capacity building and cooperative optimization of factor endowment and various comparative advantages among less developed countries.

The advantages of a dedicated collaborative approach to intellectual property by the less developed countries are simply innumerable and require a few highlights. Under this strategy, leading countries in the pack, such as Brazil, Russia, India, China and South Africa (the BRICS alliance),[4] and potential contenders thereto, are able to share their knowledge and experiences and to disseminate their best practices in navigating the TRIPS Agreement, the WTO dispute settlement and other trade and development-sensitive processes. A collaborative approach ensures context-sensitive training, education and capacity building, as well as the optimization of negotiation or bargaining leverage. Added to that, it provides what Peter Yu (2008a: 7) calls "a combine-and-conquer strategy" to counterbalance the divide-and-rule mentality of the US and its European allies. As well, the approach minimizes the prospects of retaliation, isolation and other negative forms of diplomatic backlash that arise when small states "pick fights" with powerful ones.

In addition, a focused collaborative approach would, overall, be cost efficient in regard to optimizing access to the wiggle rooms, or for exploiting the flexibilities of the current global intellectual property order and other relevant multilateral trade negotiation arrangements. Many analysts rightly contend that the less developed countries have consistently underexplored the wiggle rooms or flexibilities offered by the TRIPS and other multilateral trade agreements (Musungu et al. 2004;[5] Rolland 2007: 483; Yu 2008a: 6). Stretching or pressuring those wiggle rooms and flexibilities is now more important, perhaps, than before. This is not only because the post-TRIPS global intellectual property order and the WTO process have crystallized. It is also because pending any future reforms in the global intellectual property policy and lawmaking regime, the less developed countries will continue to play by the extant rules. Perhaps, it is only when the capacity of those flexibilities is optimally explored would appropriate and informed lessons be learned in regard to their strengths and weaknesses, and this outcome is important for fashioning future policies.

Emerging powers and their dramatic transitions in context

Increasing optimism in the ability of less developed countries to spearhead change in the global intellectual property policy and lawmaking order in the 21st century is not an isolated speculation. It is integral to confidence in their ability to realign the balance of forces in the broader global political and economic equation in the 21st century (Garten 1997; Schmitz 2006). The basis of this optimism is not far fetched. First, from the late 20th century, most regions and countries of the global south have witnessed significant political and economic transitions. Without renouncing its communist political structures, China embraced the market economy with unprecedented and unstoppable energy, marked by remarkable progress. India, the world's largest democracy, has maintained strong economic growth along with a strong profile in the bio- and digital technology sectors. America's emergence as the sole superpower after the Cold War left South American military dictatorships without America's strategic support that they had enjoyed in the Cold War era. The continent consequently shed its unviable association with brutal military dictatorships in exchange for democracy, with Brazil leading as a shinning beacon for that change. In the African region, South Africa, like a phoenix, rose from the ashes of apartheid and strategically repositioned itself for leadership in the region. Much of the rest of the continent, including Nigeria, despite regular hiccups including conflicts and military interventions in government, have transitioned via infant steps into some form of fledgling democratic cultures.

One effect of the positive political transitions in these countries and regions is the opening up of economic and political opportunities through which their voices are heard in international regulatory processes, including those dealing with intellectual property and trade, the environment and sustainable development. Also, the freeing up of democratic spaces in these nations enhances regional, bilateral and forms of multilateral cooperation. For instance, most of the countries of the south are involved at one level or the other in every conceivable form of coalition building, including regional, continental, subcontinental and special interest-driven transregional groupings.

The role and influence of leading developing countries such as Brazil, India and China in the post-TRIPS intellectual property world has become quite significant. This is so, especially in regard to the Doha Declaration and, generally, in regard to the development rounds of multilateral trade negotiations. It is also the case in relation to the specific heads of intellectual property issue linkages and the overall dynamics of various institutional forums relevant to intellectual property in global governance explored in this book, and beyond. Economic analysts have grouped Russia with Brazil, India, China and, lately, South Africa as the BRICS bloc of countries and have gradually nudged them into appreciating their enormous political and economic potential as a bloc (Schuman 2010; Wilson and Purushotaman 2003). Gradually, these countries have become engaged as an unofficial economic and political pressure bloc of great significance (Goldman Sachs 2010).[6] In 2010, the bloc announced the formal admission of South Africa into the league.[7]

With more than 25% of world land mass and 40% of its total population, the original BRIC (i.e. excluding South Africa) have a collective GDP of US$15.5

billion. Recently, the BRICS bloc of countries have begun to leverage their economic and political clout to counter, reverse or otherwise influence the US' hegemonic role in critical subjects, including intellectual property and trade. The emergence of the BRICS is another important layer on the growing south–south alignment, which builds on pre-existing historical and contemporary formations such as the Non-Aligned Movement (NAM), G77+China, and even the north–south strategic engagement forums such as Outreach 5 of the G8 and the G20 (Sotero 2009: 13).

Except South Africa, the rest of the BRIC countries rank among the five most populous countries in the world. Save for the US and Japan, which occupy the third and tenth positions, less developed countries make up 80% of the world's most populated territories. With continuing economic prosperity in the BRICS bloc and in other strategic middle income countries such as South Africa, Argentina, Mexico, Thailand, Indonesia, Malaysia and South Korea, the political and economic clout of the less developed countries and its implication for re-engaging the crisis of equity in the global intellectual property arena has never looked more promising.

Leading countries of the global south are now commonly referred to by analysts as regional or emerging powers. These countries have continued to cultivate and consolidate their regional clout as an important platform for engaging in cross-regional bridge building which is very relevant for advancing IPC4D and other trade and development oriented objectives. An example in this regard is South Africa, which, since its integration into international comity at the end of apartheid, adopted Africa as the center of its foreign policy and has shown strong leadership within the Southern African Development Community (SADC) and the African Union (AU). Also, India's engagement in the subcontinent is evident in its historical commitment to the South Asian Association for Regional Cooperation (SAAARC) and other regional groupings. Similarly, as South America's most populous country and its largest economy, Brazil's influence in the region has been quite natural, as evident in the leadership role it plays in such forums as the Mercosur (Southern Common Market) and the Union of South American Nations. Also, Indonesia and its regional partners in the ASEAN region have remained engaged in the nurturing and transformation of the South East Asian countries into a competitive regional economic and trading bloc.

Building on their regional influences, two of the original BRIC countries, India and Brazil, have formed a trilateral union with South Africa (the newest kid in the BRIC bloc) called IBSA (India–Brazil–South Africa). This association, which came into life in 2003, transcends "geographical, historical and regional differences in order to promote their individual and collective interests at a time when the current economic hardship and declining US hegemony mean greater opportunities for emerging countries in the global South" (IBSA 2009: 1). As a transregional grouping, IBSA provides a platform "for sharing of best practices between member countries and strengthens the voice of the developing world as whole" (IBSA 2009: 2) in critical areas such as trade and intellectual property negotiations. Within the short period of its existence, a report on IBSA by the Woodrow Wilson International Center for Scholars shows increased trilateral trade and cooperation among IBSA members in the G8, and an increase in "similarity among their votes in other international forums" (IBSA 2009: 9). According to the report, the combined population of IBSA countries is estimated at 1.3 billion with a nominal GDP of US$3 trillion, or in the alternative, US$5.7 trillion purchasing power parity. All the IBSA countries "encompass an area three times bigger than the European Union" (IBSA 2009:10).

With the prospect of Mexico joining IBSA,[8] only a few alliances better suit Yu's vision of a model of south–south coordination strategy for developing IPC4D. As three strategic regional leaders who also double as emerging powers, countries of the IBSA coalition are aware of the current opportunity for "re-engineering the [global] economic architecture of the Bretton Woods Institutions" (IBSA: 15) for a more representative and development oriented outcome. Divergences in the historical and political profiles and experiences of these countries should not (as has always been the reason for pessimism over south–south solidarity) be an impediment to their cooperation. In fact, bridging the development gap is a permanent issue for most, if not all less developed countries, including the regional and emerging powers among them. This realization is critical for forging IPC4D and for reconfiguring the global governance scheme for intellectual property. The recent formal admission of South Africa into the BRIC (more appropriately BRICS) bloc, however, raises concerns not only about the future of IBSA but also about the potential danger of loss of direction likely to plague the indiscriminate duplication of these alliances.

Development: a common denominator

Unlike their developed counterparts, the shared common interests of the less developed countries, including the regional and emerging powers among them, in a new development-oriented world intellectual property order, stems from diverse reasons, a few of which I identify here. First, the asymmetrical gap between the rich and poor in those countries, for example, in China, Brazil, India, South Africa and Mexico, is simply phenomenal. Even with the present unprecedented pace of economic prosperity, the rich–poor gap in those countries cannot be adequately bridged over a generation. Thus, addressing the development question, for instance, in regard to access to knowledge, essential medicines and human rights, and in regard to the distribution of miscellaneous benefits from innovation, remains a critical economic and political necessity.

Second, because most of these emerging powers are home to a majority of the world's indigenous and local communities, a humane and just resolution of the interface between intellectual property and traditional knowledge will become more urgent in the new intellectual property order. A related third point is that these emerging powers are also centers of origin of global biodiversity, and are reservoirs of cultural treasure and heritage. As such, they have a permanent and vested interest in proactively reversing the deliberate lethargy with which the developed countries have addressed those issues in the current global intellectual property regime. Last, as late entrants into the extant global intellectual property policy and lawmaking order, they are keenly aware that the system has not served their interests well. Increasingly aware of their new economic and political clout and the power in solidarity, they have an opportune moment to break the now fragile hegemony of the present global knowledge cartel.

The history of intellectual property demonstrates that when countries transition into hi-tech and creative or innovative economies, they become champions of stronger intellectual property protection, as the US, Japanese, German and South Korean experiences demonstrate (Yu 2008a: 24). It is a history of getting to the top and kicking away the ladder (Drahos and Braithwaite 2004; Lessig 2003). The logic of that history dictates that given the political and economic disparities among the countries of the south, especially in relation to the middle income or emerging regional powers like China, India, Brazil Mexico, Argentina, and South Korea, this group of countries could soon get to the "crossover point" and, singing the old tune, could begin to succumb to the problematic "high-protectionist delusions"[9] of the present day knowledge cartels. Jerome Reichman observes that intellectual property remains critically important for the advancement the emerging economies. He argues, rather bluntly, that they have two clear choices on the table:

> One is to play it safe by sticking to time-tested IP solutions implemented in OECD [Organisation for Economic Co-operation and Development] countries, with perhaps a relatively greater emphasis on the flexibilities still permitted under TRIPS (and not overridden by relevant FTAs). The other approach is to embark on a more experimental path that advanced technology countries currently find so daunting.
>
> (2009: 1126)

Similarly, broaching the issue of choices available to the high-income emerging powers in his reflections on the undetermined future of the global intellectual property order, Peter Yu observes:

> Although intellectual property in these countries will no doubt improve in the near future, there is no guarantee that these countries will be interested in retaining the existing intellectual property system once they cross over to the other intellectual property divide. Instead, these new champions may want to develop something different – something that builds upon their historic traditions and cultural backgrounds and takes account of their drastically different socio-economic conditions.
>
> (2009: 13)

Without over-flogging the issue, the ability of the emerging powers to chart a new global intellectual property order will depend, for the most part, on how they may successfully forge meaningful IPC4D. The success of this and related efforts at coalition building will be undermined if they approach it from the sometimes unhelpful confrontational binary of "us-and-them," south-and-north, or other related sentiments. Indeed, given the reality of the boomerang effect on account of the overweening reach of the current global intellectual property arrangement, both developed and less developed countries have valuable stakes in a reconfigured global intellectual property order.

It is evident in the foregoing analysis that there are more areas of shared factor endowments, and more areas of similarity in the socioeconomic, political and cultural situations of the regional and emerging powers positioned to lead the charge to reform the global intellectual property order, than there are areas of disparity and difference among them. This is probably more so in regard to those countries' engagement and experiences in the two defining technologies of the new knowledge economy, namely, bio- and digital technologies, and the latter's ubiquitous multiplier effects for many related socioeconomic sectors.

It is outside the scope of this book to explore the factors underlying the rise of these emerging economic and political powers. However, I have alluded to the positive effects of political transformation and ideological shift in some of these countries. In addition, although complex and capable of being discussed from many conceptual angles, their rise is not unconnected to the unexpected emancipatory impact of globalization and its relationship with the two epochal technologies of the knowledge economy in whose continuing evolution these countries play major roles. Further, analysts point out also that their rise coincides with the decline of the neoliberal hegemony and the Washington Consensus (Santos 2006, 2008; Söderberg 2006). Only few would deny that the emergence of these new powers implicate complex factors, not the least of which is the overbearing posture of the neoliberal hegemony toward other states, its market fetishism, and its insensitivity to context and balance, that is, its disregard for the need to pay appropriate attention to the omnibus issue of development.

Santos suggests that partly, the weakening of the neoliberal hegemony is a consequence of "[i]ts practices over recent decades [that] intensified exclusion, oppression, and the destruction of means of subsistence and sustainability of large populations of the world." This attitude created the extreme situation "where inaction and conformism" by those at the receiving end were hardly options (Santos 2008: 248). In a nutshell, this observation is true in regard to the overall outlook of the American-led global economic order following the Cold War. It is truer with regard to intellectual property and trade policies as a composite ancillary part of that global ordering.

Issues for a new global intellectual property order

Detailing the direction for a new global governance structure for intellectual property requires an entirely new project beyond the present one. Here then, only a highlight of the key issues that should engage such an order is pinpointed. First, I recognize that from most indications, the emerging regional and global powers are in a better position to chart a new course for the future of global intellectual property. Second, I assume that to press forward, a strategy of coalition building is critical. Third, any such coalition would involve diverse and complex alignments encompassing south–south and north–south actors that share a dedicated focus on development. Fourth, active engagement of the new global governance drivers and stakeholders, including NGOs, IGOs, sub-state actors from north and south with expertise in intellectual property and development is necessary for building the coalition. The importance of these so-called unconventional actors as engineers of control mechanisms in global governance cannot be underrated. Related to this is the need to boost the number of intellectual property user advocate groups to counterbalance the over-representation of rights owner lobbies in the activities of WIPO and other relevant organizations.

Pending the transition to a reconfigured global intellectual property regime, it would be necessary to increase the cooperative participation of the less developed countries in the WTO dispute process in order to explore, exploit and stretch the limits of existing flexibilities and wiggle rooms. Furthermore, the less developed countries should take more aggressive national legislative and policy initiatives to optimally exploit or leverage their residual sovereign rights to fashion domestic intellectual property policies. This is in regard to the rights that are not affected or constricted by the WTO/TRIPS and other multilateral agreements. Brazil, India and China, and regionally, the ANDEAN bloc have shown commendable leadership in this regard through their intellectual property and related reforms.[10] The rest of the less developed countries have a lot to learn from the best practices and experiences of the three countries and the Andean region in this regard.

To meaningfully initiate change, stakeholders would have to urgently pressure relevant actors and forums to put on hold the WIPO Patent Agenda, and the negotiation of various FTAs and bilateral arrangements with TRIPS-plus components. As earlier noted, in 2007, the Geneva Declaration on the Future of WIPO called for a moratorium on such arrangements as a show of good faith toward the new Development Agenda.

Refashioning a new global intellectual property order does not mean a reinvention of the wheel. Rather, it would require the agents of the desired change and their allies in IPC4D to penetrate present institutional structures of global governance of intellectual property with the objective of influencing a change in the institutional culture in the direction of development. For instance, taking into account the six issue clusters in the Development Agenda, they can push for an elaborate reorientation in the curriculum of the WIPO Academy and other national, bilateral, regional and professional intellectual property education and training programs in order to mainstream development in intellectual property education and training (de Beer and Oguamanam 2010). Since institutional culture is hard to change, the best place to start is through education and the training of a new crop of global intellectual property law and policy leaders at national, regional and global levels. In this regard, the strategic support of northern NGOs and other public interest and civil society groups with expertise on intellectual property and development in various issue linkage areas is crucial. Needless to say, education and training are critical to reforming the present misaligned global intellectual property system.

A thorough audit of the "boomerang effects" of the current intellectual property order is necessary to gain a comprehensive understanding of the mistakes and failures of the present knowledge cartel. In this regard, minimizing the social cost of intellectual property in relation to access to knowledge, promoting sequential and cumulative innovation, restoring competition to moderate the prevailing intellectual property overreach – especially in relation to the proliferation of patents of lower non-obviousness standards – and (in regard to the quickly entrenched culture of copyright abuse) using technology protection measures, are all matters of priority. Another important aspect of mitigating the social cost of intellectual property is to mainstream the notion of the creative commons, and isolate platform technology, basic and public science from overprotection under a new intellectual property norm. This must be accompanied by deliberate entrenchment of the public interest in negotiating privatization of publicly funded research to guarantee appropriate social returns and to provide ample discretion respecting access and mitigation of the social cost of such privatization.

Part of the challenge emerging economic powers face is "how to adjust the shifting relations between private and public goods [including] [e]ducation and public health, agricultural improvement, scientific research and other areas still heavily dependent on the public sector in most of those countries" (Reichman 2009b: 1124). Clearly, emerging economies have a vested interest in a new intellectual property order that addresses these questions in a transparent and dedicated manner.

One of the obvious lessons of intellectual property in global governance is the overwhelming reality of regime complexity and how the "regime game" more likely places the less developed countries in position of disadvantage in comparison to their developed counterparts. As much as regime dynamics is a permanent feature of the international process, the nature of intellectual property issue linkage across regimes remains open ended. As such, the prospects of future issue linkages to intellectual property and what regimes or intra-regime dynamics they may implicate or throw up depends, among other things, on the direction of future innovation or technology. Consequently, regime proliferation in intellectual property is a consequence of the dynamic of the rotation of interest by actors in the international process, as well as an incidence of the indeterminate proliferation of intellectual property issue linkages. In this sense, another key issue to consider in a potential reconfiguration of the global governance scheme in intellectual property is devising a strategy for efficient regime or forum management, in contrast to the present deliberate regime proliferation or regime-shifting game which actors play on the global intellectual property chessboard.

The logic of intellectual property issue linkage and its correlating regime complexity is the imperative for an intentional holistic approach to intellectual property in any attempt to reposition intellectual property regulation in global governance. The fact that multiple, evolving, and probably open-ended intellectual property issues are linked and associated with complex regimes necessarily requires renegotiating the extant space in which institutional jurisdiction is exercised in relation to intellectual property. Indeed, as much as WIPO and WTO's significance in intellectual property norm making and administration is important, there is no single, and not even few institutions today that are designed to exercise comprehensive jurisdiction over intellectual property issues in the global knowledge economy. Being an inherently complex transdisciplinary subject matter, tackling intellectual property lawmaking and policy challenges in the 21st century would require tremendous flexibility, and acute and concerted institutional networking between traditional intellectual property institutions such as WIPO/WTO and innumerable others with direct and indirect jurisdiction in specific intellectual property issue areas.

A holistic and concerted institutional approach to intellectual property re-ordering is not beneficial only to the global intellectual property arrangement. Such an approach must be premised on a similar ordering at the national level because, to fully appreciate the complexity of intellectual property in the new knowledge economy in both developed and less developed countries, domestic intellectual property agencies and authorities must understand the need for interagency collaboration as the base on which to navigate the issue linkages engaged by the discipline, and so as to entrench a culture of holism in intellectual property regulation in global governance.

A recent work that examined intellectual property training and education from a development perspective found that partly because of Nigeria's burgeoning movie industry, that country has a proactive copyright agency that dominates the intellectual property policy space with a heavy bent on copyright enforcement only. The agency, the Nigerian Copyright Commission (NCC), embarked on a reform of intellectual property curricula in Nigerian educational institutions with little or no consultation with other important sectors within that country's innovation constituencies, which are also relevant to intellectual property policy development, especially biotechnology and traditional knowledge (de Beer and Oguamanam 2010: 31). Nigeria has some parallel with India in relation to their thriving movie industries and as to their rich biodiversity and traditional knowledge endowments. It is hard to imagine an Indian approach to global intellectual property policy that focuses on its movie industry without accommodating its incredibly rich traditional biocultural knowledge, medical traditions and stakes in agricultural, pharmaceutical and biotechnology innovations.

Concluding reflections

Intellectual property in global governance implicates virtually all aspects of economic globalization and its intricate relationship with global normative and political governance. In the context of global governance, intellectual property regulation implicates an unfolding, complex regime interaction, given the indeterminate nature of technological evolution. Inherent in the pattern of this interaction is the dynamism of resistance and counterhegemonic reactions. Buoyed by the complex and interminable issue linkages to intellectual property, more and more actors continue to crowd the intellectual property policy space as agents of desirable control mechanisms relevant to the specific issue areas within their primary jurisdictions or interests. Thus, in the context of global governance, the prominence of intellectual property, a hitherto obscure and arcane discipline, is a major affirmative thesis of the new knowledge economy.

The narrative of intellectual property in global governance in this book affirms analysts' interpretive impression of global governance as both a descriptive enterprise and the study of a process in continual transition. As part of that process, intellectual property becomes a dynamic: in regard to which sociopolitical and economic arrangements are asserted and negotiated; on account of which interests are rotated on fluctuating values; in the context of which the balance among competing control forces are susceptible to ebb and flow; and in the governance of which schemes will continue to be reinvented.

As noted in Chapter 2, Rosenau was right to associate global governance with "powerful tensions, profound contradictions and perplexing paradoxes," where the controlling authorities are obscure, where critical boundaries are in a state flux defying simplistic binaries, and where the systems of rules are subject to continuing negotiation (1995: 13–14). Perhaps only few aspects of the global process more directly validate these claims than the characteristics of intellectual property in global governance as explored in this book.

Arising from the interaction of powerful tensions and embedded paradoxes, the global intellectual property system has been driven to a crossroads. Its currently unfolding future would be shaped by new forces, by a proactive engagement of old and new controlling authorities (be they obscure or self-evident) and by the unpredictable direction of new technological developments. It is a future that is set to not accept every normative claim of old order and would strive to eschew its mistakes and boomerang effects; it is set to confront the task of recalibrating intellectual property to respond to the contingencies of the ever expanding circle of diverse stakes and stakeholders. It is a future that could hardly afford to further delay mainstreaming equity and the development imperative into the core of what analysts call the calibration phase of intellectual property in global governance. Without question, these objectives are attainable with the right will and resolve. But the answer to whether they actually will be attained, and how soon, depends, at best, on the very unpredictable nature of the international process and the ancillary interests and priorities of the sociopolitical and economic actors engaged in the reform process.

Even so, the effects of a changing international norm-developing environment and the opportunities it presents are compelling and profoundly amenable to the current swirling momentum of the global intellectual property policy and law-making process. In the words of the South African Minister of International Relations and Cooperation:

> The world we live in today has changed significantly since the end of the Cold War. A new group of economically influential countries, such as Brazil, Russia, India and China are on the ascendancy, and are mapping the contours of political and economic power in the global system [. . .] In the past, images of power and the pillars of international relations were largely constructed according to a narrow and one-sided template [. . .] [Countries of] the North [. . .] viewed at each other [sic] as competitors, and failed to grasp new opportunities to provide enlightened leadership that could create new

foundations for global governance. They still viewed the world and economic relations very much in adversarial terms and as a zero-sum game.

(Nkoana-Mashabane 2010: 1–2)

Continuing, the Minister noted:

[n]ew challenges related to climate change, energy security, and those to do with coordination of trade and finance have become more salient today than ever before. The reality of interdependence is a reality in the global system today. We have shared concerns and aspirations. Overcoming these challenges and achieving a safer and better world requires concerted efforts by both the developed and developing world [. . .] Emerging powers are an important force in shaping the coordinates of a better global system, characterized by greater representation of fairness and equity.

(Nkoana-Mashabane 2010: 2)

Applying these sentiments to intellectual property in global governance, all actors agree that among others, the issues of fairness, equity, balance and access to knowledge conveniently encapsulated by the notion of development, are at the core of a new intellectual property order. Both developed and less developed countries have vested interests in reconfiguring the global governance scheme for intellectual property in the framework of development. It is matter of "fierce urgency" if we are to stem the tide of the current global intellectual property order from its present flow in the direction of the unaccountable deep social costs that threaten to drown the progress of our civilization at a time that, not many would disagree, is witness to one of the greatest technological transformations in history.

Although the rise of the countries of the south as emerging powers cannot be denied or lightly accounted, it would be too simplistic to reduce the present challenges facing intellectual property governance in the global knowledge economy to a narrow north–south binary, even if the invocation of that binary is often irresistible in an analysis of the politics of intellectual property in global governance. However, as the US National Intelligence Council rightly observed, the rise of the emerging powers has "the potential to render obsolete the old categories of the east and west, north and south, aligned and nonaligned, developed and developing. Traditional geographic groupings will increasingly lose salience in international relations [. . .] competition for [new] alliances will be more open, less fixed than in the past" (NIC 2004; quoted in Schmitz 2006: 1). This is so, as soon-to-be-displaced powers begin to re-evaluate their clout in the emergent order (Hook 2002; Schmitz 2006: 5).

Notes

1 Footnotes omitted.
2 Alluding to the potential negative effects of foundational patents in biotechnology and software on the development of innovation in synthetic biology and the option of "open source"-type model.

3 Quotation started from the abstract page.
4 Since the concept of BRIC was floated about nine years ago by Goldman Sachs Asset Management Chairman, Jim O'Neil, some countries, including the following, are touted or even self-promoted as potential contenders for membership in the coveted club: Indonesia, Mexico, Nigeria, South Africa and Turkey. On 28 December 2010, China (as the current rotating chair of BRIC) announced that the bloc has issued invitation to South Africa to join the club, following South Africa's application, thus making South Africa an official member of the economic bloc. See Mu Xuequan, "South African Joins BRIC as Full Member". Available online: http://news.xinhua net.com/english2010/china/2010-24/c_1366213.htm (accessed 27 December 2010).
5 See generally; also cited by Yu (2008a: 5).
6 For a more critical insight into the evolution and future of BRIC, see Goldman Sachs, "BRICs." Available online: http://www2.goldmansachs.com/ideas/brics/index. html (accessed 15 December 2010).
7 See *supra* note 4 and accompanying text.
8 Remark made by the South African High Commission (Ottawa) Policy Officer Anesh Maistry, at a presentation titled "South Africa as Emerging World and Regional Power," under the auspices of the Dalhousie University Centre for Foreign Policy Studies at Dalhousie University, Halifax, Nova Scotia, Canada, 25 November 2010.
9 See Reichman (2009b: 1121).
10 For instance, China's third amendment to its patent law in 2008 introduced a policy of development and promotion of innovation in China. To this end, China will require disclosure of origin of genetic resources in patent applications with the consequence of invalidation of patent when an applicant fails to disclose. The reform broaches the idea of extended exemption for scientific research and a more flexible compulsory licensing regime. Both India and China, Reichman (2009b:1162), writes, "have recently begun to formulate competition law and policy with a view to circumscribing the exclusive rights of intellectual property law." Brazil's new copyright reform proposal is hailed as progressive in part because of its more proactive approach i.e. for not allowing technology to subvert public-regarding considerations, as it makes allowances for aspects of user rights such as fair-dealing. See Michael Geist, Brazil's Approach to Anti-Circumvention: Penalties for Hindering Fair Dealing." Available online: http://www.michaelgeist.ca/content/view/5180/125/ (accessed 21 December 2010). (Referring to Article 107 of Law No. 9610 of 19 February 1998 on Copyright and Neighbouring Rights.)

Bibliography

Abbott, F. (1989) "Protecting First World Assets in the Third World: Intellectual Property Negotiations in the GATT Multilateral Framework," *Vanderbilt Journal of Transnational Law* 22: 689.

Abbott, F.M. (2002) "The Doha Declaration on the TRIPS Agreement and Public Health: Lightening a Dark Corner at the WTO," *Journal of International Economic Law* 5: 469.

Abbot, F.M. and Reichman, J.H. (2007) "The Doha Round's Public Health Legacy: Strategies for the Production and Diffusion of Patented Medicines Under the Amended TRIPS Provisions," *Journal of International Economic Law* 10: 921.

Agrawal, A. (1999) "On Power and Indigenous Knowledge," in Posey, D. (ed.) *Cultural and Spiritual Values of Biodiversity: A Complementary Contribution to Global Biodiversity Assessment*, Nairobi: UNEP.

al Attar, M., Aylwin, N. and Coombe, R.J. (2009) "Indigenous Cultural Heritage Rights in International Human Rights Law," in Bell, C. and Paterson, R.K. (eds) *Protection of First Nations Cultural Heritage: Law, Policy and Reform*, Vancouver: UBC Press.

Amani, B. and Coombe, R.J. (2005) "The Human Genome Diversity Project: The Politics of Patents at the Intersection of Race, Religion and Research Ethics," *Law and Policy* 27: 152.

Anaya, S.J. (1996) *Indigenous People in International Law*, Oxford/New York: Oxford University Press.

Andersen, R. (2008) *Governing Agrobiodiversity: Plant Genetics and Developing Countries*, Aldershot: Ashgate.

Anderson, J.E. (2009) *Law, Knowledge and Culture: The Production of Indigenous Knowledge in Intellectual Property*, Northampton, MA: Edward Elgar.

Annett, K.D. (2001) *Hidden from History: The Canadian Holocaust*, Nanaimo, BC: Kevin Annett.

Aoki, K. and Luvai, K. (2007) "Reclaiming 'Common Heritage' Treatment in the International Plant Genetic Resources Regime Complex," *Michigan State Law Review* 1: 35.

Arewa, O.B. (2006a) "Piracy, Biopiracy and Borrowing: Culture, Cultural Heritage and the Globalization of Intellectual Property," *Case Legal Studies Research Paper* 4: 19. Available online: http://works.bepress.com/o_arewa/4/ (accessed 8 November 2010).

Arewa, O.B. (2006b) "TRIPS and Traditional Knowledge: Local Communities, Local Knowledge, and Global Intellectual Property Frameworks," *Marquette Intellectual Property Review* 10: 155.

Arezzo, E. (2007) "Struggling Around the 'Natural' Divide: The Protection of Tangible and Intangible Indigenous Property," *Cardozo Art and Entertainment Law Journal* 25: 367.

Asmah, J. (2008) "Historical Thread: Intellectual Property Protection of Traditional Textile Designs: The Ghanaian Experience and African Perspectives," *International Journal of Cultural Property* 15: 271.

Bagely, M.A. (2003) "Patent First, Ask Questions Later: Morality and Biotechnology in Patent Law," *William and Mary Law Review* 45: 469.

Bains, W. (2003) *Biotechnology: From A to Z*, Oxford/New York: Oxford University Press.

Barnes, S. (2002) "Pharmaceutical Patents and TRIPS: A Comparison of India and South Africa," *Kentucky Law Journal* 91: 911.

Barsh, R.L. (1986) "Indigenous Peoples: An Emerging Object of International Law," *American Journal of International Law* 80: 369.

Battiste, M. and Henderson, J. (2000) *Protecting Indigenous Knowledge: A Global Challenge*, Saskatoon, SK: Purich.

Bell, D. (1973) *The Coming of Post-Industrial Society: A Venture in Social Forecasting*, New York: Basic Books.

Bell, D. (1976) *The Cultural Contradictions of Capitalism*, New York: Basic Books.

Benkler, Y. (2006) *The Wealth of Networks: How Social Production Transforms Markets and Freedom*, New Haven, CT: Yale University Press.

Bentley, L. (2005) "Copyright, Translations and the Relationship Between Britain and India, 1880–1914," paper presented at the Conference of the Association for Teaching and Research in Intellectual Property Law, Montreal, 11–13 July 2005.

Bhagwati, J. (2004) *In Defense of Globalization*, New York: Oxford University Press.

Binkert, B. (2006) "Why the Current Global Intellectual Property Framework Under TRIPS is not Working," *Intellectual Property Bulletin* 10: 143.

Bloche, M.G. (2002) "WTO Deference to National Health Policy: Toward an Interpretive Principle," *International Journal of Economic Law* 5: 825.

Boyle, J. (2003) "The Second Enclosure Movement and the Construction of the Public Domain," *Law and Contemporary Problems* 66: 33.

Braithwaite, J. and Drahos, P. (2000) *Global Business Regulation*, New York: Cambridge University Press.

Broughton, S., Ellingham, M, and Lusk, J. (eds) (2006) *The Rough Guide to World Music: Africa and Middle East* (vol. 1) London: Rough Guides Ltd.

Brown, M.F. (1998) "Can Culture Be Copyrighted?," *Current Anthropology* 39: 193.

Brunnée, J. (2009) "The Stockholm Declaration and the Structure and Process of International Environmental Law," in Chircop, A., McDorman, T.L. and Rolston, S.J. (eds) *The Future of Ocean Regime Building: Essays in Tribute to Douglas M. Johnston*, Leiden/Boston, MA: Martinus Nijhoff.

Brush, S.B. and Stabinsky, D. (eds) (1996) *Valuing Local Knowledge: Indigenous People and Intellectual Property Rights*, Washington, DC: Island Press.

Burger, J. (1996) "The United Nations Draft Declaration on the Rights of Indigenous Peoples," *St. Thomas Law Review* 9: 209.

Burk, D.L. (2002) "Anticircumvention Misuse," *UCLA Review* 50: 1095.

Buse, K.L., Drager, N., Fustukian, S. and Lee, K. (2002) "Globalisation and Health policy: Trends and Opportunities," in Lee, K., Buse, K.L. and Fustukian, S. (eds) *Health Policy in a Globalising World*, Cambridge: Cambridge University Press.

Callaway, E. (2010) "Immaculate Creation: Birth of First Synthetic Cell" *New Scientist*, May 5 2010. Available online: http://www.newscientist.com/article/dn18942-immaculate-creation-birth-of-the-first-synthetic-cell.html (accessed 15 December 2010).

Carin, B., Higgott, R., Scholte, J.A., Smith, G. and Stone, D. (2006) "Global Governance: Looking Ahead, 2006–2010," *Global Governance* 12: 1.

Centre for Studies in Food Security, Ryerson University, "Food Security Defined." Available online: http://www.ryerson.ca/foodsecurity/definition/ (accessed 8 November 2010).

Chambers, W.D. (2003) "WSSD and International Regime on Access and Benefit Sharing: Is a Protocol the Appropriate Legal Instrument?," *Review of European Community International Environmental Law* 12: 310.

Chapman, A.R. (2002a) "Core Obligations Related to ICECSR Article 15(1)(c)," in Chapman, A.R. and Russell, S. (eds) *Core Obligations: Building A Framework for Economic, Social and Cultural Rights*, Antwerp: Intersentia.

Chapman, A.R. (2002b) "The Human Rights Implication of Intellectual Property Protection," *Journal of International Economic Law* 5: 861.

Cheek, M.L. (2001) "The Limits of Informal Regulatory Cooperation in International Affairs: A Review of the Global Intellectual Property Regime," *George Washington International Law Review* 33: 277.

Chomsky, N. (2003) *Hegemony or Survival: America's Quest for Global Dominance*, New York: Henry Holt.

Chon, M. (2006) "Intellectual Property and the Development Divide," *Cardozo Law Review* 27: 2821.

Choudry, A. (2004) "Biotechnology, Intellectual Property, and the WTO," in Tokar, B. (ed.) *Gene Traders: Biotechnology, World Trade and Globalization of Hunger*, Burlington, VT: Toward Freedom.

Collins, F.S. (2005) "Personalized Medicine: How the Human Genome Era Will in a Health Care Revolution," paper presented to the Personalized Medicine Coalition at the National Press Club, February 2005.

Commission on Global Governance (1995a) *Issues in Global Governance: Papers Written for the Commission on Global Governance*, London: Kluwer Law International.

Commission on Global Governance (1995b) *Our Global Neighbourhood: The Report of the Commission on Global Governance*, New York: Oxford University Press.

Constitution of the United Nations Educational, Scientific and Cultural Organization, 16 November 1945. 4 UNTS 52. Available online: http://portal.unesco.org/en/ev.php-URL_ID=15244&URL_DO=DO_TOPIC&URL_SECTION=201.html (accessed 29 October 2010).

Constitution of the World Health Organization, 7 April 1948 (as amended). 14 UNTS 185. Also published as "WHO Basic Documents, 45th edn suppl.," October 2006. Available online: http://www.who.int/governance/eb/who_constitution_en.pdf (accessed 23 July 2009).

Convention on Biological Diversity, 5 June 1992. 1762 UNTS 79. Available online: http://www.cbd.int/convention/convention.shtml (accessed 22 October 2010).

Convention (No. 107) Concerning the Protection and Integration of Indigenous and Other Tribal and Semi-tribal Populations in Independent Countries, 26 June 1957. 328 UNTS 247. Available online: http://www.ilo.org/ilolex/cgi-lex/convde.pl?C107 (accessed 15 December 2010).

Convention (No. 169) Concerning Indigenous and Tribal Peoples in Independent Countries, 27 June 1989. 1650 UNTS 383. Available online: http://www2.ohchr.org/english/law/indigenous.htm (accessed 15 December 2010).

Convention Establishing the World Intellectual Property Organization, 14 July 1967. 828 UNTS 3. Available online: http://www.wipo.int/treaties/en/convention/trtdocs_wo029.html (accessed 29 October 2010).

Convention on the Means of Prohibiting and Preventing the Illicit Import, Export, and Transfer of Ownership of Cultural Property, 14 November 1970. 823 UNTS 231.

Convention for the Protection of Cultural Property in the Event of Armed Conflict, 14 May 1954. 249 UNTS 215.

Convention on the Protection and Promotion of Diversity of Cultural Expressions, 20 October 2005. 2440 UNTS. Available online: http://unesdoc.unesco.org/images/0014/001429/142919e.pdf (accessed 15 December 2010).

Convention for the Protection of the World Cultural and Natural Heritage, 16 November 1972. 1037 UNTS 151. Available online: http://whc.unesco.org/archive/convention-en.pdf (accessed 15 December 2010).

Convention for Safeguarding of the Intangible Cultural Heritage, 17 October 2003. 2368 UNTS 3. Available online: http://unesdoc.unesco.org/images/0013/001325/132540 e.pdf (accessed 15 December 2010).

Conway, G. (1997) *The Doubly Green Revolution: Food for All in the 21st Century*, Ithaca, NY: Connell University Press.

Coombe, R.J. (1991) "Objects of Property and Subject of Politics: Intellectual Property Laws and Democratic Dialogue," *Texas Law Review* 69: 1853.

Coombe, R.J. (1998) *The Cultural Life of Intellectual Properties: Authorship, Appropriation and the Law*, Durham, NC: Duke University Press.

Coombe, R.J. (2001) "The Recognition of Indigenous Peoples' and Local Communities' Knowledge in International Law," *St. Thomas Law Review* 14: 275.

Coombe, R.J. (2009) "First Nations Cultural Heritage Concerns: Prospects for Protection of Traditional Knowledge and Traditional Cultural Expressions in International Law," in Bell, C. and Robert K. Paterson, R.K. (eds) *Protection of First Nations Cultural Heritage: Law, Policy and Reform*, Vancouver: UBC Press.

Correa, C. and Musungu, S. (2002) "The WIPO Patent Agenda: The Risk for Developing Countries," *T.R.A.D.E. Working Papers 12*, Geneva: South Centre.

Cox, R.W. (1993) "Gramsci, Hegemony and International Relations: An Essay in Method," in Gill, S. (ed.) *Gramsci, Historical Materialism and International Relations*, Cambridge: Cambridge University Press.

Cox, R.W. and Sinclair, T.J. (1999) *Approaches to World Order*, Cambridge: Cambridge University Press.

Craig, C. (2002) "Locke, Labour and Limiting the Author's Right: A Warning Against a Lockean Approach to Copyright Law," *Queen's Law Journal* 28: 1.

Crawford, S. (1983) "The Origin and Development of a Concept: The Information Society," *Bulletin of Medical Library Association* 71: 380.

Crews, K.D. (2005) "Copyright Duration and the Progressive Degeneration of a Constitutional Doctrine," *Syracuse Law Review* 55: 189.

Cullet, P. (2007) "Human Rights and Intellectual Property in the TRIPS Era," *Human Rights Quarterly* 29: 403.

Daes, E.-I. (1993) Study on the Protection of the Cultural and Intellectual Property of Indigenous Peoples, Special Report of the Sub-Commission on Prevention of Discrimination Against Indigenous Peoples and Protection of Minorities Report of the Working Group on Indigenous Peoples, UN Doc E/CN.4/Sub.2/1993/28 (28 July 1993). Available online: http://www.unhchr.ch/Huridocda/Huridoca.nsf/%28Symbol%29/E.CN.4.Sub.2.1993.28.En?Opendocument (accessed 16 December 2010).

Daes, E.-I. (1998) "The United Nations and Indigenous Peoples: From 1969 to 1994." Available online: http://www.sami.uit.no/girji/n02/en/102daes.html (accessed 15 December 2010).

Darian-Smith, E. and Fitzpatrick, E. (eds) (1999) *Laws of the Postcolonial*, Ann Arbor: University of Michigan Press.

Dean, O. (2006) "Copyright in the Courts: The Return of the Lion," WIPO Magazine. Available online: http://www.wipo.int/wipo_magazine/en/2006/article_2006.html (accessed 16 November 2010).

de Beer, J. (2009a) "Defining WIPO's Development Agenda," in de Beer J. (ed.) *Implementing the World Intellectual Property Development Agenda*, Waterloo, ON: CIGI/IDRC/Wilfred Laurier University Press.

de Beer, J. (ed.) (2009b) *Implementing the WIPO Development Agenda*, Ottawa: CIGI/Winifred Laurier University Press.

de Beer, J. and Oguamanam, C. (2010) "Intellectual Property Training and Education: A Development Perspective" in *ICTDS Issue Paper No.31*. Geneva: International Commission on Trade and Sustainable Development. Available online: http://ictsd.org/i/publications/96914/?view=document (accessed 19 December 2010).

Deere, C. (2009) *The Implementation Game: The TRIPS Agreement and the Global Politics of Intellectual Property Reform in Developing Countries*, New York/Oxford: Oxford University Press.

Denhez, M. (1997) "International Protection of Expressions of Folklore: UNESCO Follow-Up to the 1989 Recommendation on the Safeguarding of Traditional Culture and Folklore," UNESCO-WIPO/FOLK/PKT/97/17 (7 April 1997).

Diamond v. Chakrabarty (1980) 447 US 303.

DiMasi, J.A. and Paquette, C. (2004) "The Economics of Follow-on Drug Research and Development: Trends in Entry Rate and Timing of Development," *Pharmacogenimics* (Suppl.) 22: 1.

Downie, J. and Herder, M. (2007) "Reflections on Commercialization of Research Conducted in Public Institutions in Canada," *McGill Health Law Publication* 1: 23.

Drahos, P. (2002) "Developing Countries and International Intellectual Property Standard Setting," *CIPR Study Paper 8*, London: Commission on Intellectual Property Rights.

Drahos, P. (ed.) (2005) *Death of Patents*, London: Lawtext Publishing Ltd.

Drahos, P. (n.d.) "The Universality of Intellectual Property: Origins and Development," Geneva: WIPO. Available online: http://www.wipo.int/tk/en/hr/paneldiscussion/papers/drahos-summary.html (accessed 17 November 2010).

Drahos, P. and Braithwaite, J. (2002) *Information Feudalism: Who Owns the Knowledge Economy?*, New York: The New Press.

Drahos, P. and Braithwaite, J. (2004) "Hegemony Based on Knowledge: The Role of Intellectual Property" *Law in Context* 21: 204.

Drahos, P. and Mayne, R. (2002) *Global Intellectual Property Rights: Knowledge, Access and Development*, Oxford: Palgrave-Macmillan.

Dutfield, G. (2001) "TRIPS-Related Aspects of Traditional Knowledge," *Case Western Reserve Journal of International Law* 33: 233.

Dutfield, G. (2006a) "Does One Size Fit All? The International Patent Regime," *Harvard International Law Review* 26: 50.

Dutfield, G. (2006b) *Protecting Traditional Knowledge: Pathways to the Future*, in *ICTSD Issue Paper No. 16*, Geneva: International Commission on Trade and Sustainable Development. Available online: http://www.iprsonline.org/unctadictsd/docs/Graham%20 final.pdf (accessed 15 December 2010).

Dutfield, G. (2009) *Intellectual Property and the Life Sciences Industry: Past Present and the Future*, 2nd edn, Danvers, MA: World Scientific.

Dutfield, G. and Suthersanen, U. (2005) "Harmonisation or Differentiation in Intellectual Property Protection? Lessons from History," *Prometheus* 23: 131.

Dutfield, G. and Suthersanen, U. (2008) *Global Intellectual Property Law*, Cheltenham/Northampton, MA: Edward Elgar.

Edward, P.G. (2008) "The Copyright Crisis: Principles for Change," *Journal of Copyright Society (USA)* 55: 165.

Ellen, R. and Harris, H. (2000) "Introduction" in Ellen, R., Parkes, P. and Bicker, A. (eds) *Indigenous Environmental Knowledge and Its Transformations: Critical Anthropological Perspectives*, Amsterdam: Harwood Academic.

el-Ojeili, C. and Hayden, P. (2006) *Critical Theories of Globalization*, Basingstoke/New York: Palgrave-Macmillan.

Eppich, C. (2002) "Patenting Dilemma: Drugs for Profit Versus Drugs for Health," *Santa Clara Law Review* 43: 289.

European Commission (2008) "Green Paper on Copyright in the Knowledge Economy," COM (2008) 466/3. Available online: http://ec.europa.eu/internal_market/copyright/ docs/ copyright-infso/greenpaper_en.pdf (accessed 26 November 2010).

European Patent Office (2007) "Scenarios for the Future." Available online: http://www. marcasepatentes.pt/files/collections/pt_PT/1/178/EPO%20Scenarios%20For%20 The%20Future.pdf (accessed 6 December 2010).

Evenson, R.E., Santaniello V. and Zilberman, D. (eds) (2002) *Economic and Social Issues in Agricultural Biotechnology*, New York: CABI Publishing.

Farley, C.H. (1997) "Protecting Folklore of Indigenous Peoples: Is Intellectual Property the Answer?," *Connecticut Law Review* 30: 1

Feacham, G.A. and Sachs, J. (2002) *Global Public Goods for Health: The Report of Working Group 2 of the Commission on Macroeconomics and Health*, Geneva: World Health Organization. Available online: whqlibdoc.who.int/publications/9241590106.pdf (accessed 29 October 2010).

Feather, J. (1988) "Authors, Publishers and Politicians: The History of Copyright and the Book Trade," *European Intellectual Property Law Review* 10: 377.

Ferkiss, V. (1979) "Daniel Bell's Concept of Post Industrial Society: Theory, Myth and Ideology," *Political Science Reviewer* 9: 61.

Ficsor, M. (2005) "The Protection of Traditional Cultural Expression/Folklore," paper presented at WIPO National Seminar on Copyright, Related Rights and Collective Management, Khartoum, Sudan, 28 February–2 March 2005, WIPO Doc WIPO/ CR/KRT/05/8. Available online: www.wipo.int/edocs/mdocs/arab/en/wipo_cr/ wipo_cr_krt_05_8.pdf (accessed 16 December 2010).

Food and Agriculture Organization of the United Nations (1989) *Farmers' Rights*, Resolution No. 5/89, FAO Conference, 25th Session, Rome, 11–20 November 1989. Available online: http://www.fao.org/docrep/x5588E/x5588E00.htm (accessed 17 January 2011).

Food and Agriculture Organization of the United Nations (1996) *Rome Declaration on Food Security*, World Food Summit, 13–17 November 1996. Available online: http://www. fao.org/docrep/003/w3613e/w3613e00.HTM (accessed 14 December 2010).

Food and Agriculture Organization of the United Nations (2010) "About FAO." Available online: http://www.fao.org/about/en/ (accessed 29 November 2010).

Food and Agriculture Organization of the United Nations, Constitution, in: *Basic Texts of the Food and Agriculture Organization of the United Nations*. Available online: http://www.fao. org/docrep/010/k1713e/k1713e01.htm#4 (accessed 29 November 2010).

Fratianni, M., Savona, P. and Kirton, J.J. (2007) *Corporate, Public and Global Governance: The G8 Contribution*, Aldershot/Burlington, VT: Ashgate.

Garten, J. (1997) *The Big Ten: The Big Emerging Markets and How They Will Change Our Lives*, New York: Basic Books.

Gathii, J.T. (2002) "Rights, Patents, Markets and Global Aids Pandemic," *Florida Journal of International Law* 14: 261.

Gay J. (ed.) (2002) *Free Software, Free Society: Selected Essays of Richard M. Stallman*, Boston, MA: GNU Press.

Genetic Resources Action International (2010) "Biodiversity Rights Legislation." Available online: http://http://www.grain.org/brl/ (accessed 15 December 2010).

Geneva Declaration on the Future of WIPO. Available online: http://www.cptech.org/ip/wipo/futureofwipodeclaration.pdf (accessed 20 November 2010).

Gervais, D. (2007) "TRIPS and Development," in Gervais, D. (ed.) *Intellectual Property, Trade and Development: Strategies to Optimize Economic Development in a TRIP Plus Era*, Oxford: Oxford University Press.

Gervais, D. (2009) "Traditional Knowledge: Are We Closer to the Answer(s): The Potential Role of Geographical Indications," *ILSA Journal of International & Comparative Law* 15: 551.

Gill, S. (2003) *Power and Resistance in the New World Order*, Hampshire/New York: Palgrave-Macmillan.

Gold, E.R. and Knoppers, B.M. (eds) (2009) *Biotechnology IP & Ethics*, Markham, ON: LexisNexis.

Goldman Sachs (2010) "BRICS." Available online: http://www2.goldmansachs.com/ideas/brics/index.html (accessed 15 December 2010).

Gonzalez, C.G. (2002) "Institutionalizing Inequality: The WTO Agreement on Agriculture," *Columbia Journal of Environmental Law* 27: 433.

Gonzalez, C.G. (2004) "Trade Liberalization, Food Security, and the Environment: The Neoliberal Threat to Sustainable Rural Development," *Transnational Law and Contemporary Problems* 14: 419.

Goodman, A. (2006) "The Origins of the Modern Patent in the Doctrine of Restraint of Trade," *Intellectual Property Journal* 19: 297.

Goss, P.J. (1996) "Guiding the Hand that Feeds: Towards Socially Optimal Appropriability in Agricultural Biotechnology Innovation," *California Law Review* 84: 1397.

Halbert, D.J. (2007) "The World Intellectual Organization: Past, Present and Future," *Journal of Copyright Society* 54: 253.

Halewood, M. (1999) "Indigenous and Local Knowledge in International Law: A Preface to *Sui Generis* Intellectual Property Protection," *McGill Law Journal* 44: 953.

Hannerz, U. (1990) "Cosmopolitans and Locals in World Culture," *Theory, Culture and Society* 7: 237.

Harding, S. (1999) "Value Obligation and Cultural Heritage," *Arizona State Law Journal* 39: 291.

Heald, P. (2003) "The Rhetoric of Biopiracy," *Cardozo Journal of International and Comparative Law* 11: 519.

Held, D., McGrew, A., Goldblatt, D. and Parraton, J. (1999) *Global Transformations: Politics, Economics and Culture*, Palo Alto, CA: Stanford University Press.

Helfer, L.R. (2002) "Intellectual Property Rights in Plant Varieties: An Overview of Options with National Governments," *FAO Legal Paper Online No. 31*. Available online: http://www.fao.org/Legal/Prs-OL/lpo31.pdf (accessed 14 December 2010).

Helfer, L.R. (2003) "Human Rights and Intellectual Property: Conflict or Coexistence?," *Minnesota Intellectual Property Review* 5: 47.

Helfer, L.R. (2004a) "Regime Shifting: The TRIPS Agreement and New Dynamics of International Intellectual Property Lawmaking," *Yale Journal of International Law* 29: 1.

Helfer, L.R. (2004b) "Human Rights and Intellectual Property: Conflicts or Co-existence?" *Netherlands Quarterly of Human Rights* 22: 167.

Helfer, L.R. (2007) "Towards a Human Rights Framework for Intellectual Property," *UC Davis Law Review* 40: 971.

Helfer, L.R. (2008) "The New Innovation Frontier? Intellectual Property and European Court of Human Rights," *Harvard International Law Journal* 40:1

Helfer, L.R. (2009) "Regime Shifting in the International Intellectual Property System," *Perspectives on Politics* 7: 39.

Helfer, L.R. and Austin, G.W. (2011) *Human Rights and Intellectual Property: Mapping the Global Interface*, Cambridge: Cambridge University Press.

Heller, M. (2008) *The Gridlock Economy: How Too Much Ownership Wrecks Markets, Stops Innovation and Costs Lives*, New York: Basic Books.

Hilton, I. (2000) "A Bitter Pill for the World's Poor," *Guardian*, 5 January.

Hodgson, D.L. (2002) "Comparative Perspectives in Indigenous Rights Movement in Africa and the Americas," *American Anthropologist* 104: 1037.

Hook, S. (2002) (ed.) *Comparative Foreign Policy: Adaptation Strategies for the Great Emerging Powers*, Upper Saddle River, NJ: Prentice-Hall.

Horton, C.M. (1995) "Protecting Biodiversity and Cultural Diversity under Intellectual Property Law: Toward a New International System," *Journal of International Environmental Law* 10: 1.

Howell, R.G. and Ripley, R. (2009) "The Interconnection of Intellectual Property and Cultural Property (Traditional Knowledge)" in Bell, C. and Paterson, R.K. (eds) *Protection of First Nations Cultural Heritage: Law, Policy and Reform*, Vancouver: UBC Press.

IBSA (2009) "Emerging Powers: India, Brazil and South Africa (IBSA) and the Future of South-South Cooperation," a Report of Woodrow Wilson International Center for Scholars, August 2009. Available online: http://www.wilsoncenter.org/events/docs/brazil.IBSAemergingpowers.pdf (accessed 4 November 2010).

International Centre for Trade and Sustainable Development (2010) "CBD Clinches ABS Protocol in Nagoya," *Bridges Trade BioRes* 10: 20. Available online: http://ictsd.org/i/news/biores/94075/ (accessed 14 December 2010).

International Convention for the Protection of New Varieties of Plants, 2 December 1961. 815 UNTS 89. Available online: http://www.upov.int/en/publications/conventions/1991/act1991.htm (accessed 29 October 2010).

International Covenant on Civil and Political Rights, 16 December 1966. 999 UNTS 171. Available online: http://www2.ohchr.org/english/law/ccpr.htm (accessed 15 December 2010).

International Covenant on Economic, Social and Cultural Rights, 16 December 1966. 993 UNTS 3. Available online: http://www2.ohchr.org/english/law/cescr.htm (accessed 26 November 2010).

International Treaty on Plant Genetic Resources for Food and Agriculture, 3 November 2001. 2400 UNTS 303. Available online: http://www.planttreaty.org/texts_en.htm (accessed 29 October 2010).

International Union for the Protection of New Varieties of Plants, Statement of Objectives. Available online: http://www.upov.int/index_en.html (accessed 29 October 2010).

Ivison, D. (2002) *Postcolonial Liberalism*, Cambridge: Cambridge University Press.

Jaffe, A.B. and Lerner, J. (2005) *Innovations and Its Discontents*, Princeton, NJ: Princeton University Press.

Jameson, F. (1991) *Postmodernism or, the Cultural Logic of Late Capitalism*, Durham, NC: Duke University Press.

Johnson, M. (ed.) (1990) *Lore: Capturing Traditional Ecological Knowledge*, Ottawa: Dene Cultural Institute/IDRC.

Kahn, H. and Bruce-Briggs, B. (1972) *Things to Come: Thinking About the Seventies and Eighties*, New York: Macmillan.

Kamau, E.C. and Winter, G. (eds) (2009) *Genetic Resources, Traditional Knowledge & the Law: Solutions for Access & Benefit Sharing*, London: Earthscan.

Kelves, D.J. and Berkowitz, A. (2001) "The Gene Patent Controversy: A Convergence of Law, Economic Interests, and Ethics," *Brooklyn Law Review* 67: 233.

Kemp, D. (2010) "Copyright on Steroids: In Search of an End to Overprotection," *McGeorge Law Review* 41: 795.

Kennedy, D. (2008) "The Mystery of Global Governance," *Ohio Northern University Law Review* 34(3): 827.

Kesan, J.P. (2000) "Intellectual Property Protection and Agricultural Biotechnology: A Multidisciplinary Perspective," *American Behavioral Scientist* 44: 464.

King, A. and Schneider, B. (1991) *The First Global Revolution: A Report of the Council of Rome*, New York: Pantheon Books.

Kingsbury, B. (2001) "Reconciling Five Competing Conceptual Structures of Indigenous Peoples' Claims in International Comparative Law," *New York University Journal of International Law and Policy* 34: 189.

Knoppers, B.M (2000) "Reflections: The Challenges of Biotechnology and Public Policy," *McGill Law Journal* 45: 559–666.

Kono, T. (2009) "Convention for the Safeguarding of Intangible Cultural Heritage: Unresolved Issues and Unanswered Question" in Kono, T. (ed.) *Intangible Cultural Heritage and Intellectual Property: Communities, Cultural Diversity and Sustainable Development*, Antwerp: Intersentia.

Krasner, S.D. (1983) *International Regimes*, Ithaca, NY: Cornell University Press.

Krasner, S.D. (2009) *Power, the State and Sovereignty: Essays on International Relations*, London/New York: Routledge.

Krimsky, S. and Wrubel, R.P. (1996) *Agricultural Biotechnology and the Environment*, Urbana, IL: University of Illinois Press.

Krisch, N. and Kingsbury, B. (2006) "Introduction: Global Governance and Global Administrative Law in the International Legal Order," *European Journal of International Law* 17: 1.

Kuhn, T.S. (1962) *The Structure of Scientific Revolution*, Chicago: University of Chicago Press.

Kumar, S. and Rai, A. (2007) "Synthetic Biology: The Intellectual Property Puzzle," *Texas Law Review* 85: 1745.

Kumar, V.S.A. (2003) "A Critical Methodology of Globalization: Politics of the 21st Century?," *Indiana Journal of Global Legal Studies* 10: 87.

Kur, A. (2009) "International Norm-Making in the Field of Intellectual Property: A Shift towards Maximum Rules?," *WIPO Journal* 1: 27.

Kurin, R. (2004) "Safeguarding Intangible Cultural Heritage in the 2003 UNESCO Convention: A Critical Appraisal," *Museum International* 56: 66.

Kymlicka, W. (1989) *Liberalism, Community and Culture*, Oxford: Clarendon.

Labonte, R., Schrecker, T., Sanders, D. and Meeus, W. (2004) *Fatal Indifference: The G8, Africa and Global Health*, Ottawa/Cape Town: IDRC/University of Cape Town Press. Available online: http://www.idrc.ca/en/ev-67872-201-1-DO_TOPIC.html (accessed 8 November 2010).

Ladner, K.L. and Dick, C. (2008) "Out of the Fires of Hell: Globalization as a Solution to Globalization: An Indigenist Perspective," *Canadian Journal of Law and Society* 23: 63.

Lee, C.C. (1996) *Dictionary of Environmental Legal Terms*, New York: McGraw-Hill.

Lesser, W. (1997) *Sustainable Use of Genetic Resources under the Convention on Biological Diversity: Exploring Access and Benefit-Sharing Issues*, Oxford: CAB International.

Lessig, L. (2003) "The Creative Commons," *Florida Law Review* 55: 763.

Lessig, L. (2004) *Free Culture: The Nature and Future of Creativity*, New York: Penguin.

Lim, A. (2001) *Global Medical Dilemma: Health Cost: The Billion-Dollar Crisis of the 21st Century*, Singapore: PG Lim.

Ling, C.Y. (2010) "Rocky Road Still Ahead for ABS Protocol." Available online: http://www.twnside.org.sg/title2/intellectual_property/info.service/2010/ipr.info.10 0401.htm (accessed 15 December 2010).

Long, D.-E. (2002) "Democratizing Globalization: Practicing the Policies of Cultural Inclusion," *Cardozo Journal of International and Comparative Law* 10: 217.

Machlup, F. (1973) *The Production and Distribution of Knowledge in the United States*, Princeton, NJ: Princeton University Press.

Mara, K. (2010) "WIPO Sees First Real Progress in 10 Years on Text for Protection of Folklore," *Intellectual Property Watch*, 26 July. Available online: http://www.ip-watch.org/weblog/2010/07/26/wipo-sees-first-real-progress-on-text-for-protection-of-folklore-in-10-years-2/ (accessed 16 December 2010).

Martin, M.F. (2009) "The End of the First-to-Invent Rule: A Concise History of Its Origin," *IDEA – The Intellectual Property Law Review* 49: 436.

Maskus, K. and Reichman, K. (2004) "The Globalization of Private Knowledge Goods and the Privatization of Public Goods," *Journal of International Economic Law* 7: 279.

Maskus, K.E. and Reichman J. (eds) (2005) *International Public Goods and the Transfer of Technology Under a Global Intellectual Property Regime*, Cambridge: Cambridge University Press.

May, C. (2006) "The World Intellectual Property Organization," *New Political Economy* 11: 433, 435.

May, C. (2007) *The World Intellectual Property Organization: Resurgence and the Development Agenda*, London/New York: Routledge.

May, C. and Sell, S. (2006) *Intellectual Property Rights: A Critical History*, Boulder, CO: Lynne Rienner Publishers, Inc.

McIntyre, B.D., Herren, H.R., Wakhungu, J. and Watson, R.T. (eds) (2009) *IAASTD, Agriculture at Crossroads: Synthesis Report*, Washington, DC: Island Press. Available online: http://www.agassessment.org/ (accessed 14 December 2010).

McLeod, K. (2001) *Owning Culture: Authorship, Ownership and Intellectual Property Law*, New York: Peter Lang.

McManis, C.R. (ed.) (2007) *Biodiversity and the Law: Intellectual Property, Biotechnology and Traditional Knowledge*, London: Earthscan.

Mehta, M.D. and Gair, J. (2001) "Social, Political, Legal and Ethical Areas of Inquiry in Biotechnology and Genetic Engineering," *Technology in Society* 23: 241.

Meyers, E. (2006) "Art on Ice: The Chilling Effect of Copyright on Artistic Expression," *Columbia Journal of Law and Arts* 30: 219.

Mezey, N. (2007) "The Paradoxes of Cultural Property," *Columbia Law Review* 107: 2004.

Mgbeoji, I. (2001) "Patents and Traditional Uses of Plants: Is a Communal Patent Regime Part of the Solution to the Scourge of Biopiracy?," *Indiana Journal of Global Legal Studies* 9: 163.

Mgbeoji, I. (2002) "Patents and Plants: Rethinking the Role of International Law in Relation to the Appropriation of Traditional Knowledge of Uses of Plants," unpublished J.S.D. dissertation, Dalhousie University.

Mgbeoji, I. (2003) "The Judicial Origins of the International Patent System: Towards a Historiography of the Role of Patents in Industrialization," *Journal of History of International Law* 5: 403.

Mgbeoji, I. (2006) *Global Biopiracy: Patents, Plants and Indigenous Knowledge*, Vancouver: UBC Press.

Mgbeoji, I. (2007) "An Overview of Indigenous Knowledge and the African Patent System," in Boon E.K. and Hens, L. (eds) *Indigenous Knowledge Systems and Sustainable Development: Relevance for Africa*, Delhi: Kamla-Raj.

Mgbeoji, I. and Allen, B. (2003) "Patent First, Litigate Later! The Scramble for Speculative and Overly Broad Genetic Patents: Implications for Access and Health Care and Biomedical Research," *Canadian Journal of Law and Technology* 2: 83.

Ministerial Declaration on the TRIPS agreement and Public Health, in *The Doha Round Texts and Related Documents*, Doha Ministerial Conference 9–14 November 2001. Geneva: World Trade Organization. Available online: http://www.wto.org/english/res_e/publications_e/doha_decl_e.htm (accessed 29 October 2010).

Mirabile, T.K. (2002) "AIDS, Africa and Access to Medicines," *Detroit College of Law Journal of International Law* 11: 175.

Monture, P.A. (1990) "Now that the Door is Open: First Nations and the Law School Experience" *Queens Law Journal* 15: 179.

Morin, J.F. (2009) "Multilateralising TRIPS-Plus Agreement: Is the US Strategy a Failure?," *Journal of World Intellectual Property* 12: 175.

Moses, T. (2000) "Invoking International Law," in Battiste, M. (ed.) *Reclaiming Indigenous Voices and Vision*, Vancouver: UBC Press.

Mossinghoff, G.J. (2005) "The First-to-Invent Rule in the US Patent System Has Provided No Advantage to Small Entities," *Journal of Patent and Trademark Office Society* 87: 514.

Mossinghoff, G.J. and Oman, R. (1997) "The World Intellectual Property Organization: A United Nations Success Story," *Journal of the Patent and Trademark Office Society* 79: 691.

Mossoff, A. (2001) "Re-thinking the Development of Patents: An Intellectual History, 1550 –1800," *Hastings Law Journal* 52: 1225.

Musungu, S.F. (2005) "Re-thinking Innovation, Development and Intellectual Property in the UN: WIPO and Beyond," in *TRIPS Issue Paper #5*, Ottawa: Quaker International Affair Program. Available online: http://www.quno.org/geneva/pdf/economic/Issues/TRIPS53.pdf (accessed 26 November 2010).

Musungu, S.F. and Dutfield, G. (2003) "Multilateral Agreements in a TRIPS-plus World: The World Intellectual Property Organization (WIPO)," in *TRIPS Issue Paper #3*, Ottawa: Quaker United Nations Office (QUNO). Available online: http://www.geneva.quno.info/pdf/WIPO%28A4%29final0304.pdf (accessed 29 October 2010).

Musungu, S.F., Villanueva, S. and Blasetti, R. (2004) "Utilizing TRIPS Flexibilities for Public Health Protection through South–South Regional Frameworks," Geneva: The South Centre.

Nagoya Protocol, on Access to Genetic Resources and the Fair and Equitable Sharing of Benefits Arising from their Utilization to the Convention on Biological Diversity. Available online: http://cbd.int/abs/doc/protocol/nagoya-protocol-en.pdf (accessed 25 May 2011).

National Intelligence Council (US) (2006) *Mapping the Global Future, Report of National Intelligence Council 2020 Project*, Washington DC. Available online: http://www.dni.gov/nic/NIC_2020_project.html (accessed 16 December 2010).

Ndiaye, N. (1986) "The Berne Convention and Developing Countries," *Columbia-VLA Journal of Law and Arts* 11: 47.

Nkoana-Mashabane, M. (2010) "The Relationship Between South Africa and the Emerging Global Powers," speech by the South African Minister of International Relations and Cooperation to the South African Institute of International Affairs, 1 November 2010. Available online: http://www.saiia.org.za/images/stories/saiia/

saia_spe_min_maite_nkoana_mashabane_20101101.pdf (accessed 26 November 2010).

Novotny, T.E. (2007) "Global Governance and Public Health Security in the 21st Century," *California Western International Law Journal* 38: 19.

Nunes, K.D. (1995) "We Can Do ... Better: Rights of Singular Peoples and the United Nations Draft Declaration on the Rights of Indigenous Peoples," *St. Thomas Law Review* 7: 421.

Oguamanam, C. (2004a) "Indigenous Peoples and International Law: The Making of a Regime," *Queens Law Journal* 30: 348.

Oguamanam, C. (2004b) "Localizing Intellectual Property in the Globalization Epoch: The Integration of Indigenous Knowledge," *Indiana Journal of Global Legal Studies* 11: 135.

Oguamanam, C. (2004c) "Protecting Indigenous Knowledge in International Law: Solidarity Beyond the Nation State," *Law Text Culture* 8: 191.

Oguamanam, C. (2005) "Genetic Use Restriction (or Terminator) Technologies (GURTs) in Agricultural Biotechnology: The Limits of Technological Alternatives to Intellectual Property," *Canadian Journal of Law and Technology* 4: 59.

Oguamanam, C. (2006a) *International Law and Indigenous Knowledge: Intellectual Property, Plant Biodiversity, and Traditional Medicine*, Toronto: University of Toronto Press.

Oguamanam, C. (2006b) "Intellectual Property Rights in Plant Genetic Resources: Farmers' Rights and Food Security in Indigenous and Local Communities," *Drake Journal of Agricultural Law* 11: 273.

Oguamanam, C. (2006c) "Regime Tension in the Intellectual Property Arena: Farmers' Rights and Post-TRIPS Counter Regime Trends," *Dalhousie Law Journal* 29: 413.

Oguamanam, C. (2007a) "Tension on the Farm Fields: The Death of Traditional Agriculture?," *Bulletin of Science, Technology and Society* 27: 260.

Oguamanam, C. (2007b) "Agro-Biodiversity and Food Security: Biotechnology and Traditional Agricultural Practices at the Periphery of International Intellectual Property Regime Complex," *Michigan State University Law Review* 215.

Oguamanam, C. (2008a) "Local Knowledge as Trapped Knowledge: Intellectual Property, Culture, Power and Politics," *Journal of World Intellectual Property* 11: 29.

Oguamanam, C. (2008b) "Patents and Traditional Medicine, Digital Capture, Creative Legal Intervention and the Dialectics of Knowledge Transformation," *Indiana Journal of Global Legal Studies* 15: 489.

Oguamanam, C. (2009a) "Beyond Theories: Intellectual Property Dynamics in the Global Knowledge Economy," *Wake Forest Intellectual Property Law Journal* 9: 104.

Oguamanam, C. (2009b) "Personalized Medicine and Complementary Alternative Medicine: In Search of Common Grounds," *Journal of Alternative and Complementary Medicine* 15: 943.

Oguamanam, C. (2009c) "Documentation and Digitization of Traditional Knowledge and Intangible cultural Heritage: Challenges and Prospects" in Kono, T. (ed.) *Intangible Cultural Heritage and Intellectual Property: Communities, Cultural Diversity and Sustainable Development* Antwerp: Intersentia.

Oguamanam, C. (2010) "Patents and Pharmaceutical R & D: Consolidating Private-Public Partnership Approach to Global Public Health Crises," *Journal of World Intellectual Property* 13: 556.

Oguamanam, C. (2011) "Genetic Resources & Access and Benefit-Sharing: Politics, Prospects and Opportunities for Canada after Nagoya," *Journal of Environmental Law and Policy* 22: 87.

Okediji, R.L. (2003) "The International Relations of Intellectual Property: Narratives of Developing Country Participation in the Global Intellectual Property System," *Singapore Journal of International and Comparative Law* 7: 315.

Okediji, R.L. (2004) "The Institutions of Intellectual Property: New Trends in an Old Debate," *American Society of International Law Proceedings* 98: 219.

Okediji, R.L. (2007) "The International Intellectual Property Roots of Geographical Indications," *Chicago-Kent Law Review* 82: 1329.

Organization for Economic Cooperation and Development (2010) "Health Data 2008: How Does the United States Compare?" Available online: http://www.oecd.org/data oecd/46/2/38980580.pdf (accessed 26 November 2010).

Oriola, T.A. (2009) "Strong Medicine: Patents, Market, and Policy Challenges for Managing Neglected Diseases and Affordable Prescription Drugs," *Canadian Journal of Law and Technology* 7: 57–123.

Oxfam (2008) "Ending the R & D Crisis in Public Health," in *Oxfam International Briefing Paper No. 22*, Oxford: Oxfam.

Pascalev, A. (2003) "You Are What You Eat: Genetically Modified Food, Integrity and Society," *Journal of Agriculture and Environmental Ethics* 16: 583.

Pistorius, T. (2006) "Developing Countries and Copyright in the Information Age," Potchefstroom Electronic Law Journal 2: 1–21. Available online: http://www. puk.ac.za/opencms/export/PUK/html/fakulteite/regte/per/issues/2006_2__Pistori us_art.pdf (accessed 21 November 2010).

Pogge, T.W. (2005) "Human Rights and Global Health a Research Program," *Metaphilosophy* 36: 182.

Portman, S. (2003) "Arrested Development: Patents and Affordability for Poorer Countries," *Patent World* 154: 281–284.

Pugatch, M.P. (2004) *The International Political Economy of Intellectual Property Rights*, Cheltenham/Northampton, MA: Edward Elgar.

Raustiala, K. (2006) "Density and Conflict in International Intellectual Property Law," *UC Davis Law Review* 40: 1021.

Raustiala, K. and Victor, D.G. (2004) "The Regime Complex for Plant Genetic Resources," *International Organization* 58: 277.

Raven, P. (2007) "The Epic Revolution and the Problem of Biodiversity Loss," in McManis, C. (ed.) *Biodiversity and the Law: Intellectual Property, Biotechnology and Traditional Knowledge*, London: Earthscan.

Raven, P.H. and Yeates, D.K (2007) "Australian Biodiversity: Threats for the Present, Opportunities for the Future," *Australian Journal of Entomology* 46: 177.

Reichman, J.H. (1989) "Intellectual Property in International Trade: Opportunities and Risks of a GATT Connection," *Vanderbilt Journal of Transnational Law* 22: 747.

Reichman, J.H. (1998) "Securing Compliance with the TRIPS Agreement after US v India," *Journal of International Economic Law* 1: 585.

Reichman, J.H. (2000) "The TRIPS Agreement Comes of Age: Conflict or Cooperation with Developing Countries?," *Case Western Reserve Journal of International Law* 32: 441.

Reichman, J.H. (2009a) "Rethinking the Role of Clinical Trial Data in International Intellectual Property Law: The Case for a Public Goods Approach," *Marquette Intellectual Property Law Review* 13: 1.

Reichman, J.H. (2009b) "Intellectual Property in the Twenty-first Century: Will Developing Countries Lead or Follow?" *Houston Law Review* 46: 1115.

Risse, M. (2008) "Is there a Human Rights to Essential Pharmaceuticals? The Global Common, the Intellectual Common, and the Possibility of Private Intellectual Property," Faculty Research Working Paper, WEP08-074, John F. Kennedy School of

Government. Available online: http://web.hks.harvard.edu/publications/getFile. aspx?Id=326 (accessed 24 July 2009).

Robinson, D. and Tobin, B. (2010) "Dealing with Traditional Knowledge under the ABS Protocol," *ICTSD Environmental and Natural Resources Programme* 4: 3. Available online: http://ictsd.org/i/environment/87124/ (accessed 15 December 2010).

Rolland, S.E. (2007) "Developing Country Coalition at the WTO: In Search of Legal Support," *Harvard International Law Journal* 48: 483.

Rosenau, J.N. (1995a) "Governance in the Twenty-first Century," *Global Governance* 11: 13.

Rosenau, J.N. (1995b) "Organisational Proliferation in a Changing World," in *Issues in Global Governance: Papers Written for the Commission on Global Governance*, London: Kluwer Law International.

Ryan, M.P. (1998) "The Function-Specific and Linkage-Bargain Diplomacy of International Intellectual Property Lawmaking," *University of Pennsylvania Journal of International Economic Law* 19: 535.

Ryan-Harshman, M. (1997) "Food Biotechnology: Food Security, Nutrition and Public Health," *Proceedings of Nutrition Society* 56: 845.

Salmon, P. (2003) "Cooperation between the World Intellectual Property Organization and the World Trade Organization," *St. John's Journal of Legal Commentary* 17: 429.

Sanders, D. (1983) "The Re-Emergence of Indigenous Question in International Law," *Canadian Human Rights Yearbook* 3: 1.

Sanders, D. (1998) "Indigenous Peoples in Comparative International Law," unpublished manuscript, archived University of British Columbia Law Library.

Santos, B.d.S. (1995) *Towards a New Common Sense: Law, Science and Politics in Paradigmatic Transition*, London: Routledge.

Santos, B.d.S. (2006) "Globalizations," *Theory, Culture & Society* 23: 389, 393.

Santos, B.d.S. (2008) "The World Social Forum and the Global Left," *Politics & Society* 36: 247.

Sassen, S. (1996) *Losing Control? Sovereignty in the Age of Globalization*, New York: Columbia University Press.

Sassen, S. (2003) "Globalization or Denationalization?," *Review of International Political Economy* 10: 1–22.

Sasson, A. (2005) *Food and Nutrition Biotechnology: Achievements, Prospects and Perceptions*, Yokohama: UN University Institute of Advanced Studies. Available online: http://www.ias.unu.edu/binaries2/Foodbiotech.pdf (accessed 14 December 2010).

Schechter, F.I. (2000) *The Historical Foundations of the Law Relating to Trademarks*, New York: Law Book Exchange.

Schmitz, G. (2006) "Emerging Powers in the Global System: The Challenges for Canada," PRB-O5-70E Parliamentary Library. Available online: http://www2.parl.gc.ca/content/lop/researchpublications/prb0570-e.pdf (accessed 14 December 2010).

Schuman, M. (2010) "The BRICS: Plotting a New World Order?," *TIME: Curious Capitalist*, 16 April 2010. Available online: http://curiouscapitalist.blogs.time.com/2010/04/16/the-brics-plotting-a-new-world-order/ (accessed 12 December 2010).

Scoones, I. (2002) "Agricultural Biotechnology and Food Security: Exploring the Debate," Working Paper No. 145, Institute of Development Studies. Available online: http://www.ntd.co.uk/idsbookshop/details.asp?id=662 (accessed 14 December 2010).

Sell, S.K. (2002) "TRIPS and the Access to Medicines Campaign," *Wisconsin International Law Journal* 20: 481.

Sell, S.K. (2003) *Private Power, Public Law and the Globalization of Intellectual Property Rights*, Cambridge: Cambridge University Press.

Sell, S.K. (2004) "The Question for Global Governance in Intellectual Property and Public Health: Structural Discursive, and Institutional," *Temple Law Review* 77: 363.

Sell, S.K., (2007) "TRIPS-Plus Free Trade Agreements and Access to Medicines," *Liverpool Law Review* 28: 41.

Sen, A. (1982) *Poverty and Famines: An Essay on Entitlement and Deprivation*, Oxford: Oxford University Press.

Serra, N., Spiegel, S. and Stiglitz, J.E. (2008) "Introduction: From the Washington Consensus towards a New Global Governance," in Serra, N. and Stiglitz, J. (eds) *The Washington Consensus Reconsidered: Towards a New Global Governance*, Clarendon/Oxford/New York: Oxford University Press.

Serra, N. and Stiglitz, J.E. (eds) (2008) *The Washington Consensus Reconsidered: Towards a New Global Governance*, Clarendon/Oxford/New York: Oxford University Press.

Shah, A. (2009) "The Pharmaceutical Corporations and Medical Research." Available online: http://www.globalissues.org/article/52/pharmaceutical-corporations-and-medical-research (accessed 25 July 2009).

Shan, Y. and Busia, K. (2002) "Medical Provisions in the Twenty-first Century," *Journal of Complementary and Alternative Medicine* 8(2): 193.

Shaver, L. (ed.) (2008) *Access to Knowledge in Brazil: New Research on Intellectual Property, Innovation and Development*, New Haven, CT: Yale University Law School.

Shaw, D.J. (2009) *Global Food and Agricultural Institutions*, London/New York: Routledge.

Sheets, J. (2000) "Copyright Misused: The Impact of the DMCA Anti-Circumvention Measures on Fair and Innovative Markets," *Hastings Commercial and Entertainment Law Journal* 23: 1.

Sherman, B. and Bentley, L. (1999) *The Making of Modern Intellectual Property Law: The British Experience, 1760–1911*, Cambridge: Cambridge University Press.

Shiva, V. (1993) *Monocultures of the Mind: Perspectives on Biodiversity and Biotechnology*, London: Zed Books.

Shiva, V. (1997) *Biopiracy: The Plunder of Nature*, Boston, MA: South End Press.

Shiva, V. (1999) *Stolen Harvest: The Hijacking of Global Food Supply*, Toronto: Hushion House.

So, A.D., Sampat, B.N., Rai, A.K., Cook-Deegan, R., Reichman, J.H., Weissman, R. et al. (2008) "Is Bayh-Dole Good for Developing Countries? Lessons from the US Experience," *PloS Biology* 6(10): e262. Available online: http://www.plosbiology.org/article/info:doi/10.1371/journal.pbio.0060262 (accessed 28 November 2010).

Söderberg, S.M. (2006) *Global Governance in Question: Empire, Class, and the New Common Sense in Managing North–South Relations*, Winnipeg: Arbeiter Ring Publications.

Srinivasan, C.S. and Thirtle, C. (2002) "Impact of Terminator Technologies in Developing Countries: A Framework for Economic Analysis," in Evenson, R.E., Santaniello, V. and Zilberman, D. (eds) *Economic and Social Issues in Agricultural Biotechnology*, New York: CABI Publishing.

Stevens, C., Greenhill, R., Kennan, J. and Devereaux, S. (2000) *The WTO Agreement on Agriculture and Food Security*, London: The Commonwealth Secretariat.

Stiglitz, J.E. (2002) *Globalization and Its Discontents*, New York: W.W. Norton & Co.

Stiglitz, J.E. (2006) *Making Globalization Work*, New York: W.W. Norton & Co.

Stiglitz, J.E. (2008a) "Economic Foundations of Intellectual Property Rights," *Duke Law Journal* 57: 1693.

Stiglitz, J.E. (2008b) "Is There a Post-Washington Consensus?," in Serra N. and Stiglitz, J.E. (eds) *The Washington Consensus Reconsidered: Towards a New Global Governance*, Oxford: Oxford University Press.

Stolte, K.M. (1998) "How Early Did Anglo-American Trademark Law Begin? An Answer to Schechter's Conundrum," *Fordham Intellectual Property, Media and Entertainment Law Journal* 8: 505.

Sunder, M. (2006) "IP3," *Stanford Law Review* 59: 257.

Takach, G.S. (2003) *Computer Law*, 2nd edn, Toronto: Irwin Law.

Takagi, Y. and Sinjela, M. (2007) "Harnessing the Power of Intellectual Property – Strategy and Programs of the WIPO Worldwide Academy," *World Patent Information* 29.

Tallaksen, E. (2005) "World 'Needs Global R and D Health Treaty,'" *SciDev*, 1 March. Available online: http://www.scidev.net/en/news/world-needs-global-rd-health-treaty. html (accessed 25 July 2009).

Taubman, A. and Leistner, M. (2008) "Analysis of Different Areas of Indigenous Resources," in von Lewinski, S. (ed.) *Indigenous Knowledge and Intellectual Property, Genetic Resources*, The Hague: Kluwer Law International.

Taylor, T.D. (2003) "A Riddle Wrapped in a Mystery: Transnational Music Sampling and Enigma's 'Return to Innocence'," in Lysloff, R.T.A and Gay, L.C. (eds) *Music and Technoculture*, Middletown, CT: Welsleyan University Press.

Ten Kate, K. and Laird, S.A. (2002) *The Commercial Use of Biodiversity: Access to Genetic Resources and Benefit-Sharing*, London: Earthscan.

Tokar, B. (2006) "WTO vs. Europe on GMOs," *Spectrezine*. Available online: http://www. spectrezine.org/environment/GMO4.htm (accessed 8 November 2010).

Torreele, E., Usdin, M. and Pierre Chirac, P. (2004) "A Needs-Based Pharmaceutical R&D Agenda for Neglected Diseases." Available online: http://www.who. int/Needs%20based%20R&D%20for%20neglected%20diseases%20Els%20Pierre% 20Martine.pdf (accessed 26 November 2010).

Torremans, P. (2004) "Copyright as a Human Right," in Torremans, P. (ed.) *Copyright and Human Rights*, London: Kluwer Law International.

Torsen, M. and Anderson, J. (2010) *Intellectual Property and Safeguarding of Traditional Cultures: Issues and Practical Options for Museums and Libraries*, Geneva: WIPO.

Travis, P., Bennett, S. Haines, A., Pang, T., Bhutta, Z., Hyder, A.A. et al. (2004) "Overcoming Health-Systems Constraints to Achieve Millennium Development Goals," *The Lancet* 364: 900. Available online: http://www.thelancet.com/journals/ lancet/article/PIIS0140-6736(04)16987-0/abstract (accessed 25 July 2009).

United Nations Committee on Economic, Social and Cultural Rights, "General Comments on the ICESCR." Available online: http://www2.ohchr.org/english/ bodies/cescr/comments.htm (accessed 22 November 2010).

United Nations Declaration on the Rights of Indigenous Peoples, UN Doc A/Res/61/295 (13 Sept 2007). Available online: http://www.un.org/esa/socdev/unpfii/en/drip.html (accessed 29 October 2010).

United Nations Development Programme (2000) "Millennium Development Goals." Available online: http://www.undp.org/mdg/ (accessed 23 July 2009).

United Nations Economic and Social Council (2006) *Committee of Experts on Public Administration: Definition of Basic Concepts and Terminologies in Governance and Public Administration*, UN Doc E/c.16/2006/4. 5 January 2006. Available online: http://unpan1.un.org/intra doc/groups/public/documents/un/unpan022332.pdf.

United Nations Educational, Social and Cultural Organization (1989) "Recommendations on the Safeguarding of Traditional Cultural and Folklore." Available online: http:// portal.unesco.org/en/ev.php-URL_ID=13141&URL_DO=DO_PRINTPAGE& URL_SECTION=201.html (accessed 16 December 2010).

United Nations Educational, Social and Cultural Organization (2006) "Convention for the Safeguarding of the Intangible Cultural Heritage to Enter into Force," press release, 20 January 2006. Available online: http://portal.unesco.org/en/ev.php-URL_ID=31424 &URL_DO=DO_TOPIC&URL_SECTION=201.html (accessed 16 December 2010).

United Nations Educational, Social and Cultural Organization (2007) Ten Keys to the Convention on the Protection and Promotion of the Diversity of Cultural Expression, UNESCO Doc CLT/CEI/DCE/2007/PI/32. Available online: unesdoc.unesco.org/ images/0014/001495/149502e.pdf (accessed 16 December 2010).

United States of America (1952) An Act to Revise and Codify the Laws relating to Patents and the Patent Office, and to Enact into Law Title 35 of the U.S. Code entitled "Patents," Washington, DC.

Universal Declaration on Cultural Diversity, adopted by the 31st session of the UNESCO General Conference in Paris, 2 November 2001). Available online: http://portal. unesco. org/en/ev.php-URL_ID=13179&URL_DO=DO_TOPIC&URL_SECTION =201.html (accessed 16 December 2010).

Universal Declaration of Human Rights, UN Doc A/810 (10 December 1948). Available online: http://www.un.org/en/documents/udhr/index.shtml (accessed 15 December 2010).

Vaidhyanathan, S. (2003) *Copyrights and Copywrongs: The Rise of Intellectual Property and How It Threatens Creativity*, New York: New York University Press. Available online: http:// www.librarything.com/author/vaidhyanathansiva (accessed 15 December 2010).

van Zanten, W. (2004) "Constructing New Terminology for Intangible Cultural Heritage," *Museum International* 56: 36.

Veneris, Y. (1984) *The Informational Revolution, Cybernetics and Urban Modeling*, PhD thesis, University of Newcastle upon Tyne, UK.

Veneris, Y. (1990) "Modeling the Transition from the Industrial to the Informational Revolution," *Environment and Planning* 22: 399.

Wallestein, I. (2005) *World Systems Analysis: An Introduction*, Durham, NC: Duke University Press.

Wassel, D. (2009) "From Mbube to Wimoweh: African Folk Music in Dual Systems of Law," *Fordham Intellectual Property Media and Entertainment Law Journal* 20: 289.

Watson, A.G. (2009) "International Intellectual Property Rights: Do TRIPS's Flexibilities Permit Sufficient Access to Affordable HIV/AIDS Medicines in Developing Countries?," *Boston College International & Comparative Law Review* 32: 143.

Watson, J.D. (2001) *The Double Helix: A Personal Account of the Discovery of the Structure of the DNA*, New York: Simon & Schuster.

Weiss, T.G. and Thakur, R. (2010) *Global Governance and the UN: An Unfinished Journey*, Bloomington, IN: Indiana University Press/CIGI/UNIHP.

Wendland, W. (2009) "Managing Intellectual Property Options When Documenting, Recording and Digitizing Intangible Cultural Heritge," in Kono, T. (ed.) *Intangible Cultural Heritage and Intellectual Property: Communities, Cultural Diversity and Sustainable Development*, Antwerp: Intersentia.

Wiessner, S. (1999) "The Rights and Status of Indigenous Peoples: A Global and Comparative and International Legal Analysis," *Harvard Human Rights Journal* 12: 57.

Williamson, J. (2008) "A Short History of Washington Consensus," in Serra, N. and Stiglitz, J.E. (eds) *The Washington Consensus Reconsidered: Towards a New Global Governance*, Clarendon/Oxford/New York: Oxford University Press.

Wilson, D. and Purushothaman, R. (2003) "Dreaming the BRICs: The Path to 2020," *Global Economics Paper No. 99*, Goldman Sachs, New York, 1 October 2003. Available online: http://www2.goldmansachs.com/ideas/brics/book/99-dreaming.pdf (accessed 15 December 2010).

WIPO Copyright Treaty (WCT), 20 December 1996. 2186 UNTS 121. Available online: http://www.wipo.int/treaties/en/ip/wct/trtdocs_wo033.html (accessed 21 November 2010).

WIPO Performances and Phonograms Treaty, 20 December 1996. 2186 UNTS 203. Available online: http://www.wipo.int/treaties/en/ip/wppt/trtdocs_wo034.html (accessed 21 November 2010).

Wood, A., Stedman-Edwards, P. and Mang, J. (eds) (2000) *The Root Causes of Biodiversity Loss*, London: Earthscan/WWF.

Wood, P.M. (2000) *Biodiversity and Democracy: Rethinking Society and Nature*, Vancouver: UBC Press.

World Health Organization (2000) "Turning the Tide of Malnutrition: Responding to the Challenge of the 21st Century," WHO/NHD/00.7, Geneva: WHO. Available online: http://www.who.int/mip2001/files/2232/NHDbrochure.pdf (accessed 14 December 2010).

World Health Organization (2001a) "Globalization, TRIPS and Access to Pharmaceuticals," *WHO Policy Perspectives on Medicines* 3. Available online: http://apps.who.int/ medicine docs/fr/d/Js2240e/5.html (accessed 22 July 2009).

World Health Organization (2001b) *Macroeconomics of Health, Investing in Health for Global Development: Report of the Commission on Macroeconomics and Health*, Geneva: WHO. Available online: http://www.paho.org/English/HDP/HDD/Sachs.pdf (accessed 22 July 2009).

World Health Organization (2002) *Global Public Goods for Health: Report of Working Group 2 of the Commission on Macroeconomics and Health*, chaired by Feachem, R.G.A. and Sachs, J.D., Geneva: WHO. Available online: http://whqlibdoc.who.int/publications/ 9241590106.pdf (accessed 26 November 2009).

World Health Organization (2006) *Report of the Commission on Intellectual Property, Innovation and Public Health*, Geneva: WHO. Available online: http://www.who.int/intellectual property/report/en/index.html (accessed 26 November 2010).

World Health Organization, "Resolution WHA52.19: Revised Drug Strategy," 8 June 1999. Available online: http://www.ops-oms.org/english/gov/ce/ce124_25.pdf (accessed 26 November 2010).

World Health Organization, "Resolution WHA56.27: Establishing the Commission on Intellectual Property Rights, Innovation," 28 May 2003. Available online: http://www.who.int/features/2003/05b/en/ (accessed 25 July 2009).

World Health Organization, "Resolution WHA61.21: Global Strategy and Plan of Action on Public Health, Innovation and Intellectual Property," 24 May 2008. Available online: http://apps.who.int/gb/ebwha/pdf_files/A61/A61_R21-en.pdf (accessed 26 November 2010). Preceded by a 2007 version, "Draft Global Strategy and Plan of Action on Public Health, Innovation and Intellectual Property." Available online: http://apps.who.int/gb/phi/pdf/igwg2/PHI_IGWG2_2-en.pdf (accessed 25 July 2009).

World Intellectual Property Organization (1998) "The Protection of Expression of Folklore: The Attempts at International Level," paper prepared by the International Bureau of WIPO, 1 November 1998. Available online: http://www.tm.ua/laws/int/ Intellectual%20Property%20Protection%20of%20Expressions%20of%20Folklore%20 Attempts%20at%20the%20International%20Level.pdf (accessed 16 December 2010).

World Intellectual Property Organization (2001) Report on Fact-Finding Missions on Intellectual Property and Traditional Knowledge (1998–1999), Geneva: WIPO.

World Intellectual Property Organization (2003) Consolidated Survey of Intellectual Property Protection of Traditional Knowledge and Folklore, WIPO/GRTKF/IC/5/7 (4 April 2003) Geneva: WIPO.

World Intellectual Property Organization (2004) IGC Report on Intellectual Property and Genetic Resources, Traditional Knowledge and Folklore: Protection of Traditional Knowledge: Overview of Policy Objectives and Core Principles, WIPO Doc WIPO/GRTKF/IC/7/5 (20 August 2004). Geneva: WIPO. Available online: http://www.wipo.int/edocs/mdocs/tk/en/wipo_grtkf_ic_7/wipo_grtkf_ic_7_5.pdf (accessed 15 December 2010).

World Intellectual Property Organization (2006a) The Protection of Traditional Knowledge: Draft Objectives and Principles, WIPO Doc WIPO/GRTKF/IC/10/5 (2 October 2006). Available online: http://www.wipo.int/edocs/mdocs/tk/en/wipo_grtkf_ic_10/wipo_grtkf_ic_10_5.pdf (accessed 16 December 2010).

World Intellectual Property Organization (2006b) The Protection of Traditional Cultural Expressions/Expressions of Folklore: Draft Objectives and Principles, WIPO Doc WIPO/GRTKF/IC/10/4 (2 October 2006). Available online: http://www.wipo.int/edocs/mdocs/tk/en/wipo/wipo_grtkf_ic_10_4.pdf (accessed 16 December 2010).

World Intellectual Property Organization (2008) The Protection of Traditional Cultural Expressions: Draft Gap Analysis, WIPO Doc WIPO/GRTKF/IC/13/4(b) (11 October 2008). Geneva: WIPO. Available online: http://www.wipo.int/meetings/en/doc_details.jsp?doc_id=131742 (accessed 15 December 2010).

World Intellectual Property Organization (2009a) The Protection of Traditional Cultural Expressions: Draft Gap Analysis: Revision, WIPO Doc WIPO/GRTKF/IC/13/5(b) Rev (11 October 2009). Geneva: WIPO. Available online: http://www.wipo.int/edocs/mdocs/tk/en/wipo/wipo_grtkf_ic_17_inf_2.doc (accessed 15 December 2010).

World Intellectual Property Organization (2009b) Australian Proposal for Extension of the Mandate of the Intergovernmental Committee on Intellectual Property, Genetic Resources, Traditional Knowledge and Folklore, WIPO Doc WO/GA/38/19 (25 September 2009). Available online: http://www.wipo.int/edocs/mdocs/govbody/en/wo_ga_38/wo_ga_38_19.pdf (accessed 16 December 2010).

World Intellectual Property Organization (2010a) "Program Activities: Draft Provisions." Available online: http://www.wipo.int/tk/en/consultations/draft_provisions/draft_provisions.html (accessed 16 December 2010).

World Intellectual Property Organization (2010b) The Protection of Traditional Cultural Expressions/Expressions of Folklore: Revised Objectives and Principles, WIPO Doc WIPO/GRTKF/IC/17/4 (21 September 2010). Available online: http://www.wipo.int/tk/en/consultations/draft_provisions/draft_provisions.html (accessed 16 December 2010).

World Intellectual Property Organization (2010c) The Protection of Traditional Knowledge: Revised Objectives and Principles, WIPO Doc WIPO/GRTKF/IC/17/5 (21 September 2010). Available online: http://www.wipo.int/tk/en/consultations/draft_provisions/draft_provisions.html (accessed 16 December 2010).

World Intellectual Property Organization (2010d) "Experts Break New Ground in Traditional Cultural Expression Talks," (press release) 23 July 2010. Available online: http://www.wipo.int/pressroom/en/articles/2010/article_0026.html (accessed 16 December 2010).

World Intellectual Property Organization, Intergovernmental Committee on Intellectual Property and Genetic Resources, Traditional Knowledge and Folklore, statement of objectives. Available online: http://www.wipo.int/tk/en/igc/ (accessed 2009).

World Trade Organization (2002) *The WTO Symposium on the Development Agenda and Beyond.* Available online: http://www.wto.org/english/tratop_e/dda_e/symp_ devagenda_ 02_e.htm (accessed 23 November 2010).

World Trade Organization, Agreement on Agriculture. Available online: http://www. wto.org/english/docs_e/legal_e/14-ag_01_e.htm (accessed 8 November 2010).

World Trade Organization, Agreement on the Application of Sanitary and Phytosanitry Measures. Available online: http://www.wto.org/english/tratop_e/sps_e/spsagr_e.htm (accessed 8 November 2010).

World Trade Organization, Agreement on Trade-Related Intellectual Property Rights. Available online: http://www.wto.org/english/tratop_e/trips_e/t_agm0_e.htm (accessed 14 December 2010).

WTO Council for TRIPS (2009) "Annual Review of the Decision on the Implementation of Paragraph 6 of the Doha Declaration on TRIPs and Public Health" IP/C/53 (4 December 2009).

Yu, G. (2007) "The Structure and Process of Negotiations at the World Intellectual Property Organization," *Chicago-Kent Law Review* 83: 1445.

Yu, P.K. (2003) "The Copyright Divide," *Cardozo Law Review* 25: 331.

Yu, P.K. (2004) "Currents and Crosscurrents in the International Intellectual Property Regime," *Loyola Law Review* 38: 323.

Yu, P.K. (2005a) "Intellectual Property and the Information Ecosystem," *Michigan State Law Review* 1: 1.

Yu, K.P. (2005b) "The Trust and Distrust of Intellectual Property Rights," *Revue Québécoise de Droit International* 18: 107.

Yu, P.K. (2006) "Of Monks, Medieval Scribes, and Middlemen," *Michigan State Law Review* 1: 1.

Yu, P.K. (2007a) "Reconceptualizing Intellectual Property Rights in Human Rights Framework," *U.C. Davis Law Review* 40: 1039.

Yu, P.K. (2007b) "International Enclosure, the Regime Complex, and Intellectual Property Schizophrenia, *Michigan State Law Review* 1: 1.

Yu, P.K. (2007c) "The International Enclosure Movement," *Indiana Law Journal* 18: 827.

Yu, P.K. (2007d) "Ten Common Questions About Intellectual Property and Human Rights," *Georgia State University Law Review* 709.

Yu, P.K. (2008a) "Building Intellectual Property Coalition for Development," *Centre for International Governance Innovation (CIGI) Working Paper Series No. 37*, Waterloo, ON: CIGI.

Yu, P.K. (2008b) "Access to Medicines, BRICS Alliances, and Collective Action," *American Journal of Law and Medicine* 34: 345.

Yu, P.K. (2008c) "Cultural Relics, Intellectual Property, and Intangible Cultural Heritage," *Temple Law Review* 81: 433.

Yu, P.K. (2009) "The Global Intellectual Property and Order and Its Undetermined Future," *WIPO Journal* 1: 1.

Index

For Product Safety Concerns and Information please contact our EU
representative GPSR@taylorandfrancis.com
Taylor & Francis Verlag GmbH, Kaufingerstraße 24, 80331 München, Germany

www.ingramcontent.com/pod-product-compliance
Ingram Content Group UK Ltd.
Pitfield, Milton Keynes, MK11 3LW, UK
UKHW021831240425
457818UK00006B/161